Stigma Syndemics

Stigma Syndemics

New Directions in Biosocial Health

Edited by Bayla Ostrach, Shir Lerman, and Merrill Singer

LEXINGTON BOOKS
Lanham • Boulder • New York • London

Published by Lexington Books
An imprint of The Rowman & Littlefield Publishing Group, Inc.
4501 Forbes Boulevard, Suite 200, Lanham, Maryland 20706
www.rowman.com

Unit A, Whitacre Mews, 26-34 Stannary Street, London SE11 4AB

British Library Cataloguing in Publication Information Available

Library of Congress Cataloging-in-Publication Data

Names: Lerman, Shir, editor. | Ostrach, Bayla, editor. | Singer, Merrill, editor.
Title: Stigma syndemics : new directions in biosocial health / edited by Shir Lerman, Bayla Ostrach, and Merrill Singer.
Description: Lanham : Lexington Books, [2017] | Includes bibliographical references and index.
Identifiers: LCCN 2017029247 (print) | LCCN 2017027715 (ebook) | ISBN 9781498552158 (Electronic) | ISBN 9781498552141 (cloth : alk. paper)
Subjects: | MESH: Socioeconomic Factors | Social Stigma | Health Status Disparities | Vulnerable Populations
Classification: LCC RA418 (print) | LCC RA418 (ebook) | NLM WA 30 | DDC 362.1--dc23
LC record available at https://lccn.loc.gov/2017029247

∞™ The paper used in this publication meets the minimum requirements of American National Standard for Information Sciences Permanence of Paper for Printed Library Materials, ANSI/NISO Z39.48-1992.

Printed in the United States of America

Contents

Introduction

Merrill Singer, Bayla Ostrach, and Shir Lerman

Social stigmatization, disproportionately affecting those already at increased risk for various health problems and with less access to needed resources, damages health through multiple pathways of interaction with biological conditions and structural environments. Given its conception of disease as the product of multiple, yet identifiable, entwined biosocial processes, syndemics provides a useful approach for assessing the role(s) of stigma in health, and thus has been a focus of research and applied interventions in anthropology, public health, and beyond.

The overarching conceptual framework of the syndemic approach received early attention from the Centers for Disease Control, which at one time maintained a *Syndemics Prevention Network* (Milstein 2002) to inform epidemiological research, and the influence of syndemics perspectives continues to grow. In 2017, *The Lancet* devoted a special issue to syndemics (Singer et al. 2017; Mendenhall 2017; Mendenhall et al. 2017; Tsai et al. 2017; Hart and Horton 2017). Researchers in public health sectors and clinicians from many specialties including oral health, chronic illness management, infectious disease prevention, and mental and sexual/reproductive health fields use syndemics approaches. Here we address many of these topics, paying attention to stigma as the key structural factor driving linked biological and social processes that threaten health.

As skillfully and richly demonstrated by the contributors in our companion volume, *Foundations of BioSocial Health: Stigma and Illness Interactions* (Lexington Books), syndemics research goes beyond simple co-morbidity or co-occurrence to describe complex overlapping and intersecting health risk factors and interactions that illuminate the multi-faceted nature of many illnesses and health conditions. Syndemics are consequential interactions between overlapping or sequential diseases or biological conditions in a population, highly influenced by social conditions that cluster diseases, heighten vulnerability, and increase the overall health burden for individuals and groups.

The preceding, related volume explored the foundations of syndemics research and the role of stigma in established syndemics. In this volume, contributors examine stigma as it drives syndemic interactions in areas that constitute new and emerging directions for syndemics research. We interrogate stigma as the structural factor that intersects and interacts with incarceration or detention; with pregnancy and other biosocially pathologized reproductive states; and with malnutrition and oral health—highly visible/detectable, and therefore potentially *stigmatizable*, aspects of bodily health.

An emerging body of syndemics research (e.g., Emard 2016; Operario et al. 2014; Martín 2013), with these two books serving as the most comprehensive contributions to date, identifies social stigmatization of diseases or individuals who suffer from them as key to promoting syndemic interactions and overall suffering. Syndemic interactions, in which stigma is a primary driving structural or social factor, affect disease interactions through the stigmatized identities of the sufferers, the stigmatization of illnesses or health conditions, or both. Explorations of stigma-driven syndemics demonstrate both the nature and significance of disease-disease interactions that occur in contexts of stigmatization, further complicating recognition, treatment, and prevention. Specifically, identification of these syndemics illustrates how stigma comes to be translated from a social condition into a damaging force in physical and/or mental health. The impact of social stigma on the pathologization of physical conditions continues to capture new academic, clinical, and applied attention, as shown by the authors of each chapter included here.

As the term "syndemic" describes various disease-disease interactions caused, exacerbated, or intensified by adverse social conditions and environments (Singer 2009; Ostrach and Singer 2012); in this book and its preceding volume, the social context of interest is structurally enforced stigmatization. All contributors, a combination of experts and emerging scholars in their respective interdisciplinary fields, address the role of stigma in producing an array of newly identified or expanded syndemics or syndemic models.

The contributors to *Stigma Syndemics: New Directions in BioSocial Health* explore biological and structural pathways of syndemic interaction in three overarching areas where the framework contributes to understanding interconnected causes of suffering, and interrelated opportunities for prevention, intervention, and change. Broadly, all of the contributions to this volume expand upon and contribute to the literature on carceral/detention syndemics; reproductive syndemics—including the proposal here of two novel pregnancy-related syndemics in which social stigma pathologizes otherwise healthy pregnancies, and oral health and malnutrition syndemics. In each of these categories, researchers from diverse disciplines, such as medical and cultural anthropology, public health, primary care, psychology, and community-based grassroots health, examine how social stigma as enacted and perpetuated through structural forces drives disease-disease and other biological or behavioral interactions that worsen health outcomes and increase suffering.

Our contributors specifically scrutinize syndemic pathways of interaction between: abortion stigma and increased risks for abortion complications (Ostrach and AbiSamra); infertility stigma and increased symptoms of endometriosis (Griffith); teen pregnancy stigma interacting with biomedicalized prenatal and birthing care to increase risks for interventions and worsened outcomes (Everson and Ostrach); racialized incarceration stigma, sexual/reproductive patterns, and challenges to parenting and family formation (Erickson); immigration detention/documentation status stigma affecting nutritional status and mental health (Carney); intellectual disability stigma and health threats among incarcerated people (Claudio et al.); bidirectional interactions between stigmatized child malnutrition and associated illnesses (Bennett), and marginalized social class status and poor oral health (Raskin).

In Ostrach and AbiSamra's chapter, the authors argue that abortion-related stigma, as an extension of gendered structural violence, represents a direct threat to reproductive health, increasing reproductive morbidity and mortality as stigma toward the abortion procedure and those who seek it contributes to more restrictive legal and care contexts that impede, prevent, complicate, or delay access to safe and high-quality abortion and post-abortion services. Ostrach and AbiSamra frame the complications of unsafe or constrained abortion care, resulting from interactions between the biological condition of pregnancy, the social reality of abortion stigma, and biomedical care in the form of abortion, as the immediate consequences of biosocial interactions between constrained care and pregnancies pathologized by structural stigma. In so doing, by relating stigma to an otherwise non-pathological condition and demonstrating how it creates and reinforces pathways of reproductive morbidity and mortality risk, they extend the syndemic framework in a new direction, offering an important conceptual tool for reproductive anthropology—as Everson also does, in a subsequent chapter on teen pregnancy stigma and iatrogenic syndemics.

Griffith's exploration of endometriosis stigma, and biological and biochemical relationships between stress, endometriosis symptoms, social constructions of and reactions to menstruation, painful intercourse, and infertility, and gendered biomedical dismissals of women's embodied gynecologic suffering, further extends the application of syndemic theoretical approaches to reproductive (and *non*-reproductive) diagnoses and experiences. Thoughtfully examining how stigma linked to both involuntary and voluntary childlessness affects both physical and social aspects of endometriosis and its biomedical management, Griffith proposes a syndemic understanding of the health consequences of the stigmatization of endometriosis and its resulting symptoms, tracing pathways of interaction between stress hormones, fertility, pain, and perceived treatment by providers, partners, family, and friends, among women diagnosed with endometriosis.

As briefly mentioned earlier, Everson, with co-authorship from Ostrach, provides another model for applying syndemic theory to stigma affecting a non-disease state, pregnancy, in this case among adolescents. Given the negative health outcomes associated with the iatrogenic effects of inappropriate and excessive biomedical prenatal and birth interventions, disproportionately applied to teens, the authors examine relationships between social and biomedical treatment of adolescent pregnancy, through a syndemic framework. Arguing that the social, political-economic, and biomedically enforced stigmatization of adolescent childbearing facilitates and scripts disapproval and mistreatment of teen mothers, Everson and Ostrach delineate a teen pregnancy stigma syndemic in which adolescents who receive biomedical maternity care encounter stigma-laden treatment by providers attempting to manage pathologized bodies, resulting in considerable health risks and worse outcomes for teens and their children.

Erickson builds on a sexual and reproductive health syndemic earlier identified among Black and Latino youth in urban settings, consisting of deleterious health consequences of biological and socio-structural interactions between poverty, discrimination, sexually transmitted infections (STIs), and early childbearing (Singer et al. 2006). To this syndemic analysis, Erickson adds the exacerbating effects high rates of racialized incarceration, and associated stigma affecting those incarcerated and their loved ones, have on sexual risk, family formation, and family stability in this population—together forming what she calls the *PDI syndemic* (*P*overty, "racial"/ethnic *D*iscrimination, *I*ncarceration). Erickson's chapter forms a bridge from the reproductive stigma syndemics in this volume to the carceral/detention-related stigma syndemics, uniting these health and social contexts ripe for stigmatization, before we turn our attention to other detention-related syndemics.

In a novel contribution to the carceral syndemics literature, Carney examines how widespread structural stigmatization of undocumented immigrants, and the stigmatized nature of immigration detention as a form of structural and state violence, produce mental distress in immigrant communities that interacts with routine food deprivation and denial of medical care in detention facilities, as immigration detention becomes a form of trauma in itself. In her chapter, she presents the syndemic implications of immigration detention stigma as it interacts with bodily traumas incurred during the experience of detention. Examining how the stigmatizing and physically damaging treatment of undocumented, primarily Latino/a, immigrants in U.S. government detention facilities affects people not only while in detention but even after, changing eating patterns and mental health status, Carney shows the far and insidious syndemic reach of our country's broken immigration policy.

Under related structural conditions, Claudio, van Dooren, Young, and Lennox examine the role of stigma in damaging interactions that affect the health of incarcerated people with intellectual disabilities. They present the consequences of exacerbating linkages between the structural nature of doubly stigmatized inmate and disability status and common physical and mental health conditions affecting incarcerated people, including many of the chronic conditions and health-affecting behaviors considered in *Foundations of BioSocial Health*: obesity, mental illness, STIs, and substance use. Another factor in the incarceration and intellectual disability stigma syndemic proposed by Claudio et al. is also a key condition that represents a rapidly expanding area in stigma syndemics research: oral health.

Bennett's devastatingly vivid ethnographic examples demonstrate how the social and structural stigmatization of impoverished populations, particularly those in unequal power relationships between the global north and south in the Americas, exacerbates and perpetuates malnutrition-related syndemics. Her chapter delineates pathways of interaction by which child malnutrition interacts synergistically with infectious diseases, including diarrheal diseases, making individuals more susceptible to pathogens, increasing the severity of the illness, and lengthening the duration of the illness, in turn producing impaired cognitive function and school performance, and cyclical stigmatization of those affected and their parents. Parents are then blamed for this structural inability to feed their children the adequate nutritious food necessary to stave off the multi-layered suffering that is, in reality caused by suboptimal social, political, and economic conditions.

Raskin, a leading oral health syndemics researcher, extends the application of syndemic theory from malnutrition and oral health to encompass an explicit discussion of stigma as a biosocial factor. Through ethnographic accounts she demonstrates in detail how the social class-based stigmatization of dental decay and gum disease, diabetes, addiction, depression, and anxiety all interact in complex ways that can worsen each condition, and shape the lived experience of afflicted suffers exposed to structural, and socially stigmatized/stigmatizing, risks for them. Raskin encourages us to consider relationships among dental and oral health/malnutrition stigma, and resulting interacting health problems, within not only microbiological and clinical contexts but also through a socio-structural and political-economic lens—a syndemics perspective. Like all of the other contributors to this volume, she adds a stigma filter to that lens, nuancing and further illuminating our view of how people marginalized and made ill by social inequality experience multi-layered, interacting forms of health and social suffering.

In the chapters that follow we present the above identified and proposed syndemics and syndemic models, analyzed in detail with supporting literature and ethnographic evidence. We do so to build on the foundations of syndemics research and stigma syndemics perspectives, and to take this approach in new directions with the interdisciplinary guidance of our talented contributors.

REFERENCES CITED

Emard, Nicholas. 2016. "Biomedical Moralities: A Syndemic Approach to Stigma, Community, and Identity in HIV-Positive Boston." https://open.bu.edu/handle/2144/16810.

Hart, Laura, and Richard Horton. 2017. "Syndemics: Committing to a Healthier Future." *The Lancet* 389 (10072): 888–889.

Martín, Yolanda C. "The syndemics of removal: trauma and substance abuse." In *Outside Justice*, pp. 91–107. Springer New York, 2013.

Mendenhall, Emily. 2017. "Syndemics: A New Path for Global Health Research." *The Lancet* 389 (10072): 889–891.

Mendenhall, Emily, Brandon A. Kohrt, Shane A. Norris, David Ndetei, and Dorairaj Prabhakaran. 2017. "Non-Communicable Disease Syndemics: Poverty, Depression, and Diabetes among Low-Income Populations." *The Lancet* 389 (10072): 951–963.

Milstein, Bobby. 2002. "Introduction to the Syndemics Prevention Network." Atlanta, GA: Centers for Disease Control and Prevention.

Operario, Don, Mei-Fen Yang, Sari L. Reisner, Mariko Iwamoto, and Tooru Nemoto. 2014. "Stigma and the Syndemic of HIV-Related Health Risk Behaviors in a Diverse Sample of Transgender Women." *Journal of Community Psychology* 42 (5): 544–557.

Ostrach, Bayla, and Merrill Singer. 2012. "At Special Risk: Biopolitical Vulnerability and HIV/STI Syndemics among Women." *Health Sociology Review* 21 (3): 258–271. doi:10.5172/hesr.2012.21.3.258.

Singer, Merrill. 2009. *Introduction to Syndemics: A Critical Systems Approach to Public and Community Health*. John Wiley & Sons.

Singer, Merrill, Nicola Bulled, Bayla Ostrach, and Emily Mendenhall. 2017. "Syndemics and the Biosocial Conception of Health." *The Lancet* 389 (10072): 941–950.

Tsai, Alexander C., Emily Mendenhall, James A. Trostle, and Ichiro Kawachi. 2017. "Co-Occurring Epidemics, Syndemics, and Population Health." *The Lancet* 389 (10072): 978–982.

Chapter One

Abortion Complication Syndemics

Structural Stigma, Pathologized Pregnancies, and Health Consequences of Constrained Care

Bayla Ostrach and Roula AbiSamra

Despite its frequent and widespread nature across diverse populations (Sedgh et al. 2012; Bartlett et al. 2004), abortion is heavily stigmatized (Cockrill and Hessini 2014; L. Harris et al. 2014). Abortion-related stigma is the widespread, institutionally enforced, gender-based phenomenon in which many people share a perception that abortion is morally deviant or unacceptable, and that individuals who seek or provide abortions are worthy of lower regard (Cockrill et al. n.d.). Kumar et al. (2009) provide some of the clearest definitions: "*Abortion stigma [is] a negative attribute ascribed to women who seek to terminate a pregnancy"; women who seek abortion come to be seen as "inferior to ideals of womanhood*" (Kumar, Hessini, and Mitchell 2009). Abortion stigma has consequences for health, through a variety of intertwined structural, biological, and biomedical pathways. The more stigmatized abortion is in a given legislative, geographic, social, or cultural context, the more likely it will be illegal or heavily restricted, and less safe (Ostrach 2016). Abortion stigma manifests within multiple levels of society: media; law and policy; institutions; communities; relationships between individuals; and within individuals themselves, as "internalized stigma." Abortion stigma leads to the marginalization of abortion and limits access to high-quality and safe care (Cockrill et al. n.d.).

Kumar calls for "*greater conceptual clarity on the power differentials that create and maintain abortion stigma*" (2013:2). Here we follow this directive by exploring how structural abortion stigma functions outside of and within biomedical settings, to shape access to abortion, constrain high-quality care, and interact with biological aspects of pregnancy and biomedical complications of the abortion procedure itself (Barot 2011; Ostrach 2016). The relative biomedical safety of abortion is determined and contextualized in large part by legality, care quality, and access, in turn influenced multi-directionally by power relationships and structural factors, including stigma (Kumar 2013). For example, most abortion-related deaths and serious injuries resulting from illegal and/or unsafe abortions occur in the developing world (Bartlett et al. 2004; Grossman, Blanchard, and Blumenthal 2008; L. H. Harris and Grossman 2011), particularly in countries where abortion remains heavily stigmatized, such as in many African, Latin American, and Asian countries (Ostrach 2016). In Latin America, where nearly all countries[1] completely outlaw abortion, the World Health Organization (WHO) estimates as many as 30 percent of deaths among pregnant women are due to unsafe (often illegal) abortion (Khan et al. 2006). Related (extra-legal) abortifacient medication requests from women in Latin America have measurably increased (Aiken et al. 2016) even though most face jail-time if caught or accused of inducing abortion.

In this chapter, to propose a syndemic model of abortion stigma, we present specific pathways of interaction between:

1. *Abortion-related stigma*, a structural factor that produces, facilitates, and perpetuates interactions between biological and biomedical factors, increasing the risk of morbidities (resulting in deleterious reproductive health threats) and mortality (death) related to:
2. *Pathologized pregnancy*, a biological condition often socially mediated to become pathogenic when concluding (or intended to conclude) in abortion; and
3. *Abortion complications* resulting from stigmatized abortion procedures performed in interaction with socially pathologized pregnancies.

Such complications include but are not limited to: acute infection (Tristan and Gilliam 2009; World Health Organization 2010), sepsis (Khan et al. 2006), bleeding, and hemorrhage (Tristan and Gilliam 2009; World Health Organization 2010; Niinimäki et al. 2009; Khan et al. 2006), uterine perforation (Tristan and Gilliam 2009), retained pregnancy tissue (World Health Organization 2010), secondary infertility (Vlassoff et al. 2008), and chronic reproductive tract infections (Vlassoff et al. 2008). Complications are made more likely by "non-compliance" with post-abortion "aftercare" instructions, more accurately signaling inability or lack of resources to attend to recommendations, inability to seek treatment for complications, and/or later entry to care—with accompanying increased risks.

Even in settings of abortion legality, stigma affects whether people can obtain abortion in a timely manner (DePiñeres, Baum, and Grossman 2014);

attend to aftercare instructions to avoid deleterious health complications (L. H. Harris 2012), and seek follow-up care if complications do occur (Shellenberg et al. 2011; Kumar, Hessini, and Mitchell 2009). Perceptions of abortion-related stigma can affect willingness to disclose having had an abortion (Shellenberg et al. 2011; Kumar, Hessini, and Mitchell 2009), with implications for obtaining medical care potentially needed for rare but possible complications from legal abortion (such as acute infections and prolonged bleeding) (Singh 2010), and the ability to attend to aftercare to prevent these (Kumar, Hessini, and Mitchell 2009).

This is not meant to suggest that abortion procedures, when performed in WHO-recognized settings of clinically acceptable care, with trained and skilled providers, are inherently unsafe. A legal or high-quality abortion is one of the safest and most common medical procedures performed—as the two co-authors were trained to say in the abortion clinics where we worked, abortion is "*safer than a root canal*" (fieldnotes)—demonstrably fifteen times safer than carrying a pregnancy to term (Raymond and Grimes 2012). Abortion, by itself, is not a threat to health. Our argument is that abortion *stigma*, by constraining access to care, endangers reproductive and public health. Improving access to legal and safe abortion, and reducing abortion-related stigma, are already recognized global public health priorities (Grimes et al. 2006; Berer 2004).

We hear about people dying from unsafe or illegal abortion in developing countries or places where it is restricted and stigmatized, but less-acknowledged and less-studied is the reality that some people affected by abortion stigma in settings of *legal* abortion are also at increased risk for complications resulting from structurally produced interactions between biological dimensions of socially pathologized pregnancies, and biomedically constrained care. We need to understand how and why these things happen, structurally *and* clinically, beyond the epidemiology, to effectively address the multi-faceted dimensions of abortion stigma's health consequences.

For millions in settings where abortion is illegal, restricted, lower-quality, and/or stigmatized, the proven relationship between stigma and safety is a major contributor to limited abortion legality and reduced social acceptability, further affecting safety in a seemingly endless, gendered, sociopolitical feedback loop (Ostrach 2016; Purcell 2015; Kumar, Hessini, and Mitchell 2009; Kumar 2013). Institutionally and culturally constraining one type of medical care as more contested, more constrained, and ultimately more vulnerable to risks for denial of care or biomedical complications constitutes a considerable health threat for patients already affected by other forms of inequality.

ABORTION STIGMA SYNDEMICS

Negative health consequences resulting from interactions between multiple biological/biomedical factors, produced and exacerbated by adverse social and structural contexts, are increasingly characterized as syndemics (Singer 2009; Ostrach and Singer 2012). In this case, it is abortion-related stigma that is the structural factor producing or reinforcing interactions between socially pathologized pregnancies ending in abortion, and possible complications[2] of abortion, in varying contexts of safety and legality, to create pathways of interaction increasing reproductive morbidity and mortality risk. Our syndemic model goes beyond the better-known syndemic framework of disease-disease interactions in adverse social conditions (Singer 2009). We extend the foundational syndemic framework to introduce a pregnancy-related stigma syndemic predicated on the interaction of particular biological and biomedical risks, within the context of an otherwise *non*-pathological biological state (pregnancy), through the widespread social sanctioning of those whose pregnancies end in abortion (Kumar, Hessini, and Mitchell 2009).

A syndemic model of abortion stigma's health consequences is an important, and thus far absent, contribution to strategies demanded by public health advocates to increase global access to safe, legal, unrestricted abortion. Our framework is needed to close the gap in abortion mortality and morbidity rates, which remain troublingly and unnecessarily high where abortion is most stigmatized. This expansion of syndemic theory to include a view of physiologic pregnancy as vulnerable to pathologization in the context of social stigma, while feminist and reproductive anthropologists have fought to define pregnancy as generally a non-disease state (Jordan 1992; Davis-Floyd 2004), echoes Everson and Ostrach's related framework for teen pregnancy stigma syndemics, elsewhere in this volume.

The role of abortion stigma's role in health outcomes cannot be underestimated—unsafe abortion is estimated to result in all of the following, each year: nearly 67,000 deaths from complications of unsafe abortion (and many more suffering from reproductive morbidity); an estimated 7.4 million disability-adjusted life years lost to unsafe abortion; 1.6 million women experience secondary infertility; 3–5 million experience chronic reproductive tract infections (Vlassoff et al. 2008). Unsafe abortion, strongly shaped by structural stigma, represents one of the greatest current threats to reproductive safety: public health estimates attribute 13 percent of all "maternal" (pregnancy-related) deaths worldwide to unsafe abortion. With an estimated 225 million women reporting an unmet need for contraceptives worldwide (Singh, Darroch, and Ashford 2014), 40 percent of pregnancies in the developing world—where abortion is more likely to be illegal, heavily restricted, or highly stigmatized—are unplanned. As elsewhere, half of these pregnancies will end in abortion (Barot 2011), many unsafe or low-quality. Unsafe abortion, estimated to constitute 49 percent of all procedures worldwide (Alan Guttmacher Institute 2015b), is therefore called a "preventable pandemic" (Grimes et al. 2006). An inability to access or fully benefit from safe abortion services and related follow-up care produces tangible threats to health (Barot 2011) and represents a considerable global concern that a syndemic framework can help address.

There is much more work to be done in examining the impact of structural abortion stigma on resulting *biomedical* aspects of constrained abortion—to qualitatively and prospectively explore how, *specifically*, stigma produces risks for health complications (Fischer et al. 2005; Saultes, Devita, and Heiner 2009; Gerdts et al. 2016; Tristan and Gilliam 2009; Khan et al. 2006; Niinimäki et al. 2009; Vlassoff et al. 2008; World Health Organization 2010), resulting in the 13 percent mortality rate of unsafe abortion, and associated morbidity rates (Singh 2006). Excellent research is underway to explore how abortion-related stigma contributes to perceptions of inaccessibility, legal climates that restrict legal abortion, and so on. But more biomedical and ethnographic research is needed to understand how people who perceive abortion stigma fare *medically* when seeking and obtaining abortion. Here we outline a theoretical and applied model for identifying abortion stigma's role in interactions between socially pathologized *biological* pregnancies, a *biomedical* procedure, and the health consequences of constrained *care*—we call for further prospective research.

Abortion stigma, by driving the illegality of abortion and other restrictions that reduce access to quality care, represents a structural threat to reproductive health (Ostrach 2016; L. Harris et al. 2014)—abortion stigma increases the reproductive morbidity risk of even legal, comparatively low-risk abortion by acting as a barrier to timely care (Ostrach 2016; Singh 2010). While the major complication rate for a first-trimester, legal abortion is less than half of 1 percent (Alan Guttmacher Institute 2016), risks increase with each week of gestation (L. H. Harris and Grossman 2011; Jones and Weitz 2009)—making stigma's relationship to delays in care-seeking directly relevant to safety.

Developing the Conceptual Model

As colleagues in, respectively, applied medical anthropology (first author) and public health (second author) who each worked in feminist abortion care before becoming applied researchers and/or reproductive justice advocates, we developed this conceptual syndemic framework based on extensive literature reviews and analysis, and ethnographic and auto-ethnographic observations over many years, to link abortion stigma to the social pathologization of pregnancies intended to end in abortion and to increased risks for abortion complications that, we argue, result from the many ways stigma restricts access to legal, safe, and/or high-quality care and related after-care. We sought to demonstrate the specific and intertwined, biological, biomedical, and structural pathways of interaction—driven by abortion stigma—that increase reproductive health risks.

From January to July 2015, the first author conducted ongoing literature searches for each of the following terms in scholarly, social science, and health research databases[3]: "*stigma abortion complications*," "*abortion stigma trimester*," "*abortion stigma follow up*," "*abortion stigma aftercare*," and "*trimester complications*."[4] She scanned identified literature, closely read publications on the research foci (stigma, abortion safety, aftercare, and/or complications) engaged in an iterative process of re-reviewing publications found more than once under these search terms or in more than one database, closely re-read outliers, and consulted with the second author to discuss implications for the developing syndemic model. We looked closely at literature that explored or suggested links between abortion-related stigma and biological and medical aspects of abortion safety, care, sequelae, and reproductive morbidity risks. The first and second authors reviewed further literature from their fields (medical anthropology and public health, respectively) including relevant publications by the *Sea Change Program*[5] and *Advancing New Standards in Reproductive Health.*

With this information, we developed a syndemic model of interactions between abortion stigma, socially pathologized pregnancies ending in abortion, and biological/biomedical complications and health consequences. We refined our model, visually represented in Figure 1.1 and delineated in the discussion section, through an iterative process of discussion and collaborative analysis that lasted over a year. During the writing process, if a pathway of interaction required further evidence, we conducted a focused search to identify further sources. For each biomedical health risk resulting from the pathways of interaction proposed in our model, we conducted a subsequent literature search during the final revision process, to provide examples. Throughout, we included relevant data from our own encounters with patients and co-workers (in 22 combined years of abortion work with seven clinics in three states and two countries, and with three abortion funding and referral hotlines) and from 35 interviews with abortion providers (conducted by the first author in other research—Ostrach and Cheyney 2014, Ostrach 2014a, Ostrach 2014b), to ethnographically and auto-ethnographically illustrate interactions identified in the literature review and analysis.

For example, abortion providers reported that, of patients who did return for follow-up care, those who were more concerned about being stigmatized for having sought an abortion might wait until their bleeding or signs of infection were "*really bad*," before returning to the clinic, while women less affected by stigma seemed more inclined to call or come in at the first sign of anything out of the range of normal. Here stigma's tendency to fuel a damaging feedback loop becomes painfully evident, as providers also expressed frustration or impatience with patients who "waited too long" to come back for follow-up, arriving at the clinic with prolonged bleeding, retained uterine tissue requiring a repeat suction procedure, or an initially preventable infection now requiring stronger antibiotics, all as a result of stigma that some providers may inadvertently reinforce by failing to hide their irritation with patients who delay seeking follow-up care. In some providers' views (obscuring structural factors), a woman who had been more "compliant" with aftercare instructions, or called sooner at the first sign of a complication, could have avoided the need for further treatment.

Abortion stigma thus affects not only patients who undergo it, but the procedure itself, and those who provide it or support a patient seeking it. Though legal abortion is very safe (Bartlett et al. 2004), risks associated with second- or third-trimester abortion are greater compared to first-trimester abortion (Harris and Grossman 2011, Grossman, Blanchard, and Blumenthal 2008). Stigma-related delays, at a structural level, add more biological and biomedical risks for those facing greater abortion restrictions; risks associated with illegal or unsafe abortion also increase with each week (Gebreselassie et al. 2005).

In another stark example from a country with ostensibly safe and legal, but highly stigmatized and heavily restricted abortion services, people in the United States have been arrested (and sometimes sentenced to prison) after a stillbirth or late miscarriage, on charges of feticide or illegally self-inducing an abortion (Paltrow 2015; Rowan 2015). One U.S. woman recently died of septic infection after attempting to self-abort a 21-week pregnancy with a coat hanger (Saultes, Devita, and Heiner 2009). As this death, which we discuss in more detail later, occurred in a state with full Medicaid coverage for abortion, few legal restrictions, and second-trimester abortion services in several large towns (fieldnotes), we suggest this self-abortion attempt may have been a consequence of stigmatized discourse surrounding second-trimester abortion, or even due to an assumption that a later abortion was illegal.

Even after a pregnant person has taken steps to seek legal abortion, stigma contributes to delayed or denied abortion and aftercare by underpinning some health professionals' refusal to care for abortion patients (Fiala and Arthur 2014). Refusal of care falls under a patchwork of laws that vary across states and countries where abortion is officially permitted (Johnson et al. 2013; Grady 2006; Marshall 2016). As a result, in some international jurisdictions a public hospital may be required by the health ministry to offer abortion services and resort to paying for the regular cross-country travel of a single willing provider, as is the case with gynecologists in Uruguay (EtShalom 2015). In others, professionals have argued in court they were within their rights in refusing not only to assist in abortion procedures but also to refuse to manage or work with staff who do, as occurred with midwives at a public hospital in Scotland (BBC News 2014). Elsewhere, nurses in New Jersey (U.S.) refused to care for an abortion patient after her procedure (Stein 2011), potentially increasing the patient's risks for complications.

Based on our auto-ethnographic research, we can add to such broad-strokes stories the conundrum of a clinic worker in Louisiana who described to the second author how her clinic is not able to stock both of the two drugs required by the Food and Drug Administration for a medication abortion, nor identify a nearby pharmacy whose staff will reliably fill a prescription for the one they do not stock (both must be taken within a specific number of hours to be effective). In fact, this clinic worker told the second author that some of her patients mention at follow-up appointments that pharmacy workers refused to fill their prescriptions for *any* medications upon seeing that the prescription originated from the abortion clinic—including prescriptions for antibiotics to prevent post-procedure infection. The first author heard many similar stories about patients' difficulties obtaining prescribed antibiotics at notoriously anti-abortion pharmacies in Oregon—even in cases when the additional medication was needed for ongoing signs of infection or other rare but possible post-abortion complication symptoms (fieldnotes, personal journals). Thanks to structural abortion stigma embodied and enacted by health care professionals beyond the oversight of the abortion clinic itself, patients are delayed in carrying out the safest recommended procedures, observing aftercare precautions, or following recommendations to treat recognized signs of infection, as well as exposed to unprofessional discrimination in healthcare.

The spillover effects of such abortion stigma may endanger even those who have not sought abortion. In clinics and on abortion hotlines, we find abortion stigma contributes to and is exacerbated by persistent myths and misconceptions about other common medications (Shoveller et al. 2007) including the "morning-after pill" (emergency contraceptives that inhibit ovulation); ergonovine, a smooth-muscle constrictor that aids in restoring uterine muscle tone; misoprostol (used similarly to ergonovine in a range of post-pregnancy situations including hemorrhage, and to induce a pharmacologic miscarriage in medication abortion) as well as lingering prejudices about people who use any of these medications—whether for abortion, abortion complications, labor and delivery complications, or other reproductive health treatments (Shoveller et al. 2007). Such stigma-driven, potentially dangerous ideas underlie the trend of consumers denied time-sensitive access to emergency contraception (Shoveller et al. 2007), or the news about a woman in Georgia whose potentially critical life-saving miscarriage treatment was delayed by an anti-abortion pharmacist (Carmon 2015).

These individuals recount the harm done to them primarily in terms of the emotional impact of stigma, though in our syndemic analysis, such encounters also directly increased their risk of biomedical harm from (undesired) pregnancy, which in fact constitutes a greater risk than an abortion, or infection following incomplete miscarriage. Yet perhaps the collateral harm done to these other, unintended victims is perfectly unsurprising, as Kumar (et al. 2009) reminds us of abortion stigma's threat to mark any person who has failed to live up to the idealized functions of womanhood, with "successful" reproduction high on that list.

STRUCTURAL, BIOLOGICAL, AND BIOMEDICAL PATHWAYS OF INTERACTION

Here we outline known and likely pathways of interaction between biological, biomedical, and structural factors mentioned. We present the role of abortion stigma in contributing to or causing deleterious biological/biomedical interactions and resulting health risks (Figure 1.1).

Pregnancy as an Entry Point for Stigmatization and Pathologization

In this syndemic, and in other research on abortion stigma (Cockrill and Nack 2013; Kumar, Hessini, and Mitchell 2009), pregnancy, an otherwise *non*-pathological biological state, is socially pathologized when the person whose body within which it biologically occurs seeks or obtains an abortion. This occurs in contexts of structural and symbolic violence where the right and agency to determine one's own bodily autonomy and reproductive destiny is systematically marginalized (Farmer 2004; Morgan and Roberts 2012; Boonstra and Nash 2014; Ginsburg and Rapp 1991).

Like other pregnancies pathologized due to assumptions about the pregnant person's social status or economic standing, a pregnancy intended, by the person in whose body it occurs, to end in abortion becomes socially contested, with repercussions for the medical care they can receive (e.g., Everson 2015; Collins and David 2009). This is seen in: adolescent pregnancy, which inspires widespread cultural judgments about who should have children and when; Black women's pregnancies, accepted as medically higher-risk for preterm labor and low birth weight without thorough discussion of the structural reasons for this; older women's pregnancies, often assumed to be the result of assisted reproductive technologies and constructed as higher-risk; and trans men's and nonbinary folks' pregnancies, an understudied topic until now given more attention in tabloids than in reproductive health studies.

Hotly contested in debates over state restrictions (Boonstra and Nash 2014), portrayed in media in ways that make women's bodies and pregnancies sensationalized public property (Joffe 2010), and subject to capricious legal restrictions and insurance rules (Roberts et al. 2014), pregnancy ending in abortion is framed as something other than a temporary biological state or physiologic pregnancy like any other. Several categories of pregnancies have historically been *more* stigmatized to begin with: those of women of color, adolescents, women in poverty, and/or unmarried women. All of these groups are statistically more likely to seek abortion services, and to encounter barriers to abortion (Ostrach and Cheyney 2014; Greene Foster et al. 2008; Boonstra and Nash 2014). Such overlapping categories of stigmatized pregnancies highlight the intersectional and compounding nature of social inequalities that impact reproductive (in)justice.

Pathologized through stigma resulting from gender role expectations and biologically reductionist views that diminish those who opt not to carry a given pregnancy to term (Kumar, Hessini, and Mitchell 2009), pregnancies concluding in abortion become the first biological factor in the mechanisms of interaction between abortion-related stigma and ensuing physical sequelae resulting from the inability to obtain a safe abortion, and/or to properly adhere to aftercare measures to prevent or treat complications. Neither pregnancy nor safe abortions inherently constitute a health risk. However, the stigmatized nature of a pregnancy ending in abortion results in the social construction of a pathological pregnancy from which deleterious reproductive harm may result. When reproductive harm does occur, sufferers are blamed for the negative outcomes, compounding abortion stigma's connection to health consequences, such as in the documented cases of low-quality care and delayed treatment for women in post-abortion and septic wards (Mayi-Tsonga et al. 2009; León, Billings, and Barrionuevo 2006).

Societal stigmatization of women's constrained reproductive decision-making perpetuates a cycle of abortion stigma with social, biological, and medical effects (Cockrill et al. 2013; Kumar, Hessini, and Mitchell 2009), reinforcing what anthropologist Marcia Ellison (2003) characterizes as structural violence shaping reproductive agency. Through pathways of structural-biological-biomedical interaction, these dynamics constitute an abortion stigma syndemic. Addressing abortion-related stigma will improve chances that those needing abortion will be able to obtain (and attend to aftercare instructions to ensure) the safest procedures and recovery possible.

To explain each of the pathways presented in Figure 1.1, we present the links represented by multiple, overlapping structural layers and describe resultant downstream risks for health complications, each of which we present with supporting literature and auto-ethnographic data. Throughout the chapter, we discuss these layers in relation to each other rather than in the (artificially) separated manner of the figure, but for the sake of explaining our syndemic model we introduce each pathway separately.

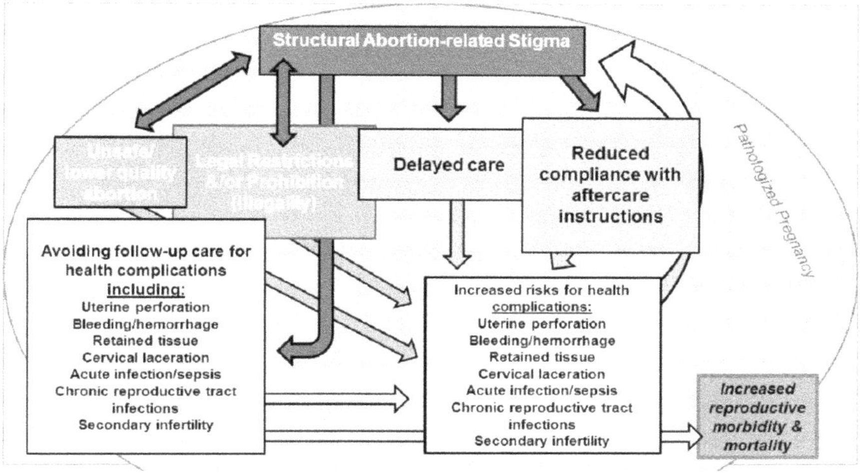

Figure 1.1. Pathways of Interaction between Abortion-Related Stigma, Pathologized Pregnancy, and Biomedical Complications.

ELEMENTS OF FIGURE 1.1

Pathologized Pregnancy

The circle around and in the background of the other elements represents the biological state of pregnancy, pathologized through socially constructed abortion-related stigma, which, in interaction with health complications resulting from constrained abortion affected by stigma, results in deleterious health complications including infection (acute and chronic), sepsis, bleeding, hemorrhage, uterine perforation, secondary infertility, and even death (Fischer et al. 2005; Saultes, Devita, and Heiner 2009; Gerdts et al. 2016; Tristan and Gilliam 2009; Khan et al. 2006; Niinimäki et al. 2009; Vlassoff et al. 2008; World Health Organization 2011). Through a syndemic relationship with abortion-related stigma, the non-disease state of pregnancy becomes socially pathologized and biomedically risky, producing risks for serious health issues that would not otherwise affect it.

STRUCTURAL ABORTION-RELATED STIGMA

The darkest gray box at the top of the diagram and corresponding dark gray arrows convey the structural factor driving this syndemic: social sanctioning expressed through abortion-related stigma (Kumar 2013). Abortion-related stigma has a bidirectional relationship with unsafe and lower-quality abortion, wherein stigma towards pathologized pregnancies ending in abortion affects care quality by, for example, discouraging providers from working in the field of abortion (Freedman et al. 2010) and limits access to safe and high-quality care by contributing to the increasing passage of state-level restrictions on facilities that provide abortion (Alan Guttmacher Institute 2015a). Lower quality abortion care contributes to stigma, a feedback loop with biomedical health consequences (Ostrach 2016; Kumar 2013; Barot 2011). Abortion-related stigma functions in a bidirectional relationship with restrictions and outright prohibition (illegal abortion), contributing to legal and social climates in which abortion is restricted or outlawed and fueling the perception that abortion is worthy of being stigmatized. This stigma, and related fear of disclosing an abortion, may reduce the ability to attend to aftercare instructions (L. H. Harris 2012) intended to reduce the risks of biomedical health complications from the abortion procedure. Structural stigma results in delays in being able to receive care, increasing the likelihood that someone may receive later abortion care, with associated greater risks for complications (L. H. Harris and Grossman 2011). Stigma contributes to the desire not to disclose having had an abortion (Shellenberg et al. 2011), which can interfere with ability or willingness to seek biomedical follow-up care for infections, bleeding, or other health consequences of interactions between pathologized pregnancies and stigmatized care.

Unsafe/Low Quality Abortion; Legal Restrictions

The dark gray boxes with white writing and corresponding arrows indicate a structural layer of interaction among abortion-related stigma, legal restrictions on abortion, and outright prohibition of abortion which directly contributes to unsafe, lower quality abortion (Barot 2011; Bartlett et al. 2004; Jones and Weitz 2009). Abortion restrictions lead to public perceptions that abortion is either so dangerous as to require heavy regulation or so deviant as to merit prohibition (Kumar, Hessini, and Mitchell 2009). Abortion restrictions lead to care that is in fact harder to obtain and/or less safe (Banerjee, Andersen, and Warvadekar 2012). Legal limitations on abortion thus have the dual effect of steering some people toward clandestine and/or self-induced abortion *and* contributing to reluctance to seek follow-up care for complications (Saultes, Devita, and Heiner 2009; Grossman et al. 2010). Constraints on legal abortion further result in delays in being able to receive safe clinical care (Grossman et al. 2014) by creating onerous barriers to providers' entering or remaining in practice, requiring patients to undergo multiple visits and waiting periods, or indirectly increasing the costs of care such that patients must spend more time preparing financially. Such delays in care lead to greater risks (L. H. Harris and Grossman 2011) for deleterious health consequences from biomedical complications of procedures performed for socially and structurally pathologized pregnancies (Kumar, Hessini, and Mitchell 2009).

Delayed Care and Reduced Compliance with Aftercare

The lighter gray boxes with black writing and corresponding arrows indicate how abortion-related stigma as a structural factor contributes to obtaining abortion later in a (pathologized) pregnancy (Jones and Weitz 2009; L. H. Harris and Grossman 2011), with increased risks for deleterious health complications including infection, sepsis, bleeding, hemorrhage, uterine perforation, retained placental or fetal tissue, cervical laceration, secondary infertility, and even death (Fischer et al. 2005; Saultes, Devita, and Heiner 2009; Gerdts et al. 2016; Tristan and Gilliam 2009; Khan et al. 2006; Niinimäki et al. 2009; Vlassoff et al. 2008; World Health Organization 2010; Grossman, Blanchard, and Blumenthal 2008). Unsafe or lower quality abortion, structurally produced and reinforced by abortion-related stigma, directly contributes to increased risks for complications (Fischer et al. 2005; Saultes, Devita, and Heiner 2009; Gerdts et al. 2016; Tristan and Gilliam 2009; Khan et al. 2006; Niinimäki et al. 2009; Vlassoff et al. 2008; World Health Organization 2010; Kumar, Hessini, and Mitchell 2009). Delayed care, and reduced compliance with aftercare, leads to the ultimate result of an abortion stigma syndemic—increased risks for deleterious health complications (as delineated throughout this chapter), and ultimately, increased reproductive morbidity and mortality.

Avoiding Follow-Up Care for Health Complications; Increased Risks for Health Complications

The lightest gray box and arrows, and the white box, illustrate the specific deleterious health consequences of difficulty attending to routine aftercare or seeking follow-up care for suspected complications, as a consequence of stigma, and of the overall health risks of interactions between pathologized pregnancies, constrained abortion, and the structural and biomedical/biological relationships between factors. Reluctance or inability to follow aftercare instructions, due to stigma, increases risks for complications: infection, sepsis, bleeding, hemorrhage, uterine perforation, retained placental or fetal tissue, cervical laceration, secondary infertility, and even death (Fischer et al. 2005; Saultes, Devita, and Heiner 2009; Gerdts et al. 2016; Tristan and Gilliam 2009; Khan et al. 2006; Niinimäki et al. 2009; Vlassoff et al. 2008; World Health Organization 2010). When abortion-related stigma contributes to legal restrictions or prohibition—pathologizing pregnancies intended to end in abortion—risks for biomedical complications increase. This can contribute to increased health consequences of interactions *between* pathologized pregnancy and stigmatized biomedical care. Such interactions increase reproductive morbidity and mortality. The various overlapping, intersecting, and additive relationships between the syndemic factors graphically represented in Figure 1.1 are further presented in detail in the following sections, with supporting literature and auto-ethnographic accounts.

Abortion Stigma, Safety, and Care Quality

Links between abortion stigma and lack of access to safe and timely care are well-known and well-documented (Ostrach 2016; L. H. Harris and Grossman 2011; Kumar, Hessini, and Mitchell 2009). Here we briefly reiterate immediate risks for reproductive morbidity and mortality that result from the restriction of practical access to safe abortion, through stigma. Abortion stigma can predict the likelihood of a wide variety of complications (Singh, Sedgh, and Hussain 2010; Mayi-Tsonga et al. 2009). Widespread abortion stigma contributes to women in much of the world having access only to clandestine or unsafe abortion, with accompanying risks for infection, sepsis, hemorrhage, and death (Khan et al. 2006; Vlassoff et al. 2008; World Health Organization 2010; Barot 2011; Grimes et al. 2006). In countries where women have no option for either legal or safe abortion, abortion stigma directly contributes to morbidity and mortality from the pathologization of ill-timed pregnancies that may end in unsafe abortion (Barot 2011; Grimes et al. 2006).

Stigma-Driven Abortion Restrictions

Even in countries where abortion is legal, but heavily restricted especially in later weeks of gestation—such as the United States (Alan Guttmacher Institute 2015a) and many countries in Europe (Chełstowska 2011; Worrell 2016b, 2016d, 2016a)—those who cannot access legal services may self-induce an abortion (Grossman et al. 2010), or seek clandestine care (Delicia 2002; Grimes et al. 2006). People concerned about abortion stigma and/or legality may use herbs, pesticides, other toxins, off-label drugs, or direct physical trauma to terminate pregnancy and avoid being seen approaching a provider to request a referral or an abortion (Shellenberg et al. 2011; Grossman et al. 2010; Worrell 2016c; Saultes, Devita, and Heiner 2009; Nyblade, Edmeades, and Pearson 2010).

Self-induction or use of clandestine care occurs not only where abortion is less accessible but also in settings where stigma contributes to assumptions that abortion is illegal, restricted, or not publicly funded (Ostrach 2013). When performed without adequate information or support, clandestine methods can result in serious health consequences (Saultes, Devita, and Heiner 2009; Gerdts et al. 2016; Khan et al. 2006; Vlassoff et al. 2008; World Health Organization 2010). Self-induction and other clandestine methods have increased in some areas as abortion becomes harder to obtain, especially in parts of the U.S. facing rapid escalation of restrictions targeting free-standing abortion clinics (Alan Guttmacher Institute 2015a; Gerdts et al. 2016; Grossman et al. 2014). Abortion stigma contributes to increasing clinic closures and restrictions (Martin 2013)—we argue this is a bidirectional dynamic.

Abortion stigma compels those most affected to rely on higher-risk abortion practices, resulting in dangerous biological and biomedical interactions between pathologized pregnancies and constrained abortion, in part through clinic closures that result from stigma-driven and stigmatizing laws (Saultes, Devita, and Heiner 2009; Gerdts et al. 2016; Khan et al. 2006; Vlassoff et al. 2008; World Health Organization 2010), and even news coverage of these laws. In a particularly chilling instance, Saultes et al. (2009) documented a case of a woman dying of septic shock after self-performing an abortion with a wire coathanger. This happened in Washington, where abortion is legal, covered by Medicaid, and where second-trimester services (which she would have needed) are available (fieldnotes). Based on our auto-ethnographic experiences in the field of abortion care, this death occurred in the context of a time when many U.S. patients, nationally, sought care while aware of news stories about clinic closures stemming from stigma-driven abortion restrictions. A woman in Tennessee faced charges of attempted murder for using a wire coat hanger in similar fashion, attempting to self-induce a 24-week abortion (Kaplan 2015). In the wake of Texas's then-tightening of abortion restrictions, facilitated by and contributing to stigmatizing abortion rhetoric, resulting in the closure of more than 20 clinics statewide, the Texas Policy Evaluation Project collected data from at least 100,000 women reporting attempts to self-abort, often through potentially dangerous means (Kaplan 2015). Though the Texas restrictions were challenged in court and overturned by the Supreme Court in mid-2016 (Domonoske 2016), closed clinics typically do not reopen. When stigma hinders access to legal, high-quality abortion, and motivates risky self-surgery, how likely is it that someone will seek appropriate biomedical follow-up care in the event of injury or infection, if faced with the threat of criminal charges?

Stigma as Deterrent to Seeking Treatment for Complications

Perhaps most threatening to health and far less studied, perceived stigma can act as a deterrent to seeking treatment for complications (Singh 2006) in settings of legal and illegal abortion. Internationally, women appear to delay seeking care for complications from unsafe abortion more than for other pregnancy-related complications (Mayi-Tsonga et al. 2009; Nyblade, Edmeades, and Pearson 2010; Grimes et al. 2006), increasing the risk of death; acute infections can progress to sepsis, bleeding can progress to hemorrhage (Khan et al. 2006). The World Health Organization recommends primary care facilities worldwide stock supply kits for basic reproductive health needs—including aftercare and follow-up medications and instruments for "common complications" of unsafe and illegal abortion (World Health Organization 2010).

Abortion stigma affects which providers people will visit, particularly in international settings where clandestine providers may offer lower quality abortion and post-abortion care, under conditions of greater secrecy (Banerjee, Andersen, and Warvadekar 2012; Grimes et al. 2006). When the degree of stigma structurally determines the quality of care available, producing interactions between pathologized pregnancies and constrained biomedical care, this threatens reproductive health and exposes abortion recipients to greater risks for infection, bleeding, and other complications (Fischer et al. 2005; Saultes, Devita, and Heiner 2009; Gerdts et al. 2016; Tristan and Gilliam 2009; Khan et al. 2006; Niinimäki et al. 2009; Vlassoff et al. 2008; World Health Organization 2010).

In one memorable case of stigma affecting access and subsequent ability to obtain follow-up care for apparent complications, the first author (hereafter "I," in this section) vividly recalls one of the first clients on an abortion referral and funding hotline in western Oregon, established after the abrupt closure of one of the only freestanding full-spectrum clinics for a large region of the state (Singer, E. and Ostrach 2017). An early call came from an undocumented Spanish-speaking woman in her 40s, whom I'll refer to as "Guadalupe." She had no transportation to a clinic; her options were to arrange travel about an hour north to one of several clinics in a larger city that offered first- and second-trimester care, with bilingual staff, and some funding assistance—or travel a half hour to a nearby small clinic offering only first-trimester care with limited appointment availability, requiring she bring her own translator. The closer clinic had a reputation for substandard care (fieldnotes). Guadalupe told me she needed to go to the closer clinic, despite its limitations—she could not tell anyone except her teenage daughter, who did not drive, about her abortion need. She thought going somewhere closer would make it easier to conceal her appointment. Guadalupe did not want travel out of her small town to be noticed—a shorter trip would risk less stigma. I arranged transportation, and went along to translate, but was dismayed to notice the clinic did little to de-stigmatize the process. Guadalupe was barely acknowledged; the faxed payment voucher had been misfiled.

During the procedure, a nurse wearing a large crucifix turned to Guadalupe and said, in Spanish (the only time Guadalupe was directly addressed or spoken to in Spanish by clinic staff), "*It's okay, God will probably forgive you, as long as you don't have* another *abortion.*" Given all my training to provide unbiased care, I was nearly speechless. In that moment, after the nurse's presumptuously stigmatizing remark, Guadalupe, lying on the exam table, turned her face toward me and began to recount an earlier, illegal abortion she received in Mexico as a young woman. She described her cervix being manually dilated with an unsterile metal instrument, on someone's kitchen table, and a short length of garden hose being passed into her uterus and left in place until a miscarriage began. Guadalupe described the infection and bleeding that followed and how pleasantly surprised she was to later carry *wanted* pregnancies to term.

She told this all to me while her legal abortion in the U.S. was performed by clinic staff who acted like we were not there. When we reached the recovery room and a different nurse cursorily told a still-sedated Guadalupe what signs of infection or excessive bleeding to look for (in English, as I translated), I idly wondered, many years before first conceptualizing this framework linking stigma, abortion access, and abortion safety, how likely she would be to call a clinic where someone had spoken to her in such a way, if she did experience complications.

Later that night, Guadalupe left a message on our hotline, sounding worried. I called back—she described passing clots "*the size of lemons*," a sign of possible retained uterine tissue that (most) clinic workers are trained to take seriously. I encouraged her to call the clinic, assuming they would have an after-hours number for emergencies. She could not understand the outgoing message; I called the clinic myself, shocked to find no option to page an on-call provider, or reach an answering service. I left a message about a patient from that day experiencing heavy bleeding, cramping, and passing large clots. I did not get a call back that night, nor in any of the days that followed, as I kept calling. But I knew Guadalupe needed alternate care for a rare but possible complication of legal abortion. She was extremely nervous that going anywhere for follow-up would reveal she'd had an abortion (Shellenberg et al. 2011). The one "free" health clinic in her town would not waive an appointment fee—apparently, checking for post-abortion infection was not considered "primary care." Though Guadalupe was feeling better when I spoke to her for the last time a few months later, after checking in regularly, I wonder to this day what stigmatizing effects the experience had on her, and on her teenage daughter's, perceptions of abortion safety.

This heartbreaking account, one of many ethnographic examples we recall, illustrates how stigma can contribute to complications from constrained care, in the context of socially pathologized pregnancy.

Crisis Pregnancy Centers—Centering Stigma

In the United States (Bryant et al. 2014), and increasingly in other countries where abortion is legal but stigmatized, unregulated "crisis pregnancy centers" run by anti-abortion organizations engage in misleading advertising and coercive "counseling" practices (Bryant et al. 2014). Such centers disseminate inaccurate medical information (Bryant et al. 2014, Bryant and Levi

2012) posing public health threats (Rosen 2012). Not inspected or held to any standards by county or state health departments or boards (as are professional medical facilities), these centers routinely operate next door to legitimate reproductive health clinics (Margo et al. 2016) and make a point of buying or renting storefront or driveway space next to or near existing abortion clinics, confusing patients attempting to attend a scheduled abortion (Everitt 2015; Margo et al. 2016). Such biased non-medical facilities advertise free pregnancy tests, ultrasounds, and options counseling, performed by unqualified workers wearing scrubs or other medical apparel (Rienzi 2009). Crisis pregnancy centers, with names chosen to appear alphabetically in phonebooks just above local abortion providers, engage in discouraging tactics designed to talk women out of having a wanted abortion, ultimately delaying abortion when wanted (Greene Foster et al. 2008; Rienzi 2009).

Though more research is needed on direct links between visiting a crisis pregnancy center and a person's subsequent ability to attend to abortion aftercare instructions or seek care for any complications, a concern among providers with whom we worked and conducted research is that some portion of people whose pregnancies are confirmed at a crisis pregnancy center may experience life-threatening ectopic pregnancies, a situation in which the lack of medical training among crisis pregnancy center staff could directly result in a dangerous missed opportunity to diagnose a serious pregnancy complication (Koenigsmark 2015). In our experience as abortion counselors and medical assistants in clinics and on hotlines, we also found that women who had been to a crisis pregnancy center or received misleading information from biased anti-abortion websites (or from protesters outside clinics) seem more hesitant to call a doctor or return to the clinic in the rare cases when bleeding, cramps, or signs of infection persist following a legal abortion procedure. This is an unsurprising but dismaying effect of abortion stigma syndemics, and warrants further prospective research.

Abortion Stigma and Medication Abortion

Another particularly worrisome complication if left untreated, "incomplete abortion" or retained tissue, is seen more often following medication or pharmacologic abortions, a protocol for terminating early pregnancy using a series of medications (typically mifepristone followed at set intervals by doses of misoprostol, or simply doses of misoprostol taken at timed intervals) to halt fetal development and induce a miscarriage (Grossman, Blanchard, and Blumenthal 2008; Akin, Kocoglu, and Akin 2005). Retained tissue or an incomplete abortion can lead to infection or to a continuing (nonviable) pregnancy (Grossman et al. 2004). Medication abortion is known to carry slightly higher risks for complications (Upadhyay et al. 2015; Ireland, Gatter, and Chen 2015), particularly infection. In one study, medication abortion had a four-fold higher risk for complications including retained tissue and hemorrhage (Niinimäki et al. 2009). Prior to the current alternate regimen used by most providers, at least in the United States (Ashok et al. 1998), an earlier medication abortion protocol that directed the insertion of misoprostol tablets vaginally (potentially introducing bacteria near the cervix or uterus) was thought to have resulted in several *Clostridium sardelli* infection deaths in a short period of time (Fischer et al. 2005) among patients in the U.S., Canada, and France.

To the extent that abortion stigma influences the feasibility of someone attending to medication abortion instructions and follow-up monitoring, or whether it is even safe for stigmatized patients to keep information about medication abortion instructions and warning signs of complications in their home, this also affects the relative safety of this early abortion option. Increasingly promoted by many business-model clinics that do not also offer suction or instrumental abortion (Singer, E. and Ostrach 2017) medication abortion is noted for greater risks for complications (Upadhyay et al. 2015; Ireland, Gatter, and Chen 2015) and a higher failure rate, that by FDA protocol would require suction or surgical follow-up often not available in the same location. Among some abortion providers in Europe and the U.S., there is increasing concern that the wider availability and promotion of medication abortion, and a corresponding drop in the availability of suction and instrumental abortion, contributes to an unforeseen stigmatization of *non*-medication abortion, and reduced availability of second-trimester abortion (fieldnotes).

In one study (Henshaw et al. 2008), those with more dangerous complications including infections, sepsis, and injury following illegal abortion had also been farther along in pregnancies and/or attempted to self-induce (such as with medication abortion pills), illustrating the bidirectionality of stigma in constraining the quality and timing of care available for pathologized pregnancies, further increasing risks for complications. Among providers, there is often discussion of the increased need for those receiving medication abortions to monitor the amount and length of bleeding, signs of infection or retained tissue, and of continuing pregnancy (Singer, E. and Ostrach 2017). Many abortion providers increasingly offer this method that requires multiple visits, medications to be administered at home, and self-monitoring of bleeding and tissue passed—all aspects of medication abortion regimens that may be complicated by external or internalized abortion stigma.

Complications of medication abortion such as infection, hemorrhage, and retained tissue (Niinimäki et al. 2009, Grossman et al. 2004), a growing concern with the increasing use of these methods for self-induction where clinics are closing as a result of stigma and in settings of illegality/restrictions, further draw our attention to the public health importance of people feeling fully able to attend to aftercare instructions and return to a high-quality care provider for follow-up and high-quality post-abortion care (Greenslade et al. 1994). Given that those who feel more stigmatized about seeking an abortion are less likely to disclose their abortion intention (Shellenberg et al. 2011), the implications for those concerned about or more affected by abortion stigma who obtain a medication abortion and then experience possible complications such as infection and bleeding (Niinimäki et al. 2009) are worrisome. If the desire not to disclose having had an abortion (Shellenberg et al. 2011) deters some from seeking follow-up care, structural stigma perpetuates the serious syndemic health consequences of interactions between a pathologized pregnancy and the biomedical aspects of constrained abortion—and perhaps even more so in relation to medication abortion, which carries more risks for complications, and requires more self-monitoring. An analysis of stigma-related syndemics could also be used to ensure that self-administered medication abortion, clandestinely attained in settings where women cannot otherwise access legal or high-quality care, could, for example, be made as safe as possible by informing the efforts of groups like *Women on Waves* to distribute information about using medication abortion pills and what to watch for in terms of complications, even in less-than-legal contexts.

That said, providers in settings with high rates of abortion mortality (such as in countries where abortion is illegal or otherwise hard to obtain) report the pharmacologic options used for medication abortion can offer a less-stigmatizing avenue for treating post-abortion complications, as women can discreetly take pills at home rather than being seen going to a hospital or clinic for vacuum aspiration to remove uterine tissue (Osur et al. 2013).

Stigma and Second-Trimester Abortion Delays

Health complication rates for legal abortion are low overall, and the absolute risks of high-quality clinical abortion continue to decline (Grossman et al. 2004). Yet stigma increases risks for complications even for abortion care provided under clinical guidelines, if it causes people to experience delays in obtaining care, or to avoid seeking needed follow-up care (Sedgh et al. 2016). Risks for complication such as bleeding, infection, uterine perforation, and retained tissue (DePiñeres, Baum, and Grossman 2014; Waddington, Hahn, and Reid 2015) are greater in later stages of pregnancy, with the risk of death, in particular, increasing with each week of pregnancy (Grossman, Blanchard, and Blumenthal 2008). This is not, of course, a reason to prevent people from obtaining later care, but rather another reason to facilitate access to earlier abortion, whenever possible, and reduce structural obstacles to later care that increase related risks.

Clinic workers and abortion researchers report those who perceive or display greater levels of abortion stigma appear to seek abortion services later in pregnancy, and more often in the second trimester (Harris and Grossman 2011; Harries et al. 2007)—this bears out in our experiences in abortion settings. Such stigma-related delays syndemically increase risks for rare but serious complications of legal abortion (Grossman et al. 2008) including bleeding, infection, and retained tissue (Tristan and Gilliam 2009), and for greater risks from later procedures and from illegal and unsafe abortion such as infection leading to sepsis, bleeding leading to hemorrhage, chronic reproductive tract infection, cervical laceration, secondary infertility, and death (Khan et al. 2006; Vlassoff et al. 2008; World Health Organization 2010; Waddington, Hahn, and Reid 2015; Barot 2011). This is one way in which the multidirectional relationship between stigma, pathologized pregnancies, and constrained care becomes frustratingly evident; second-trimester procedures, those who seek them, and providers who offer them, are all more heavily stigmatized (Norris et al. 2011). This is variously attributed to misogynistic and culturally constructed notions about the primacy of fetal "life," biologically reductionist gender roles, maternal obligation described as beginning at conception, and abortion being characterized as "dirty work" (Taylor 2008; Kumar, Hessini, and Mitchell 2009; Wolkomir and Powers 2007; Norris et al. 2011). Second-trimester abortion is thought to be less concealable, and more graphic or emotionally evocative of fetal "life" or the potential for life than are earlier procedures in which only a cluster of cells, an embryo, or a fetus, are seen on ultrasound (Kumar, Hessini, and Mitchell 2009; Norris et al. 2011).

The contents of a pregnant person's uterus, as seen or described on a coerced ultrasound or in a captive-audience mandated counseling session, do not in fact change people's minds about pursuing abortion for a given pregnancy, when they have already made a decision. At any gestation, only a tiny percentage of people, and primarily those who described themselves as unsure in their decision, hesitate to abort after viewing the yolk sac, embryo, or fetus on ultrasound (Gatter et al. 2014). Instead, such stigma-laden restrictions simply delay care and increase expenses. Those seeking abortion are aware of the disproportionate stigma toward second-trimester and later care—as clinic workers and abortion researchers, we heard women say they felt pressured to obtain care in the first trimester, or were targeted for harassment from people in their lives over attempts to undergo later care, even when their need for later care was directly due to delays in seeking earlier care as a result of structural barriers (Ostrach and Cheyney 2014), including stigma.

The stigmatized nature of abortion may further delay people from obtaining abortion by interfering with needed referrals (Harris et al. 2014), or affecting their comfort in asking their regular Ob/Gyn about terminating a pregnancy (Weitz and Cockrill 2010). Abortion stigma can interfere with asking about routine care such as an ultrasound or blood test—required in many states before terminating a pregnancy through state-level restrictions, potentially resulting in delays that produce unnecessary, avoidable, biomedical risks associated with obtaining later care. Recent evidence demonstrates that a woman denied a wanted abortion due to stigma-driven gestational limits is more likely to be in/still be in an abusive relationship several years later; she and her child(ren) are more likely to be in poverty, compared to someone *not* denied a wanted abortion (Greene Foster and Biggs 2014; L. Harris et al. 2014). For a person already facing intimate partner violence, delayed into the second trimester while seeking stigmatized abortion care, and then unable to access such care easily, delays specific to second-trimester care measurably increase the level of danger faced, both from intimate partner violence and for complications.

Providers also express anxiety about greater relative risks for deleterious health consequences from second-trimester and later procedures, exacerbated when patients are delayed from accessing earlier care. Clinical discussions emphasize the importance of later abortion recipients monitoring bleeding and signs of infection or retained tissue—indicating that if stigma deters them from doing so this would compound the very real worries providers have. Both authors often attended a U.S. national meeting of abortion providers: a popular yearly session that updates and trains physicians and clinic staff on skills for second-trimester and later abortion. We recall the good-humored, deeply understanding chuckle, followed by a profound sigh, that rippled through the room when a second-trimester session speaker one year began his remarks by saying, "*Hello, I'm ****, and I have complications*!" (personal journals). The speaker went on to describe successful clinical management of several cases in which women had been delayed until well into the second trimester, presented for care with complex abortion needs, and then experienced various complications requiring careful monitoring and skillful attention. The opening joke belied how tense and worrisome such situations can be for committed providers. They must trust that their patients, facing a larger society that stigmatizes abortion, will nevertheless remain in contact with the clinic to give updates on progress and any symptoms.

When stigma is deployed politically to restrict the legality, availability, and accessibility of second trimester (or later) abortion, making care less safe, while simultaneously functioning to prevent people from finding information needed to access earlier care, the result is a set-up. Those most at risk for delays and obstacles are backed into a sociopolitical corner: they need a highly contested and riskier procedure that is more stigmatized, and then have greater difficulty obtaining it—increasing risks for the stigma-driven health consequences of the later care they were forced to seek.

Stigma and Difficulty Attending to Aftercare

Abortion stigma impacts willingness to disclose abortion-seeking, potentially interfering with getting an abortion and/or follow-up care (Ostrach and Cheyney 2014; Cockrill and Nack 2013; Shellenberg et al. 2011; Kumar, Hessini, and Mitchell 2009). While little research has been conducted to examine the phenomenon closely, we propose that structural stigma impacts the ability to engage in self-care and infection prevention steps (Paul et al. 2011) typically recommended for a period of time after an abortion, increasing risks of complications in yet another way. No less an expert than long-time abortion provider and anthropologist Dr. Warren Hern, now one of the only surviving physicians openly providing late second-trimester and third-trimester abortion in the U.S., began writing several decades ago about the importance of working with patients to establish clear aftercare and follow-up plans to minimize complication risks (Hern 1994). If a patient avoids following abortion aftercare instructions because doing so reminds them (or signals to someone else) that they had an abortion for which they already felt stigmatized (Greene Foster et al. 2012; Shellenberg et al. 2011)—if, for example, a patient is afraid someone will see the clinic-provided aftercare instruction sheet with the word "abortion" on it, or notice a packet of antibiotics, menstrual pads, or other related supplies, and thus avoids having needed items around—this could increase risks for rare but possible complications of legal abortion (Tristan and Gilliam 2009).

Both authors noticed in years of abortion work that women who seem more affected by abortion stigma do appear less able or willing to closely follow aftercare instructions given to encourage the avoidance of rare but possible complications of legal abortion (Tristan and Gilliam 2009). Women who report more stigmatizing attitudes toward abortion nevertheless obtain abortions (Ostrach and Cheyney 2014): unintended or ill-timed pregnancies affect all people biologically able to become pregnant, and large percentages of people worldwide have an unmet need for contraceptives (Barot 2011). We conclude those more affected by stigma are at greater risk for complications including infection, sepsis, bleeding, hemorrhage, secondary infertility, and death (Fischer et al. 2005; Saultes, Devita, and Heiner 2009; Gerdts et al. 2016; Tristan and Gilliam 2009; Khan et al. 2006; Niinimäki et al. 2009; Vlassoff et al. 2008; World Health Organization 2010; DePiñeres, Baum, and Grossman 2014; Waddington, Hahn, and Reid 2015), through pathways of interaction between structural stigma, pathologized pregnancies, constrained care, and difficulty complying with aftercare. Based on our combined years of abortion provision and research, we observe that part of this equation includes those who seemingly internalize their experiences of abortion stigma by not following aftercare instructions, increasing their complication risks. Rigorous research on this aspect of our syndemic model is urgently needed.

Women who present for care seemingly more affected by abortion stigma may arrive at later gestations (Rowlands 2014), compounding their risks for complications in another way (DePiñeres, Baum, and Grossman 2014). We each encountered patients over the years who returned for follow-up care for the most common complications of legal abortion—infection and prolonged bleeding or retained tissue (Tristan and Gilliam 2009)—yet apparently suffered with them without seeking follow-up for weeks or even months at a time. Each of us can recall times when we asked a patient something like, "*Why did you wait to come back if you were having [cramps . . . bleeding that lasted more than two weeks . . . not having a period after a month . . .] etc.?*" only to have the person recount a story about a partner, family member, or anti-abortion protester who gave her such a hard time about having an abortion in the first place that seeking follow-up would have meant facing harassment all over again. We remember times when patients told us they had not taken the prophylactic antibiotics provided to prevent infection, because having them around meant reminding someone who had initially stigmatized them for seeking an abortion of it, or someone who had not known about the abortion finding out (personal notes).

Much existing literature on the efficacy of aftercare instructions and follow-up protocols puts the onus on abortion patients to be aware of what constitutes a "range of normal" bleeding and other signs and symptoms following surgical and medication abortions, emphasizing that patients must call or return to a clinic if they suspect a problem (Grossman et al. 2004). Research on unsafe abortion acknowledges the importance of reducing abortion stigma to increase access to post-abortion care (Faúndes 2012). Such research increasingly also calls for consideration of alternative strategies such as telephone follow-up, at-home pregnancy tests to rule out continuing pregnancy, or drop-in follow-up hours at clinics rather than scheduled appointments (Grossman et al. 2004)—which may also be more realistic options in settings with restricted access. All of these strategies could prove more convenient, but may not fully address structural stigma, where that is the factor deterring people from monitoring symptoms or maintaining a visual reminder of aftercare instructions, which clinic workers often note is a very real concern in situations of intimate partner violence or for young patients who live with their parents.

Links between stigma and interactions between pathologized pregnancies and biomedical complications of constrained abortion, in the context of the ability to attend to aftercare instructions, return our attention to crisis pregnancy centers and public health threats (Rosen 2012). Just as women who receive stigmatizing and false medical information from a crisis pregnancy center (Bryant and Levi 2012) may be less likely to seek follow-up care for complications such as infection or bleeding, stigma may also manifest in the form of people who have visited such centers feeling less empowered to follow aftercare instructions intended to prevent complications.

Weitz (2010) describes abortion stigma as contributing to unrealistic expectations about abortion. Those exposed to inaccurate and manipulative misinformation from Crisis Pregnancy Centers or anti-abortion websites and ads may expect recovering from abortion to be worse than it needs to be, compared to the evidence-based information they would receive from abortion providers familiar with the actual percentages and appearances of various complications and how they can be managed (Bryant et al. 2014). If exposed to stigmatizing anti-abortion myths promoting the idea that abortion will cause harm (Bryant and Levi 2012), a person may be less inclined to heed aftercare instructions based on scientific indicators of normal and abnormal symptoms, in biomedical terms. Crisis pregnancy centers often operate near abortion clinics or high schools (Everitt 2015), targeting young women and other vulnerable individuals who seek abortion at higher rates, falsely claiming that legal abortion will inevitably damage future fertility, cause breast cancer, or result in mental illness (Bryant and Levi 2012; Rosen 2012). We propose this contributes to a societal normalizing of the idea that a legal abortion might be *expected* to result in complications, and cause an abortion patient to ignore an amount of bleeding or cramping that clinician-provided, evidence-based, aftercare instructions would advise her is *not* in fact normal and means she should seek care. We argue that someone who might otherwise monitor symptoms and seek follow-up care after an abortion when faced with excessive bleeding, cramping or other symptoms, if previously told by a biased pregnancy center that the abortion would cause irreparable harm, might pay less attention to clinic-provided aftercare instructions and instead be influenced by stigma-driven misinformation to which they have been exposed by crisis pregnancy centers (Bryant et al. 2014).

In one study of medication abortion regimens taken at home (Elul et al. 2001) most women took the second of the two doses in the presence of a male partner. Though medication abortion regimens are an imperfect proxy for post-abortion medications, this suggests social support may mitigate some of the effects of stigma on following an abortion aftercare protocol at home. Though echoing findings that social support in general helps women overcome obstacles while accessing abortion (Ostrach and Cheyney 2014), this has not been widely explored in the context of biomedical aspects of abortion or follow-up.

The issue of stigma affecting ability to follow aftercare instructions is the area of our proposed syndemic least illuminated in existing literature—here lies the greatest need for prospective research. We did encounter this phenomenon directly in our own work with abortion patients, and heard about it from many fellow abortion clinic workers in other research (fieldnotes, personal journals), underscoring this aspect of the syndemic as an area ripe for ethnographic exploration.

CONCLUSIONS AND RECOMMENDATIONS

Based on our literature review and analysis, ethnographic fieldwork, and years of clinical work, we believe people more affected by abortion stigma are more at risk for and less able to avoid abortion complications, or to address them if they arise. We conclude those more affected by abortion stigma and the resulting social pathologization of their pregnancies, in interaction with constrained abortion care and reduced access to aftercare or follow-up, are at greater risk for biomedical complications such as infection, sepsis, bleeding, hemorrhage, secondary infertility, and even death (Fischer et al. 2005; Saultes, Devita, and Heiner 2009; Gerdts et al. 2016; Tristan and Gilliam 2009; Khan et al. 2006; Niinimäki et al. 2009; Vlassoff et al. 2008; World Health Organization 2010; DePiñeres, Baum, and Grossman 2014; Waddington, Hahn, and Reid 2015).

Each of these syndemic pathways of structural, biological, and biomedical interaction resulting from and related to abortion stigma overlap. Someone in a country with heavily restricted or low-quality abortion, as a result of structural stigma, is less able to access safe abortion in the first trimester, facing greater risks for complications from later abortion, if they obtain it. Where someone is able to obtain safer, early abortion, but perceives a high degree of stigma and does not or cannot follow aftercare instructions, they may be at greater risk for complications. Someone who perceives abortion stigma may avoid seeking follow-up care, if they experience complications. A person may attempt to obtain an abortion in the context of constrained care, but have difficulty finding a provider because of stigma-driven restrictions, lack of skilled providers, or a reluctance to disclose the need for an abortion—obtaining care later in pregnancy, with greater risks (L. H. Harris and Grossman 2011). In another important pathway of interaction, someone who obtains a lower-quality abortion, due to restrictions and stigma, may perpetuate societal abortion stigma by speaking negatively about the constrained care they do obtain (Kumar, Hessini, and Mitchell 2009).

In each of these scenarios, the multi-directional pathways of syndemic interaction between structural abortion stigma, socially pathologized pregnancies, constrained abortion, and biologically and biomedically interacting health consequences such as infection, sepsis, bleeding, hemorrhage, or other acknowledged physical harm resulting from stigma-driven risk factors, are evident, additive, and inextricable—tangled together in a web of stigma (Ostrach 2016). The consequences of these interactions are diverse, multi-directional, and complex, demonstrating the need for nuanced ethnographic and prospective syndemic analyses of each of the structural settings and biological features of this newly identified syndemic.

In all of these situations, abortion-related stigma facilitates and reinforces a structured biological and biomedical dynamic in which those in need of abortion and/or abortion follow-up care may be delayed in or prevented from safely obtaining it. As Purcell (2015) discusses in the context of the sociology of abortion, abortion stigma motivates those affected to avoid face-to-face contact with medical providers, compounding delays in care. Abortion stigma can affect people at different points in their care and interfere at different points: initially seeking an early abortion (likely to have a much lower risk of complications such as bleeding and acute infection which are quite rare but possible, Tristan and Gilliam 2009), attempting to attend to medically based, unbiased aftercare instructions (Paul et al. 2011), or handling symptoms of complications (whether the rare but possible complications from high-quality abortion, mentioned above, or the frequent, dangerous complications from illegal, unsafe, or self-induced abortion including chronic infection, hemorrhage, sepsis, and even death, Saultes, Devita, and Heiner 2009; Gerdts et al. 2016; Khan et al. 2006; Vlassoff et al. 2008; World Health Organization 2010). In each instance, reproductive morbidity and mortality risks increase for those facing structural stigma, through consequential relationships among biological and biomedical aspects of pathologized pregnancies, and in interaction with health consequences from stigmatized and constrained medical procedures.

Together, these interactions produce a greater burden of biologized stigmatization in the form of preventable abortion complications and health consequences. This is no indictment of abortion when performed safely—easier to do without legal restrictions and with proper access and support. Our syndemic framework instead reconfirms and supports existing public health and policy efforts to expand reproductive justice and facilitate the practical ability of all people to obtain safe, legal, high-quality abortion as needed worldwide, to lessen the devastating international burden of reproductive mortality and morbidity (Barot 2011; Ostrach 2016).

Even when abortion is legal, it is not always accessible or safe. Even when it is legal and accessible, those who perceive abortion stigma may struggle to obtain care, attend to aftercare, or seek follow-up. Abortion does not need to be stigmatized, illegal, restricted, unsafe, or inaccessible. Complications do not have to occur more often for certain populations. Abortion stigma need not result in a higher burden of reproductive deaths and injury. As providers, policymakers, and researchers, we already know how to make abortion more safe and accessible.

To do so effectively will require addressing structural abortion stigma at all levels of law, policy, care, and attitudes, and in the context of abortion provision itself. This requires clinicians, policymakers, educators, and community organizers to reduce stigma institutionally, and tackle it in popular culture and consciousness, before patients ever arrive at the clinic, or search the Internet or their neighborhoods for clandestine means. Policymakers cannot concern themselves only with law, ignoring social attitudes; abortion providers and researchers cannot concern ourselves only with protocols and aftercare instructions, ignoring social contexts embodied by patients as they sidle nervously through clinic doors flanked by shouting protesters. Abortion stigma becomes biologized and carried in people's bodies, along with pregnancies they seek to terminate, producing biological and biomedical risks for the deleterious health consequences of interactions between pathologized pregnancies, constrained abortion procedures, and biomedical health complications.

Until structural abortion stigma is acknowledged and addressed as a risk factor that interacts with biological features of pathologized pregnancy and biomedical aspects of abortion, abortion safety will be compromised—increasing complications and the ensuing health consequences. Syndemics offers a framework to think about how structures of society—the arguably more intractable elements of a medical context—are biologized in medical settings. Until we take to heart the syndemic lessons of how abortion stigma is translated into risks for delayed and denied access, reduced ability to attend to aftercare, and reluctance to seek follow-up care—increasing biological and biomedical risks—we can only ever untangle part of this web of stigma-related syndemic interactions.

NOTES

1. With the exceptions of varied circumstances in Cuba, Puerto Rico, Colombia, and the Distrito Federal in Mexico; a few other countries in the region technically allow the procedure to save a pregnant woman's life, but with unclear rules for executing this bypass process (Ostrach 2016). Recent news accounts suggest Chile might soon reconsider some of its abortion restrictions as well (Reuters 2015).
2. Including acute infection, sepsis, bleeding, hemorrhage, uterine perforation, retained tissue, secondary infertility, chronic reproductive tract infection, and even death (Fischer et al. 2005; Saultes, Devita, and Heiner 2009; Gerdts et al. 2016; Tristan and Gilliam 2009; Khan et al. 2006a; Niinimäki et al. 2009; Vlassoff et al. 2008; World Health Organization 2010).
3. *GoogleScholar*, *AnthroSource*, and *PubMed*; and related, more focused searches in the *Alan Guttmacher Institute* publication archives.
4. Because of the acknowledged conflation between the terms "illegal" and "unsafe" in the literature described, we narrowed our search to neither term, but rather simply used the term "abortion."
5. A social science research organization, funded by the *Tides Foundation*, it specifically examines effects of abortion stigma on women and providers.

REFERENCES

Akin, Ayse, Gonca Oktay Kocoglu, and Levent Akin. 2005. "Study Supports the Introduction of Early Medical Abortion in Turkey." *Reproductive Health Matters* 13 (26): 101–109.

Alan Guttmacher Institute. 2015a. "In Just the Last Four Years, States Have Enacted 231 Abortion Restrictions." January 5. http://www.guttmacher.org/media/inthenews/2015/01/05/.

———. 2015b. "Facts on Induced Abortion Worldwide: In Brief, Fact Sheet. November 2015." November. http://www.guttmacher.org/pubs/fb_IAW.pdf.

———. 2016. "Induced Abortion in the United States. Fact Sheet, 2016." http://www.guttmacher.org/pubs/fb_induced_abortion.html.

Ashok, P. W., G. C. Penney, G. M. Flett, and A. Templeton. 1998. "An Effective Regimen for Early Medical Abortion: A Report of 2000 Consecutive Cases." *Human Reproduction* 13 (10): 2962–2965.

Banerjee, Sushanta K., Kathryn L. Andersen, and Janardan Warvadekar. 2012. "Pathways and Consequences of Unsafe Abortion: A Comparison among Women with Complications after Induced and Spontaneous Abortions in Madhya Pradesh, India." *International Journal of Gynecology and Obstetrics* 118 (September): S113–20. doi:10.1016/S0020-7292(12)60009-5.

Barot, Sneha. 2011a. "Unsafe Abortion: The Missing Link in Global Efforts to Improve Maternal Health." *Guttmacher Policy Review* 14 (2): 24.

———. 2011b. "Unsafe Abortion: The Missing Link in Global Efforts to Improve Maternal Health." *Guttmacher Policy Review* 14 (2): 24–28.

Bartlett, Linda A., Cynthia J. Berg, Holly B. Shulman, Suzanne B. Zane, Clarice A. Green, Sara Whitehead, and Hani K. Atrash. 2004a. "Risk Factors for Legal Induced Abortion–related Mortality in the United States." *Obstetrics & Gynecology* 103 (4): 729–737.

———. 2004b. "Risk Factors for Legal Induced Abortion–Related Mortality in the United States:" *Obstetrics & Gynecology* 103 (4): 729–37. doi:10.1097/01.AOG.0000116260.81570.60.

BBC News. 2014. "Catholic Midwives Lose Abortion Case at UK Supreme Court." *BBC News*, December 17. http://www.bbc.com/news/uk-scotland-glasgow-west-30514054.

Berer, Marge. 2004. "National Laws and Unsafe Abortion: The Parameters of Change." *Reproductive Health Matters* 12 (24, Supplement): 1–8. doi:10.1016/S0968-8080(04)24024-1.

Boonstra, Heather D., and Elizabeth Nash. 2014. "A Surge of State Abortion Restrictions Puts Providers—and the Women They Serve—in the Crosshairs." *Guttmacher Policy Review* 17 (1): 1–17.

Bryant, Amy G., and Erika E. Levi. 2012. "Abortion Misinformation from Crisis Pregnancy Centers in North Carolina." *Contraception* 86 (6): 752–56. doi:10.1016/j.contraception.2012.06.001.

Bryant, Amy G., Subasri Narasimhan, Katelyn Bryant-Comstock, and Erika E. Levi. 2014. "Crisis Pregnancy Center Websites: Information, Misinformation and Disinformation." *Contraception* 90 (6): 601–5. doi:10.1016/j.contraception.2014.07.003.

Carmon, Irin. 2015. "When a Pharmacist Turns a Woman Away." *MSNBC*, April 14. http://www.msnbc.com/msnbc/when-pharmacist-turns-woman-away.

Chełstowska, Agata. 2011. "Stigmatisation and Commercialisation of Abortion Services in Poland: Turning Sin into Gold." *Reproductive Health Matters* 19 (37): 98–106. doi:10.1016/S0968-8080(11)37548-9.

Cockrill, Kate, Steph Herold, Ushma D. Upadhyay, Sarah Baum, Kelly Blanchard, and Dan Grossman. n.d. "What Is Abortion Stigma?" Abortion Stigma In Brief 1. http://seachange-program.org/.

Cockrill, Kate, and Leila Hessini. 2014. "Introduction: Bringing Abortion Stigma into Focus." *Women & Health* 54 (7): 593–98. doi:10.1080/03630242.2014.947218.

Cockrill, Kate, and Adina Nack. 2013. "'I'm Not That Type of Person': Managing the Stigma of Having an Abortion." *Deviant Behavior* 34 (12): 973–90. doi:10.1080/01639625.2013.800423.

Cockrill, Kate, Ushma D. Upadhyay, Janet Turan, and Diana Greene Foster. 2013. "The Stigma of Having an Abortion: Development of a Scale and Characteristics of Women Experiencing Abortion Stigma." *Perspectives on Sexual and Reproductive Health* 45 (2): 79–88.

Collins Jr., James W., and Richard J. David. 2009. "Racial Disparity in Low Birth Weight and Infant Mortality." *Clinics in Perinatology*, Current Controversies in Perinatology, 36 (1): 63–73. doi:10.1016/j.clp.2008.09.004.

Davis-Floyd, Robbie E. 2004. *Birth as an American Rite of Passage: With a New Preface*. Univ of California Press.

Delicia, Ferrando. 2002. "Clandestine Abortion in Peru, Facts and Figures." *Lima, Peru: Centro de La Mujer Peruana Flora Tristan.*

DePiñeres, Teresa, Sarah Baum, and Daniel Grossman. 2014. "Acceptability and Clinical Outcomes of First- and Second-Trimester Surgical Abortion by Suction Aspiration in Colombia." *Contraception* 90 (3): 242–248. doi:10.1016/j.contraception.2014.05.002.

Domonoske, Camila. 2016. "Supreme Court Strikes Down Abortion Restrictions In Texas." *NPR.org.* http://www.npr.org/sections/thetwo-way/2016/06/27/483686616/supreme-court-strikes-down-abortion-restrictions-in-texas.

Ellison, Marcia A. 2003. "Authoritative Knowledge and Single Women's Unintentional Pregnancies, Abortions, Adoption, and Single Motherhood: Social Stigma and Structural Violence." *Medical Anthropology Quarterly* 17 (3): 322–347.

Elul, Batya, Selma Hajri, Charlotte Ellertson, Claude Ben Slama, Elizabeth Pearlman, Beverly Winikoff, and others. 2001. "Can Women in Less-Developed Countries Use a Simplified Medical Abortion Regimen?" *The Lancet* 357 (9266): 1402–1405.

EtShalom, Yonah. 2015. "'I Wrote the Prescription; the Patient Did the Abortion': Preparation of Gynecologists for Abortion Services in Montevideo before and after 2004." MPH, Emory University.

Everitt, Amy. 2015. "Crisis Pregnancy Centers Threaten Women's Health." *Sacramento Bee*, March 11, sec. Soapbox. http://www.sacbee.com/opinion/op-ed/soapbox/article13575611.html.

Everson, Courtney Louise. 2015. "'I'm a Mom Too!'—Stigma, Support & Contested Identities among Adolescent Mothers in the United States," June. http://ir.library.oregonstate.edu/xmlui/handle/1957/56267.

Farmer, Paul. 2004. *Pathologies of Power: Health, Human Rights, and the New War on the Poor*. Vol. 4. Univ of California Press.

Faúndes, Anibal. 2012. "Strategies for the Prevention of Unsafe Abortion." *International Journal of Gynecology & Obstetrics* 119: S68–S71.

Fiala, Christian, and Joyce H. Arthur. 2014. "'Dishonourable Disobedience'—Why Refusal to Treat in Reproductive Healthcare Is Not Conscientious Objection." *Woman-Psychosomatic Gynaecology and Obstetrics* 1 (December): 12–23. doi:10.1016/j.woman.2014.03.001.

Fischer, Marc, Julu Bhatnagar, Jeannette Guarner, Sarah Reagan, Jill K. Hacker, Sharon H. Van Meter, Vadims Poukens, et al. 2005. "Fatal Toxic Shock Syndrome Associated with Clostridium Sordellii after Medical Abortion." *New England Journal of Medicine* 353 (22): 2352–60. doi:10.1056/NEJMoa051620.

Freedman, Lori, Uta Landy, Philip Darney, and Jody Steinauer. 2010. "Obstacles to the Integration of Abortion into Obstetrics and Gynecology Practice." *Perspectives on Sexual and Reproductive Health* 42 (3): 146–51. doi:10.1363/4214610.

Gatter, Mary, Katrina Kimport, Diana Greene Foster, Tracy A. Weitz, and Ushma D. Upadhyay. 2014. "Relationship between Ultrasound Viewing and Proceeding to Abortion." *Obstetrics & Gynecology* 123 (1): 81–87.

Gebreselassie, Hailemichael, Maria F. Gallo, Anthony Monyo, and Brooke R. Johnson. 2005. "The Magnitude of Abortion Complications in Kenya." *BJOG: An International Journal of Obstetrics & Gynaecology* 112 (9): 1229–1235.

Gerdts, Caitlin, Liza Fuentes, Daniel Grossman, Kari White, Brianna Keefe-Oates, Sarah E. Baum, Kristine Hopkins, Chandler W. Stolp, and Joseph E. Potter. 2016. "Impact of Clinic Closures on Women Obtaining Abortion Services After Implementation of a Restrictive Law in Texas." *American Journal of Public Health*, no. 0: e1–e8.

Ginsburg, Faye, and Rayna Rapp. 1991. "The Politics of Reproduction." *Annual Review of Anthropology* 20: 311–343.
Grady, Allison. 2006. "Legal Protection for Conscientious Objection by Health Professionals." *Virtual Mentor* 8 (5): 327–31. doi:10.1001/virtualmentor.2006.8.5.hlaw1-0605.
Greene Foster, Diana, and M. Antonia Biggs. 2014. "Effect of an Unwanted Pregnancy Carried to Term on Existing Children's Health, Development and Care." *Contraception* 90 (3): 305.
Greene Foster, Diana, Heather Gould, Jessica Taylor, and Tracy A. Weitz. 2012. "Attitudes and Decision Making among Women Seeking Abortions at One US Clinic." *Perspectives on Sexual and Reproductive Health* 44 (2): 117–124.
Greene Foster, Diana, Rebecca A. Jackson, Kate Cosby, Tracy A. Weitz, Philip D. Darney, and Eleanor A. Drey. 2008. "Predictors of Delay in Each Step Leading to an Abortion." *Contraception* 77 (4): 289–293.
Greenslade, Forrest C., Harrison McKay, Merrill Wolf, and Katie McLaurin. 1994. "Post-Abortion Care: A Women's Health Initiative to Combat Unsafe Abortion." *Advances in Abortion Care/IPAS* 4 (1): 1.
Grimes, David A., Janie Benson, Susheela Singh, Mariana Romero, Bela Ganatra, Friday E. Okonofua, and Iqbal H. Shah. 2006. "Unsafe Abortion: The Preventable Pandemic." *The Lancet* 368 (9550): 1908–1919.
Grossman, Daniel, Kelly Blanchard, and Paul Blumenthal. 2008. "Complications after Second Trimester Surgical and Medical Abortion." *Reproductive Health Matters* 16 (31): 173–182.
Grossman, Daniel, Charlotte Ellertson, David A. Grimes, and Dilys Walker. 2004. "Routine Follow-up Visits after First-Trimester Induced Abortion." *Obstetrics & Gynecology* 103 (4): 738–745.
Grossman, Daniel, Kelsey Holt, Melanie Peña, Diana Lara, Maggie Veatch, Denisse Córdova, Marji Gold, Beverly Winikoff, and Kelly Blanchard. 2010. "Self-Induction of Abortion among Women in the United States." *Reproductive Health Matters* 18 (36): 136–146.
Grossman, Daniel, Kari White, Kristine Hopkins, and Joseph E. Potter. 2014. "The Public Health Threat of Anti-Abortion Legislation." *Contraception* 89 (2): 73.
Harries, Jane, Phyllis Orner, Mosotho Gabriel, and Ellen Mitchell. 2007. "Delays in Seeking an Abortion until the Second Trimester: A Qualitative Study in South Africa." *Reproductive Health* 4 (1): 7.
Harris, Laura, Sarah CM Roberts, M. Antonia Biggs, Corinne H. Rocca, and Diana Greene Foster. 2014. "Perceived Stress and Emotional Social Support among Women Who Are Denied or Receive Abortions in the United States: A Prospective Cohort Study." *BMC Women's Health* 14 (1): 76.
Harris, Lisa H. 2012. "Stigma and Abortion Complications in the United States." *Obstetrics & Gynecology* 120 (6): 1472–1474.
Harris, Lisa H., and Daniel Grossman. 2011. "Confronting the Challenge of Unsafe Second-Trimester Abortion." *International Journal of Gynecology & Obstetrics* 115 (1): 77–79.
Henshaw, Stanley K., Isaac Adewole, Susheela Singh, Akinrinola Bankole, Boniface Oye-Adeniran, and Rubina Hussain. 2008. "Severity and Cost of Unsafe Abortion Complications Treated in Nigerian Hospitals." *International Family Planning Perspectives*, 40–50.
Hern, Warren M. 1994. "Surgical Abortion: Management, Complications, and Long-Term Risks." *Gynecology and Obstetrics.* 1994 (59). http://www.drhern.com/pdfs/surgabgo.pdf.
Ireland, Luu Doan, Mary Gatter, and Angela Y. Chen. 2015. "Medical Compared with Surgical Abortion for Effective Pregnancy Termination in the First Trimester." *Obstetrics & Gynecology* 126 (1): 22–28.
Joffe, Carol. 2010. "Anti-Choice Woman-Hating Goes Mainstream." *RH Reality Check*. May 24. http://rhrealitycheck.org/article/2010/05/24/womanhating-goes-mainstream-among-antichoicers/.
Johnson Jr, Brooke R., Eszter Kismödi, Monica V. Dragoman, and Marleen Temmerman. 2013. "Conscientious Objection to Provision of Legal Abortion Care." *International Journal of Gynecology & Obstetrics*, Conscientious objection to the provision of reproductive healthcare, 123, Supplement 3 (December): S60–62. doi:10.1016/S0020-7292(13)60004-1.

Jones, Bonnie Scott, and Tracy A. Weitz. 2009. "Legal Barriers to Second-Trimester Abortion Provision and Public Health Consequences." *American Journal of Public Health* 99 (4): 623.

Jordan, Brigitte. 1992. *Birth in Four Cultures: A Crosscultural Investigation of Childbirth in Yucatan, Holland, Sweden, and the United States*. Waveland Press.

Kaplan, Sarah. 2015. "Tenn. Woman Charged with Attempted Murder for Failed Coat Hanger Abortion." *Washington Post*, December 14. https://www.washingtonpost.com/news/morning-mix/wp/2015/12/14/tenn-woman-charged-with-attempted-murder-for-failed-coat-hanger-abortion/.

Khan, Khalid S., Daniel Wojdyla, Lale Say, A. Metin Gülmezoglu, and Paul FA Van Look. 2006. "WHO Analysis of Causes of Maternal Death: A Systematic Review." *The Lancet* 367 (9516): 1066–1074.

Koenigsmark, Tess. 2015. "Crisis Pregnancy Centers Should Be Accountable for Lies, Misinformation." *CT Viewpoints*. July 31. http://ctviewpoints.org/2015/07/31/pregnancy-center-accountability/.

Kumar, Anuradha. 2013. "Everything Is Not Abortion Stigma." *Women's Health Issues* 23 (6): e329–e331.

Kumar, Anuradha, Leila Hessini, and Ellen MH Mitchell. 2009. "Conceptualising Abortion Stigma." *Culture, Health & Sexuality* 11 (6): 625–639.

León, Rodolfo Gómez Ponce de, Deborah L. Billings, and Karina Barrionuevo. 2006. "Woman-Centered Post-Abortion Care in Public Hospitals in Tucumán, Argentina: Assessing Quality of Care and Its Link to Human Rights." *Health and Human Rights* 9 (1): 174–201. doi:10.2307/4065395.

Margo, Judy, Lois McCloskey, Gouri Gupte, Melanie Zurek, Seema Bhakta, and Emily Feinberg. 2016. "Women's Pathways to Abortion Care in South Carolina: A Qualitative Study of Obstacles and Supports." *Perspectives on Sexual and Reproductive Health* 48 (4): 199–207.

Marshall, Claire. 2016. "The Spread of Conscience Clause Legislation." *American Bar Association Human Rights* 39 (2). Accessed April 30. http://www.americanbar.org/publications/human_rights_magazine_home/2013_vol_39/january_2013_no_2_religious_freedom/the_spread_of_conscience_clause_legislation.html.

Martin, Lisa. 2013. "Targeted Regulation of Abortion Providers (TRAP) Legislation: Missed Opportunities for pro-Choice Communities to Combat Abortion Stigma." In APHA. https://apha.confex.com/apha/141am/webprogramadapt/Paper282958.html.

Mayi-Tsonga, Sosthene, Litochenko Oksana, Isabelle Ndombi, Thierno Diallo, Maria Helena De Sousa, and Aníbal Faúndes. 2009. "Delay in the Provision of Adequate Care to Women Who Died from Abortion-Related Complications in the Principal Maternity Hospital of Gabon." *Reproductive Health Matters* 17 (34): 65–70.

Morgan, Lynn M., and Elizabeth FS Roberts. 2012. "Reproductive Governance in Latin America." *Anthropology & Medicine* 19 (2): 241–254.

Niinimäki, Maarit, Anneli Pouta, Aini Bloigu, Mika Gissler, Elina Hemminki, Satu Suhonen, and Oskari Heikinheimo. 2009. "Immediate Complications after Medical Compared with Surgical Termination of Pregnancy." *Obstetrics & Gynecology* 114 (4): 795–804.

Norris, Alison, Danielle Bessett, Julia R. Steinberg, Megan L. Kavanaugh, Silvia De Zordo, and Davida Becker. 2011. "Abortion Stigma: A Reconceptualization of Constituents, Causes, and Consequences." *Women's Health Issues* 21 (3): S49–S54.

Nyblade, Laura, Jeffrey Edmeades, and Erin Pearson. 2010. "Self-Reported Abortion-Related Morbidity: A Comparison of Measures in Madhya Pradesh, India." *International Perspectives on Sexual and Reproductive Health* 36 (03): 140–48. doi:10.1363/3614010.

Ostrach, Bayla. 2013. "'Yo No Sabía . . . '—Immigrant Women's Use of National Health Systems for Reproductive and Abortion Care." *Journal of Immigrant and Minority Health/ Center for Minority Public Health* 15 (2): 262–72. doi:10.1007/s10903-012-9680-9.

———. 2014a. "Critical Medical Anthropology as a Roadmap—Understanding Access to Abortion in the Catalan Health System." *Medical Anthropology Quarterly* 1 (1): (online).

———. 2014b. "Did Policy Change Work? Oregon Women Continue to Encounter Delays in Medicaid Coverage for Abortion." *Anthropology in Action* 21 (3): 20–30.

———. 2016. "This Tangled Web of Reproductive Morbidity Risk: Abortion Stigma, Safety & Legality." *Frontiers in Women's Health* 1 (2): (online).

Ostrach, Bayla, and Melissa Cheyney. 2014. "Navigating Social and Institutional Obstacles Low-Income Women Seeking Abortion." *Qualitative Health Research*, June, 1049732314540218. doi:10.1177/1049732314540218.

Ostrach, Bayla, and Merrill Singer. 2012. "At Special Risk: Biopolitical Vulnerability and HIV/STI Syndemics among Women." *Health Sociology Review* 21 (3): 258–71. doi:10.5172/hesr.2012.21.3.258.

Osur, Joachim, Traci L. Baird, Brooke A. Levandowski, Emily Jackson, and Daniel Murokora. 2013. "Implementation of Misoprostol for Postabortion Care in Kenya and Uganda: A Qualitative Evaluation." *Global Health Action* 6. http://www.ncbi.nlm.nih.gov/pmc/articles/PMC3636418/.

Paltrow, Lynn M. 2015. "How Indiana Is Making It Possible to Jail Women for Having Abortions." *The Public Eye*. http://www.politicalresearch.org/2015/03/29/how-indiana-is-making-it-possible-to-jail-women-for-having-abortions/.

Paul, Maureen, Steve Lichtenberg, Lynn Borgatta, David A. Grimes, Phillip G. Stubblefield, and Mitchell D. Creinin. 2011. *Management of Unintended and Abnormal Pregnancy: Comprehensive Abortion Care*. John Wiley & Sons.

Purcell, Carrie. 2015. "The Sociology of Women's Abortion Experiences: Recent Research and Future Directions." *Sociology Compass* 9 (7): 585–96. doi:10.1111/soc4.12275.

Raymond, Elizabeth G., and David A. Grimes. 2012. "The Comparative Safety of Legal Induced Abortion and Childbirth in the United States:" *Obstetrics & Gynecology* 119 (2, Part 1): 215–19. doi:10.1097/AOG.0b013e31823fe923.

Reuters. 2015. "Chile's Lawmakers Take Key Step toward Decriminalizing Abortion | Reuters," August 4. http://www.reuters.com/article/us-chile-abortion-idUSKCN0QA01M 20150805.

Rienzi, Mark L. 2009. "History and Constitutionality of Maryland's Pregnancy Speech Regulations, The." *J. Contemp. Health L. & Pol'y* 26: 223.

Roberts, Sarah CM, Heather Gould, Katrina Kimport, Tracy A. Weitz, and Diana Greene Foster. 2014. "Out-of-Pocket Costs and Insurance Coverage for Abortion in the United States." *Women's Health Issues* 24 (2): e211–e218.

Rosen, Joanne D. 2012. "The Public Health Risks of Crisis Pregnancy Centers." *Perspectives on Sexual and Reproductive Health* 44 (3): 201–205.

Rowan, Andrea. 2015. "Prosecuting Women for Self-Inducing Abortion: Counterproductive and Lacking Compassion." *Guttmacher Policy Review* 18 (3).

Rowlands, Sam. 2014. *Abortion Care*. Cambridge University Press.

Saultes, Teresa A., Diane Devita, and Jason D. Heiner. 2009. "The Back Alley Revisited: Sepsis after Attempted Self-Induced Abortion." *Western Journal of Emergency Medicine* 10 (4). http://escholarship.org/uc/item/2mx5w2gr.

Sedgh, Gilda, Veronique Filippi, Onikepe O. Owolabi, Susheela D. Singh, Ian Askew, Akinrinola Bankole, Janie Benson, et al. 2016. "Insights from an Expert Group Meeting on the Definition and Measurement of Unsafe Abortion." *International Journal of Gynecology & Obstetrics*. http://www.sciencedirect.com/science/article/pii/S0020729216001028.

Sedgh, Gilda, Susheela Singh, Iqbal H. Shah, Elisabeth \AAhman, Stanley K. Henshaw, and Akinrinola Bankole. 2012. "Induced Abortion: Incidence and Trends Worldwide from 1995 to 2008." *The Lancet* 379 (9816): 625–632.

Shellenberg, Kristen M., Ann M. Moore, Akinrinola Bankole, Fatima Juarez, Adekunbi Kehinde Omideyi, Nancy Palomino, Zeba Sathar, Susheela Singh, and Amy O. Tsui. 2011. "Social Stigma and Disclosure about Induced Abortion: Results from an Exploratory Study." *Global Public Health* 6 (sup1): S111–S125.

Shoveller, Jean, Cathy Chabot, Judith A. Soon, and Marc Levine. 2007. "Identifying Barriers to Emergency Contraception Use Among Young Women from Various Sociocultural Groups in British Columbia, Canada." *Perspectives on Sexual and Reproductive Health* 39 (1): 13–20. doi:10.1363/3901307.

Singer, E., (Elyse Ona), and Bayla Ostrach. 2017. "The End of Feminist Abortion Counseling? Examining Threats to Women's Health." In *Transcending Borders*, 255–270. Palgrave-

MacMillan (Springer imprint). http://link.springer.com/chapter/10.1007/978-3-319-48399-3_16.
Singer, Merrill. 2009. *Introduction to Syndemics: A Critical Systems Approach to Public and Community Health*. John Wiley & Sons.
Singh, Susheela. 2006. "Hospital Admissions Resulting from Unsafe Abortion: Estimates from 13 Developing Countries." *The Lancet* 368 (9550): 1887–1892.
———. 2010. "Global Consequences of Unsafe Abortion." *Women's Health* 6 (6): 849–860.
Singh, Susheela, Jacqueline E. Darroch, and Lori S. Ashford. 2014. "Adding It Up: The Costs and Benefits of Investing in Sexual and Reproductive Health 2014." http://www.popline.org/node/637887.
Singh, Susheela, Gilda Sedgh, and Rubina Hussain. 2010. "Unintended Pregnancy: Worldwide Levels, Trends, and Outcomes." *Studies in Family Planning* 41 (4): 241–250.
Stein, Rob. 2011. "New Jersey Nurses Charge Religious Discrimination over Hospital Abortion Policy." *Washington Post*, November 27. https://www.washingtonpost.com/national/health-science/new-jersey-nurses-charge-religious-discrimination-over-hospital-abortion-policy/2011/11/15/gIQAydgm2N_story.html.
Taylor, Janelle S. 2008. *The Public Life of the Fetal Sonogram: Technology, Consumption, and the Politics of Reproduction*. Rutgers University Press.
Upadhyay, Ushma D., Sheila Desai, Vera Zlidar, Tracy A. Weitz, Daniel Grossman, Patricia Anderson, and Diana Taylor. 2015. "Incidence of Emergency Department Visits and Complications after Abortion." *Obstetrics & Gynecology* 125 (1): 175–183.
Vlassoff, Michael, Jessica Shearer, Damian Walker, and Henry Lucas. 2008. *Economic Impact of Unsafe Abortion-Related Morbidity and Mortality: Evidence and Estimation Challenges*. Vol. 59. Institute of Development Studies. https://www.ids.ac.uk/files/dmfile/RR59.pdf.
Waddington, Ashley, Philip M. Hahn, and Robert Reid. 2015. "Determinants of Late Presentation for Induced Abortion Care." *J Obstet Gynaecol Can* 37 (1): 40–45.
Weitz, Tracy A. 2010. "Rethinking the Mantra That Abortion Should Be' Safe, Legal, and Rare.'" *Journal of Women's History* 22 (3): 161–172.
Weitz, Tracy Ann, and Kate Cockrill. 2010. "Abortion Clinic Patients' Opinions about Obtaining Abortions from General Women's Health Care Providers." *Patient Education and Counseling* 81 (3): 409–414.
Wolkomir, Michelle, and Jennifer Powers. 2007. "Helping Women and Protecting the Self: The Challenge of Emotional Labor in an Abortion Clinic." *Qualitative Sociology* 30 (2): 153–169.
World Health Organization. 2010. "Packages of Interventions for Family Planning, Safe Abortion Care, Maternal, Newborn and Child Health." W.H.O. http://www.clacaidigital.info:8080/xmlui/handle/123456789/307.
———. 2011. "World Health Organization Sexual and Reproductive Health: Preventing Unsafe Abortion." http://www.who.int/reproductivehealth/topics/unsafe_abortion/en/index.html.
Worrell, Marc. 2016a. "Abortion Law Andorra." *Women on Waves*. Accessed March 10. http://www.womenonwaves.org/en/page/4753/abortion-law-andorra.
———. 2016b. "Abortion Law France." *Women on Waves*. Accessed March 10. http://www.womenonwaves.org/en/page/4775/abortion-law-france.
———. 2016c. "How to Do an Abortion with Pills (Misoprostol, Cytotec)?" *Women on Waves*. Accessed March 10. http://www.womenonwaves.org/en/page/702/how-to-do-an-abortion-with-pills--misoprostol--cytotec.
———. 2016d. "Malta." *Women on Waves*. Accessed March 10. http://www.womenonwaves.org/en/page/4343/malta.

Chapter Two

The Syndemic of Endometriosis, Stress, and Stigma

Véronique A. S. Griffith

Endometriosis, an epidemic and a chronic disease in which endometrial-like tissue (tissue biologically similar to the uterine lining) becomes ectopic and is found, abnormally, outside the uterus affects over 176 million women or 1 in 10 women worldwide, and approximately 1.5 million women in the United Kingdom (U.K.). It is characterized by extremely painful menstrual periods, chronic pelvic pain, pain during sexual intercourse (known as dyspareunia) and infertility. The symptoms often severely impact quality of life so that women affected with the disorder may struggle to work, or even simply to walk (Tulandi et al. 2004, Redwine 2004, Fritz 2005, Rogers et al. 2009).

In this chapter, I use a syndemic model to discuss the stigmatization of endometriosis and how this contributes to disease-disease interactions between endometriosis and stress. The syndemic concept, where two or more diseases interact in a specific structural context and thereby have a greater negative impact on the health of individuals than would otherwise occur, (Singer 2014) has been applied in the past to conditions such as acquired Human Immunodeficiency Virus (HIV) infections and tuberculosis which interact deleteriously in contexts of gendered inequality, poverty, war, and violence (Kwan and Ernst 2011, Freudenberg and Galea 2006). But the concept of syndemics also applies to other disease interactions in social conditions such as stigmatization, stress, and structural violence. In the case of endometriosis, I argue that stigma manifests as an embodied representation of structural violence,[1] where women are harmed through increasing levels of stress and worsening endometriosis symptoms. In such settings, women's suffering is seen as acceptable and of little consequence, thus normalizing the stress-producing stigmatization of their lived experiences with bodily and social suffering (Griffith 2015).

The endometriosis-stress-stigma syndemic I propose in this chapter is based on an ethnographic study, primarily conducted in the North-East of England, contextualized with further information from women with endometriosis across the wider United Kingdom and a content analysis of online sources. I aim to show how social stigma enacted toward women related to menstruation, sexual intercourse, and childlessness, exacerbates perceived symptoms of endometriosis. High levels of stress, which result from the stigma-laden environment within which women with endometriosis live, lead to worsening symptoms of endometriosis in three interlinked biosocial ways. First, stigma-induced stress socially limits access to medical care and treatment by causing women to avoid and be discouraged from seeking help from medical professionals by key figures such as mothers and school nurses. Second, stress may directly increase symptoms of endometriosis, increasing pain, infertility, and dyspareunia (pain with sexual activity). This occurs as abnormal cortisol levels, related to stress, are bi-directionally linked to infertility with effects on fertilization, production of gametes (eggs) (Harrison, Rowan and Mathias 2005, Harlow et al. 1997), and embryo implantation and development (Lima et al. 2006). Moreover, perceived pressure to engage in vaginal intercourse (in heterosexual relationships) is also associated with worsening dyspareunia and pain (Fritzer et al. 2013). Third, stress is thought to biologically increase the spread of endometriosis with increased development of new blood vessels associated with endometriosis (Tariverdian et al. 2007), and increased formation of endometrial lesions in animal models (Appleyard et al. 2015 and Cuevas et al. 2012). In a vicious cycle, worsened endometriosis symptoms contribute to stigma-induced stress as women struggle to live up to culturally shaped ideals of womanhood. Infertility or difficult menstruation associated with endometriosis is further stigmatized. And, the biological and social aspects of endometriosis and its sequelae interact and compound each other to both worsen and be worsened by cultural stigma that affects the availability and quality of care. The endometriosis-stress-stigma syndemic proposed here thus constitutes an important contribution to the field of stigma-linked syndemics, reproductive health, and ethnographic research on endometriosis that must be understood by health-care professionals seeking to improve treatment interventions.

BACKGROUND

The Stigma of Menstruation

Menstruation is particularly relevant to endometriosis as heavy and painful periods are common symptoms that women with endometriosis experience.

Historically and in many cultures, people saw menstrual blood as polluting (Douglas 1966, Meggitt 1964, Balzer 1981, Sanday 1981, Paige and Paige 1981). Buckley et al. (1988) first challenged the idea that menstrual fluid was considered polluting universally and that menstruation was by definition linked to women's subordination, showing that menstrual blood could also be empowering (Buckley et al. 1988, Hoskins 2002). It has more recently been suggested that the "classic menstrual-blood-as-pollution model be discarded" in favour of a more nuanced understanding of situationally specific menstrual taboos (Gottlieb 2002, 386).

"Menstrual blood is a stigmatizing mark" that fits Goffman's three categories of stigma: the "abominations of the body," the "blemishes of individual character," and the stigma related to specific marginalized social groups (Goffman 1963, 4; Johnston-Robledo and Chrisler 2013, 10). While menstruation itself may be considered an abomination, its visible presence equally may be viewed as an individual character flaw. In addition, menstrual blood remains symbolic of the "tribal identity of femaleness" (Johnston-Robledo and Chrisler 2013, 10).

The social discomfort associated with menstruation is linked to three separate taboos in North American culture (Kissling 1996b). The first, the concealment taboo, refers to the idea that menstruation is something to be ashamed of and therefore to be hidden (Kissling 1996b). The second, the activity taboo, relates to social restrictions on menstruating women. The third, the communication taboo, alludes to the concept that one should not speak of menstruation (Kissling 1996a).

As much of the original data on which this chapter is based were collected in the United Kingdom, I primarily present a more detailed background on British menstrual culture. Laws (1990) in her book on what she calls British "menstrual etiquette" discusses the presence of both the concealment and communication taboos in British culture. Menstruation becomes something to be hidden, to be concealed both visually and orally in British culture (Laws 1990, O'Flynn 2006). With regards to the concealment taboo, British women use linguistic strategies including slang, pronouns, and euphemisms to discuss menstruation in a more comfortable fashion (Kissling 1996, O'Flynn 2006). Furthermore, the Independent Broadcasting Authority in Britain prohibited commercials for menstrual products on specific television networks until 1988 citing "'uncomfortable' or 'indiscrete' references to menstruation" (Laws 1990, 46 in O'Keefe 2006, 537). To this day, menstrual pads and tampons "are designed to be undetectable," and television ads of menstrual products make no direct mention of menstruation or blood, even going as far as to use blue liquid not red liquid to show the efficacy of the products (O'Keefe 2006, 537). These advertisements continue to reinforce negative attitudes towards menstruation including secrecy and shame (Power 1995).

An earlier qualitative study of semi-structured interviews of twenty women with endometriosis in Australia found that women not only anticipated social sanctioning as a result of disclosure of menstrual problems but also were often reprimanded when they did so (Seear 2009). The disclosure of menstrual problems may lead to difficulties due to its interpretation by men "as an excuse to get out of duties that they believe women owe them" (Seear 2009, 1124). Thus, women conceal menstruation to protect themselves from any gendered ostracization (Seear 2009).

For women with endometriosis, this menstrual etiquette finds its way into both the doctor's office (Cox et al. 2004) and the workplace (Denny 2004). This is further bolstered by the finding that problems around menstruation are not to be spoken of in the workplace, and that menstrual-related absences are explained through allusions to being generally unwell or feeling abdominal discomfort (O'Flynn 2006).

The Stigma of Sex

Discussions of stigma in existing literature linked to sex are limited and generally reported in connection with homosexuality, HIV, and other sexually transmitted infections, and sex work (Herek 2007, Preston 2004, Rushing 2005, Cunningham 2002). A sexual relationship (which becomes particularly important in endometriosis as pain during sex is a major symptom) remains largely an intimate affair, limited to the private sphere. It becomes something not talked about openly, a stigmatized topic of discussion and a communication taboo.

The landmark United States Supreme Court case Griswold v Connecticut (1956) can help elucidate the notion of sexual health stigma. Estelle Griswold opened a birth control clinic, was arrested, and found guilty of using contraception. Her appeal went to the Supreme Court, which found that the Connecticut statute was unconstitutional as the protection of the privacy of the marital relationship was essential. The Court found the intimacy of the then-"marriage relationship," now-"sexual relationship" was intrinsically private, something not to be intruded upon by outsiders not a party to that relationship (Griswold v. Connecticut, 381 U.S. 379 [1965]). In the U.K., sexuality is covered under article 8 of the Human Rights Act of 1998, which states that: "Everyone has the right to respect for his private and family life, his home and his correspondence."[2] Sexuality remains part of one's "private life."[3]

Considering the sexual relationship as private remains a current concept where sex is more present as a subject for discussion and representation especially in the media and on the Internet, its practices remain hidden away (Attwood 2009). In British culture, this is said to translate to an ambivalence about sex with social license granted around sexual innuendo and humor, but at the same time "a moralistic censure of explicit discussion of sexuality or sexual practice" (Alldred and David 2007, 2). Thus, a communication taboo still exists where conversations about sex result in discomfort, embarrassment, resistance, and coyness (Alldred and David 2007).

Communication taboos regarding dyspareunia have been reported by Cox (2004) and Fritzer (2013). Their findings that women felt it necessary to have sex despite pain and to feign enjoying intercourse are echoed by Elmerstig (2008) in a study of adolescent Swedish women and coital pain. They found that women "continue to have sexual intercourse despite pain and discomfort . . . pretend . . . not to feel pain or discomfort, or feign enjoyment . . . as part of . . . striving to be an ideal woman" (Elmerstig 2008, 360). Women with endometriosis in Austria "sacrificed their own pleasure and had sexual intercourse despite pain with the focus on the partner's pleasure instead of themselves" (Fritzer 2013, 395).

The Stigma of Childlessness

Western society has been characterized as pro-natalist and "pro-birth," in which parenthood is something to strive for (Miall 1985, 384). The two major fertility norms are that "married couples reproduce," and that "married couples should want to reproduce" (Veevers 1980, 3 in Miall, 1985, 384). Because childlessness goes against these norms, childlessness becomes "a form of deviant behavior in that it is statistically unusual and violates prevailing norms of acceptable conduct" (Miall 1985, 384).

Such ideology places childlessness firmly in contrast to femininity and the definition of what it means to be a woman: "Pronatalist cultural discourses have contextualized the meaning of the term 'woman' around the inevitability of a desire for motherhood, and the centrality of motherhood to understandings of feminine identity" (Gillespie 2001, 142). If a woman's purpose is socially constructed as that of becoming a mother, and she cannot or chooses not to become a mother, then, by her society's standards, is she still a woman? Childlessness, in the context of gender roles and resulting stigma, thus represents what Gillepsie calls "failed femininity" in contrast to socially constructed and globally dominant "normal" womanhood (Morell 1994, Ulrich and Weatherall 2000) constructed as "heterosexual, fertile, life-giving, selfless and fecund" (Gillespie 2001, 142).

Such literature makes a distinction between voluntary childlessness or childlessness by choice, and involuntary childlessness or childlessness related to infertility or sub-fecundity (Miall 1986). Women who wish to but are unable to have children are seen as people to be pitied and therefore to be supported in their moment of need (Gillespie 2000). In contrast, women who choose not to have children are seen as selfish and unfeminine (Gillespie

2000). Ultimately both forms of childlessness are stigmatized and stigmatizing and often result in isolation.

It is a matter of debate whether the stigma attached to female infertility relates to the association with a physical deformity or to "deviation from group identity" (Whiteford and Gonzalez 1994). While Miall (1985) suggests that infertility is more likely associated with a physical deformity, Whiteford et al. speculate that "the stigma attached to infertility rests not on the perceptions of a physical deformity, but on the sense of having broken a group norm" (Whiteford and Gonzalez 1994, 29). They argue this is so because the only visible sign of infertility is the lack of children. Involuntary childlessness is nevertheless associated with the notion of the "failed body" with Nancy Scheper-Hughes (1979) for example finding that Irish women who suffered serial stillbirths and miscarriages were both pitied and blamed. Medical discourses link the term infertility to notions of disease and illness. Thus, infertility becomes something to be diagnosed and treated, while also becoming a source of stigma for the childless woman (Gillespie 2000).

METHODS

This chapter is based on an ethnographic study using multiple qualitative methods, conducted primarily in the North-East of England, with additional data collected from across the United Kingdom and through online sources. I conducted semi-structured interviews with and collected questionnaires from 35 women suffering from endometriosis, and semi-structured interviews with 20 gynecologists (15 registrars[4] and 5 consultants[5]) and 10 chronic-pain medical professionals, for a total of 65 participants. The first group represented four populations of patients: members of a local support group in the North-East of England; members of a national support group; patients attending a local gynecology clinic (in the North-East of England); and members of online groups (Pinterest and Facebook) who were primarily from the U.S., Canada, the U.K., and Australia. I designed the question lists for both women with endometriosis and medical professionals to capture their understandings of endometriosis and their experiences of the patient-medical professional interaction. I administered questionnaires to members of the national support group, whereas members of the local support group and the patients from the gynecology clinic undertook semi-structured interviews for between forty-five minutes to two hours. The questions for both groups were the same. I did not contact the members of the online groups directly, but rather collected and analyzed their publicly posted visual representations of endometriosis. I also carried out participant-observation in a gynecology clinic once to twice a week for eight months and at six endometriosis support group meetings lasting approximately two hours each.

For triangulation purposes, as mentioned above, I analysed visual representations found on two different websites. The first set of data is of uploaded art made by endometriosis sufferers to represent endometriosis and their experiences of endometriosis. The second set of visual data represents images already existing on the Internet that members of the site felt represented endometriosis. In large part, this second data set involved not only visual images but also pieces of text interspersed. I thematically coded all types of data collected using content analysis. The National Health Service (NHS) in the U.K. and the Department of Anthropology, Durham University, U.K. approved all components of this research study prior to the start of data collection.

THE CYCLE OF STIGMA, STRESS, AND WORSENING ENDOMETRIOSIS

Endometriosis and Stress

Stress contributes to worsening endometriosis symptoms and symptoms of endometriosis increase stress in a bi-directional pathway. In addition, gendered stigma around endometriosis increases stress in a sociobiological pathway. Together these pathways interact to form the endometriosis-stress-stigma syndemic. Women with endometriosis have increased perceived stress levels (Tariverdian et al. 2007, Lazzeri et al. 2015, Petrelluzzi et al. 2008, Siedentopf et al. 2008) and associated altered levels of cortisol (Lima et al. 2006, Petrelluzzi et al. 2008). Cortisol is a hormone that has anti-inflammatory properties. Infertility, dyspareunia, and pelvic pain due to endometriosis are thought to cause "considerable physical and psychological stress because of their devastating effects on affective, sexual, and reproductive behavior, damaging the patient's self-esteem and impairing her quality of life" (Petrelluzzi et al. 2008, 390). Lazzeri et al. (2015), for example, found that in women with a long history of endometriosis, repeated surgical treatments were associated with higher levels of perceived stress. Petrelluzzi et al. (2012) found improvement in the physical functioning of women with endometriosis and normalization of their cortisol levels through physical therapy including breathing exercises and massage, and psychological interventions including behavioral cognitive therapy, suggesting that reducing psychological stress and improving coping resulted in perceived improvement of endometriosis symptoms.

Stress has been linked to increased pain levels, may in fact "contribute to the neuroendocrine processes that give rise to pain syndromes" (Melzack 1999, 99), and can alter pain thresholds (McEwen et al. 2010). Vachon-Presseau et al. (2013) found elevated cortisol levels in patients with chronic back pain and associated smaller hippocampal volume in the brain, and stronger pain-evoked activity. This, they think, suggests a stress model of chronic pain where a "sustained endocrine stress response . . . may contribute to . . . persistent pain states" (Vachon-Presseau et al. 2013). Moreover, social pressure to have intercourse may worsen dyspareunia (Fritzer et al. 2013), a sociobiological pathway that will be explained in more detail below.

Stress responses also affect the distribution of metabolic activity away from reproductive systems (Harrison, Rowan and Mathias 2005). Increased immune mediators due to stress may impact fertility (Harlow et al. 1997) on several levels such as fertilization, gamete production, and embryo implantation and development (Lima et al. 2006), and thus can biologically reduce fertility function. Altered cortisol levels (a sign of stress) in follicular fluid may also be linked to infertility, with total follicular cortisol levels reduced in infertile women with minimal or moderate endometriosis (Smith et al. 2002). In addition, after ovulation, high local levels of cortisol with its anti-inflammatory properties may allow for the oviduct to remain free of leukocytes (a type of white blood cell) whose presence could impair egg fertilization (Andersen 2002 and Lazzeri et al. 2015). In other words, stress hormones can affect conception further compounding the stress caused by infertility, in a vicious cycle. Psychological stress may increase oxidative damage[6] (Aschbacher et al. 2013) with negative effects on both egg and sperm viability, further leading to infertility (Gupta et al. 2006).

Stress thus may not only increase symptoms of endometriosis but also have an impact on the pathophysiology of the disease itself. Perceived stress in endometriosis patients may cause angiogenesis (development of new blood vessels) in endometriotic implants,[7] which in turn leads to the spread of endometriosis (Tariverdian et al. 2007). In addition, in a rat model of endometriosis, stress has been shown to increase the number and the size of endometriotic cysts and endometriosis vesicles (Appleyard et al. 2015 and Cuevas et al. 2012). Several papers have linked stress to the propagation of endometriosis through the effect of stress on cellular immunity. Lima et al. (2006) suggested that stress, by inhibiting "natural killer" cells in peritoneal fluid, increases the possibility of endometrial cells reaching the peritoneum through retrograde menstruation implanting. "Natural killer" cells act as a vacuum to pick up and destroy menstrual blood that has migrated backwards through the fallopian tubes, blood that if left may form endometriosis. Thus, if they are not allowed to function properly, in this case because of stress, endometriosis may be more likely to form.

Petrelluzzi et al. (2012) found that corticotropin-releasing hormone (CRH), a pro-inflammatory agent, increases due to psychological stress. This hormone has been strongly expressed in endometriotic implants and the mast cells surrounding these lesions. It may be that CRH and other inflammatory mediators exert more local inflammation due to increased stress (Petrelluzzi et al. 2012). Furthermore, such increased inflammation may result in increased adhesion (scar tissue) formation, a common cause of chronic pain in endometriosis. In addition, increased levels of CRH may worsen endometriosis symptoms through further reducing progestin levels (which are known to be decreased in endometriosis), interfering with fallopian tube mobility possibly increasing retrograde menstrual flow (Petrelluzzi 2012).

All of this literature demonstrates important biological pathways through which stress as both a psychological and physical state, in fact a biolog*ized* physical experience, contributes to, exacerbates, and interacts with the disease of endometriosis. It is clear that stress can increase all of the following symptoms and factors worsening endometriosis: angiogenesis, inflammation, pain, infertility, and dyspareunia, through the production of catecholamines and corticosteroids, as well as oxidative damage. Therefore, stress may not only worsen the symptoms of endometriosis but also contribute to the spread or severity of the disease itself within the body. As I will demonstrate in the next section, the social stigmatization of childlessness and sex related to endometriosis, and cultural stigma surrounding menstruation, contributes to increased stress levels for women living with endometriosis, producing the endometriosis-stigma-stress syndemic in which endometriosis increases stigma-induced stress and stress increases endometriosis symptoms. Overall, "a perpetual vicious circle may be present in patients with endometriosis, sustained by the disease-related inflammation and increased stress perception and reduced quality of life as a consequence of chronic pain and infertility" (Siedentopf et al. 2008, 451).

Stigma-Induced Stress in Endometriosis

Results of this study show that endometriosis is stigmatized and stigmatizing, seen still as a "women's disease" of the reproductive organs. Women report experiencing communication taboos related to stigma associated with three aspects of endometriosis symptoms or its sequelae—menstruation, dyspareunia, and involuntary childlessness. These taboos increase levels of perceived stress in women with endometriosis. The notion that "it's a woman's lot to suffer," that women are meant to have pain both during menstruation and during sexual intercourse, also limits women's ability to seek care.

In addition, the stigmatization of endometriosis leads women to hide their illness and pretend to be healthy, taking on what I term the "mask of health." Their hesitance in communicating their endometriosis experiences as well as the perceived need to hide the illness lead women to feel they are "suffering in silence." Ultimately, stigmatization of endometriosis increases women's levels of perceived stress, in turn exacerbating their disease progression and symptoms.

"It's Not Something You Talk About, Is It?"

My female participants reported creating a virtual map in their heads of who could and could not be told certain information. They were very clear that someone had to be in the "inner" circle to be told about their illness. The women distinguished two classes of information: a general understanding of endometriosis, and details about their specific experience of the disease. Even to hear a general explanation of endometriosis required one of two things: a certain amount of trust/closeness or a specific reason/necessity such as in the context of a job where the boss needed to know why they were absent from work.

A majority of women with endometriosis (n=20 of a total 35) reported feeling unable to discuss the condition. "It's not something you talk about, is it?" they stated. This feeling, they often explained was related to endometriosis being "a women's disease" or being about "women's bits." Mandy[8] said that:

> I struggled socially in my teens because I didn't go out as much as my friends. It also made things tricky with gatherings if I'd had to cry off certain activities and been unable to explain why because I don't necessarily know people that well, or because middle-aged men are involved who would be uncomfortable with being told about "women's things!" Boyfriends sometimes found it tough too, if I didn't feel much like being intimate at times—I'm lucky that my husband is very patient and understanding.

An image one woman with endometriosis posted online in a community forum, representing a female doll with her mouth duct-taped in the shape of an X, also speaks to the issue that the gendered, gynecological, nature of endometriosis makes it an intrinsically taboo subject. Next to the doll is written "The Voice of A Woman is Obscene." The woman who posted it, Samantha, stated:

> Last week was a hard week for me, #[9] endometriosis, processing a few things for myself. One of the issues that popped into my head was gender roles. I found this picture on a blog and it started me thinking about women, or silence or limited ability to speak openly about issues society sees as taboo such as menstrual health. We need to talk about it, why should we lower our voices when we talk about our bodies.

Haley responded by writing: "So true. And why are we as women left feeling inferior when we have issues?" Gillian, in her post, asked: "Is it still a 'man's world' we live in? Sometimes it seems that way." Many women with endometriosis believe that taboos relating to endometriosis are associated with gender. For them, women are treated as inferior and if it were a disease affecting men, it would be taken more seriously.

In an online post, Helen explained the reason endometriosis is not to be discussed:

> In feminist, or more relevant, psychoanalytic terms . . . the female biology strikes inherent fear to patriarchal norms . . . the boundaries society abides by are gender biased and "woman's issues" simply do not comfortably fit within that boundary . . . when i talk about endo[10] i find a real wall of taboo is formed as i talk about reproductive parts etc. THEN as soon as i say it can also effect lungs/eyes/kidneys/brain people find it more accessible and "serious;" It seems to me that the only way to break these taboo walls is to talk, talk, talk and keep on talking until we are heard . . . it will happen as long as we don't give up.

For her, it is the woman's body that causes fear. Since it is a disease of women's "reproductive parts," it does not fit within acceptable societal boundaries and becomes a taboo subject. Endometriosis only becomes a "serious" and "accessible" condition when she moves away from the link to women's genitalia and on to other parts of the body such as lungs or brain.

Abigail confirmed, in her post, the idea that it is endometriosis' link to menstrual and sexual health that allows it to remain surrounded by silence:

> I never understood why we should be silent about menstrual or sexual health as it pertains to women. Nobody understands conditions like endo because of this great silence and taboo against it. It's almost like even in our "advanced" and "modern" world, men are still afraid of us because they still don't understand why we have cycles and bleed and then stop for no reason other than it's a natural process. And the women who have a menstrual health problem are chastised by those who choose to believe that all periods are created equal. Probably more of an ignorance than an intentional snub, but ignorance can be fixed by education.

For Abigail, our "modern" world is in fact not so advanced. The taboos around menstrual and sexual health remain because "men are still afraid" of women and their unexplained menstrual cycles. This then impacts women who have menstrual health problems, as one of the by-products of this is the belief that "all periods are created equal."

Jane also acknowledged the existence of the taboo from "an old world" in the "new world":

> I think the taboo of talking about periods and other female reproductive problems is an example of every one of us living between old and new worlds. It is still not socially acceptable for us to talk about a prevalent problem. But in today's world if we want awareness and answers we need to talk about it. We need to break out of the limbo stuck between the old and new.

The women themselves appear to acknowledge that endometriosis is a "woman's disease" linked to structural violence. It is a disease they see as linked to women's silence and to gendered taboos. These women feel that because endometriosis is linked exclusively to women and to increased menstrual bleeding, pelvic pain, pain with sexual activity, and infertility, the broader society does not want to discuss it. Women with endometriosis feel discriminated against, subjected to enforced silence. Their context is one of structural violence where women experience gendered oppression and loss of equal status with men, and with women who are not suffering from endometriosis and therefore fit more neatly into ascribed female gender roles.

Menstruation: The First Communication Taboo

Talking about endometriosis requires discussing menstruation, the uterus (womb), and the idea that cells related to the endometrium (lining of the uterus) are found outside the uterus. Stories where menstruation was not to be spoken of were abundant, creating a barrier to medical care, and invariably were linked by women to receiving a late diagnosis. The woman speaking below, Charlotte, had symptoms of endometriosis since her first period at age 13 but was not diagnosed until age 32. For her, she could not have known that what she experienced was abnormal as she did not understand what a normal period was: "In my family, it wasn't ever to be talked about, it wasn't something we really ever discussed. I always had heavy periods and just thought it was normal."

Participants spoke of a communication taboo with regards to heavy[11] menstrual flow. However, this seemed related to the visual image of heavy bleeding (associated with endometriosis) and perhaps not simply linked to menstruation itself. Here, it was not the menstruation itself they were hesitant to discuss, but the presence of blood flooding the bed or the bathroom floor as one woman describes it. For these women, blood is not something to be talked about as it is a bit "unseemly."

Women also described an evolution regarding their feelings towards the communication taboo with stories of feeling unable to speak about endometriosis often placed in the past. In a support group meeting, Alice explained:

> I have no "fear" anymore. If people are uncomfortable I don't care anymore. I don't want anyone else to have to go through what I went through. So I talk about it. If I tell just one person about endometriosis then maybe that knowledge will trickle down. If just one person had talked about endometriosis at work for example during lunch I might have thought oh I have that, I have that, I have that even I had not wanted to join in the conversation. Or if someone had talked about their periods and those were normal I would have thought oh is my period not normal then. Maybe I would have gone to the GP sooner?

This inability to discuss menstruation was linked to women not knowing their suffering was abnormal and therefore delaying their access to care. Not having support and possible treatment likely increased women's experiences of stress and then worsened their symptoms of endometriosis, contributing to the biological-biological-social pathway in this syndemic.

Dyspareunia: The Second Communication Taboo

Talking about endometriosis often required women to discuss dyspareunia (pain during sex). This second type of communication taboo appeared more prominently than the other stigmas. Women in the local support group did not talk much about specifics (sexual positions that were more or less comfortable in relation to painful intercourse, for example) as compared to women in online support groups.

Discussions about sexual intercourse were always considered to be delicate in nature. Women stated they would not discuss such issues with their parents, or family members at all. Even discussions with doctors were considered at best awkward, with many women describing going to the doctor's office with the intention of asking about sexual issues and being unable to even start such a conversation. This discussion was first and foremost to be had with their sexual partners.

Therefore, many discussions among members of support groups (either online or in person) focused on how to talk to their partners. These discussions were separated into two types: how to introduce endometriosis to new or potential partners; and how to discuss changes in physical condition with their current partners. This generally focused on how to tell him (no one discussed any female partners) that sexual intercourse was painful. (Interestingly, women with endometriosis did not speak of their partners noticing without being told, or themselves initiating such a conversation.) Talking to one's partner about pain during intercourse was difficult, as women with endometriosis reported feeling considerable internalized social pressure to have sexual intercourse despite the pain it caused. Some women (10) spoke of feeling pressure to pretend to enjoy the sex. This pressure did not come necessarily from their male partners, but was an unspoken societal norm to conform to their perceived and expected role as sexual partners, and as women.

One example of this involved a discussion at a support group meeting. We were all drinking coffee and tea, having cake, talking and laughing. The support group meeting resembled a group of young friends having a good talk about their lives, and their partners. Janet shared:

> I'm not sure if I should tell my boyfriend that it hurts again to have intercourse. I've just been putting up with it, I lock myself in the bathroom afterwards and have a bath which helps a bit but . . . I don't think he knows. I want the lights off so he won't see the tears.

Some women also felt pressure to ensure that their partners enjoyed the sex despite their own pain. In an interview, Sally explained:

> And even relationship-wise you know it's painful. If we sleep together, I bleed. Afterwards you know I can be in pain for a couple of days. So that's quite difficult as well. It can't be great for him, that you know yeah I'll sleep with you but actually I'll be in agony for hours afterwards it must make them feel great.

During the support group meeting, Elizabeth talked of her ex-boyfriend who she believed ended the relationship in large part due to endometriosis. This related to a fairly common fear: that their partners would leave them because of decreased sexual activity. Margaret, in her interview, said: "We just don't have sexual intercourse anymore—it's a miracle we're still together."

Some women worried that the inability to have sex impacted their womanhood. It was not uncommon to hear "it challenges my femininity." The inability to have sex somehow was felt as a failure to fulfill their role as a wife or a partner. Susan added, in an interview: "It concerns me that I will not be able to be that person to them having sex and stuff."

Women with endometriosis also feared how future sexual partners might react to the news of pain during sex and the possible inability to have sexual intercourse:

> And I know a friend of mine [who] has got endometriosis finds it very difficult now 'cause she's single and she worries about what's gonna happen if she has a relationship and about kids and all this, that, and the other.

Women with endometriosis also felt uncomfortable discussing sexual issues with their doctors, indicating a barrier to receiving appropriate care. As mentioned, many reported going to the doctor with the plan to ask about pain during sexual intercourse and leaving without approaching the topic. Janet, for example, made an appointment to see her gynecologist to talk to him about dyspareunia, only to leave without saying anything. "It was like trying to talk about sex with my father," she explained.

Feeling unable to access treatment due to social stigma related to talking about heavy bleeding, painful intercourse, etc. can in fact worsen women's dyspareunia (pain with sex) and other symptoms of endometriosis as it goes untreated. In addition, pressure to have sexual intercourse and the associated fear of not being able to perform sexually, may result in broken partnerships and increased stress levels, which in turn biochemically exacerbates the pathophysiology of endometriosis. Fritzer et al. (2013) demonstrated that pressure to have intercourse and associated stress may in fact worsen dyspareunia. Just as stress increases pain during sexual intercourse, painful sex associated with endometriosis increases women's stress as they may want to avoid sexual intercourse or may have sex even though it is painful, with the resulting stress in turn increasing their symptoms in a vicious social stigma/stress/endometriosis syndemic cycle. Reducing sexual activity in an effort to avoid pain will, however, limit women's ability to get pregnant, increasing their chances of experiencing stigma and stress, related to potential infertility often associated with endometriosis. Women with endometriosis are in a gendered social and physical bind, it seems.

Childlessness: The Third Communication Taboo

Women with endometriosis discuss both involuntary and voluntary childlessness. While some women with endometriosis cannot have children, they still want to. Other women do not want children but feel that their biomedical treatment has been in large part linked to the assumption that they will want children at some point. Even if they have decided not to have children now, it is assumed by medical professionals that they may change their minds in the future.

Much of the stigma relating to voluntary childlessness discussed by my participants appears to originate from the medical professionals themselves. The women believed that medical professionals took their symptoms more seriously when the women were looking to get pregnant, suggesting an iatrogenic reinforcement of stigma and prolonging of suffering in women not seeking pregnancy. In an interview, Lacey said, "It was not until I wanted to have children that they took me seriously and really investigated the problem." Women with endometriosis also felt medical professionals did not believe or trust women's decisions about having children or not. For them, medical decisions that could have improved their quality of life were not taken, in order to preserve fertility—regardless of their desires. These women had no intention of getting pregnant and expressed frustrations that some surgical treatment options that might have relieved endometriosis symptoms but resulted in sterilization were denied to them. Women stated that medical professionals expected them to change their minds as if it were not possible for a woman to prefer or choose childlessness.

In addition, women with endometriosis were unable to discuss involuntary childlessness with most people. Generally, it seemed a topic they reserved for their partners and in special cases their mothers. Women spoke of their extended families' knowing about the involuntary childlessness but usually felt the family was less than understanding and put pressure on the couple. Laura stated that her extended family would say: "Oh, you'll have a kid, it'll be fine." She went on to say:

> They were dismissing anything that John (her husband) or I said. And that felt a bit like they do not believe me. It's (endometriosis) made me more careful about who I would have a relationship with and what kind of person. And so

> my husband now is fantastic, you know supportive. I don't think they ever really get it. It's difficult cause they can't see and you get used to managing your pain so unless it's really bad and you kind of go aaah, I try and get on with it. But he's really good whereas I've had other relationships where at what point you tell somebody you've got something like this? Do you not tell them? Do you go with somebody that wants children because that's the kind of person I would like or do you go with somebody that doesn't want children because you might not be able to give them children so it's always the thing isn't it?

Even on the online groups the discussion as to whether one should discuss successes with fertility, pregnancy issues related to endometriosis, or problems with children became quite heated. Some women believed this type of discussion does not belong in a forum about endometriosis. Instead, any mention of the word "pregnancy," or "children" was considered by some to be severely upsetting due to the grief over past reproductive losses or challenges felt by some members of the group. Some even stated that in writing posts mentioning pregnancy or children one should include a "trigger warning," something increasingly used when discussing matters relating to rape, sexual abuse, and eating disorders online.

Ironically, the stress linked to the social stigma of childlessness through infertility, or to reactions to voluntary childlessness, likely increases these women's inability to have children if they do wish to, since it has been shown that stress hormones interact with hormones responsible for normal ovulatory cycles such as FSH (Follicle Stimulating Hormone), LH (Luteinizing Hormone), prolactin, and GnRH (Gonadotropin Releasing Hormone) (Schenker et al. 1992). Women with endometriosis who encounter less than understanding and supportive responses to their decisions and experiences with fertility from health professionals and friends or family members may in fact experience more endometriosis symptoms, as the resulting stigma-driven stress has an impact on their reproductive hormones.

"It's a Woman's Lot to Suffer"

The notion that stigma relating to endometriosis is gendered and socially constructed can be seen through the women's common experience expressed in, "it's a woman's lot to suffer." Statements like: "Because you're a woman you're just meant to put up with it" were common and used most often related to the pain of menstruation (a main symptom of endometriosis is severe pain, with many women unable to walk properly due to the pain or confined to their beds for several days), and linked to the notion that women's symptoms were often dismissed by the medical community and by family members, school nurses, and others.

Women with endometriosis often stated that when they were teens their symptoms were dismissed as either "just period pain" or "bowel cramps." As Mary explained in a questionnaire:

> I have had symptoms of endometriosis since my late teens. However, I did not know they were endometriosis symptoms. I told my mum about them and she said they were probably "bowel cramps."

Several women reported their parents being told by doctors: "Oh it's her age; it'll settle down." Pain associated with menstruation is apparently normalized for teens and young women, likely delaying diagnosis and access to care for some young people with endometriosis. This dismissal of endometriosis symptoms reinforces the idea that "it's a woman's lot to suffer" and led many women to believe for many years that what they were experiencing was indeed "normal," as Nancy wrote on her questionnaire: "In my teens it was very bad—I missed out on quite a lot because I was laid up suffering with it. As I got older I just learned to cope, really—I believed there would never be any help forthcoming, that it was 'normal' for some women to go through this, and that I just had to deal with it."

Ultimately, the women reported that the difference between endometriosis pain and varying degrees of normal menstrual pain became blurred. Naomi had many times been told "You've got endometriosis. What's that? So just period pain?" Therefore, as it is apparently socially indistinguishable from "normal" period pain, endometriosis became the ultimate "normal" state of a "woman's lot to suffer." This idea became so ingrained that even "GPs[12] think period pain is 'normal.'"

The concept that "it's a woman's lot to suffer" could also relate to other aspects of endometriosis-related pain such as dyspareunia (pain during sex). As discussed previously, women with endometriosis felt they should not complain if they had pain during sexual intercourse. It was a task they were meant to accomplish regardless of the pain involved, and if they were unable to have sex, it meant, to them, they were somehow deficient as women.

The idea, ensconced in stigma around menstruation and sex, that "it's a woman's lot to suffer," reinforces social stigma that interacts with biological pathways between psychological and physiological manifestations of stress for women with endometriosis that exacerbate disease severity, progression, and symptoms. It limits women's ability to access care and treatment for their symptoms, in a climate of structural violence that reinforces gender roles within which women feel the need to have painful sex or avoid talking about heavy bleeding. Seeking advice from their mothers, school nurses, or doctors, being told "it is normal," meant women stopped asking for help. This resulted in women's spending more time without care and silently enduring worsening symptoms.

"It's a woman's lot to suffer," for women with endometriosis, thus becomes a socially enforced, stigmatizing notion applied to all aspects of endometriosis, producing biologized stress that interacts with biological aspects of the disease to worsen suffering. Yet women want to resist this passive sufferer role—a quotation on endometriosis by Susan Sarandon, widely posted by other sufferers online, says:

> When all you know is pain you don't know that that is not normal. It is not a woman's lot to suffer, even if we've been raised that way. It is not OK to miss a part of your life because of pain and excessive bleeding. It is not OK to be bed-ridden for two-to-three days a month. It is not OK to [have] pain during sex. It is not OK to have major bloating and nausea (attributed to Susan Sarandon).[13]

The Mask of Health

As women perceived and internalized that there should be minimal public discussion of endometriosis, they understood a need to hide the condition. They discussed tools and strategies they used to "pass" as healthy. This "mask of health" was one they used repeatedly and on a daily basis. It helped them get through each day. When they could come home and lie on the couch with the hot water bottle, this was when the mask came off. The mask was used as a support mechanism for accomplishing day-to-day tasks. When they were unable to carry out these tasks as expected, they felt they had failed and therefore gave in to the reality of the illness and its limitations.

Women discussed putting on a face to go out every day and pretend that everything was going well. Putting on make up became a way of masking their paleness or tiredness. While this was not a topic often discussed during my interviews, it was a common topic in support group meetings. "We put on a brave face before we go out, don't we? When we are at home we lie down on the couch with the hot water bottle on and don't move unless absolutely necessary."

> I always look pale if I don't put on make up. I won't go out of the house without putting on make up. Otherwise I might have people asking me if I am feeling ok.

This necessity to put on a brave face, to camouflage one's suffering with makeup, became a requirement the women placed on themselves. Hiding the pain was a daily event. What the women presented to the outside world was the image of a healthy woman.

The one exception to this rule of putting on the "mask of health" was during a doctor's visit. In support group meetings, women spoke of the necessity of going to the doctor "looking a mess." It was felt that this was one method by which doctors would be more inclined to believe that one was ill, as endometriosis was otherwise not taken seriously. Marie explained that "because we are so used to pretending we are healthy" we "forget to show our true situation" and "we are suffering but we turn up at the doctor's like we would to go anywhere else." Women would give each other specific suggestions as to the best way to present oneself in the clinic. They would explain that there is a fine line between looking ill and looking depressed. So they would joke about showering being a "good thing to do," while simultaneously suggesting that they not put on make up for a clinic visit. For example, during one support group meeting Alice explained: "Go to the doctor's looking a mess, don't wash your hair, don't put on make up. The worst is when you go in and [the doctor] says 'you are looking well today.' And you think 'yes but I feel awful.'"

Therefore, the "mask of health," not only reinforces the stigma and invisibility linked to endometriosis but remains a barrier to care. Women with endometriosis here clearly acknowledged that hiding their illness limited their access to treatments as their doctors may not be convinced of their suffering, ultimately increasing their symptoms of endometriosis. In the setting of a clinic the "mask of health" then potentially limits women's ability to take on the sick role (Parsons 1951). It is the "seeing" of the symptoms by the doctor that could allow for the treatment they are severely lacking. In addition, the stress of needing to maintain a "healthy" appearance may itself be another element which contributes to the stigma-stress-endometriosis pathway.

Suffering in Silence

Women with endometriosis often discussed feeling that they were "suffering in silence." This was linked to the stigmas previously discussed: "[Endo]'s also made things tricky at gatherings if I'd have to cry off certain activities and been unable to explain why because I don't necessarily know people that well, or because middle-aged men are involved and would be uncomfortable with being told about 'women's things!'" The silence, the inability to express their emotions and feel their voices are heard, becomes a common feeling amongst women with endometriosis, even during a day out shopping with the family:

> If you're out with them (family) for the day for example going shopping I can't walk around as much as everyone else can do. So you can kind of try and hint that actually I might need to go and sit down, I'm getting a bit tired. But unless you quite forcefully say I can't do this anymore and worry about upsetting other people, you make yourself do stuff I think, don't you, when actually inside you're absolutely dying. You think: I know I'm going to be really ill here.

For Trudy, the silence is due to her inability to explain her experience of endometriosis to others, a struggle linked to the gendered stigmas previously discussed. "I still feel like this today becuz no one around knows truly how I felt going through this." The muted silence has everything to do with Trudy's feeling that others do not know what she has gone through. In this, the image forms the expression of her isolation. This loneliness associated with endometriosis was a common feeling amongst my informants. Statements such as: "It makes you feel lonely doesn't it?" and "If you don't have [endometriosis], how can you understand? You can't, can you?" were relatively common.

"Suffering in silence," due to internalized, gendered stigma, causes women to feel isolated, increasing their stress levels, and likely biologically exacerbating their symptoms. It also forces them to continue to push their bodies despite feeling ill at that particular moment, increasing their physical suffering in yet another way. This may ultimately cause them to push through the pain as opposed to taking the time to rest, potentially increasing their pain levels. Thus, stigma-induced "suffering in silence" increases levels of stress and therefore symptoms of endometriosis. These both increase the felt necessity to hide symptoms, which further exacerbates stress and delays care-seeking, further exacerbating the endometriosis and further fueling the stress and the stigma, all in interaction with each other.

DISCUSSION

While several concepts elucidated in this study have been reported before in the literature including the concept of striving to be an ideal woman discussed in this study (Denny 2004, Cox 2004), menstrual etiquette in women with endometriosis (Seear 2009), Denny (2004) and Cox (2004) and communication taboos around dyspareunia (Cox 2004 and Fritzer 2013), interestingly, stigma relating to childlessness is remarkably absent from the endometriosis literature. In addition, the "mask of health" that women feel the need to use, or the resulting "suffering in silence" and the isolation seen in this study have not been previously documented. Furthermore, to my knowledge, the concept of a syndemic has yet to be applied to endometriosis.

My finding that women with endometriosis experience increased levels of stigma-induced stress correlates with those of Tariverdian et al. (2007) who reported that women with endometriosis experienced increased levels of perceived stress. Stigma-induced stress makes symptoms of endometriosis worse by limiting women's ability to seek help from clinicians. This results in delayed diagnosis and treatment times and ultimately causes women to have worsened symptoms of endometriosis.

In addition, increased stress through abnormal cortisol levels have been linked to the propagation of endometriosis in a rat model (Appleyard et al.

2015 and Cuevas et al. 2012). Women with endometriosis have also been shown to have abnormal cortisol levels (a marker of increased stress) and have been shown to increase their functionality through decreased stress levels (Petrelluzzi et al. 2012). Stress has also been linked both to increased pain levels and to infertility (Melzack 1999 and McEwen et al. 2010) while pressure to have intercourse may worsen dyspareunia (Fritzer et al. 2013).

The endometriosis-stress-stigma syndemic I present in this chapter is best illustrated as a cycle (see Figure 2.1) in which worsening symptoms of endometriosis result from and also contribute to social and gendered stigma that produces psychological and physiological symptoms of stress which further interact with and exacerbate the physical symptoms of endometriosis, in a context of structural violence producing and perpetuating harmful gender role expectations that limit access to care. The social stigma in this case is linked to three communication taboos.

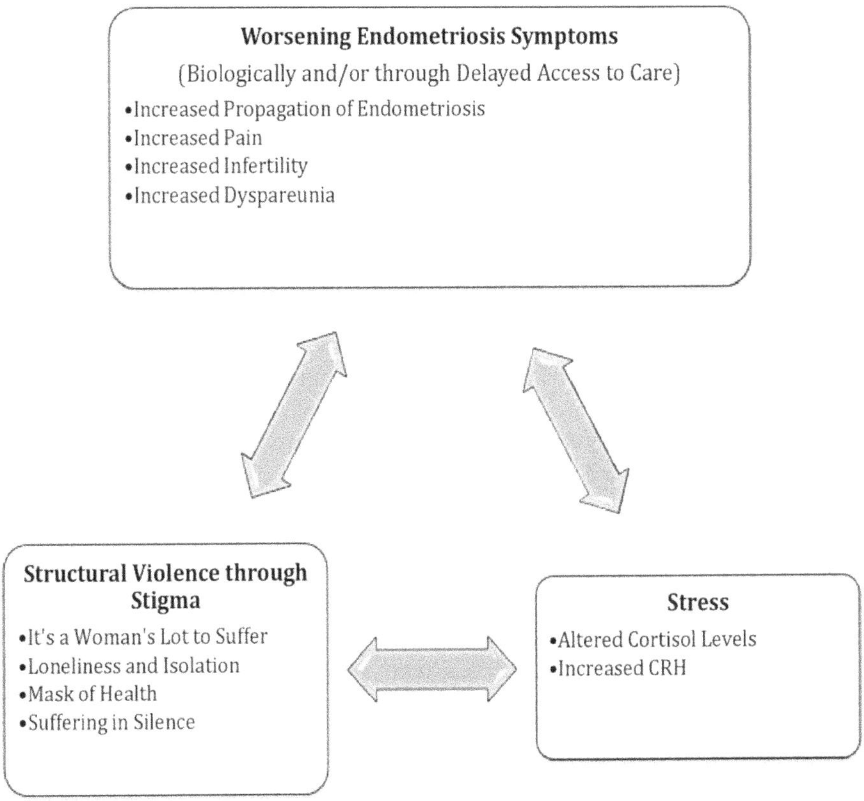

Figure 2.1. Elements of the Endometriosis, Stress, and Stigma Syndemic.

Owing to the three types of communication taboos (menstrual, childlessness and dyspareunia), women feel unable to discuss specific aspects of endometriosis effectively, even once silence is broken in order to obtain a diagnosis. They believe, "it's a woman's lot to suffer" and understand endometriosis as a dismissed and unimportant illness from which they nevertheless suffer greatly, and a concept which they actively seek to resist through online forums. Women with endometriosis conclude they are required to hide the illness and to put on what I have called a "mask of health," causing them to feel increased levels of isolation and ultimately stress, worsening their symptoms and suffering through the interactions between physiological and psychological stress and their endometriosis. This gives birth to the repetitive cycle of stigma-induced stress worsening the endometriosis condition, which in turn exacerbates the stress.

CONCLUSION

Heightened levels of stress resulting from the stigmatization of endometriosis and its symptoms increase symptoms and severity of endometriosis, and bi-directionally influence disease pathophysiology. Stress has been linked to increased pain levels, while pressure to have intercourse may worsen pain during sexual activity. This increased dyspareunia may also mean patients have intercourse less frequently and therefore fewer chances to become pregnant, increasing stigma related to childlessness. Stress also may increase the spread of endometriosis as well as biologically decreasing the viability of oocytes leading to infertility. In addition, though not explored here, stress over a female partner's endometriosis also is thought to potentially affect male fertility through increased erectile dysfunction and potentially through decreased sperm viability—this is currently an understudied topic (Nargund 2015).

The worse the symptoms of endometriosis, the more women may experience stigma-induced stress; the more they experience stigma-induced stress, the worse their symptoms become, in a stigma-driven biosocial interaction. The social construction, and resulting stigmatization, of endometriosis as a "women's disease" and the related endometriosis-stress-stigma syndemic must be understood by healthcare professionals seeking to provide care to the endometriosis patient. Stigma relating to topics such as menstruation, sexual intercourse, and childlessness exacerbate symptoms of endometriosis by lengthening times to diagnosis and prompting women to avoid seeking help. The isolation in turn leads to further stress, which exacerbates pain levels and retards treatment-seeking behavior. Worsened symptomatology then creates yet more stigma-induced stress as women strive to fulfill socially imposed ideals of "womanhood."

Examining these results from the lens of syndemics provides an entirely new view on endometriosis, where gendered social stigma creates significant stress that biologically interacts with and worsens endometriosis suffering. This contribution provides a novel approach to conceptualizing and approaching endometriosis with hopes of reducing stigma and improving care for women with endometriosis. Understanding this endometriosis-stigma-stress syndemic may lead to new forms of research on endometriosis and impact the practices of medical professionals.

NOTES

1. Structural violence is a concept first used by Galtung (1969) and then by Farmer (1999) to explain a type of violence without a direct actor, but rather a violence that is built into a social system (such as racism, classism, or gender discrimination) which ultimately leads to unequal power, unequal access to resources, and unequal access to health-care in this case.
2. http://www.legislation.gov.U.K./U.K.pga/1998/42/schedule/1/part/I/chapter/7.
3. https://www.citizensadvice.org.U.K./law-and-rights/civil-rights/human-rights/what-rights-are-protected-under-the-human-rights-act/your-right-to-respect-for-private-and-family-life/.
4. A registrar in the system of NHS (National Health Service) in the U.K. would be the equivalent of a resident in the U.S. system. Also, please note that one registrar was training to be a GP (General Practitioner) not a gynecologist.
5. A consultant in the system of the NHS in the U.K. would be equivalent to an attending in the U.S. system.
6. Oxidative damage is the damage to cells created by reactive oxygen species (ROS), which are chemically reactive molecules containing oxygen such as oxygen ions or peroxides.
7. Endometriotic implants are the displaced tissue biologically related to the uterine lining in endometriosis.
8. Note that all names used in this chapter are pseudonyms to protect the anonymity of the participants.
9. A hashtag (#) is a symbol used online to symbolize the user's recognition that whatever they have posted or written they consider to be related to that hashtag, in this case endometriosis.
10. Note that women often use the term "endo" to mean endometriosis. Where the participants have used "endo" as opposed to endometriosis I have left their own words.
11. What is considered "heavy" menstrual flow is ultimately a contested notion. Here, I used the women's own terminology. If she considered her flow to be "heavy," I maintained her terminology.
12. General Practitioners, equivalent to Primary Care Doctors in the United States
13. http://www.pinterest.com/pin/112730796895370820/. Accessed December 11, 2014.

REFERENCES

Alldred, Pam. *Get real about sex: The politics and practice of sex education*. McGraw-Hill Education (UK), 2007.

Andersen, C. Yding. "Possible new mechanism of cortisol action in female reproductive organs: physiological implications of the free hormone hypothesis." *Journal of Endocrinology* 173, no. 2 (2002): 211–217.

Aschbacher, Kirstin, Aoife O'Donovan, Owen M. Wolkowitz, Firdaus S. Dhabhar, Yali Su, and Elissa Epel. "Good stress, bad stress and oxidative stress: insights from anticipatory cortisol reactivity." *Psychoneuroendocrinology* 38, no. 9 (2013): 1698–1708.

Appleyard, Caroline B., Myrella L. Cruz, Siomara Hernández, Kenira J. Thompson, Manuel Bayona, and Idhaliz Flores. "Stress management affects outcomes in the pathophysiology of an endometriosis model." *Reproductive Sciences* (2014): 1933719114542022.

Attwood, Feona. Introduction to *Mainstreaming sex: The sexualization of western culture*, edited by Feona Attwood. IB Tauris, 2014.

Balzer, Marjorie Mandelstam. "Rituals of gender identity: markers of Siberian Khanty ethnicity, status, and belief." *American Anthropologist* 83, no. 4 (1981): 850–867.

Buckley, Thomas. *Blood magic: The anthropology of menstruation*. Univ of California Press, 1988.

Cox, Helen, Lorraine Henderson, Ros Wood, and Glenda Cagliarini. "Learning to take charge: women's experiences of living with endometriosis." *Complementary Therapies in Nursing and Midwifery* 9, no. 2 (2003): 62–68.

Cuevas, Marielly, Idhaliz Flores, Kenira J. Thompson, Dinah L. Ramos-Ortolaza, Annelyn Torres-Reveron, and Caroline B. Appleyard. "Stress exacerbates endometriosis manifestations and inflammatory parameters in an animal model." *Reproductive Sciences* 19, no. 8 (2012): 851–862.

Cunningham, S. D., J. Tschann, J. E. Gurvey, J. Dennis Fortenberry, and Jonathan M. Ellen. "Attitudes about sexual disclosure and perceptions of stigma and shame." *Sexually transmitted infections* 78, no. 5 (2002): 334–338.

Denny, Elaine. "Women's experience of endometriosis." *Journal of Advanced Nursing* 46, no. 6 (2004): 641–648.

Douglas, Mary. *Purity and Danger: an analysis of the concepts of taboo*. London: Routledge & Kegan Paul, 1966.

Elmerstig, Eva, Barbro Wijma, and Carina Berterö. "Why do young women continue to have sexual intercourse despite pain?." *Journal of Adolescent Health* 43, no. 4 (2008): 357–363.

Farmer, Paul. *Infections and inequalities: The modern plagues*. Los Angeles: Univ of California Press, 1999.

Freudenberg, Nicholas, Marianne Fahs, Sandro Galea, and Andrew Greenberg. "The impact of New York City's 1975 fiscal crisis on the tuberculosis, HIV, and homicide syndemic." *American Journal of Public Health* 96, no. 3 (2006): 424–434.

Fritz, M.A. "Endometriosis" in *Clinical gynecologic endocrinology and infertility*, edited by Leon Speroff and Marc A. Fritz. Lippincott Williams & Wilkins, 2005.

Fritzer, N., D. Haas, P. Oppelt, D. Hornung, M. Wölfler, U. Ulrich, G. Fischerlehner, M. Sillem, and G. Hudelist. "More than just bad sex: sexual dysfunction and distress in patients with endometriosis." *European Journal of Obstetrics & Gynecology and Reproductive Biology* 169, no. 2 (2013): 392–396.

Galtung, Johan. "Violence, peace, and peace research." *Journal of Peace Research* 6, no. 3 (1969): 167–191.

Gillespie, Rosemary. "Contextualizing voluntary childlessness within a postmodern model of reproduction: Implications for health and social needs." *Critical Social Policy* 21, no. 2 (2001): 139–159.

———. "When no means no: Disbelief, disregard and deviance as discourses of voluntary childlessness." *Women's Studies International Forum* 23, no. 2 (2000): 223–234.

Goffman, Erving. *Stigma: Notes on the management of spoiled identity*. Englewood Cliffs, NJ: Prentice-Hill Inc.

Gottlieb, Alma. "Afterword." *Ethnology* 41, no. 4 (2002): 381.

Griffith, Véronique A.S. *It's a Woman's Lot to Suffer, Isn't It?: Endometriosis, Gender and Stigma*. Annual Anthropology Postgraduate Conference 2015, Durham University, 2015.

Gupta, Sajal, Ashok Agarwal, Natalie Krajcir, and Juan G. Alvarez. "Role of oxidative stress in endometriosis." *Reproductive Biomedicine Online* 13, no. 1 (2006): 126–134.

Harlow, Christopher R., Julian M. Jenkins, and Robert ML Winston. "Increased follicular fluid total and free cortisol levels during the luteinizing hormone surge." *Fertility and Sterility* 68, no. 1 (1997): 48–53.

Harrison, Victoria, Karen Rowan, and John Mathias. "Stress reactivity and family relationships in the development and treatment of endometriosis." *Fertility and Sterility* 83, no. 4 (2005): 857–864.

Herek, Gregory M. "Confronting sexual stigma and prejudice: Theory and practice." *Journal of Social Issues* 63, no. 4 (2007): 905–925.

Hoskins, Janet. "Blood mysteries: Beyond menstruation as pollution." *Ethnology* 41, no. 4 (2002): 299–301.

Human Rights Act of 1998. http://www.legislation.gov.uk/ukpga/1998/42/schedule/1/part/I/chapter/7.

Hummelshoj, Lone *Mentionitis: Educating others about endometriosis.* Retrieved December 8, 2014, from endometriosis.org: global forum for news and information: http://endometriosis.org/news/opinion/mentionitis-educating-others-about-endometriosis/ n.d.

Johnston-Robledo, Ingrid, and Joan C. Chrisler. "The menstrual mark: Menstruation as social stigma." *Sex Roles* 68, no. 1–2 (2013): 9–18.

Kwan, Candice K., and Joel D. Ernst. "HIV and tuberculosis: a deadly human syndemic." *Clinical Microbiology Reviews* 24, no. 2 (2011): 351–376.

Kissling, Elizabeth Arveda. "Bleeding out loud: Communication about menstruation." *Feminism & Psychology* 6, no. 4 (1996a): 481–504.

———. "'That's just a basic teen-age rule': Girls' linguistic strategies for managing the menstrual communication taboo." (1996b): 292–309.

Lazzeri, Lucia, Cinzia Orlandini, Silvia Vannuccini, Serena Pinzauti, Claudia Tosti, Errico Zupi, Rosella Elena Nappi, and Felice Petraglia. "Endometriosis and perceived stress: impact of surgical and medical treatment." *Gynecologic and Obstetric Investigation* 79, no. 4 (2015): 229–233.

Laws, Sophie. *Issues of blood: The politics of menstruation*. Hampshire: Macmillan: 1990.

Lima, A. P., M. D. Moura, and A. A. M. Rosa e Silva. "Prolactin and cortisol levels in women with endometriosis." *Brazilian Journal of Medical and Biological Research* 39, no. 8 (2006): 1121–1127.

McEwen, Bruce S., and Madhu Kalia. "The role of corticosteroids and stress in chronic pain conditions." *Metabolism* 59 (2010): S9–S15.

Meggitt, Mervyn J. "Male-female relationships in the Highlands of Australian New Guinea." *American Anthropologist* 66, no. 4 (1964): 204–224.

Melzack, Ronald. "Pain and stress: A new perspective." *Psychosocial factors in pain: Critical perspectives* (1999): 89–106.

Miall, Charlene E. "Perceptions of informal sanctioning and the stigma of involuntary childlessness." *Deviant Behavior* 6, no. 4 (1985): 383–403.

Morell, Carolyn Mackelcan. *Unwomanly conduct: The challenges of intentional childlessness*. London: Virago, 1994.

Nargund, Vinod H. "Effects of psychological stress on male fertility." *Nature Reviews. Urology* 12, no. 7 (2015): 373–382.

O'Flynn, Norma. "Menstrual symptoms: the importance of social factors in women's experiences." *Br J Gen Pract* 56, no. 533 (2006): 950–957.

O'Keefe, Theresa. "Menstrual blood as a weapon of resistance." *International Feminist Journal of Politics* 8, no. 4 (2006): 535–556.

Paige, Karen, and Jeffery M. Paige. *The politics of reproductive ritual*. Los Angeles: Univ of California Press, 1981.

Petrelluzzi, K. F. S., M. C. Garcia, C. A. Petta, D. M. Grassi-Kassisse, and Regina C. Spadari-Bratfisch. "Salivary cortisol concentrations, stress and quality of life in women with endometriosis and chronic pelvic pain: research report." *Stress* 11, no. 5 (2008): 390–397.

Petrelluzzi, Karina Friggi Sebe, Marcia Carvalho Garcia, Carlos Alberto Petta, Daniel Araki Ribeiro, Nancy Ramacciotti de Oliveira Monteiro, Isabel Cristina Céspedes, and Regina Celia Spadari. "Physical therapy and psychological intervention normalize cortisol levels and improve vitality in women with endometriosis." *Journal of Psychosomatic Obstetrics & Gynecology* 33, no. 4 (2012): 191–198.

Parsons, Talcott. *The social system*. London: Routledge & Kegan Paul, 1951.

Preston, Deborah Bray, Anthony R. D'Augelli, Cathy D. Kassab, and Richard E. Cain. "The influence of stigma on the sexual risk behavior of rural men who have sex with men." *AIDS Education and Prevention* 16, no. 4 (2004): 291–301.

Power, Paula. "Menstrual complexities." *Health Education* 95, no. 2 (1995): 17–21.

Rogers, Peter AW, Thomas M. D'Hooghe, Asgerally Fazleabas, Caroline E. Gargett, Linda C. Giudice, Grant W. Montgomery, Luk Rombauts, Lois A. Salamonsen, and Krina T. Zondervan. "Priorities for endometriosis research: recommendations from an international consensus workshop." *Reproductive Sciences* 16, no. 4 (2009): 335–46.

Rushing, Rosanne, Charlotte Watts, and Sharon Rushing. "Living the reality of forced sex work: perspectives from young migrant women sex workers in northern Vietnam." *Journal of Midwifery & Women's Health* 50, no. 4 (2005): e41–e44.

Sanday, Peggy Reeves. *Female power and male dominance: On the origins of sexual inequality*. Cambridge: Cambridge University Press, 1981.

Schenker, Joseph G., Dror Meirow, and Eran Schenker. "Stress and human reproduction." *European Journal of Obstetrics & Gynecology and Reproductive Biology* 45, no. 1 (1992): 1–8.

Scheper-Hughes, Nancy. *Saints, scholars, and schizophrenics: Mental illness in rural Ireland.* London: Univ of California Press, 1979.

Seear, Kate. "The etiquette of endometriosis: stigmatisation, menstrual concealment and the diagnostic delay." *Social Science & Medicine* 69, no. 8 (2009): 1220–1227.

Siedentopf, Friederike, Nadja Tariverdian, Mirjam Rücke, Heribert Kentenich, and Petra C. Arck. "Immune status, psychosocial distress and reduced quality of life in infertile patients with endometriosis." *American Journal of Reproductive Immunology* 60, no. 5 (2008): 449–461.

Singer, Merrill. "Syndemics" in *The Wiley Blackwell Encyclopedia of Health, Illness, Behavior, and Society,* edited by William C. Cockerham, Robert Dingwall, and Stella R. Quah, 1–4. John Wiley and Sons (2014).

Smith, M. P., S. D. Keay, F. C. Margo, C. R. Harlow, P. J. Wood, D. J. Cahill, and M. G. R. Hull. "Total cortisol levels are reduced in the periovulatory follicle of infertile women with minimal–mild endometriosis." *American Journal of Reproductive Immunology* 47, no. 1 (2002): 52–56.

Tariverdian, Nadja, Theoharis C. Theoharides, Friederike Siedentopf, Gabriela Gutiérrez, Udo Jeschke, Gabriel A. Rabinovich, Sandra M. Blois, and Petra C. Arck. "Neuroendocrine-immune disequilibrium and endometriosis: an interdisciplinary approach." *Seminars in Immunopathology* 29, no. 2 (2007): 193–210.

Redwine, David B. *Surgical management of endometriosis*. New York: Martin Dunitz, 2004.

The Daily Telegraph. *Sex is still a taboo subject in the home.* Retrieved November 2014, from The Daily Telegraph: http://www.telegraph.co.uk/women/mother-tongue/4176425/Sex-still-a-taboo-subject-in-the-home.html 2009.

Tulandi, Togas and David Redwine. *Endometriosis.* New York: Marcell Drekker, 2004.

Turner, Bryan. S. "Aging and identity: Some reflections on the somatizisation of the self" in *Images of Ageing: Cultural Representations of Later Life*, edited by Mike Featherstone and Andrew Wernick. London: Routledge (1995).

Ulrich, Miriam, and Ann Weatherall. "Motherhood and infertility: Viewing motherhood through the lens of infertility." *Feminism & Psychology* 10, no. 3 (2000): 323–336.

Vachon-Presseau, Etienne, Mathieu Roy, Marc-Olivier Martel, Etienne Caron, Marie-France Marin, Jeni Chen, Genevieve Albouy et al. "The stress model of chronic pain: evidence from basal cortisol and hippocampal structure and function in humans." *Brain* 136, no. 3 (2013): 815–827.

Whiteford, Linda M., and Lois Gonzalez. "Stigma: The hidden burden of infertility." *Social Science & Medicine* 40, no. 1 (1995): 27–36.

Chapter Three

Pathologized Pregnancies and Deleterious Health Outcomes

Iatrogenic Effects of Teen Pregnancy Stigma

Courtney L. Everson and Bayla Ostrach

ADOLESCENT PREGNANCY IN THE UNITED STATES

Despite declining trends in adolescent pregnancy over the last half century, nearly a quarter of a million women[1] in between the ages of 15 and 19 gave birth in the United States (U.S.) in 2015 (Martin et al. 2017), representing 6 percent of all births. Geography, race/ethnicity, socioeconomic status (SES), and other factors interweave to contribute to the alarmingly negative perinatal health outcomes and lifelong social inequities suffered by childbearing adolescents and their children (Ventura, Hamilton, and Matthews 2014). Women ages 15 to 19 experience some of the highest preterm delivery (9.91 percent), low birth weight (9.48 percent), and infant mortality rates (8.52/1000 live births) of all age groups (Martin et al. 2017; Mathews, MacDorman, and Thoma 2015). Low birth weight and prematurity are leading causes of neonatal death in the U.S., as well as have severe morbidity consequences for the neonate, including respiratory issues, higher susceptibility to infection, and delayed developmental and learning disabilities (Centers for Disease Control 2015; March of Dimes 2013; Mathews, MacDorman, and Thoma 2015; U.S. Department of Health & Human Services 2015).

Moreover, race and class intersect to disproportionately burden subgroups and drive these alarming rates. Preterm delivery rates of adolescents ages 15 to 19 by race and ethnicity are highest among non-Hispanic Black women (12.05 percent), followed by non-Hispanic white (9.56 percent), and Hispanic women (8.89 percent) (Martin et al. 2017). Similarly, low birth weight rates are highest among non-Hispanic black women (13.63 percent), followed by non-Hispanic white women (8.45 percent), and Hispanic women (8.07 percent) (Martin et al. 2017). Infant mortality rates are highest among non-Hispanic black women (11.69/1000), followed by non-Hispanic white women (8.48/1000), and Hispanic women (6.26/1000) (Mathews, MacDorman, and Thoma 2015). The landscape of birth outcomes in the United States is one of serious inequity.

Poverty is also a documented correlate with negative perinatal outcomes (Barcelos and Gubrium 2014; Finer and Zolna 2014; Jeha et al. 2015; Kearney and Levine 2012; Smithbattle 2007; Ventura, Hamilton, and Matthews 2014), and childbearing adolescents disproportionately come from low socioeconomic families of origin. As Kearney and Levine (2012:142) explain:

> Our reading of the totality of evidence [on adolescent childbearing] leads us to conclude that being on a low economic trajectory in life leads many teenage girls to have children while they are young and unmarried and that poor outcomes seen later in life (relative to teens who do not have children) are simply the continuation of the original low economic trajectory.

The "poor outcomes seen later in life" include teen mothers and their infants experiencing lower educational attainment; higher rates of poverty, food insecurity, and unstable housing; decreased mother-infant bonding; and delayed early childhood development (Jutte et al. 2010; Kearney and Levine 2012; Nicolson et al. 2013; Ventura, Hamilton, and Matthews 2014). Underlying social inequities are thus reproduced through intergenerational cycles of poverty and teenage pregnancy (Kearney and Levine 2012; Porter and Holness 2011; Smithbattle 2007). Teen childbearing is claimed to pose an "economic drain on society" and a "financial burden on taxpaying citizens" (Bute and Russell 2012:712), wherein $9.4 to $28 billion per year is spent on adolescent births in the U.S. through a combination of social service programs, lost tax revenue, and the high expenses of public health, foster care, and legal systems (U.S. Department of Health & Human Services 2015).

Such statistics on the social and economic "costs" of young pregnancy are used to support prevailing meta-narratives that construct pregnant teens as "social problems" (Linders and Bogard 2014) afflicted with a "moral disease" (Inhorn 2006), and parenting adolescents are deemed the "undeserving poor" (Silver 2008). Multiple studies demonstrate how adolescents are intensely stigmatized during the childbearing process, from pregnancy through to birth and then into mothering (Boath, Henshaw, and Bradley 2013; Erdmans and Black 2015; Everson 2015; Mantovani and Thomas 2014; Shanok and Miller 2007; SmithBattle 2013; Whitley and Kirmayer 2008; Wiemann et al. 2005; Yardley 2008). Stigma affects young childbearing women even before they become pregnant through public campaigns that target this "social menace" (Grover and Sandhu 2009). For example, the Bloomberg Mayoral Administration's 2013 teen pregnancy prevention campaign in New York City used the teary-eyed faces and "voices" of children (notably featuring racial minorities) and statistical "facts" to show the perils of young childbearing, with ad-lines like: "I'm twice as likely not to graduate high school because you had me as a teen," or "Got a good job? I cost thousands of dollars each year" (Taylor 2013).

Adolescent women for whom pregnancy may not be directly stigmatized by their ethnic culture or family members still encounter stigmatizing societal messages that even a wanted pregnancy is at odds with a dominant cultural logic that dictates a script for young women to follow—a script that determines the correct order for high school completion, establishing a stable relationship, college (in some economic/class strata), and *then* children (Aparicio, Pecukonis, and O'Neale 2015; Erickson 1998; Middleton 2011; Wilson and Huntington 2006). This kind of dominant cultural logic also drives young people's avoidance of pregnancy when they see it as a barrier to goal achievement (Cheney et al. 2014), though this appears to be mediated by class and potentially by ethnicity, revealing additional ways that intersectional stigma is reinforced in an unequal society. If the "script" internalized by middle-class white teenagers is that they can graduate from college and be successful if they just manage to not get pregnant (Cheney et al. 2014; Erdmans and Black 2015; Peterson et al. 2012), how then is a teenager who *does* get pregnant (and decides to carry to term) perceived? What message is then given if anti-teen pregnancy campaigns (Taylor 2013), displayed prominently on bus shelters in targeted (poor) neighborhoods in New York City, show predominantly teens of color?

Implied in such campaigns are thus not only the "costs" of young pregnancy, but the moral digression that adolescent pregnancy symbolizes—a digression from heteronormative notions of the "moral" family and the "good" mother—a mother constructed as white, married (to an employed husband), and a middle- to upper-class adult (Bute and Russell 2012; Everson 2012; James and Rashid 2013). Images of the "bad teen mother" are inextricably linked to meta-narratives regarding "acceptable" motherhood, where transitions from adolescence to adulthood occur in a preferred order: economic independence through education and employment, followed by a stable marriage and eventually children (Barcelos 2014; Ellison 2003; Wilson and Huntington 2006). Childbearing adolescents functionally contradict this life course trajectory and deviate from these societally normalized and enforced "optimal" circumstances of motherhood, resulting in intense stigmatization that fuels social marginalization and poor outcomes.

SYNDEMICS AND TEEN PREGNANCY STIGMA

In this chapter, we propose a syndemic model of teen pregnancy stigma that demonstrates dynamic relationships between the structural stigmatization of young pregnancy, the biosocial pathologization of these pregnancies, the subsequent medical interventions used to control the now-pathologized pregnancy, and the resulting negative perinatal health outcomes. We begin from the premise that pregnancy is a biological condition itself with socially and culturally imbued meanings (Cheyney 2010; Davis-Floyd 2004; Davis-Floyd, Sargent, and Rapp 1997; Jordan 1992; Rothman 1991; Trevathan 2010). When pathologized, however, in this case through stigmatization of adolescent childbearing specifically, pregnancy becomes a biological condition treated *like* a disease, with ensuing iatrogenic risks, rather than as an optimal, undisrupted physiologic process with benefits for both childbearing person and neonate.

Such bidirectional, structural and biological interactions occur in a context of biomedical management and regulation of adolescent childbearing, against larger sociocultural backdrops that marginalize these women and their babies. In this paper, we expand on existing syndemics theory by arguing that some syndemics, rather than resulting from interactions solely between two or more diseases in structural context (Singer 2009), can instead involve a non-diseased biological state, such as pregnancy, when it is mediated by biosocial factors that pathologize and result in iatrogenic interventions that have deleterious health consequences. Specifically, we emphasize how an otherwise physiologic, evolutionary human process (American College of Nurse-Midwives [ACNM], Midwives Alliance of North America [MANA], National Association of Certified Professional Midwives [NACPM] 2012; Davis-Floyd and Cheyney 2009; Trevathan 2010)—pregnancy—can become both conceptually *and* biologically pathologized through the extensive stigma ascribed to certain pregnancies and persons.

A variety of recognized reproductive syndemics are already linked to pregnancy, but in most of these cases, an existing disease-disease interaction is worsened in the case of pregnancy, rather than occurring exclusively in the context of stigma. Already identified "pregnancy syndemics," broadly defined, include infectious and tropical disease interactions with HIV in the context of development in sub-Saharan Africa, worsening suffering for pregnant women (Singer 2013), and efforts to relate SAVA (substance abuse, violence, AIDS) to pregnancy and alcohol use (Russell, Eaton, and Petersen-Williams 2013). Some scholars also describe as syndemic certain relationships between pregnancy and psychosocial symptoms in public health research, though the exact nature of the biological or bio-behavioral interactions, and how these are driven by social contexts, is not made abundantly clear (Coulter et al. 2014).

To our knowledge, the teen pregnancy stigma syndemic we propose here, and the chapter elsewhere in this volume (co-authored by this chapter's second author) proposing an abortion stigma syndemic, are the first new syndemics to feature pregnancy as a distinct biological factor, with pregnancies biosocially pathologized by stigmatization as a main component. We make the case for this syndemic relationship by positing that an otherwise non-diseased biological state, long championed as a healthy physiologic process by feminist and reproductive anthropologists (Davis-Floyd 2004; Davis-Floyd 2001; Rothman 1991), can be viewed as diseased when ensnared in a harmful syndemic. When the structural factor of social stigmatization constructs a pregnancy as pathological, threatening, or risky in some way to society, a particular pregnancy becomes treated as a "disease" rather than a physiologic process. This has deep implications for the biomedical management of (young) pregnant bodies. Specifically, we explore the structural-biosocial-biomedical pathways of interaction among:

- *Structural factors:* Intersectional stigmatization of teen childbearing, specifically—combined with medicalization of childbearing in biomedical care, broadly—leads to social and medical pathologization of adolescent pregnancy, through;
- *Biosocial processes:* Labeled a social and medical pathology, adolescent pregnancies are subject to management and regulation via excessive biomedical interventions, which act on the biological condition of pregnancy, and;
- *Biomedical interventions:* Excessive and unnecessary interventions, including early inductions, in interaction with the biological condition of pregnancy, produce iatrogenic birth effects with both short- and long-term implications for perinatal health.

Drawing on ethnographic research as well as the existing body of social and health sciences literature on adolescent childbearing and other pregnancy-linked syndemics, we illustrate how the application of a syndemic model can elucidate the dynamic interplay between macro-level factors (notably, ageism, classism, racism, and sexism) and micro-level (individual) biologies/pathologies and biographies of childbearing adolescents.

METHODS

Between January to July 2015, we conducted a series of focused literature searches using primary social science and health research databases, including: Medline (FirstSearch), Google Scholar, AnthroSource, Academic Search Premier, and EbscoHost. We focused on examining recent and ovarian research on teenage childbearing experiences, birth physiology, health and social outcomes, and pregnancy syndemics. We used the following keywords in varying combinations: teen(age) pregnancy; adolescent pregnancy; pregnancy syndemics; adolescent birth; teen(age) birth; stigma (stigmatization); induction; pathology (pathologized); iatrogenic; outcomes; intervention; health. Abstracts from resulting literature were initially reviewed to determine relevance, and then thorough reading of applicable articles was undertaken (Bryman 2012). Additionally, we used backward chaining and forward chaining to find additional literature related to the subject matter (Booth 2008).

We concentrated on articles that discussed young pregnancy stigma, pathologization, and structural factors, and their relationships to health-seeking behavior, experiences, care processes, interventions, and short- and long-term health outcomes. We concluded the review when searches began to heavily repeat information we previously found and no new literature of immediate relevance emerged (i.e., saturation in the review was accomplished). We also relied on reports from the National Centers for Health Statistics to understand population-level trends for young childbearing women in the United States. Finally, we drew on the first author's extensive ethnographic research with pregnant and parenting teens in the U.S. over the last ten years. IRB approval was secured from Oregon State University. Collectively, these sources allowed us to develop a proposed syndemic model of stigmatized young pregnancy that biosocially produces deleterious perinatal health outcomes. As the model emerged, we re-engaged the literature for areas requiring further elaboration and evidence in order to support the proposed pathways of interaction. During final revisions to this chapter, we re-reviewed a set of focused literature to update references and further illuminate specific dyadic interactions between pathologized pregnancies and iatrogenic interventions affecting the laboring person and the neonate.

FROM STIGMATIZATION TO BIOSOCIAL PATHOLOGIZATION TO IATROGENIC EFFECTS OF BIRTH INTERVENTIONS

In the sections that follow, we outline pathways of syndemic interaction between multiple structural, biosocial, and biomedical factors that act on the biological condition of pregnancy and, we argue, most clearly coalesce to perpetuate cycles of health inequity for childbearing adolescents and their children. In Figure 3.1, we illustrate the proposed syndemic, beginning with the stigmatizing processes inflicted on young pregnancies and births. The stigma ascribed to childbearing adolescents leads to the biosocial pathologization of their pregnancies, enacted through biomedical care. Posited as a social and medical pathology, regulation and control take place through extensive (often unnecessary) biomedical management and interventions that carry known iatrogenic risks and subsequently produce deleterious birth outcomes. These structural, biosocial, and biomedical factors, and the syndemic interactions between them, are discussed below.

The Stigmatization of Teen Pregnancy

Since Goffman's (1986) original work on stigma, much contribution has been made to the study of stigma as a key element in health and social inequities, identity making, self-efficacy, and social exclusion processes (Barcelos 2014; Bohren et al. 2015; Brubaker and Wright 2006; Earnshaw et al. 2013; Luttrell 2011; Metzl and Hansen 2014; Nelson 2001; SmithBattle 2013; Wenham 2011; Yardley 2008). An increasing focus in health and social sciences literature today is on the social-structural dimensions of stigma, including the role of intersecting social identities and locations in producing variations in experiences of stigma and health consequences. Attention to intersectionality and its relationship with stigmatizing processes is called "intersectional stigma" (Mantovani and Thomas 2014). We argue that intersectional stigma is particularly poignant in the case of childbearing adolescents, where the stigma ascribed to their age intersects with the stigma attached to other marginalized mothering identities they may hold, most notably as childbearing women of color (Attanasio and Kozhimannil 2015; Brubaker 2007; Earnshaw et al. 2013; Erdmans and Black 2015; Henderson,

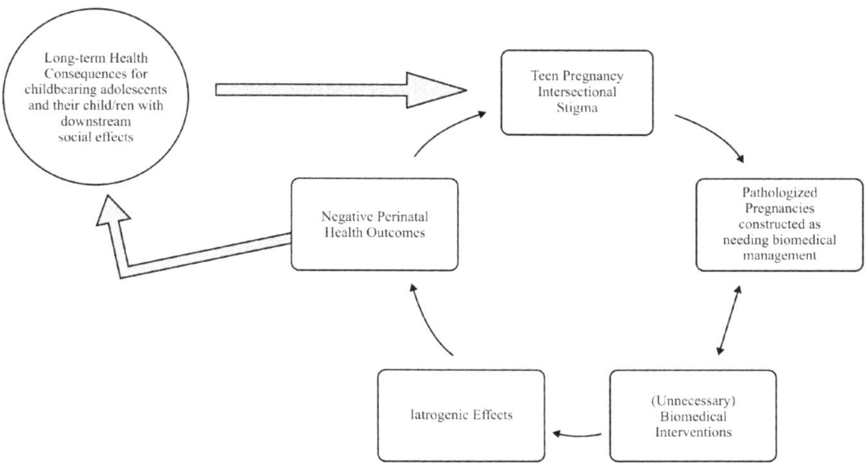

Figure 3.1. Proposed syndemic model of structural-biosocial-biomedical pathways of interaction between teen pregnancy stigma, pathologized pregnancies, iatrogenic interventions, and deleterious health outcomes.

Gao, and Redshaw 2013; Reid et al. 2016; Rosenthal and Lobel 2016), those in poverty (Belle Doucet 2003; Bloch and Taylor 2014; James-Hawkins and Sennott 2014; Porr, Drummond, and Olson 2012), single women (Broussard, Joseph, and Thompson 2012), as well as those facing unintentional pregnancies (Ellison 2003; James and Rashid 2013). In effect, it is not only the well-documented stigma ascribed to someone's age that is of consequence (Boath, Henshaw, and Bradley 2013; Ellis-Sloan 2014; Erdmans and Black 2015; Everson 2015; Mantovani and Thomas 2014; McDermott and Graham 2005; Rodriguez 2008; Shanok and Miller 2007; Sharpe 2015; Silver 2008; Solivan et al. 2015; SmithBattle 2013; Whitley and Kirmayer 2008; Wiemann et al. 2005; Wilson and Huntington 2006; Yardley 2008), but the ways in which stigmatizing processes attached to teen motherhood are compounded, and fueled, by other markers of (real and assumed) difference held, resulting in intersectional stigma during care of these "disgraceful" social groups (Mantovani and Thomas 2014).

A long-standing tradition in anthropology and the social sciences explores birthing practices, motherhood, and the political, social, and biological constructions of birthing bodies (Cheyney 2010; Craven 2010; Davis-Floyd 2004; Einstein and Shildrick 2009; Erickson 1998; Rapp 2001; Rothman 1991). Such literature sheds light on the ways in which social identities, locations, power, and controlled resource access intersect to produce differentials in birthing care, or what has been labeled "'stratified reproduction'—the hierarchical organization of reproductive health, fecundity, birth experiences, and child rearing that supports and rewards the maternity of some, while despising or outlawing the mother-work of others" (Rapp 2001:469). The intersectional stigma attached to young pregnancy is a primary mechanism by which such "despising" and "outlawing" occurs, largely through the power of labeling and stereotyping, which in turns leads to social exclusion, "damaged" identities, pathologizing processes, and discriminatory treatment (Bohren et al. 2015; Brubaker and Wright 2006; Nahar and van der Geest 2014; Spangler 2011; Wenham 2011; Yardley 2008). Cranny-Francis and colleagues (2003:140) provide a germane definition of stereotyping and its role in the production of stigmatizing processes and rhetoric:

> Stereotyping is part of the maintenance of social and symbolic order. It sets up a symbolic frontier between the "normal" and the "deviant," the "normal" and the "pathological," the "acceptable" and the "unacceptable," what "belongs" and what does not or is "other," between "insider" and "outsider." Us and them.

We apply Scambler's (2006, 2009) and Scambler and Paoli's (2008) conceptual framework on felt and enacted stigma in order to illustrate how stigma is a crucial, but often overlooked, element at play in the production of health inequities and the ways in which biosocial pathologization unfolds. In felt stigma, an individual internalizes notions of shame associated with their condition or position, and the individual may hold deep fears about being discriminated against and, thus, engage in behaviors (such as non-disclosure, avoidance) that circumvent potentially stigmatizing situations. In enacted stigma, an individual is the target of discrimination by others and subsequently experiences unequal or punitive treatment. We argue that through processes of internalization (felt stigma) and discriminatory treatment (enacted stigma), stigmatizing processes can become embodied and biologized, physically affecting a childbearing adolescent's biological condition of pregnancy through interaction with iatrogenic biomedical interventions, thus producing adverse health outcomes.

A large body of anthropological literature (Cassidy and Tom 2015; Davis-Floyd, Sargent, and Rapp 1997; Einstein and Shildrick 2009; Rapp 2001; Rothman 1991; Van Hollen 2003; Zacher Dixon 2015) has demonstrated the ways in which childbearing processes are pathologized and childbirth has become increasingly medicalized. The argument here is that if childbirth is a pathological process—rather than a physiologic one—then biomedical management and control must take place under the authoritative knowledge of the obstetric hierarchy. Stigmatizing processes thus combine with the institutional medicalization of childbearing in biomedical care. What unfolds is a formidable interplay between age-, race-, and class-based oppression with the authoritative knowledge of biomedical birthing care (Davis-Floyd, Sargent, and Rapp 1997; Ellison 2003; Jordan 1992; Spangler 2011). This interplay labels the adolescent pregnancy as medical pathology, and the childbearing teen as social pathology, each to be disciplined, managed, and regulated.

Biomedical Management of the Pathologized Young Pregnant Body

Employing Foucault's concepts of biopower and governmentality, Barcelos (2014) examines the ways in which teen pregnancy stigma manifests to create prevailing meta-narratives of adolescent childbearing as social pathology, and illustrates how the management of adolescent pregnancy occurs at both population (e.g., teen pregnancy prevention campaigns) and individual levels (i.e., pregnant teen bodies[2]). Constructed as a social pathology, pregnant teens—especially women of color, those in poverty, and single women (intersectionality, see above)—represent a threat to appropriate citizenry, sexuality, and motherhood—a threat that must be regulated and monitored: "The pregnant teen body is abject (Lupton 1999, 138) and irresponsible, a failure of rational public health and a threat to the neoliberal state, the normative family, and the discipline of public health" (Barcelos 2014:83). Barcelos argues that in prevention campaigns and clinical care, childbearing adolescents are held up as symbolic and literal reminders of the "dangers" of being a teen parent. Regulation of adolescent childbearing is normalized by framing pregnant teen bodies as "risky bodies" and subsequently institutionalized through biomedical management that silences young mothers and ignites abusive care.

We extend this notion of "risky bodies" and subjectivities identified by Barcelos (2014) to understand how the now-pathologized pregnant teen body becomes medically managed, much as the bodies of poor women of color and women on Medicaid are constructed as having "unruly bodies" to be surveilled and micro-managed, as in Bridges' (2011) work on prenatal care in a public hospital in New York City. Notably, such management occurs not only through care processes, as delineated below, but also through care rhetoric in obstetric settings. Breheny and Stephens (2010:311) document in detail the discourses of teenage motherhood dominating medical and nursing journals, claiming that, "The construction of teenage motherhood as a disease means that it makes sense to respond to it [in] terms of surveillance and control." The monitoring and regulation enacted over childbearing adolescents is arguably more pronounced than that exhibited during the medical care of other pregnant women precisely because of the added elements of intersectional stigma ascribed to pregnant teens. As such, we argue that pregnant teens are more likely to be subjected to invasive medical management of their pregnancies. The connection between stigma, pathologization, and increased invasive care can manifest in a variety of transecting ways.

For example, previous research (Anderson and McGuinness 2008; Arthur, Unwin, and Mitchell 2007; Brubaker 2007; Brubaker and Dillaway 2008; Dillaway and Brubaker 2006; Everson 2015, 2016; Low et al. 2003; Nichols et al. 2014; Sauls 2004; SmithBattle 2013; Wenham 2011) demonstrates how enacted stigma takes place during biomedical care of childbearing adolescents through processes that systematically exclude young women from their own medical care. A primary pathway by which exclusion from care occurs is through silencing and lack of decision-making power, in which young women are often not given (nor told they have) informed choice or consent during antenatal, labor/birth, and postpartum care. Exclusion also occurs through outright abuse, or what Perez D'Gregorio (2010) has termed "obstetric violence" to denote the dehumanizing treatment of women by medical providers through appropriation of the body, unnecessary intervention, degrading treatment, and dismissal of autonomy and informed choice. During extensive fieldwork with childbearing adolescents in the U.S., the first author documented multiple cases of obstetric violence against teens, including forced episiotomies, outright lies, humiliating rhetoric, overly aggressive vaginal exams, and the routine use of interventions like pharmacological induction, artificial rupture of membranes, and epidural pressures (Everson 2015, 2016).

Enacted stigma then combines with felt stigma to further the embodiment of inequality during teen childbearing. Experiences of disrespect and obstetric violence can lead to internalization of their communicated "less than" status as women and mothers by medical providers, where disempowerment, disconnectedness, and trauma in childbirth manifests and fuels negative self-concept (Anderson and McGuinness 2008; Arthur, Unwin, and Mitchell 2007; Brubaker and Wright 2006; Everson 2015, 2016; Nichols et al. 2014; Sauls 2004; Smithbattle, Lorenz, and Leander 2013). This internalization of shame and blame can influence a teen's sense of self-efficacy and diminish their ability to participate in their own care, whereby performative acts of silence are adopted due to deep fear and oppressive messaging.

For example, because they are commonly not given explanation of procedures or granted informed consent—and in internalizing messages of "not being good enough"—they may be less likely to ask questions about biomedical interventions that interact with their bodies, or advocate for themselves during pregnancy and delivery, deferring to those in authority and remaining silent for fear of being further labeled as incapable, selfish, or incompetent (Boath, Henshaw, and Bradley 2013; Everson 2012, 2015, 2016; Rodriguez 2008; Porter and Holness 2011; Wenham 2011; Whitley and Kirmayer 2008; SmithBattle 2013). In a self-fulfilling biosocial prophecy, this non-engagement then provides illusory "proof" that teen moms are indeed "incapable, bad moms" in need of biomedical regulation (i.e., interventions) of their pathologized pregnancies.

Previous research (Arthur, Unwin, and Mitchell 2007; Boath, Henshaw, and Bradley 2013; Daniels, Noe, and Mayberry 2006; Downe et al. 2009; Everson 2012, 2015, 2016; Gray 2002; Hodgkinson et al. 2014; Low et al. 2003; Mantovani and Thomas 2014; Mantovani and Thomas 2015; Wenham 2011; Whitley and Kirmayer 2008; Yardley 2008, 2009) also documents the high levels of stress that come from trying to access medical services, and the ways in which pregnant teens commonly stop seeking care in order to avoid stigmatizing situations. Felt stigma, thus, impacts not only self-concept and self-efficacy (Brubaker and Dillaway 2008; Porr, Drummond, and Olson 2012; Smithbattle, Lorenz, and Leander 2013), but may lead to avoidance behaviors that heighten susceptibility to poor health (Gray 2002).

For example, the first author (Everson 2015, 2016) has documented how during biomedical care, teens are frequently made to feel unsafe in disclosing symptoms, which leads to delayed diagnosis of true clinical issues, and this furthers the need for intervention to manage the situation because preventative measures or early diagnosis did not occur. Additionally, even when participants did disclose, their concerns were often silenced and dismissed under the rhetoric that teens are "too selfish" and "too stupid" to know what they are talking about. This had severe consequences for getting timely care, especially in emergent situations. Most significantly, the very fact that a teen's pregnancy is biosocially pathologized through intersectional stigma means interventions to "fix" the dysfunctions are seen as necessary and thus normalized in biomedical care (Barcelos 2014; Brubaker and Dillaway 2008; Bute and Russell 2012). Here, the triple jeopardy of age, race, and class intersect with the power-over care practices of U.S. technocratic birth to situate young women as passive objects (rather than active agents), and uphold the purported authoritative knowledge of biomedicine. Consequently, childbearing adolescents are at significant risk for medically managed, nonphysiologic birth and associated deleterious health outcomes (Romano and Lothian 2008; Lothian 2014b), as a result of the combined effects of felt and enacted stigma that biosocially pathologize teen pregnancy.

Physiologic Birth and its Threatened Status in Biomedical Birthing Care

In order to highlight how excessive and unnecessary interventions fuel poor health outcomes for childbearing adolescents and neonates, we provide here a brief overview of the benefits of physiologic birth. In doing so, we emphasize what is taken from adolescent childbearing women when their pregnancies are disproportionately pathologized, and then move into the iatrogenic effects of interventions that, in and of themselves, are dangerous. Physiologic birth is defined as "one that is powered by the innate human capacity of the woman and fetus. This birth is more likely to be safe and healthy because there is no unnecessary intervention that disrupts normal physiologic processes" (ACNM, MANA, NACPM 2012:2). Physiologic childbirth has multiple hallmarks, including:

> Characterized by spontaneous onset and progression of labor; includes biological and psychological conditions that promote effective labor; results in the vaginal birth of the infant and placenta; results in physiological blood loss; facilitates optimal newborn transition through skin-to-skin contact and keeping the mother and infant together during the postpartum period; and supports early initiation of breastfeeding. (ACNM, MANA, NACPM 2012:2)

The benefits of physiologic birth, grounded in our evolutionary history as a species (Davis-Floyd and Cheyney 2009; Small 2011; Trevathan 2010), has long been recognized in midwifery care models (Davis-Floyd 2001, 2004; Jordan 1992; Rothman 1991) and increasingly in biomedical research as well (ACNM, MANA, NACPM 2012; Buckley 2015; Romano and Lothian 2008; Sakala, Romano, and Buckley 2016; World Health Organization 1996). A vaginal birth without interventions carries fewer risks and greater benefits for the person giving birth and for the neonate, both immediately and long-term.

Physiologic birth, when not subjected to interference, promotes optimal neonatal neurological development, facilitates parent-infant bonding, supports immediate initiation of optimal breastfeeding, sustains maternal mental health, improves infant growth, diminishes incidences of chronic disease later in life for the neonate, and confers short- and long-term immunological benefits to the neonate from exposure to the vaginal microbiome (ACNM, MANA, NACPM 2012; Bodner et al. 2010; Buckley 2015; Cho and Norman 2013; Dominguez-Bello et al. 2010; Goer and Romano 2012; Kramer et al. 2008; Mueller et al. 2015; Sakala, Romano, and Buckley 2016; Romano and Lothian 2008; Sevelsted et al. 2015). Additionally, physiologic birth supports optimality of the neuroendocrine system by protecting the evolved hormonal physiology of labor (Buckley 2015; Sakala, Romano, and Buckley 2016), which facilitates safe passage of the neonate through the birth process and optimal neonatal transitions (e.g., thermoregulation and cardio-respiratory transitions). Protecting the hormonal physiology of labor also decreases the need for interventions (e.g., by facilitating endogenous hormones that promote effective cervical dilation and uterine contractions, and increase maternal ability to cope with pain) that carry their own inherent dangers and can cause iatrogenic effects for both childbearing person and neonate, as detailed in the next section.

In response to the growing recognition of the benefits of physiologic birth and the inherent dangers of medical interventions during labor and birth, a significant number of health organizations, researchers, and consumer advocacy agencies alike (Lothian 2014) have detailed the need for care practices (see Lamaze International 2007) and environments (see Sakala and Corry 2008) that support physiologic birth and decrease the use of interventions without clinical indication. Given the known interactions between biological pregnancies and biomedical interventions that produce deleterious health consequences, it is critical for reproductive justice advocates and care providers alike to acknowledge—as we do in this proposed syndemic—that pregnant teens are biosocially pathologized during biomedical care due to intersectional stigma and, thus, placed at increased risk for excessive and (unnecessary)[3] interventions.

(Unnecessary) Interventions and Negative Perinatal Health Outcomes

Childbearing adolescents pose an unusual paradox in terms of birth intervention rates as compared to other age groups and national trends in the United States. Despite the "cascade of interventions" (Amis 2014; Declercq et al. 2013; Childbirth Connection 2015; Lothian 2014a; Petersen et al. 2013; Rossignol et al. 2014)—a term used to describe a set of excessive and iterative medical procedures that routinely occur in hospital births with serious consequences for health and birth outcomes (described in more detail, below)—studies document lower (but not necessarily acceptable) rates of cesarean and operative vaginal delivery for childbearing adolescents compared to their adult counterparts (Martin et al. 2017; Torvie et al. 2015). In contrast, teens experience higher rates of epidural analgesia and induction of labor (Osterman and Martin 2011; Osterman and Martin 2014), which are typically associated with higher cesarean rates (Declercq et al. 2013; Lothian 2014a; Petersen et al. 2013). The U.S. has an overall national cesarean rate of 32.0 percent; for women under the age of 20, the cesarean rate is 20.4 percent (Martin et al. 2017). However, the international health community recommends a targeted cesarean rate of no more than 10–15 percent (World Health Organization 2015) because, at the population level, cesarean rates greater than 10 percent are not associated with reduced maternal or neonatal mortality, and, in fact, cesareans above this threshold are implicated in increased reproductive mortality and morbidity (American College of Obstetricians and Gynecologists [ACOG] et al. 2014; World Health Organization 2015). A cesarean rate of even 21 percent for teen moms is thus unacceptably high by international standards.

Epidural analgesia usage (narcotic painkillers administered through a spinal injection during labor, which interfere with a laboring person's ability to feel their contractions and disrupt the body's natural production of oxytocin that helps maintain effective contractions and lowers maternal stress and pain) gradually decreases with increasing age; women under the age of twenty experience the highest epidural analgesia use rate at 64 percent, while rates for women ages twenty to thirty-four hover around 60 percent on average (Osterman and Martin 2011). In a review of singleton births at 37 to 44 weeks' gestation in the U.S., Ananth, Wilcox, and Gyamfi-Bannerman (2013) found that at least 25 percent of labor inductions and/or cesarean deliveries among women under the age of twenty were clinically *non*-indicated (i.e., not medically necessary and thus likely inappropriate). Only 56.6 percent of the young women in this sample experienced a spontaneous onset of labor and subsequent vaginal birth (Ananth, Wilcox, and Gyamfi-Bannerman 2013). Teen moms were thus disproportionately denied the benefits of physiologic birth, for themselves and their infants.

Given the known benefits of spontaneous labor and uninterrupted physiologic birth—as reviewed above—combined with the inherent risks posed by medical interventions (Bannister-Tyrrell et al. 2014; Bonsack, Lathrop, and Blackburn 2014; Declercq, Barger, and Weiss 2011; Glantz 2012; Herrera-Gómez et al. 2015, 2017; Kjerulff et al. 2017; Hincz et al. 2014; Zenzmaier et al. 2017), the U.S. has made national efforts (and some strides) over the past several years to reduce clinically unnecessary cesarean deliveries and early inductions (i.e., labor induction prior to 39 completed weeks) (ACOG et al. 2014; American Public Health Association [APHA] 2014; ACOG Committee on Practice Bulletins 2009; Clark et al. 2010; Centers for Medicare and Medicaid Services 2012; Hartmann et al. 2012). For childbearing adolescents, however, early inductions continue to occur at alarmingly high rates, and cesarean rates remain less than optimal. Pregnant teens, affected by interactions between structural stigma, biosocial pathologization of their biological condition, and iatrogenic interventions, are not yet reaping the benefits of gradual obstetric reform.

Notably, the ACOG (American College of Obstetricians and Gynecologists) Practice Bulletin on clinical management guidelines for labor induction still identifies, but does not define, "psychosocial indications" as an appropriate reason for pharmacological or mechanical induction (ACOG Committee on Practice Bulletins 2009), in which artificial hormones (i.e., prostaglandins, synthetic oxytocin, misoprostol) or mechanical devices (i.e., balloon catheters, laminaria tents) are given to a pregnant woman to force the start of her labor (Jozwiak et al. 2012; Ramirez 2011). These methods may also be used for artificial augmentation of labor (i.e., accelerate the pace of labor) (Kenyon et al. 2013). This catch-all category of "psychosocial indications" is particularly problematic in light of the stigma-driven, biosocial pathologization of childbearing teens' pregnancies, where both dominant societal rhetoric and biomedical practices treat them as incapable, morally deviant, and irresponsible "children having children"—arguable bases from which to electively (and inappropriately) induce under "psychosocial indications."

Pharmacologic or mechanical induction of labor is thus a birth intervention of particular concern to our syndemic, as it clearly produces a bidirectional, biological, and biomedical interaction with health consequences. Labor induction involves two primary risk conduits for the laboring person and fetus/neonate. First, any intervention can disrupt the hormonal physiology of labor and, as briefly summarized above, uninterrupted physiologic birth is essential for: fetal readiness at birth (i.e., pre-labor lung maturity), fetal protection during passage through the birth canal (i.e., buffering from labor hypoxia via increases in epinephrine-norepinephrine receptors), labor progression (i.e., increased oxytocin receptors to facilitate effective contractions), maternal ability to cope with pain and stress (i.e., pain-reducing, pleasure-increasing effects of beta-endorphins), fetal-to-neonatal transitions (i.e., catecholamine surges to promote respiratory transitions and thermoregulation), and optimal breastfeeding initiation as well as mother-infant bonding (i.e., increased oxytocin and prolactin receptors) (Buckley 2015; Sakala, Romano, and Buckley 2016). When pharmacological induction (of any timing) occurs, these protective and beneficial effects of physiologic childbearing are inhibited. Simply put, a neonate that does not undergo a spontaneous labor (i.e., a labor that started and progressed without artificial interference) may not have finished all of the biological processes necessary to be ready for life outside the womb and, in turn, such biomedical disruptions may impact the ability to achieve optimal immediate- and long-term health and growth.

Second, induction of labor is considered the tipping point for the "cascade of interventions" (Amis 2014; Declercq et al. 2013; Childbirth Connection 2015; Lothian 2014a; Petersen et al. 2013; Rossignol et al. 2014), or the recognized ways in which one biomedical birth intervention may lead to unanticipated or new problems during labor, which may then "need" to be monitored, prevented, or corrected by another intervention. This can introduce additional complications or variations from physiologic labor progression that need to be treated with even more interventions, and the cascade continues with the final culmination most often being a cesarean delivery that was not otherwise medically necessary, but which is commonly constructed in a biomedical setting as being an "emergency" delivery necessitated, in many cases, by the outcome of an earlier intervention that followed predictably from another intervention (Kjerulff et al. 2017; Lothian 2014a; Zenzmaier et al. 2017).

A common cascade of interventions scenario can be seen in Figure 3.2, and follows this flow: a labor begins by pharmacological induction such as with synthetic oxytocin (e.g., Pitocin); synthetic oxytocin is known to increase contraction intensity (but not necessarily efficiency) while also not providing the same pain-reducing effects of endogenous opiate-like pain relief hormones (beta-endorphins) that would otherwise be released during physiologic labor (Buckley 2015; Sakala and Corry 2008). The increased intensity of synthetically enhanced non-physiologic labor, without the concomitant release of opiate-like beta-endorphins that accompany spontaneous contractions in physiologic labor, may lead to a laboring woman being encouraged to use epidural anesthesia for synthetic pain relief which, in turn, causes a significant drop in maternal blood pressure and decreased oxygen flow to the fetus. Fetal distress is then diagnosed and labor progression remains slow, producing a predictable "emergency" where a cesarean is recommended—and justified for reasons of the neonate's well-being and/or the laboring woman's "exhaustion" (after a labor made more physically difficult by the non-physiologic contractions brought on by artificial induction)—at the urging of the biomedical team that offered or promoted the synthetic labor to begin with (Amis 2014; Declercq et al. 2013; Childbirth Connection 2015; Herrera-Gómez et al. 2015, 2017; Kjerulff et al. 2017; Lothian 2014a; Petersen et al. 2013; Rossignol et al. 2014; Zenzmaier et al. 2017).

As Simpson and Atterbury (2003:770) note, "It is unlikely that all women are provided with a complete discussion of the cascade of interventions that frequently accompany labor induction." This may be particularly true for childbearing adolescents who are already less likely to receive informed consent and explanation during biomedical care (Brubaker 2007; Brubaker and Dillaway 2008; Everson 2015, 2016; Low et al. 2003; Nichols et al. 2014). The damaging effects of this cascade of interventions likely lend themselves to multiple intrapartum and postpartum syndemics for both

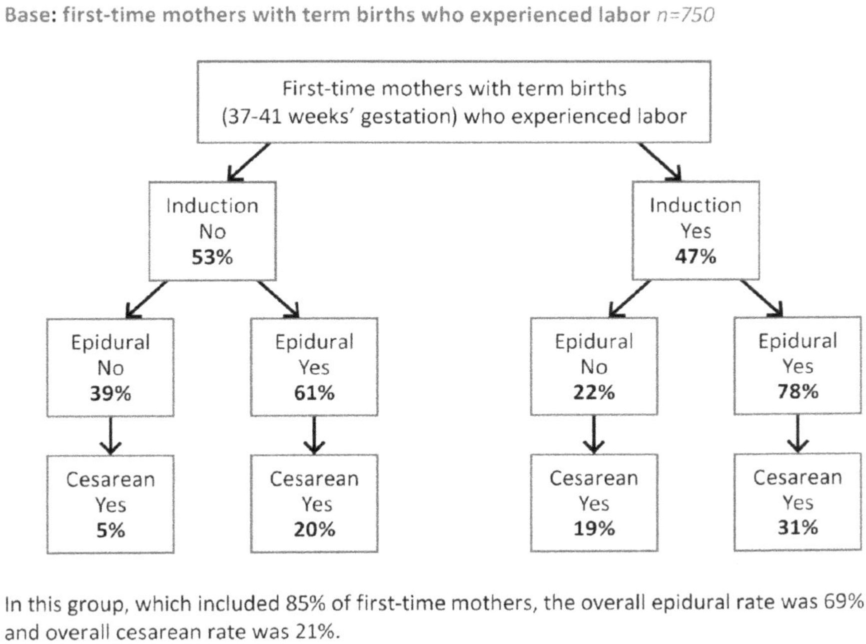

Figure 3.2. Cascade of intervention example. *Source*: Cascade of intervention results from Childbirth Connection's™ national Listening to Mothers III survey (reproduced from Declercq et al. 2013).

halves of the birth dyad, with immediate and long-term health risks for the childbearing person and neonate. Here, we are focusing on the role that stigma-driven, biosocial pathologization of adolescent pregnancies plays in positioning young women as especially vulnerable to certain biomedical aspects of this cascade, and to the resulting deleterious health consequences of interactions between their biological pregnancies and the iatrogenic effects of biomedical interventions targeting these pregnancies.

In addition to the health consequences of induction in interrupting the hormonal physiology of labor, each successively introduced intervention in the cascade (epidurals, cesarean section, etc.) carries its own inherent risks, any of which can interact syndemically with a pathologized (biological) pregnancy in the context of structural stigma. Epidurals, for example, are associated with maternal and neonatal complications, such as operative vaginal delivery (forceps or vacuum extraction), cesarean sections, labor dystocia (obstructed or stalled labor), maternal fever, perineal trauma (trauma to any part of the genitalia as a result of cutting or tearing), NICU admission for the neonate (which can affect bonding and breastfeeding), immediate and later breastfeeding difficulties, respiratory complications, nausea, vomiting, dizziness, hypotension (low blood pressure), maternal urinary incontinence, fetal distress, severe headaches and backache, and, in extreme circumstances, temporary to permanent nerve damage (Bannister-Tyrrell et al. 2014; Herrera-Gómez et al. 2015; Hincz et al. 2014; Jones et al. 2012; Loewenberg-Weisband et al. 2014; Lothian 2014a; Shrestha, Devgan, and Sharma 2014).

Cesareans also carry inherent maternal and neonatal health risks, including maternal wound infections, neonatal breathing difficulties (e.g., transient tachypnea and respiratory distress syndrome), postpartum hemorrhage, blood clots, breastfeeding problems, and postpartum depression, as well as escalated increased risks for future pregnancies, such as uterine rupture, adhesions (where the placenta attaches to the cesarean scar in subsequent pregnancies), infections (including hospital-acquired infections increasingly resistant to treatment), and excessive bleeding during repeat cesareans (Blanchette 2011; Bodner et al. 2010; Chang et al. 2015; Goer, Romano, and Sakala 2012; Houston et al. 2015; Lyell 2011; Spong et al. 2012). Of significant importance for intergenerational health and the deepening of structural health inequities through widening gaps in chronic illness rates, cesarean deliveries are also implicated in the disruption of the microbial colonization processes in birth. Colonization largely happens during the neonate's transition through the birth canal during a vaginal delivery and, subsequently, during immediate skin-to-skin contact with the mother after birth (Collado et al. 2012; Dahlen et al. 2014; Dominguez-Bello et al. 2010; Mueller et al. 2015).

Infants delivered by cesarean section are deprived of this important exposure to the vaginal microbiome, which transfers key immunological substances to the neonate, irreplaceably establishing their own crucial microbiota from the moment of birth. Increasing cesarean section rates are explored in a growing body of research as a primary contributing factor to worldwide epidemic rates of asthma, obesity, diabetes, necrotizing fasciitis, and other long-term health consequences of not experiencing physiologic birth, and thus not acquiring the early seeding of the vaginal microbiome with its accompanying immune advantages (Dahlen et al. 2014). With these troubling risks of disruptions to physiologic birth gaining more attention, the implications for childbearing adolescents and their neonates, who may be at even greater risk through teen pregnancy stigma syndemics, are critical to consider not only in the context of reproductive justice, but also for global public health and structural health inequalities.

Early Inductions

The iatrogenic effects of ubiquitous medical interventions in birth are alarmingly clear. For young childbearing adolescents, an additional layer of risk comes into play with *early* induction, both because of the inherent risks induction poses and due to the iatrogenic neonatal prematurity that can result from interactions between the intervention and the biological condition of pregnancy. Thus, as induction—in and of itself—holds risks, what happens when labor induction takes place prior to full-term pregnancy, when a fetus has not yet reached optimal development? Early inductions of labor have been on the rise since the 1980s, and the proportion of neonates born prior to 39 weeks' gestation increased almost 60 percent between 1981 and 2006 (Osterman and Martin 2014). Since 2006, births occurring prior to 39 weeks decreased by 12 percent due to concerted efforts in obstetric and public health communities to reduce non-clinically indicated early inductions. These concerted efforts arose from recognition of the known iatrogenic effects of induction, and growing global concerns about preterm labor and low-birthweight rates, which increase with early induction (Amis 2014; APHA 2014; Bonsack, Lathrop, and Blackburn 2014; Glantz 2012; Loftin et al. 2010; Osterman and Martin 2014; Simpson and Atterbury 2003; Simpson and Atterbury 2003).[4]

However, resulting declines in births before full-term have not been observed for all childbearing persons—inequities by maternal age persist. Most notably, between 2006 and 2012, declines in induction between 35 and 37 weeks gestation were witnessed for all maternal age groups[5] *except* childbearing adolescents under the age of twenty. In fact, quite the opposite occurred: between 2006 and 2012, childbearing adolescents experienced a 10 percent *increase* in labor induction at 35 weeks' gestation, a 5 percent increase at 36 weeks, and a 5 percent increase at 37 weeks (Osterman and Martin 2014)—demonstrating the degree to which pregnant teens are subjected to comparatively more interventions, by this measure. Rates did decline slightly for women under the age of 20 at 38 weeks' gestation by 6 percent, though this was the smallest change seen across all age groups (Osterman and Martin 2014). Rising induction rates are but one example of how stigma-driven, biosocial pathologization of adolescent childbearing bodies results in interactions between the biological condition of pregnancy and non-clinically indicated biomedical interventions, together resulting in negative perinatal health consequences.

Non-clinically indicated procedures in biomedical care are commonly described as "unnecessary" or "elective," but contrary to common perception, "elective" means by physician choice (not the patient's choice)[6] and without medical indication to do so, thus leading to their designation as "unnecessary" interventions (Lothian 2014a; Lothian 2014b; Moore and Low 2012). The significant risks of early elective inductions are well-documented, with neonatal morbidity and mortality significantly greater among neonates born prior to 39 weeks' gestation. Risks include breathing problems (e.g., respiratory distress syndrome, transient tachypnea, pneumonia, and assisted ventilation—largely due to fetal lung immaturity), infection, hypothermia, hypoglycemia, 5-minute Apgar scores <7 (a composite measure used as a proxy for long-term morbidity), low birth weight, small for gestational age, hyperbilirubinemia (jaundice), breastfeeding difficulties (in part due to under-developed gastrointestinal tracts), and admission to the NICU (ACOG 2013; Ananth, Wilcox, and Gyamfi-Bannerman 2013; Barton et al. 2011; Bastek et al. 2008; Bonsack, Lathrop, and Blackburn 2014; Engle 2011; Osterman and Martin 2014; Raju et al. 2006; Moore and Low 2012).

These health risks are said to be a consequence of iatrogenic prematurity when they involve early elective induction, cesarean, or any other medical intervention that causes the newborn to be more physiologically immature and/or of low birth weight (Amis 2014; Institute of Medicine 1985; Loftin et al. 2010). In addition to such morbidity, the health effects of iatrogenic prematurity then coalesce to increase neonatal mortality (NM). Compared to neonates born at 39 weeks' gestation, the relative risk of NM at 35, 36, 37, and 38 weeks' gestation is 6.4, 3.7, 2.3, and 1.4, respectively; infant mortality rates also significantly rise with early delivery (ACOG 2013). For all measures, morbidity and mortality decrease with each increasing week of gestation. What these statistics mean is that biomedical care, with its accompanying high rate of interventions like early induction, may increase the health risks for childbearing persons and their babies. When these interventions are disproportionately targeted to interact with teen pregnancies, the deleterious outcomes are, by extension, a product of structural relationships between stigma and biosocial-biomedical-biological processes. Adolescent women facing a pregnancy that is biosocially pathologized due to structural stigma and the authoritative knowledge of biomedical birthing care are more likely to experience misuse of interventions that interact with the biological conditions of their pregnancies, with the predictable deleterious health consequences we have outlined above. In the case of teen pregnancy, intersectional stigma powerfully reinforces or is used to justify the pathologization of adolescent pregnancies and this, in turn, facilitates the use of biomedical interventions. These interventions then interact with the biology of pregnancy to produce negative health consequences for teen women and their children, who thereby receive a less than optimal start to life. Stigma is thus the first structural ingredient in a complex, but common syndemic recipe.

Long-Term Health and Well-Being Implications

Complications from preterm delivery are the leading cause of death for children under the age of five, and delivery prior to 39 weeks' gestation is associated with negative long-term child developmental trajectories due to the large percentage of brain growth that occurs in the final gestational weeks (Liu et al. 2015; March of Dimes 2013; McGowan et al. 2011; Raju et al. 2006). Changes in the microbial ecology of the gastrointestinal tract—due to differentials in gestational age from early induction, separation of the mother-baby dyad at birth, and cesarean section—may also have long-term impacts on health, including the development of autoimmune and allergic diseases (Cho and Norman 2013; Collado et al. 2012; Dahlen et al. 2014; Dominguez-Bello et al. 2010; Mueller et al. 2015; Neu and Rushing 2011). Preterm deliveries contribute not only to human suffering through ongoing morbidity and mortality, but also have profound economic implications—prematurity costs the U.S. more than $26.2 billion per year (March of Dimes 2013). Late preterm deliveries (34 through 36 weeks) account for 74 percent of all preterm births, and labor induction is cited as a primary driver of these deliveries (Loftin et al. 2010; Moore and Low 2012). Childbearing adolescents experience not only the highest rates of early induction (Osterman and Martin 2014), but some of the highest rates of total preterm delivery, as well as late preterm delivery, at 9.91 percent and 6.86 percent, respectively (Martin et al. 2017). Iatrogenic preterm birth, resulting from non-clinically indicated early induction, is one of the clearest possible indicators of the interactions between biomedical interventions and the biological condition of pregnancy, underscored, in this case, by structural stigma and biosocial pathologization.

Moreover, childbearing adolescents are at the beginning of the reproductive phase of the life course, and are likely to have additional children. As such, we must consider the long-term threats of these medical interventions to reproductive options and perinatal health equity in subsequent deliveries. For example, despite clinical evidence suggesting a trial of labor (TOL) after cesarean to be preferable in many cases to an automatic repeat cesarean, and multiple studies demonstrating the safety of vaginal birth after cesarean (VBAC), this option is frequently limited in locales across the U.S., as many hospitals require an automatic repeat cesarean, citing concerns over uterine rupture as the reason why they will not allow a TOL or VBAC (Bernstein, Matalon-Grazi, and Rosenn 2012; Cox 2011; Cunningham et al. 2010; Guise, Eden, et al. 2010; Guise, Denman, et al. 2010). Repeat cesareans carry their own level of inherent risk to both fetus and childbearing person, including adhesions, bowel injury, infections, hysterectomy, wound bleeding, prolonged hospital stays, and increased maternal mortality (Guise, Eden, et al. 2010; Guise, Denman, et al. 2010; Lyell 2011). Approximately 25 percent of childbearing adolescents give birth to another child within two years of an initial delivery, and one in five births to adolescent women are repeat births (Barnet et al. 2009; US Department of Health & Human Services 2015).

Rapid repeat deliveries may further the social exclusion and stigma experienced by young childbearing women, while deepening economic, social, and health inequities. The children of teen and prior teen mothers face negative health, social, and educational outcomes as well, and (if daughters) are statistically more likely to become young mothers themselves (East, Reyes, and Horn 2007; Jutte et al. 2010; Porter and Holness 2011; Smithbattle 2007). Childbearing adolescents may also experience reduced self-efficacy and increased negative self-concept associated with the disempowering, stigmatizing experiences of biomedical care and ubiquitous medical interventions (Anderson and McGuinness 2008; Arthur, Unwin, and Mitchell 2007; Brubaker and Wright 2006; Everson 2015; Nichols et al. 2014; Sauls 2004; Smithbattle, Lorenz, and Leander 2013). In this way, cycles of poverty, young childbearing, and negative perinatal health perpetuate in the context of stigma-driven, biosocial pathologization of pregnancy, contributing to "legacies of disadvantage" and lifelong structural vulnerability (Everson 2015, 2016; Metzl and Hansen 2014; Smithbattle 2007; Quesada, Hart, and Bourgois 2011).

Teen pregnancy stigma, then, not only drives iatrogenic health outcomes at birth in multidirectional ways, but also through intergenerational effects. Stigma-driven, biosocial pathologization of teen pregnancy produces biomedical-biological interactions that carry damaging lifelong health consequences for both the adolescent and neonate. This, in turn, may produce further structural stigma and impact future pregnancies of both woman and child, lending itself to a syndemic cycle of pathologized teen pregnancy that extends far beyond a given teen mother or a singular event. This cycle occurs not only because of societal and structural factors, but because of the perpetuation of institutionalized stigma within the biomedical system and the ways that birthing care is structured in U.S. hospitals, causing pregnant teens to embody inequality through their experiences with iatrogenic birth interventions and resulting damaging health consequences.

CONCLUSION

Interactions between labor induction, the recognized cascade of interventions in biomedical birthing care, iatrogenic prematurity, and resulting short- and long-term health consequences for the dyad of birthing persons and their children—in the context of teen pregnancy stigma and pathologization—give great cause for reproductive, public, and perinatal health concern. When we consider the current and increasingly high rates of early elective induction for pregnant teens, a clear need to re-evaluate the iatrogenic effects of interventions among childbearing adolescents, as well as the socio-structural milieus that facilitate these damaging health interactions, emerges. Economic costs, combined with the negative health outcomes experienced by young childbearing women and their children, further compound, and iteratively drive, the health and social burdens of teen pregnancy stigma. We have argued that a teen pregnancy stigma syndemic exists in which intersectional structural stigma propels the biosocial pathologization of young childbearing adolescents, which in turn leads to increased (and inappropriate) biomedical interventions that interact with the biological condition of pregnancy to produce deleterious health consequences.

As one of the bidirectional aspects of the syndemic we propose, the iatrogenic effects of medically managed deliveries contribute to the larger stigma-driven low-support, high-stress environments childbearing adolescents encounter—social environments that are implicated in negative outcomes and cycles of disadvantage (Entringer, Buss, and Wadhwa 2015; Everson 2015; Porter and Holness 2011; Smithbattle, Lorenz, and Leander 2013; Yardley 2008). Moreover, iatrogenic interventions may reproduce teen pregnancy stigma and pathologizing processes by reinforcing meta-narratives in the U.S. that focus on the economic and health "costs" of young pregnancies. These structural frameworks of shame and blame contribute to biosocial pathways of interaction when the stigma enacted upon (and often internalized by) childbearing adolescents is expressed in, and reinforced by, health-damaging interactions between biological pregnancy and biomedical interventions.

Finally, the stigma-driven pathologization that underlies the proposed syndemic may be extended to other pregnancies as well. We propose that additional pregnancy-related syndemics, in which the stigmatization of the people in whose bodies the pregnancies occur—such as women of color, older women, people who participate in the continuum of assisted reproductive technologies (as recipients and surrogates), transmen, and so on—should be studied to further understand the biosocial mediation of biomedical interventions with biological pregnancy, and to expand the continuum of reproductive justice. Considerations of such structural, biosocial, and biological interactions, and their health consequences in pregnancy, can be used to inform a wide array of efforts to reduce health inequities.

NOTES

1. Although we primarily use the term "women" to refer to those experiencing pregnancy and birth in this chapter, we want to acknowledge the diversity of gender identities and embodied experiences of pregnancy that occur across the gender spectrum. At times, and for language variety, we use more gender-inclusive terms. Increasingly acknowledged in the literature on family formation, pregnancy, and birth, we are aware that transmen, gender-variant, genderfluid, and genderqueer people also become pregnant and give birth (Ellis, Wojnar, and Pettinato 2015). The impacts of stigmatization, pathologization of pregnancy, and iatrogenic interventions is equally worthy of future research in non-binary gender populations.

2. We use the terms "body" and "bodies" throughout this paper to mean the holistic nature of embodied experiences, drawing on Scheper-Hughes' and Lock's 1987 conceptualization of the body(ies), wherein they posit three constructs to create a more nuanced and contextualized analysis: the individual body, or "the lived experience of the body-self" (7); the social body, or "the representational uses of the body as a natural symbol with which to think about nature, society, and culture" (7); and the body politic, or "the regulation, surveillance, and control of bodies (individual and collective) in reproduction and sexuality, in work and in leisure, in

sickness and other forms of deviance and human difference" (7–8). The pathways of interaction discussed herein illustrate these three forms, and demonstrate the intrinsically socio-politically constituted nature of the syndemic.

3. We bracket the term "unnecessary" in the phrase "unnecessary interventions" to indicate a two-fold concern over interventions—first, any intervention carries a level of inherent risk and, thus, an inherent ability to produce deleterious outcomes; and second, the potential for iatrogenic effects is greatly pronounced when the intervention is not clinically indicated. Non-clinically indicated procedures are commonly described as "unnecessary" or "elective."

4. Gestational age definitions changed with early induction prevention campaigns: Early preterm is defined as deliveries prior to 34 completed weeks gestation; late preterm is delivery between 34 to 36 completed weeks gestation; early term is delivery between 37 to 38 completed weeks gestation; full term is delivery between 39 to 40 completed weeks gestation; late term is delivery at 41 weeks; and postterm is delivery at 42 completed weeks gestation or beyond (Osterman and Martin 2005).

5. The exception is women over the age of 40 who saw a slight, but not statistically significant, increase of labor induction at 37 weeks' gestation between 2006 and 2012.

6. There is increasing evidence that Brazil, a country with an extremely high cesarean section rate often blamed on women's requests, has disparities in these rates largely due to ethnicity, income, and provider preference/suggestion (Hopkins 2000).

REFERENCES

American College of Nurse Midwives [ACNM], Midwives Alliance of North America [MANA], National Association of Certified Professional Midwives [NACPM]. 2012. "Supporting Healthy and Normal Physiologic Childbirth: A Consensus Statement by the American College of Nurse-Midwives, Midwives Alliance of North America, and the National Association of Certified Professional Midwives." *Journal of Midwifery & Women's Health* 57 (5): 529–32. doi:10.1111/j.1542-2011.2012.00218.x.

American College of Obstetricians and Gynecologists [ACOG]. 2013. "ACOG Committee Opinion No. 561: Nonmedically Indicated Early-Term Deliveries." *Obstetrics and Gynecology* 121 (4): 911–15. doi:10.1097/01.AOG.0000428649.57622.a7.

ACOG Committee on Practice Bulletins. 2009. "ACOG Practice Bulletin No. 107: Induction of Labor." *Obstetrics and Gynecology* 114 (2 Pt 1): 386–97. doi:10.1097/AOG.0b013e31 81b48ef5.

ACOG, Society for Maternal-Fetal Medicine [SMFM], Aaron B. Caughey, Alison G. Cahill, Jeanne-Marie Guise, and Dwight J. Rouse. 2014. "Safe Prevention of the Primary Cesarean Delivery." *American Journal of Obstetrics and Gynecology* 210 (3): 179–93. doi:10.1016/j.ajog.2014.01.026.

Amis, Debby. 2014. "Healthy Birth Practice #1: Let Labor Begin on Its Own." *The Journal of Perinatal Education* 23 (4): 178–87. doi:10.1891/1058-1243.23.4.178.

Ananth, Cande V., Allen J. Wilcox, and Cynthia Gyamfi-Bannerman. 2013. "Obstetrical Interventions for Term First Births in the United States." *Paediatric and Perinatal Epidemiology* 27 (5): 442–51. doi:10.1111/ppe.12068.

Anderson, Cheryl, and Teena M. McGuinness. 2008. "Do Teenage Mothers Experience Childbirth as Traumatic?" *Journal of Psychosocial Nursing and Mental Health Services* 46 (4): 21–24.

Aparicio, Elizabeth, Edward V. Pecukonis, and Shalita O'Neale. 2015. "'The Love That I Was Missing': Exploring the Lived Experience of Motherhood among Teen Mothers in Foster Care." *Children and Youth Services Review* 51 (April): 44–54. doi:10.1016/j.childyouth.2015.02.002.

American Public Health Association [APHA]. 2014. "Reducing Non Medically Indicated Elective Inductions of Labor." Policy Statement. Washington, D.C.: American Public Health Association.

Arthur, Angela, Sally Unwin, and Theresa Mitchell. 2007. "Teenage Mothers' Experiences of Maternity Services: A Qualitative Study." *British Journal of Midwifery* 15 (11): 672.

Attanasio, Laura, and Katy B. Kozhimannil. 2015. "Patient-Reported Communication Quality and Perceived Discrimination in Maternity Care." *Medical Care* 53 (10): 863–71. doi:10.1097/MLR.0000000000000411.

Bannister-Tyrrell, Melanie, Jane B. Ford, Jonathan M. Morris, and Christine L. Roberts. 2014. "Epidural Analgesia in Labour and Risk of Caesarean Delivery." *Paediatric and Perinatal Epidemiology* 28 (5): 400–411. doi:10.1111/ppe.12139.

Barcelos, Christie A. 2014. "Producing (potentially) Pregnant Teen Bodies: Biopower and Adolescent Pregnancy in the USA." *Critical Public Health* 24 (4): 476–88. doi:10.1080/09581596.2013.853869.

Barcelos, Christie A., and Aline C. Gubrium. 2014. "Reproducing Stories: Strategic Narratives of Teen Pregnancy and Motherhood." *Social Problems* 61 (3): 466–81. doi:10.1525/sp.2014.12241.

Barnet, Beth, Jiexin Liu, Margo DeVoe, Anne K. Duggan, Melanie A. Gold, and Edward Pecukonis. 2009. "Motivational Intervention to Reduce Rapid Subsequent Births to Adolescent Mothers: A Community-Based Randomized Trial." *Annals of Family Medicine* 7 (5): 436–45. doi:10.1370/afm.1014.

Barton, John R., Lucy A. Barton, Niki B. Istwan, Cheryl N. Desch, Debbie J. Rhea, Gary J. Stanziano, and Baha M. Sibai. 2011. "Elective Delivery at $34^{0}(/)^{7}$ to $36^{6}(/)^{7}$ Weeks' Gestation and Its Impact on Neonatal Outcomes in Women with Stable Mild Gestational Hypertension." *American Journal of Obstetrics and Gynecology* 204 (1): 44.e1–5. doi:10.1016/j.ajog.2010.08.030.

Bastek, Jamie A., Mary D. Sammel, Emmanuelle Paré, Sindhu K. Srinivas, Michael A. Posencheg, and Michal A. Elovitz. 2008. "Adverse Neonatal Outcomes: Examining the Risks between Preterm, Late Preterm, and Term Infants." *American Journal of Obstetrics and Gynecology* 199 (4): 367.e1–8. doi:10.1016/j.ajog.2008.08.002.

Belle Doucet, Deborah, Joanne. 2003. "Poverty, Inequality, And Discrimination As Sources Of Depression Among U.S. Women." *Psychology of Women Quarterly* 27 (2): 101–13. doi:10.1111/1471-6402.00090.

Bernstein, Sarah N., Shira Matalon-Grazi, and Barak M. Rosenn. 2012. "Trial of Labor versus Repeat Cesarean: Are Patients Making an Informed Decision?" *American Journal of Obstetrics and Gynecology* 207 (3): 204.e1–6. doi:10.1016/j.ajog.2012.06.057.

Blanchette, Howard. 2011. "The Rising Cesarean Delivery Rate in America: What Are the Consequences?" *Obstetrics and Gynecology* 118 (3): 687–90. doi:10.1097/AOG.0b013e318227b8d9.

Bloch, K, and T Taylor. 2014. "Welfare Queens and Anchor Babies: A Comparative Study of Stigmatized Mothers in the United States." In *Mothering in the Age of Neoliberalism*, edited by Melinda Vandenbeld Giles, Ch. 10. Bradford, ON: Demeter Press.

Boath, Elizabeth Hardie, Carol Henshaw, and Eleanor Bradley. 2013. "Meeting the Challenges of Teenage Mothers with Postpartum Depression: Overcoming Stigma through Support." *Journal of Reproductive and Infant Psychology* 31 (4): 352–69. doi:10.1080/02646838.2013.800635.

Bodner, Klaus, Franz Wierrani, Werner Grünberger, and Barbara Bodner-Adler. 2010. "Influence of the Mode of Delivery on Maternal and Neonatal Outcomes: A Comparison between Elective Cesarean Section and Planned Vaginal Delivery in a Low-Risk Obstetric Population." *Archives of Gynecology and Obstetrics* 283 (6): 1193–98. doi:10.1007/s00404-010-1525-y.

Bohren, Meghan A., Joshua P. Vogel, Erin C. Hunter, Olha Lutsiv, Suprita K. Makh, João Paulo Souza, Carolina Aguiar, et al. 2015. "The Mistreatment of Women during Childbirth in Health Facilities Globally: A Mixed-Methods Systematic Review." *PLOS Med* 12 (6): e1001847. doi:10.1371/journal.pmed.1001847.

Bonsack, Carrie F., Anthony Lathrop, and Mary Blackburn. 2014. "Induction of Labor: Update and Review." *Journal of Midwifery & Women's Health* 59 (6): 606–15. doi:10.1111/jmwh.12255.

Booth, Andrew. 2008. "Unpacking Your Literature Search Toolbox: On Search Styles and Tactics." *Health Information & Libraries Journal* 25 (4): 313–17. doi:10.1111/j.1471-1842.2008.00825.x.

Breheny, Mary, and Christine Stephens. 2010. "Youth or Disadvantage? The Construction of Teenage Mothers in Medical Journals." *Culture, Health & Sexuality* 12 (3): 307–22. doi:10.1080/13691050903513234.

Bridges, Khiara. 2011. *Reproducing Race: An Ethnography of Pregnancy as a Site of Racialization*. University of California Press.

Broussard, C. Anne, Alfred L. Joseph, and Marco Thompson. 2012. "Stressors and Coping Strategies Used by Single Mothers Living in Poverty." *Affilia* 27 (2): 190–204. doi:10.1177/0886109912443884.

Brubaker, Sarah Jane. 2007. "Denied, Embracing, and Resisting Medicalization African American Teen Mothers' Perceptions of Formal Pregnancy and Childbirth Care." *Gender & Society* 21 (4): 528–52. doi:10.1177/0891243207304972.

Brubaker, Sarah Jane, and Heather E. Dillaway. 2008. "Re-Examining the Meanings of Childbirth: Beyond Gender and the 'Natural' versus 'Medical' Dichotomy." In *Advancing Gender Research from the Nineteenth to the Twenty-First Centuries*, 12:217–44. Advances in Gender Research 12. Emerald Group Publishing Limited. http://www.emeraldinsight.com/doi/abs/10.1016/S1529-2126%2808%2912012-4.

Brubaker, Sarah Jane, and Christie Wright. 2006. "Identity Transformation and Family Caregiving: Narratives of African American Teen Mothers." *Journal of Marriage and Family* 68 (5): 1214–28.

Bryman, Alan. 2012. *Social Research Methods*. 4th edition. Oxford; New York: Oxford University Press.

Buckley, Sarah. 2015. "Hormonal Physiology of Childbearing: Evidence and Implications for Women, Babies, and Maternity." Washington, D.C.: Childbirth Connection Programs, National Partnership for Women & Families.

Bute, Jennifer J., and Laura D. Russell. 2012. "Public Discourses about Teenage Pregnancy: Disruption, Restoration, and Ideology." *Health Communication* 27 (7): 712–22. doi:10.1080/10410236.2011.636479.

Cassidy, Tanya, and Abdullahi El Tom. 2015. *Ethnographies of Breastfeeding: Cultural Contexts and Confrontations*. Bloomsbury Publishing.

Centers for Disease Control. 2015. "Preterm Birth | Maternal and Infant Health | Reproductive Health | CDC." http://www.cdc.gov/reproductivehealth/maternalinfanthealth/pretermbirth.htm.

Centers for Medicare and Medicaid Services. 2012. "Reducing Early Elective Deliveries in Medicaid and CHIP." Baltimore, MD: Centers for Medicare and Medicaid Services. http://www.medicaid.gov/Medicaid-CHIP-Program-Information/By-Topics/Quality-of-Care/Downloads/EED-Brief.pdf.

Chang, Shiow-Ru, Kuang-Ho Chen, Hong-Nerng Ho, Yeur-Hur Lai, Ming-I. Lin, Chien-Nan Lee, and Wei-An Lin. 2015. "Depressive Symptoms, Pain, and Sexual Dysfunction over the First Year Following Vaginal or Cesarean Delivery: A Prospective Longitudinal Study." *International Journal of Nursing Studies* 52 (9): 1433–44. doi:10.1016/j.ijnurstu.2015.04.019.

Cheney, Ann M., Bayla Ostrach, Ruthanne Marcus, Cynthia Frank, Cassandra Ball, and Pamela I. Erickson. 2014. "A Culture of Future Planning: Perceptions of Sexual Risk among Educated Young Adults." *Qualitative Health Research* 24 (10): 1451–62. doi:10.1177/1049732314548595.

Cheyney, Melissa. 2010. *Born at Home: The Biological, Cultural and Political Dimensions of Maternity Care in the United States*. Cengage Learning.

Childbirth Connection. 2015. "Cascade of Intervention in Childbirth." *Understandig & Navigating the Maternity Care System*. http://www.childbirthconnection.org/article.asp?ck=10182.

Cho, Clara E., and Mikael Norman. 2013. "Cesarean Section and Development of the Immune System in the Offspring." *American Journal of Obstetrics and Gynecology* 208 (4): 249–54. doi:10.1016/j.ajog.2012.08.009.

Clark, Steven L., Donna R. Frye, Janet A. Meyers, Michael A. Belfort, Gary A. Dildy, Shalece Kofford, Jane Englebright, and Jonathan A. Perlin. 2010. "Reduction in Elective Delivery at <39 Weeks of Gestation: Comparative Effectiveness of 3 Approaches to Change and the

Impact on Neonatal Intensive Care Admission and Stillbirth." *American Journal of Obstetrics and Gynecology* 203 (5): 449.e1–6. doi:10.1016/j.ajog.2010.05.036.

Collado, Maria Carmen, Maria Cernada, Christine Baüerl, Máximo Vento, and Gaspar Pérez-Martínez. 2012. "Microbial Ecology and Host-Microbiota Interactions during Early Life Stages." *Gut Microbes* 3 (4): 352–65. doi:10.4161/gmic.21215.

Coulter, Robert, Shari Kessel Schneider, Amy Herrick, and Lydia O'Donnell. 2014. "Sexual Behaviors and Outcomes Associated with Syndemics for Lesbian and Bisexual Girls." In *ResearchGate*. https://www.researchgate.net/publication/266809334_Sexual_behaviors_and_outcomes_associated_with_syndemics_for_lesbian_and_bisexual_girls.

Cox, Kim J. 2011. "Providers' Perspectives on the Vaginal Birth after Cesarean Guidelines in Florida, United States: A Qualitative Study." *BMC Pregnancy and Childbirth* 11: 72. doi:10.1186/1471-2393-11-72.

Cranny-Francis, Anne, Wendy Waring, Pam Stavropolous, and Joan Kirby. 2003. *Gender Studies: Terms and Debates*. Houndmills, Basingstoke, Hampshire; New York: Palgrave Macmillan.

Craven, Christa. 2010. *Pushing for Midwives: Homebirth Mothers and the Reproductive Rights Movement*. Philadelphia: Temple University Press.

Cunningham, F. Gary, Shrikant I. Bangdiwala, Sarah S. Brown, Thomas Michael Dean, Marilynn Frederiksen, Carol J. Rowland Hogue, Tekoa King, et al. 2010. "NIH Consensus Development Conference Draft Statement on Vaginal Birth after Cesarean: New Insights." *NIH Consensus and State-of-the-Science Statements* 27 (3): 1–42.

Dahlen, Hannah Grace, Soo Downe, Holly Powell Kennedy, and Maralyn Foureur. 2014. "Is Society Being Reshaped on a Microbiological and Epigenetic Level by the Way Women Give Birth?" *Midwifery* 30 (12): 1149–51.

Daniels, Pamela, Godfrey Fuji Noe, and Robert Mayberry. 2006. "Barriers to Prenatal Care Among Black Women of Low Socioeconomic Status." Text. March. http://orst.library.ingentaconnect.com/content/png/ajhb/2006/00000030/00000002/art00008.

Davis-Floyd, R. 2001. "The Technocratic, Humanistic, and Holistic Paradigms of Childbirth." *International Journal of Gynaecology and Obstetrics: The Official Organ of the International Federation of Gynaecology and Obstetrics* 75 Suppl 1 (November): S5–23.

———. 2004. *Birth as an American Rite of Passage: With a New Preface*. University of California Press.

Davis-Floyd, Robbie, and Melissa Cheyney. 2009. "Birth and the Big Bad Wolf: An Evolutionary Perspective." In *Childbirth across Cultures*, 1–22. Springer. http://link.springer.com/10.1007/978-90-481-2599-9_1.

Davis-Floyd, Robbie, Carolyn F. Sargent, and Rayna Rapp. 1997. *Childbirth and Authoritative Knowledge: Cross-Cultural Perspectives*. Berkeley: University of California Press.

Declercq, Eugene, Mary Barger, and Judith Weiss. 2011. "Contemporary Childbirth in the United States: Interventions and Disparities." In *Reducing Racial/Ethnic Disparities in Reproductive and Perinatal Outcomes*, edited by Arden Handler, Joan Kennelly, and Nadine Peacock, 401–27. Springer US. http://link.springer.com/chapter/10.1007/978-1-4419-1499-6_16.

Declercq, Eugene, Carol Sakala, Maureen Corry, Sandra Applebaum, and Ariel Herrlich. 2013. *Listening to Mothers III: Pregnancy and Birth*. New York, NY: Childbirth Connection.

Dillaway, Heather, and Sarah Jane Brubaker. 2006. "Intersectionality and Childbirth: How Women from Different Social Locations Discuss Epidural Use." *Race, Gender & Class*. 13 (3/4): 16–41.

Dominguez-Bello, Maria G., Elizabeth K. Costello, Monica Contreras, Magda Magris, Glida Hidalgo, Noah Fierer, and Rob Knight. 2010. "Delivery Mode Shapes the Acquisition and Structure of the Initial Microbiota across Multiple Body Habitats in Newborns." *Proceedings of the National Academy of Sciences* 107 (26): 11971–75.

Downe, S, K Finlayson, D Walsh, and T Lavender. 2009. "'Weighing up and Balancing Out': A Meta-Synthesis of Barriers to Antenatal Care for Marginalised Women in High-Income Countries." *BJOG: An International Journal of Obstetrics & Gynaecology* 116 (4): 518–29. doi:10.1111/j.1471-0528.2008.02067.x.

Earnshaw, Valerie A., Lisa Rosenthal, Jessica B. Lewis, Emily C. Stasko, Jonathan N. Tobin, Tené T. Lewis, Allecia E. Reid, and Jeannette R. Ickovics. 2013. "Maternal Experiences with Everyday Discrimination and Infant Birth Weight: A Test of Mediators and Moderators among Young, Urban Women of Color." *Annals of Behavioral Medicine: A Publication of the Society of Behavioral Medicine* 45 (1): 13–23. doi:10.1007/s12160-012-9404-3.

East, Patricia L., Barbara T. Reyes, and Emily J. Horn. 2007. "Association between Adolescent Pregnancy and a Family History of Teenage Births." *Perspectives on Sexual and Reproductive Health* 39 (2): 108–15. doi:10.1363/3910807.

Einstein, Gillian, and Margrit Shildrick. 2009. "The Postconventional Body: Retheorising Women's Health." *Social Science & Medicine (1982)* 69 (2): 293–300. doi:10.1016/j.socscimed.2009.04.027.

Ellison, Marcia A. 2003. "Authoritative Knowledge and Single Women's Unintentional Pregnancies, Abortions, Adoption, and Single Motherhood: Social Stigma and Structural Violence." *Medical Anthropology Quarterly* 17 (3): 322–47.

Ellis, Simon Adriane, Danuta M. Wojnar, and Maria Pettinato. 2015. "Conception, Pregnancy, and Birth Experiences of Male and Gender Variant Gestational Parents: It's How We Could Have a Family." *Journal of Midwifery & Women's Health* 60 (1): 62–69.

Ellis-Sloan, Kyla. 2014. "Teenage Mothers, Stigma and Their Presentations of Self.'" *Sociological Research Online* 19 (1): 9.

Engle, William A. 2011. "Morbidity and Mortality in Late Preterm and Early Term Newborns: A Continuum." *Clinics in Perinatology* 38 (3): 493–516. doi:10.1016/j.clp.2011.06.009.

Entringer, Sonja, Claudia Buss, and Pathik D. Wadhwa. 2015. "Prenatal Stress, Development, Health and Disease Risk: A Psychobiological Perspective—2015 Curt Richter Award Paper." *Psychoneuroendocrinology* 62 (December): 366–75. doi:10.1016/j.psyneuen.2015.08.019.

Erdmans, Mary Patrice, and Timothy Black. 2015. *On Becoming a Teen Mom: Life before Pregnancy*. Oakland, California: University of California Press.

Erickson, Pamela I. 1998. *Latina Adolescent Childbearing in East Los Angeles*. University of Texas Press.

Everson, Courtney. 2012. "'Lost Cause' Mothers: Stigma, Power, and Resistance in the Performativity of Adolescent Motherhood." 111th American Anthropological Association. San Francisco.

———. 2015. "'I'm a Mom Too!' – Stigma, Support & Contested Identities among Adolescent Mothers in the United States." PhD Dissertation, Corvallis, OR: Oregon State University. http://hdl.handle.net/1957/56267.

———. 2016. "Structural Vulnerability and Obstetric Violence among Childbearing Adolescents in the United States: Narratives of Care." Society for Applied Anthropology, *76th Annual Meeting*. Vancouver, BC.

Finer, Lawrence B., and Mia R. Zolna. 2014. "Shifts in Intended and Unintended Pregnancies in the United States, 2001-2008." *American Journal of Public Health* 104 Suppl 1 (February): S43–48. doi:10.2105/AJPH.2013.301416.

Glantz, J. Christopher. 2012. "Obstetric Variation, Intervention, and Outcomes: Doing More but Accomplishing Less." *Birth (Berkeley, Calif.)* 39 (4): 286–90. doi:10.1111/birt.12002.

Goer, Henci, and Amy Romano. 2012. *Optimal Care in Childbirth: The Case for a Physiologic Approach*. Classic Day Publishing.

Goer, Henci, Amy M Romano, and Carol Sakala. 2012. "Vaginal or Cesarean Birth: What Is at Stake for Women and Babies?" New York: Childbirth Connection.

Goffman, Erving. 1986. *Stigma: Notes on the Management of Spoiled Identity*. Reissue edition. New York: Touchstone.

Gray, Alison J. 2002. "Stigma in Psychiatry." *Journal of the Royal Society of Medicine* 95 (2): 72–76.

Grover, Namita, and Keerat Sandhu. 2009. "Teenage Pregnancy: Too Much Too Soon." *Journal of South Asian Federation of Obstetrics & Gynecology* 1 (3): 41–43.

Guise, Jeanne-Marie, Mary Anna Denman, Cathy Emeis, Nicole Marshall, Miranda Walker, Rongwei Fu, Rosalind Janik, Peggy Nygren, Karen B. Eden, and Marian McDonagh. 2010.

"Vaginal Birth after Cesarean: New Insights on Maternal and Neonatal Outcomes." *Obstetrics & Gynecology* 115 (6): 1267–78. doi:10.1097/AOG.0b013e3181df925f.

Guise, Jeanne-Marie, Karen Eden, Cathy Emeis, Mary Anna Denman, Nicole Marshall, Rongwei Rochelle Fu, Rosalind Janik, Peggy Nygren, Miranda Walker, and Marian McDonagh. 2010. "Vaginal Birth after Cesarean: New Insights." *Evidence Report/technology Assessment*, no. 191 (March): 1–397.

Hartmann, KE, JC Andrews, RN Jerome, RM Lewis, FE Likis, JN McKoy, TS Surawicz, and SH Walker. 2012. "Strategies to Reduce Cesarean Birth in Low-Risk Women." Comparative Effectiveness Review 80. Rockville, MD: Agency for Healthcare Research and Quality.

Henderson, Jane, Haiyan Gao, and Maggie Redshaw. 2013. "Experiencing Maternity Care: The Care Received and Perceptions of Women from Different Ethnic Groups." *BMC Pregnancy and Childbirth* 13: 196. doi:10.1186/1471-2393-13-196.

Herrera-Gómez, A., O. García-Martínez, J. Ramos-Torrecillas, E. De Luna-Bertos, C. Ruiz, and F. M. Ocaña-Peinado. 2015. "Retrospective Study of the Association between Epidural Analgesia during Labour and Complications for the Newborn." *Midwifery* 31 (6): 613–16. doi:10.1016/j.midw.2015.02.013.

Herrera-Gómez, Antonio, Elvira De Luna-Bertos, Javier Ramos-Torrecillas, Francisco Manuel Ocaña-Peinado, Olga García-Martínez, and Concepción Ruiz. 2017. "The Effect of Epidural Analgesia Alone and in Association With Other Variables on the Risk of Cesarean Section." *Biological Research for Nursing*, 1099800417706023. doi:10.1177/1099800417706023.

Hincz, Piotr, Lech Podciechowskil, Mariusz Grzesiak, Wojciech Horzelski, and Jan Wilczyflski. 2014. "Epidural Analgesia during Labor: A Retrospective Cohort Study on Its Effects on Labour, Delivery and Neonatal Outcome." *Ginekologia Polska* 85 (12): 923–28.

Hodgkinson, Stacy, Lee Beers, Cathy Southammakosane, and Amy Lewin. 2014. "Addressing the Mental Health Needs of Pregnant and Parenting Adolescents." *Pediatrics* 133 (1): 114–22. doi:10.1542/peds.2013-0927.

Hopkins, K. 2000. "Are Brazilian Women Really Choosing to Deliver by Cesarean?" *Social Science & Medicine (1982)* 51 (5): 725–40.

Houston, Kathryn A., Anjali J. Kaimal, Sanae Nakagawa, Steven E. Gregorich, Lynn M. Yee, and Miriam Kuppermann. 2015. "Mode of Delivery and Postpartum Depression: The Role of Patient Preferences." *American Journal of Obstetrics and Gynecology* 212 (2): 229.e1–229.e7. doi:10.1016/j.ajog.2014.09.002.

Inhorn, Marcia C. 2006. "Defining Women's Health: A Dozen Messages from More than 150 Ethnographies." *Medical Anthropology Quarterly* 20 (3): 345–78.

Institute of Medicine. 1985. *Preventing Low Birthweight: Summary*. National Academies Press.

James, E. Angel, and Moira Rashid. 2013. "'Welfare Queens' and 'Teen Moms': How the Social Construction of Fertile Women Impacts Unintended Pregnancy Prevention Policy in the United States." *Policy, Politics & Nursing Practice* 14 (3–4): 125–32. doi:10.1177/1527154413510408.

James-Hawkins, Laurie, and Christie Sennott. 2014. "Low-Income Women's Navigation of Childbearing Norms Throughout the Reproductive Life Course." *Qualitative Health Research*, September, 1049732314548690. doi:10.1177/1049732314548690.

Jeha, D., I. Usta, L. Ghulmiyyah, and A. Nassar. 2015. "A Review of the Risks and Consequences of Adolescent Pregnancy." *Journal of Neonatal-Perinatal Medicine*, March. doi:10.3233/NPM-15814038.

Jones, Leanne, Mohammad Othman, Therese Dowswell, Zarko Alfirevic, Simon Gates, Mary Newburn, Susan Jordan, Tina Lavender, and James P. Neilson. 2012. "Pain Management for Women in Labour: An Overview of Systematic Reviews." *The Cochrane Database of Systematic Reviews* 3: CD009234. doi:10.1002/14651858.CD009234.pub2.

Jordan, Brigitte. 1992. *Birth in Four Cultures: A Crosscultural Investigation of Childbirth in Yucatan, Holland, Sweden, and the United States*. 4th edition. Prospect Heights, Ill: Waveland Pr Inc.

Jozwiak, Marta, Kitty WM Bloemenkamp, Anthony J Kelly, Ben Willem J Mol, Olivier Irion, and Michel Boulvain. 2012. "Mechanical Methods for Induction of Labour." In *Cochrane*

Database of Systematic Reviews. John Wiley & Sons, Ltd. http://onlinelibrary.wiley.com/doi/10.1002/14651858.CD001233.pub2/abstract.

Jutte, Douglas P., Noralou P. Roos, Marni D. Brownell, Gemma Briggs, Leonard MacWilliam, and Leslie L. Roos. 2010. "The Ripples of Adolescent Motherhood: Social, Educational, and Medical Outcomes for Children of Teen and Prior Teen Mothers." *Academic Pediatrics* 10 (5): 293–301. doi:10.1016/j.acap.2010.06.008.

Kearney, Melissa S., and Phillip B. Levine. 2012. "Why Is the Teen Birth Rate in the United States so High and Why Does It Matter?" *The Journal of Economic Perspectives: A Journal of the American Economic Association* 26 (2): 141–66.

Kenyon, Sara, Hironobu Tokumasu, Therese Dowswell, Debbie Pledge, and Rintaro Mori. 2013. "High-Dose versus Low-Dose Oxytocin for Augmentation of Delayed Labour." In *Cochrane Database of Systematic Reviews*. John Wiley & Sons, Ltd. http://onlinelibrary.wiley.com/doi/10.1002/14651858.CD007201.pub3/abstract.

Kjerulff, Kristen H., Laura B. Attanasio, Joyce K. Edmonds, Katy B. Kozhimannil, and John T. Repke. 2017. "Labor Induction and Cesarean Delivery: A Prospective Cohort Study of First Births in Pennsylvania, USA." *Birth (Berkeley, Calif.)*, March. doi:10.1111/birt.12286.

Kramer, Michael S., Frances Aboud, Elena Mironova, Irina Vanilovich, Robert W. Platt, Lidia Matush, Sergei Igumnov, et al. 2008. "Breastfeeding and Child Cognitive Development: New Evidence from a Large Randomized Trial." *Archives of General Psychiatry* 65 (5): 578–84. doi:10.1001/archpsyc.65.5.578.

Lamaze International. 2007. "Position Paper: Promoting, Supporting, and Protecting Normal Birth." *The Journal of Perinatal Education* 16 (3): 11–15. doi:10.1624/105812407X217084.

Linders, Annulla, and Cynthia Bogard. 2014. "Teenage Pregnancy as a Social Problem: A Comparison of Sweden and the United States." In *International Handbook of Adolescent Pregnancy*, edited by Andrew L. Cherry and Mary E. Dillon, 147–57. Springer US. http://link.springer.com/chapter/10.1007/978-1-4899-8026-7_7.

Liu, Li, Shefali Oza, Daniel Hogan, Jamie Perin, Igor Rudan, Joy E. Lawn, Simon Cousens, Colin Mathers, and Robert E. Black. 2015. "Global, Regional, and National Causes of Child Mortality in 2000-13, with Projections to Inform Post-2015 Priorities: An Updated Systematic Analysis." *Lancet (London, England)* 385 (9966): 430–40. doi:10.1016/S0140-6736(14)61698-6.

Loewenberg-Weisband, Yiska, Sorina Grisaru-Granovsky, Alexander Ioscovich, Arnon Samueloff, and Ronit Calderon-Margalit. 2014. "Epidural Analgesia and Severe Perineal Tears: A Literature Review and Large Cohort Study." *The Journal of Maternal-Fetal & Neonatal Medicine: The Official Journal of the European Association of Perinatal Medicine, the Federation of Asia and Oceania Perinatal Societies, the International Society of Perinatal Obstetricians* 27 (18): 1864–69. doi:10.3109/14767058.2014.889113.

Loftin, Ryan W, Mounira Habli, Candice C Snyder, Clint M Cormier, David F Lewis, and Emily A DeFranco. 2010. "Late Preterm Birth." *Reviews in Obstetrics and Gynecology* 3 (1): 10–19.

Lothian, Judith A. 2014a. "Healthy Birth Practice #4: Avoid Interventions Unless They Are Medically Necessary." *The Journal of Perinatal Education* 23 (4): 198–206. doi:10.1891/1058-1243.23.4.198.

———. 2014b. "Promoting Optimal Care in Childbirth." *The Journal of Perinatal Education* 23 (4): 174–77. doi:10.1891/1058-1243.23.4.174.

Low, Lisa Kane, Karin Martin, Carolyn Sampselle, Barbara Guthrie, and Deborah Oakley. 2003. "Adolescents' Experiences of Childbirth: Contrasts with Adults." *Journal of Midwifery & Women's Health* 48 (3): 192–98.

Luttrell, Wendy. 2011. "Where Inequality Lives in the Body: Teenage Pregnancy, Public Pedagogies and Individual Lives." *Sport, Education and Society* 16 (3): 295–308. doi:10.1080/13573322.2011.565962.

Lyell, Deirdre J. 2011. "Adhesions and Perioperative Complications of Repeat Cesarean Delivery." *American Journal of Obstetrics and Gynecology* 205 (6 Suppl): S11–18. doi:10.1016/j.ajog.2011.09.029.

Mantovani, Nadia, and Hilary Thomas. 2014. "Stigma, Intersectionality and Motherhood: Exploring the Relations of Stigma in the Accounts of Black Teenage Mothers 'Looked After' by the State." *Social Theory & Health* 12 (1): 45–62. doi:10.1057/sth.2013.19.
———. 2015. "Resilience and Survival: Black Teenage Mothers 'Looked After' by the State Tell Their Stories About Their Experience of Care." *Children & Society* 29 (4): 299–309. doi:10.1111/chso.12028.
March of Dimes. 2013. "The Impact of Premature Birth on Society." http://www.marchofdimes.org/mission/the-economic-and-societal-costs.aspx.
Martin, Joyce A, Brady E Hamilton, Michelle J K Osterman, Anne K. Driscoll, and T. J. Mathews. 2017. "Births: Final Data for 2015." National Vital Statistics Reports 66 (1): 1–70.
Mathews, T. J., Marian F. MacDorman, and Marie Thoma. 2015. "Infant Mortality Statistics from the 2013 Period Linked Birth/Infant Death Data Set." *National Vital Statistics Reports* 64 (9): 1–30.
McDermott, Elizabeth, and Hilary Graham. 2005. "Resilient Young Mothering: Social Inequalities, Late Modernity and the 'Problem' of 'Teenage' Motherhood." *Journal of Youth Studies* 8 (1): 59–79. doi:10.1080/13676260500063702.
McGowan, Jennifer E., Fiona A. Alderdice, Valerie A. Holmes, and Linda Johnston. 2011. "Early Childhood Development of Late-Preterm Infants: A Systematic Review." *Pediatrics*, May, peds.2010–2257. doi:10.1542/peds.2010-2257.
Metzl, Jonathan M., and Helena Hansen. 2014. "Structural Competency: Theorizing a New Medical Engagement with Stigma and Inequality." *Social Science & Medicine (1982)* 103 (February): 126–33. doi:10.1016/j.socscimed.2013.06.032.
Middleton, Sue. 2011. "'I Wouldn't Change Having the Children—Not at All.' Young Women's Narratives of Maternal Timing: What the UK's Teenage Pregnancy Strategy Hasn't Heard." *Sexuality Research and Social Policy* 8 (3): 227–38. doi:10.1007/s13178-011-0058-x.
Moore, Jennifer, and Lisa Kane Low. 2012. "Factors That Influence the Practice of Elective Induction of Labor." *The Journal of Perinatal & Neonatal Nursing* 26 (3): 242–50. doi:10.1097/JPN.0b013e31826288a9.
Mueller, Noel T., Elizabeth Bakacs, Joan Combellick, Zoya Grigoryan, and Maria G. Dominguez-Bello. 2015. "The Infant Microbiome Development: Mom Matters." *Trends in Molecular Medicine* 21 (2): 109–17.
Nahar, Papreen, and Sjaak van der Geest. 2014. "How Women in Bangladesh Confront the Stigma of Childlessness: Agency, Resilience, and Resistance." *Medical Anthropology Quarterly* 28 (3): 381–98. doi:10.1111/maq.12094.
Nelson, Hilde Lindemann. 2001. *Damaged Identities, Narrative Repair*. Ithaca, NY: Cornell University Press.
Neu, Josef, and Jona Rushing. 2011. "Cesarean versus Vaginal Delivery: Long Term Infant Outcomes and the Hygiene Hypothesis." *Clinics in Perinatology* 38 (2): 321–31. doi:10.1016/j.clp.2011.03.008.
Nichols, Tracy R., Margaret Brown, Sheryl L. Coley, Allyson Kelley, and Kelly Mauceri. 2014. "'I Managed It Pretty Good': Birth Narratives of Adolescent Mothers." *The Journal of Perinatal Education* 23 (2): 79–88. doi:10.1891/1058-1243.23.2.79.
Nicolson, Susan, Fiona Judd, Frances Thomson-Salo, and Sarah Mitchell. 2013. "Supporting the Adolescent Mother-Infant Relationship: Preliminary Trial of a Brief Perinatal Attachment Intervention." *Archives of Women's Mental Health* 16 (6): 511–20. doi:10.1007/s00737-013-0364-9.
Osterman, Michelle J K, and Joyce A Martin. 2011. "Epidural and Spinal Anesthesia Use During Labor: 27-State Reporting Area, 2008." *National Vital Statistics Reports* 59 (5): 1–14.
Osterman, Michelle J. K., and Joyce A. Martin. 2014. "Recent Declines in Induction of Labor by Gestational." *NCHS Data Brief* 155: 1–8.
Petersen, Antje, Ulrich Poetter, Claire Michelsen, and Mechthild M. Gross. 2013. "The Sequence of Intrapartum Interventions: A Descriptive Approach to the Cascade of Interven-

tions." *Archives of Gynecology and Obstetrics* 288 (2): 245–54. doi:10.1007/s00404-013-2737-8.
Peterson, Brennan D., Matthew Pirritano, Laura Tucker, and Claudia Lampic. 2012. "Fertility Awareness and Parenting Attitudes among American Male and Female Undergraduate University Students." *Human Reproduction* 27 (5): 1375–82.
Porr, Caroline, Jane Drummond, and Karin Olson. 2012. "Establishing Therapeutic Relationships with Vulnerable and Potentially Stigmatized Clients." *Qualitative Health Research* 22 (3): 384–96. doi:10.1177/1049732311421182.
Porter, Luz S., and Nola A. Holness. 2011. "Breaking the Repeat Teen Pregnancy Cycle." *Nursing for Women's Health* 15 (5): 368–81. doi:10.1111/j.1751-486X.2011.01661.x.
Quesada, James, Laurie Kain Hart, and Philippe Bourgois. 2011. "Structural Vulnerability and Health: Latino Migrant Laborers in the United States." *Medical Anthropology* 30 (4): 339–62. doi:10.1080/01459740.2011.576725.
Raju, Tonse N. K., Rosemary D. Higgins, Ann R. Stark, and Kenneth J. Leveno. 2006. "Optimizing Care and Outcome for Late-Preterm (near-Term) Infants: A Summary of the Workshop Sponsored by the National Institute of Child Health and Human Development." *Pediatrics* 118 (3): 1207–14. doi:10.1542/peds.2006-0018.
Ramirez, Mildred M. 2011. "Labor Induction: A Review of Current Methods." *Obstetrics and Gynecology Clinics of North America*, Practical Approaches to Controversies in Obstetric Care, 38 (2): 215–25. doi:10.1016/j.ogc.2011.02.012.
Rapp, R. 2001. "Gender, Body, Biomedicine: How Some Feminist Concerns Dragged Reproduction to the Center of Social Theory." *Medical Anthropology Quarterly* 15 (4): 466–77.
Reid, Allecia E., Lisa Rosenthal, Valerie A. Earnshaw, Tené T. Lewis, Jessica B. Lewis, Emily C. Stasko, Jonathan N. Tobin, and Jeannette R. Ickovics. 2016. "Discrimination and Excessive Weight Gain during Pregnancy among Black and Latina Young Women." *Social Science & Medicine (1982)* 156 (March): 134–41. doi:10.1016/j.socscimed.2016.03.012.
Rodriguez, Cheryl. 2008. "Beyond Today and Pass Tomorrow: Self-Efficacy Among African-American Adolescent Mothers." *Voices* 8 (1): 18–22. doi:10.1111/j.1548-7423.2008.tb00048.x.
Romano, Amy M., and Judith A. Lothian. 2008. "Promoting, Protecting, and Supporting Normal Birth: A Look at the Evidence." *Journal of Obstetric, Gynecologic, & Neonatal Nursing* 37 (1): 94–105.
Rosenthal, Lisa, and Marci Lobel. 2016. "Stereotypes of Black American Women Related to Sexuality and Motherhood." *Psychology of Women Quarterly*, February, 0361684315627459. doi:10.1177/0361684315627459.
Rossignol, Michel, Nils Chaillet, Faiza Boughrassa, and Jean-Marie Moutquin. 2014. "Interrelations Between Four Antepartum Obstetric Interventions and Cesarean Delivery in Women at Low Risk: A Systematic Review and Modeling of the Cascade of Interventions." *Birth* 41 (1): 70–78. doi:10.1111/birt.12088.
Rothman, Barbara Katz. 1991. *In Labor: Women and Power in the Birthplace*. New York: W. W. Norton & Co Inc.
Russell, Beth S., Lisa A. Eaton, and Petal Petersen-Williams. 2013. "Intersecting Epidemics among Pregnant Women: Alcohol Use, Interpersonal Violence, and HIV Infection in South Africa." *Current HIV/AIDS Reports* 10 (1): 103–10. doi:10.1007/s11904-012-0145-5.
Sakala, Carol, and Maureen Corry. 2008. *Evidence-Based Maternity Care: What It Is and What It Can Achieve*. New York, NY: Milbank Memorial Fund.
Sakala, Carol, Amy M. Romano, and Sarah J. Buckley. 2016. "Hormonal Physiology of Childbearing, an Essential Framework for Maternal-Newborn Nursing." *Journal of Obstetric, Gynecologic, and Neonatal Nursing: JOGNN / NAACOG* 45 (2): 264–75. doi:10.1016/j.jogn.2015.12.006.
Sauls, Donna J. 2004. "Adolescents' Perception of Support During Labor." *The Journal of Perinatal Education* 13 (4): 36–42. doi:10.1624/105812404X6216.
Scambler, Graham. 2006. "Sociology, Social Structure and Health-Related Stigma." *Psychology, Health & Medicine* 11 (3): 288–95. doi:10.1080/13548500600595103.
———. 2009. "Health-Related Stigma." *Sociology of Health & Illness* 31 (3): 441–55. doi:10.1111/j.1467-9566.2009.01161.x.

Scambler, Graham, and Frederique Paoli. 2008. "Health Work, Female Sex Workers and HIV/AIDS: Global and Local Dimensions of Stigma and Deviance as Barriers to Effective Interventions." *Social Science & Medicine (1982)* 66 (8): 1848–62. doi:10.1016/j.socscimed.2008.01.002.

Scheper-Hughes, Nancy, and Margaret M. Lock. 1987. "The Mindful Body: A Prolegomenon to Future Work in Medical Anthropology." *Medical Anthropology Quarterly*, New Series, 1 (1): 6–41.

Sevelsted, Astrid, Jakob Stokholm, Klaus Bønnelykke, and Hans Bisgaard. 2015. "Cesarean Section and Chronic Immune Disorders." *Pediatrics* 135 (1): e92–98. doi:10.1542/peds.2014-0596.

Shanok, Arielle F., and Lisa Miller. 2007. "Stepping up to Motherhood Among Inner-City Teens." *Psychology of Women Quarterly* 31 (3): 252–61. doi:10.1111/j.1471-6402.2007.00368.x.

Sharpe, Gilly. 2015. "Precarious Identities: 'Young' Motherhood, Desistance and Stigma." *Criminology and Criminal Justice*, February, 1748895815572163. doi:10.1177/1748895815572163.

Shrestha, Bikash, Amit Devgan, and Mukti Sharma. 2014. "Effects of Maternal Epidural Analgesia on the Neonate—a Prospective Cohort Study." *Italian Journal of Pediatrics* 40: 99. doi:10.1186/s13052-014-0099-x.

Silver, Lauren. 2008. "The Politics of Regulation: Adolescent Mothers and the Social Context of Resiliency." *Voices* 8 (1): 1–11. doi:10.1111/j.1548-7423.2008.tb00040.x.

Simpson, Kathleen Rice, and Jana Atterbury. 2003. "Trends and Issues in Labor Induction in the United States: Implications for Clinical Practice." *Journal of Obstetric, Gynecologic, and Neonatal Nursing: JOGNN / NAACOG* 32 (6): 767–79.

Singer, Merrill. 2009. *Introduction to Syndemics: A Critical Systems Approach to Public and Community Health*. John Wiley & Sons.

———. 2013. "Development, Coinfection, and the Syndemics of Pregnancy in Sub-Saharan Africa." *Infectious Diseases of Poverty* 2: 26. doi:10.1186/2049-9957-2-26.

Small, Meredith. 2011. *Our Babies, Ourselves: How Biology and Culture Shape the Way We Parent*. Reprint edition. Vintage.

Smithbattle, Lee. 2007. "Legacies of Advantage and Disadvantage: The Case of Teen Mothers." *Public Health Nursing (Boston, Mass.)* 24 (5): 409–20. doi:10.1111/j.1525-1446.2007.00651.x.

———. 2013. "Reducing the Stigmatization of Teen Mothers." *MCN. The American Journal of Maternal Child Nursing* 38 (4): 235–41; quiz 242–43. doi:10.1097/NMC.0b013e3182836bd4.

Smithbattle, Lee, Rebecca Lorenz, and Sheila Leander. 2013. "Listening with Care: Using Narrative Methods to Cultivate Nurses' Responsive Relationships in a Home Visiting Intervention with Teen Mothers." *Nursing Inquiry* 20 (3): 188–98. doi:10.1111/j.1440-1800.2012.00606.x.

Solivan, Amber E., Maeve E. Wallace, Kathryn C. Kaplan, and Emily W. Harville. 2015. "Use of a Resiliency Framework to Examine Pregnancy and Birth Outcomes among Adolescents: A Qualitative Study." *Families, Systems, & Health* 33 (4): 349–55. doi:10.1037/fsh0000141.

Spangler, Sydney A. 2011. "'To Open Oneself Is a Poor Woman's Trouble': Embodied Inequality and Childbirth in South-Central Tanzania." *Medical Anthropology Quarterly* 25 (4): 479–98.

Spong, Catherine Y., Vincenzo Berghella, Katharine D. Wenstrom, Brian M. Mercer, and George R. Saade. 2012. "Preventing the First Cesarean Delivery: Summary of a Joint Eunice Kennedy Shriver National Institute of Child Health and Human Development, Society for Maternal-Fetal Medicine, and American College of Obstetricians and Gynecologists Workshop." *Obstetrics and Gynecology* 120 (5): 1181–93.

Taylor, Kate. 2013. "City Campaign Targeting Teenage Pregnancy Draws Criticism." *The New York Times*, March 6. http://www.nytimes.com/2013/03/07/nyregion/city-campaign-targeting-teenage-pregnancy-draws-criticism.html.

Torvie, Ana J., Lisa S. Callegari, Melissa A. Schiff, and Katherine E. Debiec. 2015. "Labor and Delivery Outcomes among Young Adolescents." *American Journal of Obstetrics and Gynecology*, April. doi:10.1016/j.ajog.2015.04.024.

Trevathan, Wenda. 2010. *Ancient Bodies, Modern Lives: How Evolution Has Shaped Women's Health*. 1 edition. New York: Oxford University Press.

U.S. Department of Health & Human Services. 2015. *Child Health USA 2014*. Rockville, MD: U.S. Department of Health and Human Services. http://mchb.hrsa.gov/chusa14/health-status-behaviors/infants/preterm-birth-low-birth-weight.html.

———. 2015. "Teen Pregnancy and Childbearing." *Office of Adolescent Health*. http://www.hhs.gov/ash/oah/adolescent-health-topics/reproductive-health/teen-pregnancy/index.html.

Van Hollen, Cecilia. 2003. *Birth on the Threshold: Childbirth and Modernity in South India*. University of California Press.

Ventura, Stephanie J., Brady E. Hamilton, and T. J. Matthews. 2014. "National and State Patterns of Teen Births in the United States, 1940-2013." *National Vital Statistics Reports: From the Centers for Disease Control and Prevention, National Center for Health Statistics, National Vital Statistics System* 63 (4): 1–34.

Wenham, Aniela. 2011. "Mothers in the Making: A Qualitative Longitudinal Study Exploring the Journey of Becoming and Being a Teenage Mother." PhD Dissertation, Heslington, York, UK: University of York.

Whitley, Rob, and Laurence J. Kirmayer. 2008. "Perceived Stigmatisation of Young Mothers: An Exploratory Study of Psychological and Social Experience." *Social Science & Medicine (1982)* 66 (2): 339–48. doi:10.1016/j.socscimed.2007.09.014.

Wiemann, Constance M., Vaughn I. Rickert, Abbey B. Berenson, and Robert J. Volk. 2005. "Are Pregnant Adolescents Stigmatized by Pregnancy?" *The Journal of Adolescent Health: Official Publication of the Society for Adolescent Medicine* 36 (4): 352.e1–8. doi:10.1016/j.jadohealth.2004.06.006.

Wilson, Helen, and Annette Huntington. 2006. "Deviant (M)others: The Construction of Teenage Motherhood in Contemporary Discourse." *Journal of Social Policy* 35 (01): 59–76. doi:10.1017/S0047279405009335.

World Health Organization. 1996. *Care in Normal Birth: A Practical Guide*. Geneva: World Health Organization. http://whqlibdoc.who.int/hq/1996/WHO_FRH_MSM_96.24.pdf?ua=1.

———. 2015. *WHO Statement on Caesarean Section Rates*. Geneva: World Health Organization.

Yardley, Elizabeth. 2008. "Teenage Mothers' Experiences of Stigma." *Journal of Youth Studies* 11 (6): 671–84. doi:10.1080/13676260802392940.

———. 2009. "Teenage Mothers' Experiences of Formal Support Services." *Journal of Social Policy* 38 (02): 241–57. doi:10.1017/S0047279408002821.

Zacher Dixon, Lydia. 2015. "Obstetrics in a Time of Violence: Mexican Midwives Critique Routine Hospital Practices." *Medical Anthropology Quarterly* 29 (4): 437–54. doi:10.1111/maq.12174.

Zenzmaier, Christoph, Hermann Leitner, Christoph Brezinka, Willi Oberaigner, and Martina König-Bachmann. 2017. "Maternal and Neonatal Outcomes after Induction of Labor: A Population-Based Study." *Archives of Gynecology and Obstetrics* 295 (5): 1175–83. doi:10.1007/s00404-017-4354-4.

Chapter Four

The Multiple Stigmas of the PDI Syndemic

Poverty, "Racial"/Ethnic Discrimination, Incarceration, and Reproductive and Familial Risk

Pamela I. Erickson

Syndemic theory seeks to explain the tendency for multiple, concurrent, and interacting epidemics to develop under conditions of health and social disparities (Singer et al. 2006, Singer 2009). Instead of focusing on discrete, bounded diseases, the syndemic approach focuses on connections, interactions, and underlying causal conditions rooted in the social contexts in which diseases cluster. The syndemic approach promotes investigation of both micro and macro levels of disease interaction, seeking to explain both the specific pathways and mechanisms of contact and exchange between two or more comorbid health conditions and the social and environmental determinants of such disease interactions and their clustering in a population. Syndemic theory, thus, focuses on environments of risk and the social structures that promote them. Syndemics, like social epidemiology, seeks to trace socio-biological embodiment—"how we literally incorporate biologically the material and social world in which we live from conception to death"—and to investigate these pathways in order to understand the social and biological determinants of ill health more comprehensively (Krieger 2001:672).

THE PDI SYNDEMIC

Social, Economic, and Political Contributions

There is a growing global literature on the social determinants of health disparities and inequities spearheaded by the World Health Organization's report on *The Social Determinants of Health* that clearly shows a relationship between social and economic deprivation and poorer health (see Marmot 2005). Social discrimination also has a clear relationship to health disparities, exacerbating poor health outcomes due to social and economic deprivation. Groups or classes of people who are discriminated against (e.g., racial or ethnic minorities, sexual minorities, women, people living with obesity) have poorer health than those who are not discriminated against. For example, the burden of disease associated with being an African-American in the United States is well documented (Williams et al. 2003, Franks et al. 2006) as is the heightened global risk to women of being infected with HIV (Ostrach and Singer 2012).

Economic deprivation and social discrimination interact in a syndemic and synergistic relationship that further exacerbates poor health outcomes. Economic deprivation affects living conditions: affordable housing, availability of healthy food, health care, good school and job opportunities, personal safety, exposure to toxins and other hazards in the environment, and exposure to violence and crime. Thus, it has a direct effect on health from conception to death. Discrimination and the internalization of the stigma of belonging to a group that is discriminated against affect all the systems of the body that are designed to deal with internal and external stress (the autonomic system, the hypothalamic-pituitary-adrenal [HPA] axis, and the cardiovascular, metabolic, and immune systems) putting them into chronic over or under activity, which itself can cause ill health and exacerbate disease progression (McEwen 1998). For example, the chronic triggering of the flight-or-fight response elevates cortisol levels and contributes to sustained hypertension, which then leads to other chronic health problems (Krieger 2000).

The social determinants of health described above are continually at play in the background where specific syndemics produce disease interactions in stigmatized populations such as the one I will describe here among African-American and Puerto Rican young adults (age 18–25) in inner city Hartford, CT. I build on a syndemic previously identified in this population that consists of poverty, discrimination, sexual and reproductive risk, sexually transmitted infections (STIs), and early childbearing among African-American and Puerto Rican young adults in Hartford, Connecticut (CT.) (Singer et al. 2006). To this syndemic, I add the exacerbating effects that high rates of incarceration in this population have on sexual risk, family formation, and family stability. I call this more complicated syndemic the PDI syndemic (*P*overty, "racial"/ethnic *D*iscrimination, *I*ncarceration).

The PDI syndemic originates within the structural context of inner-city poverty, discrimination, and lack of opportunity during childhood and adolescence (e.g., school, jobs) that leads to low educational attainment, unemployment or underemployment, and resort to the informal (possibly illicit) sector (e.g., drug use and distribution, theft, survival sex) for subsistence. This, in the context of intense policing in low-income minority communities, often leads to run-ins with the legal system (e.g., juvenile justice, arrest and incarceration), which is itself a result of larger political-economic and structural factors that maintain the social domination of African-Americans and other minority populations. Incarceration exacerbates the already heightened sexual risk-taking in this population (Singer et al. 2006) and leads to greater sexual risk for those incarcerated and their sexual partner(s) both within (e.g., fellow inmates or corrections officers) and outside of jail (e.g., bringing STIs/HIV acquired inside jail from sexual encounters or injection drug use during incarceration to partners on the outside). Such behaviors increase both STI and HIV risk and disease interactions. Moreover, incarceration threatens relationships and undermines family formation and family stability, playing a key role in the "epidemic" of single mothers, absent fathers, and "broken" families in the inner city (Roberts 2003–2004). Multiple incarcerations, which are not uncommon in this population, further weaken the stability of relationships and the family.

All of these insults to this population lead to their being multiply stigmatized for being poor, undereducated, unemployed, drug-users, non-white, sexual risk-takers, young and mostly single parents, and violent criminals/prisoners/ex-prisoners/felons. These multiple stigmas interact with socioeconomic and political processes that exacerbate health problems and perpetuate the marginalized social status of this group, a textbook case of structural violence (Farmer 2006).

Biological Contributions

The human beings at the center of this syndemic are young adults (age 18–24). The main biological health risks to this age group include those resulting from sexual behavior and drug or alcohol use (e.g., pregnancy complications, HIV, and several other STIs, including chlamydia, genital herpes, HPV, trichomoniasis, and gonorrhea) and from violence. Many STIs create lesions on the genitals that attract and serve as entry points for HIV and other STI infections that can then be passed on to sexual partners. For example, having herpes simplex virus type 2 (HSV-2) is associated with a two to four times greater risk of infection with HIV and when they co-occur the natural course of both diseases is changed (Singer 2009). A similar but potentially more serious interaction is HIV and hepatitis C virus (HCV), which occurs because of the increasing potential for liver disease with chronic HCV that is apparently due to the inability of the immune system to control HCV when HIV is also present. In addition, the presence of either HIV or HCV can also reduce the efficacy of treatment regimens for one or the other pathogen (Singer 2009). Many other non-sexually transmitted infectious and non-infectious diseases of poverty (e.g., tuberculosis, malnutrition) are also syndemic with STIs and HIV. Living in a poverty environment entails greater exposure to and risk for poor health, which is exacerbated by the chronic stress induced by the poverty and violence of the inner city.

Women are at particularly heightened risk for acquiring STIs and HIV due to multiple interacting biological and social factors (Ostrach and Singer 2012). First, the female reproductive system is mostly internal and offers a more favorable moist, warm environment to pathogens than does the male reproductive system. Male to female transmission is documented at two to four times higher than the reverse (United Nations Population Fund 2004). In addition many contraceptive methods used by women (e.g., injectable, oral, and patch contraceptives) contain progestin that can thin the lining of the vaginal epithelial cells, making them vulnerable to tears and lacerations during intercourse and may also cause increased vaginal bleeding, as do contraceptive devices such as copper IUDs (Morrison et al. 2004). It is also important to note that young age, pregnancy, and menopause can also change the vaginal environment making it more susceptible to tears (Ostrach and Singer 2012). Finally, the social status of women (e.g., male dominance in the gender hierarchy, sexism, economic dependence on a man, psychological and physical abuse, unbalanced sex ratio due to incarceration, and early death of men through violence) can result in greater sexual risk-taking and vulnerability to exploitation among women.

Violence in the inner city can result in serious bodily, psychological, and emotional harm. Both violence and living with multiple stigmatizations can trigger the hypothalamic-pituitary-adrenal (HPA) axis into action to protect the body from perceived danger. The HPA axis is a complex of direct influences and feedback interactions among the hypothalamus, the pituitary gland, and the adrenal glands. The interaction among these organs is a major part of our neuroendocrine system that controls reactions to stress and regulates many body processes (e.g., digestion, the immune system, mood and emotions, sexuality, and energy storage and expenditure). It evolved to protect the body from danger, but when set into chronic activation can have many negative physical and mental health consequences, especially over time (Guillans 2015). For example, chronic activation of this system has been linked to hypertension, depression, and anxiety, and it has also been implicated in altered circadian rhythms (e.g., sleep disorders), blood sugar dysregulation (e.g., diabetes), inflammatory signaling (e.g., food allergies), gastrointestinal irritation, chronic inflammatory diseases (e.g., rheumatoid arthritis), and obesity to name a few (Krieger 2000, Guilliams 2015).

The interaction and synergistic effects of the social, economic, and political systems that affect inner-city young adults over the life-course interact simultaneously with the biological changes incurred due to STIs, violence, multiple stigmas, and chronic activation of the HPA axis, placing the young adults who participated in our project at risk of poor health in the present and at risk for future chronic health problems. Throughout this chapter I will describe the ways these structural and biological factors, in the context of stigma, intersect and interact in participants' experiences to produce negative social and health outcomes.

METHODS

I use data collected from 414 young African-American and Puerto Rican adults who participated in the Hartford, CT., component of Project PHRESH.comm (Philadelphia and Hartford Research and Education on Sexual Health and Communication)[1] to illustrate this syndemic. PHRESH was a five-year (2003–2008), mixed-methods study funded by the Centers for Disease Control and Prevention (CDC) as a cooperative agreement with the Center for Health, Intervention, and Prevention (CHIP) at the University of Connecticut (UConn) and the Family Planning Council in Philadelphia, PA (FPCP). The major goal of this project, for which I was the Principal Investigator, was to understand strategies and patterns of communication and negotiation surrounding sexual behavior and prevention strategies for STI and pregnancy in sexually active, at-risk, inner city, minority populations.

The PHRESH team (investigators from CDC, FPCP, and UConn) designed a mixed-methods approach to address these issues beginning with a qualitative investigation of the "culture" of sexual and romantic behavior among these emerging adults (Arnett 2000), experience-near data to assess communication and negotiation strategies and actual prevention behavior, and a final structured survey to validate the major themes found in the qualitative data. Sequential fielding of the methods allowed data from each method to inform data collection and analysis for subsequent methods. This flexible strategy allowed us to follow up on unexpected themes that emerged at each step and to triangulate findings across methods.

Qualitative methods included focus group discussions (FGDs), semi-structured sexual and romantic life history interviews (SRIs), coital diaries (CDs),[2] and systematic cultural assessments involving free listing, ranking, and pile sorting (SCAs). These methods yielded an in-depth and nuanced understanding of the sexual culture of emerging adults in Hartford and the processes they used to make decisions within sexual and romantic relationships ranging from casual to serious. A final structured interview (SI) using venue-based sampling strategies collected quantitative data that we used to verify and further explore the qualitative findings. Each method is described briefly below.

Qualitative Methods

Focus Group Discussions (FGDs), 2004

The first method fielded included focus group discussions designed to collect cultural data and to explore salient terms and issues of concern to the study through a guided group discussion of the following aspects of heterosexual relationships: 1) types of relationships and sexual behaviors, 2) attitudes towards monogamy and abstinence, 3) knowledge and understanding of condoms and safer sex, 4) the physical and emotional risks encountered in relationships, and 5) structural factors at work in the inner city context that inform and constrain the choices available to young adults. We conducted eight extended (5–6 hours) focus groups of 6–12 participants homogenous by gender and ethnicity (i.e., Puerto Rican females, African-American males, etc.). A total of 73 individuals participated in this method. FGDs provided a general idea of the social context of sexual and romantic relationships and a basic understanding of what participants considered normative behavior with respect to condom use.

Themes from the FGDs included a large range of relationship types, from casual to serious, and sexual only to romantic and sexual. Sex was often used to gain access to resources (e.g., money, drugs, a car, diapers, hair braiding, shoes, etc.) or to one's children. Condom use was normative in casual relationships, but sex without a condom was preferred in all types of relationships. In serious relationships, condom cessation signified trust, and couples often used STI testing to achieve this transition (Abraham et al. 2011). Multiple partners were normative and infidelity expected, although not desired. Both men and women seek and enjoy sex.

Sexual Relationship Life History Interviews (SRIs), 2005–2006

The sexual relationship life history interviews were 1–2 hour, open-ended interviews in which participants were asked to tell the story of their self-identified most important sexual and romantic relationships from first to most recent and completed a pile sort of relationship types from the FGDs. Their stories provided a general picture of the different ways young people begin their sexual lives, transition from one partner to the next, whether and with whom they used condoms and contraception, and their feelings about their different relationships. Most participants talked about four or five partners (range 1–9). A total of 62 young adults participated in this method.

The individual narratives provided a counterpoint to the group norms for behavior set forth by the focus group participants. These stories reveal a wide variety of experiences punctuated by feelings of happiness and sadness, love and loss, agency and victimization, hope and fear. Virtually all participants were affected, some more and some less, by the violence, illegal activities, and poverty of their neighborhoods and by the high rates of incarceration, especially of young men.

Qualitative Data Analysis

The tape-recorded focus groups, interviews, and diary debriefings were transcribed verbatim, yielding 5,952 pages of text that was coded for major and emergent themes by a team of coders using ATLAS.ti, For the SRIs and CDs, modified percent agreement (MPA) was used as a measure of inter-coder agreement for a core set of codes applied to all data. MPA scores were used to reconcile disagreement between coders on code meaning and text segmentation (Hatfield-Timajchy et al. 2009). Three quarters of the SRIs and just over half of the CDs were coded by two to three coders, reconciled, and finalized. FGDs were coded by a single coder.

Quantitative Methods

Systematic Cultural Assessment (SCA), 2004 and 2006

In this method we used free list and pile sort activities to understand the cognitive structure of the following domains: 1) relationship types, 2) sexual behaviors, 3) ideal partner characteristics, 4) physical and emotional risks of relationships, and 5) infidelity/cheating behaviors and reasons. For each domain, items were free listed in FGDs and narrowed to terms mentioned by more than one group (range 24–50 terms per domain). These items were then pile sorted (free or directed) by individual participants (62 for domain 1, 40 for domains 3–5) and analyzed using multidimensional scaling and hierarchical clustering.

Participants listed many kinds of relationship types that were primarily sexual (about 2/3) or romantic (1/3). Infidelity was thought to be possible in only the most committed of relationships (e.g., marriage, hubby/wifey, "official" boyfriend/girlfriend) and was deemed understandable under many different instrumental circumstances (e.g., desire for a type of sex that partner is not willing to engage in, gaining access to children from another relationship, access to resources, etc.) (Macauda et al. 2011). There were no differences in outcome by sex or ethnicity.

Structured Interviews (SI), 2008

The structured interview (SI) was the final method fielded. Participants were recruited using a venue-based sampling strategy and interviewed face-to-face in the field in 2008. The 30–45 minute survey included questions covering seven general areas: 1) demographic information, 2) fertility history, 3) sexual history, 4) sexual, reproductive, and contraceptive behavior with *serious* partners in the last six months, 5) sexual, reproductive, and contraceptive behavior with *casual* partners in the last six months, 6) attitudes towards condoms and cheating (infidelity), 7) STI/HIV history and screening, and 8) history of incarceration. A total of 241 participants completed the survey. Data were analyzed with SPSS®. In general, the quantitative data substantiated the themes from the qualitative data. Relevant findings for this paper will be reported in the text.

Data Triangulation

Our data analysis strategy incorporated the triangulation of all methods. We identified themes in the qualitative data and compared them across methods. SCA techniques were used to describe the cognitive models regarding relationship types, infidelity, and emotional and physical risks of relationships and to test gender and ethnic differences in these models, which were not significant. We included questions in the SI related to themes that emerged from the qualitative methods (e.g., STI testing, infidelity, and incarceration) to validate qualitative findings. This paper makes primary use of the FGD and SRI text data with corroborating statistical information from the SI.

Participant Recruitment

African-American and Puerto Rican participants ages 18–25 were recruited using purposive sampling through street outreach at either general street settings or specialized activity sites (e.g., parks, laundromats, convenience stores, etc.) where they were approached and engaged in conversation by outreach workers of similar sex and ethnicity. If they met the inclusion criteria,[3] the project was explained and they were asked if they wanted to participate. Participants for the SI gave verbal consent and all other participants provided written consent. This research protocol was approved by the Institutional Review Boards of the University of Connecticut, the Centers for Disease Control and Prevention, the Family Planning Council of Philadelphia, and the Hispanic Health Council in Hartford. Participants received compensation roughly corresponding to $15 per hour for their time and were also provided with bus tokens if needed.

Participant Characteristics

Participants for all methods had a mean age of 20 years. Thirty-four percent of female participants and 66 percent of male participants reported more than five lifetime sexual partners, and 57 percent of respondents reported that they had sex with more than one person of the opposite sex in the last year. A high proportion (18 percent) reported having ever had an STI and 96 percent reported ever having used a condom.

In the SI, males reported an average of 16 lifetime sexual partners, while females reported an average of nine.[4] Twenty percent reported having ever been diagnosed with an STI, with more females reporting infection than males (29 percent vs. 10 percent). This gender difference is notable in that STIs commonly produce hidden epidemics. For example, the CDC estimates that in the United States there are nearly 20 million cases of new STIs annually caused by eight different viruses and bacteria, many of them undiagnosed (Satterwhite et al. 2013). Only 61 percent of participants reported using a condom at last vaginal sex, although condom usage was higher among African-Americans (71 percent) than Puerto Ricans (59 percent).

THE SEXUAL CULTURE

I begin this section by describing the sexual culture underlying the syndemic of poverty, discrimination, and incarceration that contributes to sexual and reproductive risk, sexually transmitted infections (STIs), and early childbearing among African-American and Puerto Rican young adults in Hartford (Singer et al. 2006) and the repercussions of high rates of incarceration in the population that further exacerbate the underlying syndemic, creating the larger PDI syndemic proposed here.

The sexual culture underlying this syndemic among African-American and Puerto Rican emerging adults in inner-city Hartford is characterized by early sexual initiation, multiple sexual partners, early childbearing, and high rates of STI. The vast majority (74 percent) of our respondents had sex by the time they are 15 years old (Erickson et al. 2013). Multiple partners are normative and the vast majority of participants (74 percent) had five or more lifetime sexual partners (range 1–100). Unplanned and early pregnancy and parenting were also common with a little over half of respondents (54 percent) indicating they had one or more children and of these 59 percent were under age 18 when they became pregnant. Nevertheless, parenthood was most often welcomed and having a child to care for seemed to give new meaning especially to the mothers' and also to some of the fathers' lives—a cultural script that has been previously described among urban, low-income Latinas in East Los Angeles (Erickson 1998). Some of these young families managed to live together, usually in one of their parent's households, but most did not. Many mothers were no longer romantically involved with the father(s) of their children (only 3 percent were married, but cohabitation was more common in this population than marriage), but fathers were often still involved with their children when possible. The baby mama/baby daddy relationship type was recognized as an important relationship that captures this tendency for parents who are no longer together to remain involved with their children. In fact, this relationship was described as "the one that will be with you for life" whether you want it or not. These relationships also caused a significant amount of stress (sometimes referred to by participants as "baby mama/daddy drama") in people's lives. Nevertheless, children were welcomed and very much a part of these young people's lives, hopes, and dreams.

Participants recognized many different relationship types from one-night stands to live-in committed relationships to baby mama/baby daddy (see Singer et al. 2006). Cluster analysis of the pile sort of the 30 most salient relationship types revealed that they clustered into three general categories: 1) those that were primarily sexual in nature, 2) those that were primarily romantic and emotionally meaningful in which one could "catch feelings" for another person, and 3) those that were consensual but were used instrumentally to gain access to resources (e.g., money, things, drugs, access to one's children). The participants did not consider this last category to be sex work. Rather it was understood as an essential resource exchange strategy within an environment of scarce resources that both men and women used when needed.

The use of infectious disease terminology for falling in love (i.e., catching feelings) reflected the overall sense of doom that pervaded participants' discourse about relationships both in the FGDs and the SRIs. While monogamy and commitment were often desired, there was an overwhelming sense of lack of trust in romantic partners among both men and women. Free lists of risks and benefits of having a romantic relationship corroborated this idea that catching feelings and entering into a serious relationship was risky. The qualitative data supported this generalized fear of commitment and the sense of uncertainty about the possibility of sexual fidelity in committed relationships. In the SRI interviews, "less than 5 percent of participants had ever been in a serious relationship in which neither they nor their partner had side partners. The majority (72 percent), both males (69 percent) and females (76 percent), had a secondary partner during one or more of their serious relationships or had a serious partner who they thought had cheated on them (males 79 percent, females 86 percent)" (Singer et al. 2006:2016). Such fears are likely related to the fact that some sexual relationships, especially secondary ones, are motivated by the very real need for access to resources.

Having multiple partners and not using condoms are well-known risk factors for STI transmission, and the generally high rates of STIs in our sample attested to this. In the SI, 18 percent, in the FGDs 11 percent, and in the SRIs, 22 percent of respondents indicated they had had an STI at some time in their lives, with females more likely to report STI history than males. In Hartford at the time of our study, HIV/AIDS was epidemic among minority populations, but gonorrhea and chlamydia were the most commonly reported STIs (Singer et al. 2006). While our question about STIs was not specific, it is likely that gonorrhea and chlamydia were the most common infections among the respondents in our different methods, although some may have been infected with HIV. While we did not collect actual biological data on disease interaction, the potential for such interaction is evident both in the reported rates of STI infection and the known patterns of interactions among STIs.

Condom use was commonly mentioned as the way to prevent STIs, but while condom use with casual partners was a normative ideal among our participants, actual use with casual partners depended on the context of the sexual encounter—where it occurred, whether condoms were available, whether drugs and alcohol were involved—all of which made condom use less likely. In addition, respondents told us that they gauged how "clean" (i.e., disease free) a potential sexual partner was based on their reputation and how they looked and smelled (Singer et al. 2006). This cultural logic often led to non-use of condoms since most respondents were very clear that they enjoyed sex more without them. When a person "looked clean" condoms were frequently not used.

In established serious relationships condom use was not at all normative and introducing or reintroducing them would be interpreted as a lack of trust in a partner or proof of one's own infidelity. Thus, partners in a serious relationship had to depend on their partner using a condom in side relationships so as not to bring STIs into the main relationship. Many women talked about finding out their partner was cheating when they contracted an STI, and this often signaled the end of the relationship.

Couples often negotiated the status of developing romantic relationships by talking about whether or not to stop using condoms, which indicated a developing trust in the partner and the desire for a more serious relationship. Thus, shifting to non-use of condoms and/or use of female contraceptive methods only is a well-known cultural sign that a relationship is serious or becoming serious (Cheney et al. 2014). Couples often used mutual STI testing when they were in this phase of negotiating their relationship to demonstrate they were disease-free before they actually stopped using condoms (Abraham et al. 2011).

Thus, we see that condom use was a complex cultural symbol among the young adults in our study. It signaled the kind of relationship one had and how much trust the partners had in each other. In addition, condoms were associated with disease prevention and people generally did not like to use them, preferring "raw" sex. Thus, active condom use was dependent primarily on an accurate assessment of the risk of contracting an STI from any given potential partner (Is s/he clean, known, safe?) and one's agency in negotiating condom use with a partner (e.g., harder for women, harder when under the influence of drugs or alcohol, harder when romantically involved). Such assessments can be difficult and fraught with emotion and depend on the context of the sexual encounter. Given this understanding of the cultural meaning of condoms, it is not surprising that they are used less often than might be prudent, placing participants at risk for STIs/HIV.

It was clear from the FGDs and SRIs that participants understood the need to protect themselves from STI/HIV and the role of condoms in doing so, but the pattern of less than ideal condom use with casual partners and low use with serious partners discussed above was corroborated in the SI. At first sex with a casual partner, 87 percent of participants used condoms, but at last sex with that partner this dropped to 78 percent. With serious partners 78 percent had used a condom at first sex, but only 39 percent at last sex with that partner (Hock-Long et al. 2013). Concurrent multiple partners were reported by only 5 percent in the SI, 18 percent of participants said they had only one current casual partner, and 77 percent had only one serious partner at the time of the survey (Hock-Long et al. 2013). These patterns of condom use and nonuse combined with the tendency for multiple, serial, and sometimes concurrent partners allowed continuing STI transmission, reinfection, and likely co-infections in this population. In addition, while both men and women were active sexual participants, there was still a traditional gender hierarchy and many of the SRI participants talked about violent incidents in their relationships (e.g., hitting, slapping, knifing, destroying property, stalking and guarding of women) on the part of either or both partners, suggesting the possibility that sexual violence (and its physical, biological, psychological, and emotional sequelae) is also likely an issue. Since violence was not a main issue under study, however, the only information we had on this was what participants volunteered in the SRIs. Nevertheless, women were at a disadvantage in the gender hierarchy and this may have made them more willing to take sexual risks to preserve a relationship, thereby increasing their risk of STI/HIV.

I now turn to the impact of high rates of incarceration on sexual culture, families, and the PDI syndemic itself.

THE IMPACT OF INCARCERATION

Our qualitative data suggested that incarceration was a common experience that significantly affected relationships and family building. The FGDs revealed extensive use of sexual and relationship terminology that was based on penal and violent language such as *jailbird* for a type of relationship, *domestic* for a relationship characterized by abuse and interpersonal violence, *lockdown* for relationships with a jealous partner who keeps track of your movements, and *bang bang* for rough sex to name just a few (Hatcherson 2009). In the SRIs, 43 percent of the 62 participants talked about the impact of jail on their lives and relationships. Perhaps this is not surprising since between 1980 and 2010 the total incarcerated population in Connecticut grew from 3,845 to 18,052, an increase of 369.5 percent, and in 2003, the year our study began, the majority (72 percent) of prisoners incarcerated in Connecticut were African-American (44 percent) or Hispanic (28 percent) (Connecticut General Assembly, Connecticut Prison Statistics from the Office of Fiscal Analysis Department of Corrections database 2010[5] and 2003[6]). In order to quantify the extent of incarceration in our population, we added questions to the SI regarding history of incarceration, which documented that 60 percent of male participants had been in jail at least once, 67 percent of those for 30 or more days. Perhaps somewhat more surprising was that 25 percent of female participants had been in jail at least once, 47 percent of them for 30 or more days with no significant differences by race/ethnicity.

While high rates of incarceration of young black males has become a prominent social issue in the United States, it was only beginning to make the news at the time of our study, and Michelle Alexander's book, *The New Jim Crow*, that brought the issue to public attention was only published in 2010. However, the problem had been addressed earlier by Loïc Wacquant (2002), who saw the prison and the ghetto as a new strategy to isolate and maintain a black underclass separate and unequal, which he called the hyperghetto.[7] Dorothy E. Roberts (2003–2004), Kirkland and Ellis Professor, Northwestern University School of Law, characterized the cultural impact of the mass incarceration of African-American men over the last three decades that had turned prison into "a common and predictable experience for African-American men in their twenties" and also noted that the fastest growing segment of the prison population was African-American women (Roberts: 1274). Roberts also described the extent of incarceration: "On any given day, nearly one-third of black men in their twenties are under the supervision of the criminal justice system—either behind bars, on probation, or on parole." (Roberts: 1272). Moreover she noted that "the exit and re-entry of inmates is geographically concentrated in the poorest, minority neighborhoods" where "As many as 1 in 8 of the adult male residents is sent to prison each year and 1 in 4 is behind bars on any given day" (Roberts: 1276). This cycling of African-Americans from the ghetto to the prison and back is what Wacquant (2002) termed the 'ghetto as prison and prison as the ghetto, a new form of discrimination and subjugation that permanently ensures the exclusion of African-Americans, especially men, from the wider society.

Roberts (2003–2004:1281–1294) outlined the consequences of these changes on communities affected by high rates of incarceration that: 1) damage social networks (children, families, and friends) by causing economic strain and psychological stress, the burden of which falls on women; 2) skew the sex ratio and distort social norms regarding relationships and family formation, (i.e., competition for men creates the tendency to multiple partners, weakens family stability, and weakens women's power in relationships, all of which are particularly damaging psychologically to children); 3) encourage distrust of the justice system; 4) create conditions that valorize prison and its culture of violence, rape, and brutality; and 5) destroy social citizenship (i.e., ex-convicts, especially felons, have difficulty gaining employment and participating fully in society). Many of these socio-political consequences of incarceration are reflected in our qualitative data, which shows that high rates of incarceration affect the sexual culture of inner-city minority populations in all aspects from sexual initiation, to relationship development, to break-ups, to parenting, and even how they talk about sex and relationships.

I turn now to the voices of the young people who participated in our study and from whom we came to understand the impact of incarceration on their lives and by extension on their health.

Incarceration's Impact on the Language of Relationships

Violent language and jail terminology were used to describe many sexual acts and relationships (Hatcherson 2009). Explicitly violent relationships named by FGD participants included aggressive, violent, and dominant. Many women and some men recounted incidents of domestic violence, which they called simply "domestic." Thus, saying a relationship was domestic meant it was violent. Other relationships were psychologically or emotionally violent, such as brain surgeon (someone who lies to get sex), pimp (someone who runs a string of sex workers with whom he is also sexually intimate), family freeway (someone who has sex with all the women in the family—sisters, mothers, aunts, cousins), and running a train (where a group of friends has sex with the same woman serially). Another relationship type described in an African-American female FGD was called jailbird, as these female African-American participants explained:

> Participant 3: [Jailbird]—that's like someone you done known and he telling you, I'm about to get locked up. I gotta do my biz for three months, so when I come out, we banging [having rough sex]. We bang bang. But you keep contact with the person the whole time they in jail, and then when they get out, it's all that stress and he trying to pound it [have rough sex].

Interviewer: So he's kind of like a shag partner, in some respects?

Participant 1: No, he a jail partner.

Interviewer: Is that a different category, jail partner?

Group: Yeah!

Participant 3: . . . put jailbird.

Participant 1: 'cause it's still going to be that rough sex and when he get out of jail, 'cause he going to tear it down.

In the same FGD one young woman described the cycling in and out of prison this way:

> Basically, that's most of what they [jailbirds] do . . . like come home, hop two months, go to jail two, three years, come back another two, three months, go back to jail.

Both men and women compared being in a serious relationship to incarceration. In the African-American male FGDs, participants said that in marriage/live-in relationships "you a prisoner and she the officer, basically"; "yeah, she's the guard, she's running it." However, men in serious relationships often described policing their partner's behavior and attempting to isolate and control them as this participant explains:

> Now wifey, that somebody you got to keep distant from everybody else. That's somebody you love. You can't let her be chillin' with your boys. She basically stays at home and takes care of the kids. She don't be around your friends.

Women in the FGDs reported that they knew they were in a serious relationship "when he keep you locked down, can't see your friends, you don't even go out no more!" and when "you be crying all the time." Thus, for most of our participants, jealousy, threats, obsession, and paranoia were normative in a serious or committed relationship, and this resulted in the mistrust and fear surrounding "catching feelings" that is part of the sexual culture. The psychological impact of this kind of everyday language about sexual and romantic relationships begs further study as to its emotional effects and interactions with other diseases or illnesses. However, while it may be unnerving for outsiders to hear, it is clear that this language and associated behavior developed in the context of the pervasive presence of incarceration in the community that as Roberts noted tends to "valorize prison and its culture of violence, rape, and brutality" (Roberts 2003–2004:1281–1294).

Incarceration's Impact on Sexual Initiation

The sexual culture of our participants is characterized by early sexual initiation as described earlier, and most participants were under the age of consent when they began their sexual careers. Older men, however, were often worried about the legal consequences of having sex with underage women, but it was not uncommon for them to do so anyway. This Puerto Rican female participant recounts a discussion with the man with whom she first had sex:

> P: [He said] "When you were 13, I was 21. Remember?" He was: "I could have went to jail for your ass."

As noted in the introduction of the syndemic earlier in the chapter, young women are biologically more at risk of STI infection due to the immaturity of their vaginal epithelial cells, and in these situations may be socially more vulnerable to sexual or romantic coercion possibly putting them at higher risk for both STI/HIV and the physical and emotional sequelae of coerced sex (Ostrach and Singer 2012).

Incarceration's Impact on Relationships

As discussed earlier, the sexual culture of our participants was characterized by a pervasive lack of trust, and new relationships were particularly affected by uncertainty due to incarceration, as this African-American female participant explained:

> I met Jamal like in between what I was going through with Brad. We had sex, and so the next day I went for, you know, the 72-hour pill [emergency contraception]. So, um, and he never called me. So basically, I thought it was just a one-night stand and come to find out he was in jail. He had his cousin call me, and he was on the other line, and that's how I find out.

An African-American male participant (SRI) had a similar experience in a new relationship:

> [I just met her and] we had sex every day for two weeks straight. So I guess it [the relationship] was good. I can't really say because I'm not so high and mighty on myself, I just . . . she umm . . . she got locked up. She went to jail for something. They [police] rushed her house and the wrong kind of drugs [were] inside her house. I mean, if you got weed you're not gonna go to jail for a long time, but if it's meth [methamphetamine] or something else, you're going away for a long time. Yeah, I think there was Special K [ketamine] in there, too. So she . . . she's in [jail]. So that's how our relationship ended. I'm not gonna write. You're not my pen pal. Don't call me.

Longer-term relationships are also affected by the uncertainty of incarceration, as these two African-American female SRI participants noted:

> Participant 1: Um, we were in a relationship for what, a year,'til he started going to jail, and that was like: "I'm not gonna be running back for jail," so I ended up not messing with him.
>
> Participant 2: I definitely thought it was going to be a serious relationship. I don't think he knew he was going to jail. He was in there for 18 months. It's too long for me [not to have sex or a partner].

Incarceration's Impact on Family and Parenting

Incarceration often has negative effects on parenting and family formation in relationships of different attachment levels and longevity as these SRI participants indicated:

> African-American Female Participant: Like I knew where he hung out and stuff like that, but we didn't know a lot about each other. We just knew that one day we was going to have sex with each other, and one day we did [have sex], and we both got a child out of it (laughing).
>
> Interviewer: OK, and then after that you didn't see him again?
>
> African-American Female Participant: No, I didn't have sex with him again, and he's in jail, he's in and out of jail.
>
> Puerto Rican Male Participant: I was incarcerated from 15 to 17, and then I got incarcerated when I was 21 until I was 23.
>
> Interviewer: Ok, so from 14 to 15, are you just having like a lot of like one-night stands, a lot of jumps and stuff 'cause you're like in the clubs and you're selling [drugs].
>
> Puerto Rican Male Participant: It's like, like I said, I wasn't nobody big [in drugs]. I just knew how to make money and keep it going, you know. Oh, I had sex with female COs [correction officers] in jail, don't get me wrong. 'Cause I knew them from the world. That's why . . . I used to serve them [sell drugs to them outside].
>
> From 17 to 21, I'm just enjoying my life, having fun, getting on with making up for what I lost, making money.
>
> In between his two incarcerations he met Jenni and had a baby with her.

> Interviewer: When you're with Jenni, you're 20, she's 19, and you had a baby, but then this whole thing kind of happens . . .
>
> Puerto Rican Male Participant: When I was 21, that's when I kind of left her. I felt she was fucking some other dude with my daughter over there. She walking home late at night. It was probably like 11 when I got that call. She got the baby with her. People get into a fight from what I hear. A couple more people start fighting and gunshots go off and things happened, and I blamed her for that. And that day, I was going to kill her in the hospital, I swear to god.
>
> That was [happened] in New York. I lived up there by myself for a while trying to work things with her just to be close to my kid. I couldn't do it no more so I moved back to Connecticut.

After breaking off with Jenni, he moved to Massachusetts and had another partner, Cassie. Then he was incarcerated again.

> Puerto Rican Male Participant: Then I moved to Massachusetts. I was trying to get away from the atmosphere [in CT] because I knew what would happen if I let myself get sucked back into that type of atmosphere [drug dealing], you know what I mean? Then I met Cassie. She took me in, but I didn't love her.
>
> Then I got incarcerated again from 21 to 23. And then I met my wife after I got out, and I'm happy. I'm just—I'm happy. I'm content right now. I can't ask for more. Maybe I could ask for, you know, getting on my feet a little better, a little faster but I ain't, but taking it slow.

He does not have any contact with Jenni or his daughter.

A final example of how incarceration disrupts relationships, lives, and families comes from a Puerto Rican female SRI participant married to a jailbird.

> We knew we was gonna have Yesenia. Like we knew we would eventually have a baby. And we waited 'til Yesenia was three and we started all over again. And I had Serena last year. But Serena he fucked up. That's when he was doing his cheating and shit. He wasn't there when I gave birth to her, but we planned her. We knew before he went to jail that time that I was pregnant.
>
> So I don't ask [him] for much—"You're not here." My sister-in-law plays the role of my baby daddy. She gives me whatever I need. I married into a good family at least when it came to take care of my kids and financially-wise they can take care of my kids. So, thank God for that. And he's just a fuck-around.

> Out of all the guys I've had he's like . . . the worry. He's the one understanding [me] the most, but fucks up the most, too. And he's always in and out of jail. I think it's fucked up that my kids gotta grow up without a father.
>
> But he's told me that if he gets jail time for me to live my life. When he comes out he'll come get what he left and we'll start over where we left off at. Because he knows I'm not waiting four years. "I didn't put you there, you did it to yourself. So, you go ahead with your business, I'm not gonna have no kids with nobody else. I won't bring another man into your bed, but I cannot guarantee you or promise you that I will be faithful." And he understands that. [If I sleep with someone else] I won't let feelings get attached, because my baby's daddy's in my picture. Always gonna be in my picture and nothing gonna change that. Can't nobody take his place.

This young woman is committed to her children's father and will take him back when he comes out of jail, but she feels free to have side partners while he is inside and worries about the impact of her children not having a father around, but she also says:

> I tried so many times to get rid of him (laughs). Moved to Connecticut [from New York] trying to get rid of him! How the fuck that motherfucker find me so fast? Like it's scary . . . it's scary because like . . . he's so determined.
>
> I know I love him. I won't get rid of him. I hate him sometimes. He's done a lot of bad, but I won't get rid of him.

She loves him, hates him, perhaps fears him, will have other partners while he is in jail without letting her feelings get out of hand, will accept him when he comes back, and then repeat the whole cycle again because he is a jailbird.

DISCUSSION

The multiple uncertainties of the experience of incarceration among the young adults in our sample affect every single aspect of relationship and family building making it very difficult for those affected by it to achieve stability and security, putting them at risk for chronic stress and activation of the HPA axis, which is a major cause of disease in and of itself but also exacerbates the effects of other co-occurring biological (e.g., STI/HIV, alcohol or drug dependence/addiction), psychological (e.g., PTSD), and emotional (e.g., anxiety, depression, chronic fear) diseases. High incarceration rates and their sequelae are, thus, an important part of the PID syndemic.

Our qualitative research provided us with a deeper understanding of the lived experience of high incarceration rates. Our data illustrate the compounding impact of the turnstile relationship (in and out of prison) that many of the men and women in our study endured and that further increases the already unstable and unpredictable nature of life in the hyperghetto (Wacquant 2002). Incarceration can push people to take advantage of brief periods between incarcerations to have sex and possibly children, which they might otherwise not consider under less stressful conditions. Incarceration also results in frequent break-ups that exacerbate the already normative pattern of having multiple relationships (a major risk factor for STIs/HIV) for romantic and resource access purposes by alternately adding and removing people from the sexual pool—the same people who are perceived to have the right to sex once they come out. In addition, the long-term partner of someone in jail often takes side partners during the incarceration period (a culturally normative behavior), increasing the risk for STI/HIV. Children grow up without their father's presence and families are undermined, increasing feelings of stress, worry, loss, depression, and anxiety. Once in the turnstile, it is hard to get out because of limited economic opportunities available in addition to the added stigma created by having been incarcerated. Poverty alone makes life insecure and unstable; jail time, often related to drugs and violence, magnifies the problem by forcing our participants into acting for today rather than planning for the future. Incarceration interacts synergistically with the syndemic of poverty and sexual risk-taking described earlier in this chapter and is intimately tied to the sexual and reproductive health disparities faced by inner-city young adults. It exacerbates the risks for, and the health consequences of physical, biological, psychological, emotional, and social illnesses and the negative effects these can have on each other.

The multiple stigmas of poverty, discrimination, incarceration, sexually transmitted infections (STIs), early parenting, single motherhood, and absent fathers are borne by these young people throughout their lives and are undoubtedly implicated in higher rates of disease while they are young (i.e., STIs, substance use/abuse, physical and emotional violence, depression). Specific disease interactions known to exacerbate each other include the two most common STIs in Hartford, chlamydia and gonorrhea at the time of the study (Singer et al. 2006), both of which create lesions on the genitals that attract and serve as entry points for HIV and other STIs that can be passed on to sexual partners. It is also probable that many of the young people in our study will develop chronic diseases in later life (e.g., asthma, hypertension, heart disease, diabetes, depression, chronic obstructive pulmonary disease, obesity, diabetes) due to the stressors that are related to the physical, social, economic, and political environment in which they live and to the stigmatization and discrimination they face every day of their lives from the broader society as poor, undereducated, minority men and women. The added stigma and negative effects of incarceration on families only heightens the risk for disease. Among young adults in Hartford, substance use, both recreational and as self-medication for the insults and injuries of stigmatized lives, commonly creates the climate for greater sexual risk-taking and interpersonal violence that in turn can lead to further interactions between biological, physical, psychological, and emotional sequelae such as addiction, physical trauma, unintended pregnancy, STIs, fear, anxiety, and depression. The PDI syndemic has particularly negative effects on the stability of relationships and the family and on the health and well being of so many young adults and their children. The truly exacerbating effects of high rates of incarceration on health and personal welfare discussed in this chapter should give us pause. We must recognize, address, and reverse the social determinants of this syndemic (i.e., social and economic inequity and discrimination) in order to end it and free our young people from the burden of illness created by both structural violence and their stigmatized lives.

NOTES

1. This research was supported by Award Numbers U58/CCU123064 from the Centers for Disease Control. Its contents are solely the responsibility of the author and do not necessarily represent the official views of CDC. The study was approved by the University of Connecticut Institutional Review Board from 2004 to 2014.

2. The Coital Diaries (n=38) were not used in this analysis and are not discussed in this section.

3. Participants were eligible if they met the basic eligibility criteria: age 18–25, had had sex with a member of the opposite sex in the last year, born in the United States or Puerto Rico, self-identified as African-American or Puerto Rican, and spoke English (FGD, SCA, SI methods) or English or Spanish (SRI and CD methods—Hartford only). The language criteria were imposed for practical reasons to maintain consistency between the Hartford and Philadelphia sites. All Spanish interviews were translated into English. There were two SRIs and three CDs completed in Spanish; most Puerto Ricans in this age group spoke English. The CD method had more stringent eligibility criteria—having had sex at least three times in the last 30 days with a member of the opposite sex and having had sex with more than one person in the last 30 days. An additional eligibility criterion for SI participants was not having participated in any of the other PHRESH methods.

4. For our participants, the "lifetime" in question was from sexual initiation to their age at the time of the study (i.e., 18–25 years).

5. http://www.cga.ct.gov/2010/rpt/2010-R-0030.htm. First accessed October 2011, last accessed November 5, 2016.

6. http://www.cga.ct.gov/2003/olrdata/jud/rpt/2003-R-0837.htm. First accessed October 2011, last accessed November 5, 2016.

7. According to Wacquant (2002), the hyperghetto is the fourth stage in Americans' domination of African Americans. The first was slavery (1619–1865) during which African slaves worked their owners' plantation. The second was Jim Crow (1865–1965) where freed African slaves worked as sharecroppers in the South. The third was the ghetto (1915–1968) when African-Americans moved North to work in the industrial economy at menial jobs and were isolated in urban ghettos. The current stage is the hyperghetto (1968–) in which African-Americans are perceived as welfare recipients and/or criminals and isolated in urban ghettos and jails as a source of surplus labor.

REFERENCES

Abraham, Traci, Mark Macauda, Pamela Erickson, and Merrill Singer. "And Let Me See Them Damn Papers! The Role of STI/AIDS Screening among Urban African American and Puerto

Rican Youth in the Transition to Sex without a Condom" *AIDS and Behavior* 15(2011): 1359–1371.

Alexander, Michelle. *The New Jim Crow: Mass Incarceration in the Age of Colorblindness.* The New Press, 2010.

Arnett, Jeffrey Jensen. "Emerging adulthood: A theory of development from the late teens through the twenties." *American Psychologist* 55(2000): 469–480.

Cheney, Ann M., Bayla Ostrach, Ruthanne Marcus, Cynthia Frank, Cassandra Ball, Pamela I. Erickson. A Culture of Future Planning: Perceptions of Sexual Risk Among Educated Young Adults. *Qualitative Health Research* 24(2014):1451–1462.

Erickson, Pamela I. *Latina Adolescent Childbearing in East Los Angeles.* Austin: University of Texas Press, 1998.

Erickson, Pamela I., Louise Badiane, and Merrill Singer."The Social Context and Meaning of Virginity Loss among African American and Puerto Rican Youth in the Inner City." *Medical Anthropology Quarterly* 27(2013): 313–329.

Farmer, Paul E., Bruce Nizeye, Sara Stulac, Salmaan Keshavjee 2006. Structural Violence and Clinical Medicine. *PLoS Medicine* 3(2006) e449: 0001–0006.

Franks, Peter, Peter Muennig, Erica Lubetkin, and Haomiao Jia. "The Burden of Disease Associated with Being African-American in the United States and the Contribution of Socio-economic Status." *Social Science and Medicine* 62(2006): 2469–2478.

Guilliams,Thomas G. 2015. *The Role of Stress and the HPA Axis in Chronic Disease Management.* The Point Institute, 2015.

Hatcherson, Jean. "Social Construction of Intimate and Sexual Relationships, Sexual Risk Taking, and Parenting Among Low-Income, Inner City African Americans." Ph.D. diss., University of Connecticut, 2009.

Hatfield-Timajchy Kendra, Karen Andes, Amy Cassidy. "Beyond Polemics: The Merits and Challenges of Assessing Intercoder Agreement in a Qualitative Research Study." Poster presented at 137th annual meeting of the American Public Health Association, November 7–11, 2009, Philadelphia, PA.

Hock-Long, Linda, Dare Henry-Moss, Marion Carter, Kendra Hatfield-Timajchy, Pamela I. Erickson, Amy Cassidy, Mark Macauda, Merrill Singer, and Jesse Chittams. "Condom Use with Serious and Casual Heterosexual Partners: Findings from a Community Venue-Based Survey of Young Adults." *AIDS and Behavior* 17(2013):900–913.

Krieger, Nancy. "Theories for Social Epidemiology in the 21st Century: An Ecosocial Perspective." *International Journal of Epidemiology* 30(2001): 668–677

Krieger, Nancy 2000. "Discrimination and Health," in *Social Epidemiology,* edited by Lisa F. Berkman and Ichiro Kawachi, 36–75. New York: Oxford University Press, 2000.

Macauda, Mark, Pamela Erickson, Merrill Singer, and Claudia Santelices. "A Cultural Model of Infidelity among African American and Puerto Rican Young Adults." *Anthropology and Medicine* 18(2011): 351–364.

Marmot, Michael. "Social Determinants of Health Inequalities." *Lancet* 365(2005): 1099–1104.

NcEwen, Bruce S. "Protective and Damaging Effects of Stress Mediators: Allostasis and Allostatic Load." *New England Journal of Medicine*. 338(1998): 171–179.

Morrison, Charles S., Patricia Bright, Emelita Wong, Cynthia Kwok, Irina Yacobson, Charlotte Gaydos, Heidi Tucker, Paul D. Blumenthal, Paul D. Hormonal Contraceptive Use, Cervical Ectopy, and the Acquisition of Cervical Infections. *Sexually Transmitted Diseases* 31(2004): 561–567.

Ostrach, Bayla, and Merrill Singer. "At Special Risk: Biopolitical Vulnerability and HIV/STI Syndemics among Women." *Health Sociology Review* 21(2012): 258–271.

Roberts, Dorothy E. "The Social and Moral Costs of Mass Incarceration in African American Communities." *Stanford Law Review* 56(2003–2004): 1271–1305.

Satterwhite, Catherine L., Elizabeth Torrone, Elissa Meites, Eileen Dunne, Reena Mahajan, Ocfemia, M. Cheryl Banez, John Su, Fujie Xu, and Hillard Weinstock. "Sexually Transmitted Infections among U.S. Women and Men: Prevalence and Incidence Estimates, 2008," *Sexually Transmitted Diseases* 40(2013): 187–193.

Singer, Merrill. Introduction to Syndemics: A Critical Systems Approach to Public and Community Health. San Francisco, CA: John Wiley and Sons, 2009.

Singer, Merrill C., Pamela I. Erickson, Louise Badiane, Rosemary Diaz, Dugeidy Ortiz, Traci Abraham, and Anna Marie Nicolaysen. "Syndemics, Sex, and the City: Understanding Sexually Transmitted Diseases in Social and Cultural Context." *Social Science and Medicine* 63(2006): 2010–2021.

United Nations Population Fund. Addressing Gender Perspectives in HIV Prevention. *HIV Prevention Now Programme Briefs No. 4* (2004). New York, NY.

Wacquant, Loïc. "From Slavery To Mass Incarceration: Rethinking the 'Race Question' in the US." *New Left Review* 13(2002). Accessed September 6, 2014, at http://newleftreview.org.ezproxy.lib.uconn.edu/II/13/loic-wacquant-from-slavery-to-mass-incarceration.

Williams, David R., Harold W. Neighbors, and James S. Jackson. "Racial/Ethnic Discrimination and Health: Findings from Community Studies." *American Journal of Public Health* 93 (2003): 200–208.

Chapter Five

Sickness in the Detention System

Syndemics of Mental Distress, Malnutrition, and Immigration Stigma in the United States

Megan A. Carney

The stigma of being an "illegal immigrant" in the United States has perpetuated hostility toward individuals and groups perceived as falling under this category, while also generating intense fear and anxiety around the punitive repercussions of being undocumented. Findings from previous research support the general belief that immigration enforcement practices are a source of mental distress in immigrant communities (Gonzales and Chavez, 2012; Talavera, Núñez-Mchiri, and Heyman, 2010; Menjívar, 2013). The fear linked to this distress prevents many individuals from seeking care for both physical and mental health problems (Chavez, 2012; Hacker et al., 2011). Meanwhile, in the past decade, the United States has continued to amplify a "racialized removal program" (Golash-Boza and Hondagneau, 2013) characterized by mass detention of undocumented immigrants in private facilities and subsequent deportation of individuals to countries of origin. While in detention, individuals are often denied adequate care or food, and the experience of detention becomes a form of trauma in itself. From ethnographic fieldwork with immigration rights activists and community-based mental health agencies, as well as semi-structured interviews with former detainees and relatives of detainees and deportees in Washington state, in this chapter I explore the syndemics of immigration stigma, mental health decline in immigrant communities, and the bodily traumas—particularly in the form of malnutrition—incurred during the experience of detention and as this syndemic affects Latino communities. The syndemic resulting from the confluence of stigma, mental health decline, and bodily trauma has an increasingly deleterious effect on the overall health of immigrants in the United States who already experience a marginalized health status (Sargent and Larchanche, 2011; Viruell-Fuentes, Miranda, and Abdulrahim, 2012).

Economic marginalization of Latino immigrants in the United States produces significant health disparities, particularly among women (Quesada, Hart, and Bourgois, 2011). Participation in the secondary job market translates into no benefits or health insurance for most Latino immigrants, subsequently perpetuating a long list of unmet health care needs (Zambrana, Dorrington, and Hayes-Bautista, 1995; Zlolniski, 2006). Stress that migrants associate with the pressure to acquire work and to work longer hours may negatively affect health while also preventing sick or injured workers from seeking medical attention (Gleeson, 2010). Rates of diabetes, heart disease, and cancer are significantly higher among Latinos than the general population, and reported rates of depression and mental illness are also comparatively higher among Latinos, especially for women and those whose dominant language is Spanish (Vélez-Ibáñez, 1996).

The post-9/11 environment of policing and intense xenophobia in the United States intensified existing health disparities through practices of political exclusion. As reported by the Migration Policy Institute's website (2011):

> In the decade since 9/11, immigration policy has been viewed principally through the lens of national security, a development that has given rise to major new border security and law enforcement initiatives, heightened visa controls and screening of international travelers and would-be immigrants, the collection and storage of information in vast new interoperable databases used by law enforcement and intelligence agencies, and the use of state and local law enforcement as force multipliers in immigration enforcement.

Specifically, recent punitive actions toward perceived undocumented persons in the United States heightened immigrants' fears and anxieties about profiling and deportation, thereby yielding negative health outcomes in the near term (Chen and Vargas-Bustamente, 2011; Coleman and Kocher, 2011; Gonzales and Chavez, 2012; Gonzales, Suarez-Orozco, and Dedios-Sanguineti, 2013; Hacker et al., 2011; Salas, Moya and Gurrola, 2013; Sargent and Larchanche, 2011; Toomey et al., 2013; Willen et al., 2011). Moreover, state surveillance of those suspected to be lacking legal authorization reproduces exclusion and undermines desires for stability and belonging.

As *zones of confinement* (Carney, 2013), multiple spheres of everyday life are gradually encroached upon by the "network of detention structures" (Fassin, 2011), and other "sites of exception," thereby confining certain groups of people to social death by restricting physical and social mobility. This language of "confinement" has emerged several times over the course of my research, both in referencing the policing of immigrants in everyday life in the United States and in the experience of being detained, specifically through the use of the Spanish verb *encerrar*. The word may translate as "to shut up," "to lock up," or "to confine." In describing life as an unauthorized migrant for instance, one of my key informants stated: "Here we live like little caged animals [*animalitos encerrados*]," while another also deployed this term in describing her experience of detention (*me encerró*). Immigration enforcement, and detention and deportation in particular, does not only implicate those apprehended by state authorities; the life chances and futures of entire families and communities hinge precariously on the fates of detainees and deportees. Therefore, while detention centers register quite literally as the most physically confining of possible zones of confinement, multiple exclusions are produced and enacted along a spectrum of confining spaces of social life located far beyond the confines of formal detention. In other words, the embodiment of vulnerability that characterizes life inside detention centers connects to and mirrors life on the outside. Death, illness, and mental distress in detention are not isolated events at isolated locales, but rather emerge from a constellation of sites controlling and restricting people's mobility, sovereignty, and life chances (Fassin, 2011; De Genova and Peutz, 2010).

RESEARCH METHODOLOGY

My research seeks to underscore the broader health outcomes of an amplified restrictive immigration regime (Menjívar, 2013) in the United States. While my fieldwork has included interviews with previously detained individuals, I have not been solely focused on the lived experience of detention per se. Since early 2013, I have been researching the effects of US immigration enforcement policies and associated activities for immigrants' subjectivities, self-perceptions of health, care-seeking behaviors, and responses by health service providers with a regional emphasis on the city of Seattle, Washington, and surrounding areas in King County. I examine the lived experience of heightened mental distress among immigrant women as well as the social life of mental health practice across a variety of sites including community clinics, social service agencies, and detention centers. My research focuses on Latino communities, with a particular emphasis on Mexican and Central American immigrants, for the reason that these groups have been disproportionately targeted by recent detention and deportation efforts in the United States (accounting for more than 97 percent of all deportations) (Golash-Boza and Hondagneu-Sotelo, 2013). Relatedly, I focus on immigrant women, as recent research suggests that the vast majority of detainees and deportees (at least 85 percent) are men, thereby implying that women who are left behind are disproportionately burdened with financial, emotional, and psychological stressors such as household expenses, childcare, family grief, and distress (Das Gupta, 2013; Golash-Boza and Hondagneu-Sotelo, 2013). Thus, while presenting some of the findings of my research herein, I alternate discussion of the perspectives and lived experiences of those both *inside* and *outside* the immigrant detention system.

More than 14 percent of Washington state residents are foreign-born, originating primarily from Asia (41 percent) and Latin America (30.5 percent) (Migration Policy Institute, 2015). Between 2000 and 2011, Washington experienced an increase of 48 percent in its foreign-born inhabitants (Migration Policy Institute, 2015). Mexico, the Philippines, and Vietnam rank among the top three countries of origin of foreign-born residents (City of Seattle, 2015). In actual numbers, Washington is home to more than one million immigrants, of whom an estimated 230,000 are without formal[1] status (Pew Hispanic Center, 2014). Mexican immigrants account for the largest share (62 percent) of the state's unauthorized population (Pew Hispanic Center, 2014). Seattle in particular has gradually transitioned from its Anglo settler origins toward a more diverse city of immigrants. Immigrants from various parts of Asia have been arriving since the early twentieth century, and those from Latin America have been arriving since the early 1970s. Despite the concentration of wealth in the Seattle region, poverty remains high at 12.6 percent for the entire Seattle-Tacoma-Bellevue metropolitan area (US Census Bureau, 2013). Notably, this area is also home to one of the largest detention facilities in the United States. The Tacoma Northwest Detention Center (Figure 5.1), a privately operated, 1,575-bed facility owned by the prison contractor GEO Corp and is located less than 50 miles from Seattle. In addition to being one of the largest, it is also the only detention center located in the Pacific Northwest region.

Ethnographic data appearing in this chapter stem from in-depth interviews with twenty (20) immigrant women, as well as from informal interviews with multiple mental health therapists, community-based clinic administrators, social workers, attorneys, and immigration rights activists. I recruited participants for in-depth interviews through community-based organizations providing mental and behavioral health services including everything from psychiatric care to domestic violence intervention and substance abuse treatment. Prior to recruitment, I met several times with the leadership within these organizations to explain my research objectives and interest in collaboration. These individuals expressed some apprehension around my interviewing clients who were suffering from behavioral or mental health problems. While I was very competent in Spanish and had prior experience doing long-term fieldwork with immigrant populations, I did not have any credentials in counseling. Thus, together we developed a memorandum of understanding that outlined recruitment and interview protocols, including plans for referring clients to specific services in cases of severe distress. With permission

Figure 5.1. Visitors arriving to the front entrance of the Northwest Detention Center, Tacoma. *Source*: Photo by author.

from the leaders of these organizations, fliers that advertised the study were distributed in both English and Spanish and posted to the community boards at multiple programs sites.

My study participants originated from Mexico, Guatemala, Honduras, and Peru and were living in the Seattle-Bellevue-Tacoma metropolitan area, and as a condition of the sampling criteria, had experienced being apprehended and detained firsthand or through a relative or close friend. In-depth interviews were conducted in Spanish, or some mix of Spanish and occasional English. Portions of interview transcriptions that appear in this chapter I have translated from Spanish to English.

IMMIGRANT DETENTION IN THE UNITED STATES

From 2008 to 2014, spanning the Obama presidency, more than a record two million people entered the immigrant detention system in the United States (Marchevsky and Baker, 2014). Despite instances of inhumane and degrading treatment repeatedly highlighted by former detainees and calls by human and civil rights organizations to end the practice of privatized detention, the private prison industry continues to manage the majority of immigrant detention centers with minimal, if any, government oversight. Detention Watch Network reports that only eight of the 350 U.S.-based detention facilities are actually operated by the Department of Homeland Security (DHS) (Detention Watch Network, 2012). DHS reduces expenditures by entering contracts with private companies such as GEO Corp to oversee detention. Whereas a private facility costs DHS only about $90 per day for each detainee, the cost per detainee at one of its own facilities is about $122 per day. In 2007, DHS issued a daily bed quota of 34,000, essentially guaranteeing steady revenues to the private detention industry (Detention Watch Network, 2012). Individual detainee lengths of stay range from several days to several years and depend on a number of variables such as access to legal counsel, strength of ties to kin in the United States, and time to immigration hearing. Although most detainees are unsuccessful in obtaining an authorized release, detention is still a routine and profitable step prior to "voluntary" or mandated deportation.

From 1993 to 2011, deportations in the United States increased nine-fold; deportations of Mexicans and Central Americans increased 10- and 12-fold, respectively (DHS Yearbook of Immigration Statistics, 2012; Golash-Boza and Hondagneu-Sotelo, 2013). More than half of deportations in 2011 were classified as "removals" rather than "returns," marking a noticeable shift from the previous century.[2] Whereas Border Patrol conducts returns when apprehending people at border posts or along perilous migration routes at the U.S.-Mexico border, removals involve an immigration hearing or waiving the right to a hearing. This shift in the composition of deportations coincided with the privatization of immigrant detention, namely because removals yield monetary profits. Unlike individuals categorized as "returns" who are maybe detained for only a few days, individuals categorized as "removals" may be detained up to several years. Tanya Maria Golash-Boza and Pierrette Hondagneu-Sotelo highlight that "Nearly all of these recent deportees have been Latino men, creating a crisis in Latino families and communities" (272). Thus they deem current detention and deportation procedures in the United States as comprising a gendered racial removal program.

IMMIGRATION STIGMA

Janis Jenkins and Elizabeth Carpenter-Song (2008) "understand stigma to be intersubjective, that is, produced and experienced in the interactive spaces between individuals in culturally defined social worlds" (p. 382). The presence of stigma is usually attributed to an ostensible moral failing or character flaw located within the individual or mapped across a particular group. In the case of immigration in the United States, individuals who lack authorized status are regarded as morally inferior or depraved (Menjívar and Kanstroom, 2013). Furthermore, because there is a racialization of "illegality" in the United States that associates undocumented status with skin color (specifically brownness or blackness), immigration stigma contributes to hypervisibility and the perpetuation of second-class citizenship among all people of color (Horton and Barker, 2010; Rivera, 2014). Nicholas De Genova contends that migrant "illegality," predicated on the erasure of legal personhood, maroons the individual into "a space of forced invisibility, exclusion, subjugation, and repression" (2002:427). Simultaneously a juridical status, sociopolitical condition, and way of being in the world (Plascencia, 2012; Willen, 2007), "illegality" renders an individual "physically present but legally absent, existing in a space outside of society" (Coutin, 2007:9). Roberto Gonzales and Leo Chavez offer a revision to this definition by suggesting that "to be illegally present is not to be 'outside of society' but to be allowed to participate in some aspects of society (e.g., schooling) but not others (e.g., work)" (2012:258). Similarly, in U.S. society, immigrants without recognized legal status are expected to work and contribute, but are restricted from full use of health care and other social benefits reserved for citizens.

Jenkins and Carpenter-Song (2008) further explain that "the experience of being stigmatized can be a struggle against dehumanization" (p. 382) that must be understood in relation to "particular local worlds" (p. 383). For instance, undocumented individuals are not the only ones to experience "illegality," as mixed-status households and families collectively negotiate the effects of "illegality" on a regular basis. If one understands the intricacies of stigmatization, then it is not surprising how tensions may escalate among members of mixed-status households. Specifically, migrants with formal status may distinguish themselves from the realm of "illegality" by both internalizing and reproducing stigma. In other words, "the management of stigma, for some, appears paradoxically to involve 'othering' those perceived to be more impaired than oneself" (Jenkins and Carpenter-Song, 2008:391). Conversely, another instance of reproducing stigma manifests in the form of internalizing the stigma and its associated negative attitudes and perceptions (Jenkins and Carpenter-Song, 2008:391), similar to the logic in Bourdieu's (2004) discussion of symbolic violence. Immigrants are often regarded as an illegitimate social group toward whom society must display distrust (Larchanche, 2012). This illegitimacy is constructed through "long-standing prejudices, economic insecurities, and social fears" (Larchanche, 2012:859), and allows for the repudiation of basic human rights to immigrants in detention.

As Carolyn Sargent and Stephanie Larchanche argue, "Immigration status—documented or undocumented—has significant implications for migrant health and access to health services" (2011:347). Instead of finding improved access to more affordable and adequate health services through migration, Sarah Willen, Jessica Mulligan, and Heide Castañeda emphasize the ways that "'illegality' often places im/migrants in positions of considerable health risk" (2011:336). Viewed as undeserving, migrants without formal status experience multiple barriers to health care, discrimination in health care settings, and ultimately, declined health status (Castañeda, 2012; Chavez, 2012; Coutin, 2010; Gonzales and Chavez, 2012; Holmes, 2012; Larchanche, 2012; Sargent and Larchanche, 2011; Willen, 2007, 2012).

MENTAL DISTRESS: DEPRESSION AND ANXIETY

Inside: I receive a call from a number I do not recognize and allow it to go to voicemail. I'm caught off guard moments later listening to a woman explain that she is responding to the flier I posted at a community clinic almost one year ago; it's the first call I've received in many months. I return Mabel's[3] call that evening, and in the five minutes we speak she frantically explains how that morning she received orders for deportation, and that it is not the first time. Worried about her immediate security, I ask how soon she has to leave. She explains that because her attorney has already started the appeal process, she will likely be able to postpone the deportation date. We arrange to meet at her apartment the following week.

One of the most telling things about meeting Mabel was her preference for showing me her story through documents rather than telling me in words. She repeated over and over again how things "were complicated" and that it was too difficult for her to talk about her experiences. Within a few minutes of being in her home, she had brought me hundreds of papers: signed letters from the community clinic, a life history narrative composed by her attorney, and affidavits. There was a perverse poeticism to me piecing the fragments of her life together through these documents while she sat quietly beside me. Even more disturbing though were the details of this unfinished story.

Mabel is 34 years old and lives with her two children—ages 6 and 1—and husband in an apartment in the Seattle neighborhood of Bellevue that they rent from someone described by Mabel as being very generous and allowing them to stay there virtually rent-free. Prior to living in this apartment, over about one year ago, her family had been homeless for some time.

Mabel has been struggling with her petition for legal status for the past four years. She has been detained, deported, and ordered for deportation again. Most recently, her petition for asylum was denied and she was ordered to leave the country. Her lawyer was furious with the judge for seeming to ignore the details of her case. Mabel migrated with the assistance of a smuggler to the United States from Guatemala City in 2005, fleeing an extremely abusive father. I learned the details of this abuse through reading Mabel's testimony that described years of sexual abuse, rape, and death threats. Her father repeatedly invoked the language of "property" in relating to Mabel. He told her that she was his "property" and that he could do what he wanted with her, including kill her. Mabel's sister was also subjected to this abuse and she recently attempted suicide. She is still living in Guatemala.

United States Immigration and Customs Enforcement (ICE) officials apprehended Mabel in 2011 when she was driving with her then 2-year-old son. They arrested her, leaving her son behind and alone in the car (a detail that immigration activists hear all too often). She then did not see her son or husband for the next year, except for a few visits they made to the Northwest Detention Center in Tacoma. Her son exhibited severe symptoms of having suffered a traumatic event thereafter, and has since been living with what is, for now, diagnosed as autism. Mabel learned of my study while taking her son to the community clinic for therapy; she expresses a desire for therapy for her own traumas but has yet to begin any treatment.

Only a few months into her stay, ICE officials decided to transfer Mabel to a detention center in Arizona. She did not see her family at all during this time. She said that both centers failed to provide her with adequate health care, treated her like an animal, deprived her of contact with her son and husband, and even threatened to isolate or coerce her should she show signs of emotional distress. She was "scared to cry for [fear of] what they might do to her." She was held in Arizona for eight months, deported to Guatemala, and illicitly returned to Seattle some months later.

Outside: Mabel's son, Jorge, exhibited symptoms of suffering a traumatic event the first time he went to visit his mother at the detention center. Unable to touch his mother because of rules prohibiting physical contact, he began screaming and banging his head uncontrollably against the partition separating him from his mother. A letter from the clinic where Jorge goes to receive care, addressed to the immigration judge, explains Jorge's condition as follows: "One year after the trauma of witnessing his mother being taken away by ICE, Jorge's development is markedly and severely delayed. Jorge only knows approximately 10 words and has difficulty engaging in play normal for his age. Jorge continues to act out aggressively towards himself and becomes easily frustrated."

Recent research underscores the myriad forms of mental distress linked to the everyday specter of immigration enforcement in the United States. For instance, Karen Hacker and colleagues (2011) find high levels of stress manifest as a result of disturbances in the community, such as workplace raids conducted by Immigration and Customs Enforcement (ICE), everyday policing, and racial profiling of immigrants. Similar studies allude to the ways that fears about deportation pose risks to psychosocial wellbeing and interfere with access to health services (Salas, Ayon, and Gurrola, 2013). In addition, these studies find that immigrants directly attribute the onset of certain physical and mental health problems, such as hypertension and depression, to their deportation fears. Other sources of anxiety include fears about collaboration between local law enforcement and ICE, concern about not being able to furnish proper documentation when in the presence of authorities, and missing health appointments or forgoing care for health problems altogether (Chen and Vargas-Bustamente, 2011; Gonzales and Chavez, 2012; Sargent and Larchanche, 2011; Willen et al., 2011).

In addition to the stigma that surrounds much immigration such as the stigma of being "illegal" and an ostensible drain on the state (Chavez, 2008), there is also the general stigma around mental health that prevails in many parts of the world. Mental health specialists emphasize that although mental health problems afflict immigrant communities disproportionately, the stigma attached to these forms of suffering—in addition to lack of ability to pay for care—often precludes possibilities for discussion, diagnosis, and appropriate treatment. Critical medical social scientists note the stigmatizing effects of psychiatric diagnosis and mental health approaches, which reinforce social exclusion while also reifying biomedical categories (Fassin and Rechtman, 2009). Thus, this stigma poses significant challenges for connecting immigrant populations with preventative resources and treatment for mental health problems and in some cases jeopardizes petitions for formal status: "Mental health conditions also weaken immigrants' abilities to obtain and retain documentation" (Kenworthy, 2012:124).

Along with "illegality," research has shown that the experience of "deportability" (De Genova, 2002) translates to negative mental health outcomes in the immediate term (Hacker et al., 2011; Silove et al., 2000; Willen et al., 2011). Nicholas De Genova and Nathalie Peutz (2010) describe deportability as both "the palpable risk and visceral fear of deportation" and "anticipatory anxieties and painful memories of deportation—[of one's] own or of [one's] family members" (p. 19). Yet there is less knowledge of how repeated exposure to and fear about intensified surveillance and interior enforcement affect the mental health and wellbeing of immigrant communities in the long-term (Golash-Boza and Hondagneu-Sotelo, 2013; Hacker et al., 2011) or of how these activities shape responses by service providers to heightened mental distress.

Empirical evidence from narratives I collected doing ethnographic fieldwork corroborates findings from previous research that mental health conditions often begin as part of the detention experience. Refugees and asylum-seekers for instance, often report re-traumatization from being subjected to inhumane treatment while in detention. Asylum seekers are often survivors of torture, political persecution, and war, yet the rigorous procedures underlying the asylum process, coupled with reports of neglect and abuse during detention, together aggravate the precarious emotional and mental states of some detainees (Silove et al., 2000). In addition, it is almost mandatory that an asylum-seeker perform her/his original exposure to trauma in order to substantiate her/his claim for asylum (Cabot, 2013; Giordano, 2014). Critical scholars underscore what is "the singular and comparatively privileged place of trauma in immigration law" (Kenworthy, 2012:124), and how biomedical practitioners are implicated in this process: "a diagnosis carries much more weight than a narrative" (Fassin and Rechtman, 2009:265). When re-traumatized in detention, asylum seekers may actually fail to provide appropriate answers in the screening process for asylum, thereby jeopardizing their chances for legal entry to the United States.[4]

Mental health issues may also arise when detention centers isolate family members from one another. Some family members of undocumented status are unable to visit detainees because centers require formal identification of all visitors. The Northwest Detention Center in Tacoma forbids physical contact between detainees and visitors and enforces this rule through the use of plexiglass partitions in visitation rooms. Many mothers have shared with me how this is particularly disheartening for children who desire to express physical affection with a parent or other close relative who is in detention. Moreover, detention centers often segregate detainees based on age, effectively tearing detained children from parents in some instances (Adams et al., 2011).

In subjecting detainees to dehumanizing treatment, detention centers are part and parcel of a system that naturalizes and normalizes the social suffering of immigrants in the United States and reproduces the stigmatized domain of "illegality" (De Genova and Peutz, 2010). In short, the immigrant-detention system reinforces the stigma of "illegal" immigration. Elsewhere I have argued that detention centers function as important sites of subjectivization, instilling migrants with docility toward the state through exacting what I call "affective discipline" (Carney, 2013). Affective modes of discipline relegate migrants into a state of self-imposed exile and coax them to accept the conditions of their "abjectivity" (Gonzales and Chavez, 2012; Willen, 2007), of their identification as "nobodies" (Green, 2011), and of their corporeal suffering as "natural and deserved" (Quesada, Hart, and Bourgois, 2011:342). The immigrant-detention system thus exacerbates depressive and anxious symptoms among individuals both inside and outside the physical confines of detention centers, conditioning immigrant communities to regard mental distress as something that one deserves (Carney, 2013). In this way, the stigmatizing structural forces of immigration detention produce biological implications for mental health and distress. Moreover, as I will discuss in the next section, the stigma-induced risks for mental health conditions including depression and anxiety deleteriously interact, at a biological level, with malnutrition produced by the conditions of immigration detention, exacerbating health problems and detainees' suffering both during detention and after.

MALNUTRITION

Inside: While pregnant, Pilar migrated with her brother and a smuggler from Guatemala through Mexico, fleeing death threats following her eyewitness of a homicide. She left behind two children, then ages 8 and 2, with her mother. Seeking asylum in the United States, she arrived to the border entry in San Diego, where she was then immediately detained by ICE. "*Me agarró*" (they took me), she said. She remained at the detention center for four months. During this time, she was extremely underfed. She noted how detainees were frequently served contaminated foods and suffered from bouts of food poisoning: "The food, well, we spotted maggots in it." Harsh conditions at the center compounded her experience of not getting enough to eat:

> The place for sleeping was a small space on the floor. There's a piece of metal coming off the floor, it's a piece like this [*tracing a table structure with her hands*], like as if it were a table, a piece of metal and there is space above and space below. The mattress is like, a mattress like you'd use for doing exercises. It's very thin; it's a piece of sponge. It is very difficult to sleep there. Your back hurts very much. It's very uncomfortable.

Feeling sleep-deprived and suffering from chronic back pain, Pilar struggled to maintain her appetite, especially for food she feared would make her physically ill.

A significant body of research demonstrates links between depressive and anxiety disorders, and malnutrition (Alaimo, Olson, and Frongillo, 2002; Casey et al., 2004; Huddleston-Casas, Charnigo, and Simmons, 2009; Laraia et al., 2006; Polivy et al., 1994; Sindler, Wellman, and Stier, 2004). These experiences are often mutually reinforcing at both emotional and biological levels. For instance, stress may curb appetite and yield to disordered eating while malnutrition in itself can have profound effects on physiological processes in the body, including hormonal changes that can alter mood. Thus the stressful conditions both inside and outside detention centers may impinge on one's overall psychosocial wellbeing and desire to eat, thereby leading to malnutrition.

Deprivation of food and water ranks as the most commonly reported form of abuse among former detainees. The nongovernmental organization No More Deaths, which provides humanitarian aid to migrants in the desert, found in its own "Culture of Cruelty" study of short-term detention (defined as lasting two to three days) that centers denied food to 2,981 individuals and provided insufficient food to 11,384 people out of the 12,895 interviewed, including children, teenagers, and women. Furthermore, only 20 percent of those surveyed who had been held in custody for more than two days actually received a meal (Adams et al., 2011).

Migrants may already be suffering from severe hunger and dehydration when apprehended by border patrol, making the deprivation of food in detention centers a particularly cruel form of stigmatization, and exacerbating other structural risks. With increased militarization of the U.S.-Mexico border, migrants arriving from Mexico and Central America cross treacherous, life-threatening desert environments (Androff and Tavassoli, 2012; De Leon, 2012; Holmes, 2013). Dehydration and malnourishment are common during these journeys through the desert, as migrants are exposed to extreme temperatures and cannot carry adequate supplies (De Leon, 2012).

When apprehended by border agents, migrants will often have suffered without food and water for days, only then to be denied either or both while in custody (Adams et al., 2011). The "Culture of Cruelty" report found that detention center staff consistently dismissed requests for sufficient food, including requests from children and pregnant women. Former detainees I interviewed described centers as only supplying packets of crackers, or serving uncooked, frozen, or otherwise inedible food such as dry beans, cat food, or moldy or insect-filled food, and reported that centers typically ignored religious dietary restrictions. Dehumanizing treatment by center staff also frequently accompanies the provision of food: staff might discard food belonging to detainees into the trash, feed it to dogs or horses in front of detainees, and throw unpackaged food at detainees or onto the floor (Adams et al., 2011). As a result of being underfed while in custody, many former detainees cite weight loss (Patel and Jawetz, 2008). This systematic food deprivation brings with it immediate and long-term physical and mental health risks; malnutrition is a known syndemic risk factor, as it interacts with a variety of infectious (Ostrach and Singer, 2012) and non-infectious diseases such as diabetes (Mendenhall, 2012), including in concert with depression (Lerman, 2017, 2015; Mendenhall, 2012). As I argue here, in the case of immigration detention, the stigma-driven structural factor of food deprivation produces long-lasting impacts on detainees' risks for syndemic interactions between acute and chronic malnutrition, and mental health problems including anxiety and depression. These intertwined and mutually reinforcing diseases and conditions not only affect detainees while they are in ICE custody, but also after they are released; family members of detainees are also affected by the stigma and stress of worry and fear about and for detained family members and by the economic impact of losing household members whose income may help pay for their own food or health care, to detention.

These intertwined risks are not merely the unfortunate reality for individuals who, for economic reasons, become vulnerable to U.S. immigration policy—they are a systematic matter of government choice. Human and civil rights organizations note that outsourcing immigrant-detention to private prison companies, a cynical cost-cutting strategy by DHS, compromises any ability to enforce minimal standards, to secure detainee rights, and to intervene in cases of misconduct toward detainees. One spokesperson for the American Civil Liberties Union told the *Wall Street Journal* in 2009, "We have serious concerns about for-profit prison companies because they are notorious for cutting essential costs that need to be provided to maintain a safe and constitutional environment for prisoners" (Counterpunch, 2009). DHS has drafted a list of forty-one Performance-Based National Detention Standards,[5] a list that includes an exhaustive 26-page document for food services alone. Currently, however, there are no procedures in place for enforcing these standards. A report to the United Nations Special Rapporteur on Human Rights of Migrants notes that while the standards issued by ICE are "theoretically mandatory for all . . . [they] are merely guidelines" (Patel and Jawetz, 2008:202). In other words, none of the standards issued by ICE are legally binding or closely monitored.

The array of food-related abuses reported by former detainees contrasts significantly with the food service standards outlined by DHS. The 26-page document on food service, comprising section 4.1 under the category of "care" in the Performance-Based National Detention Standards, begins with emphasizing provision of "a nutritionally balanced diet that is prepared and presented in a sanitary and hygienic food service operation" (ICE, 2011:203). The list of standards includes a directive for feeding detainees three meals per day, two of which should be hot. The document also provides details for meals (in terms of time allotment and dining spaces), food preparation, menu planning, security, detainee workers (who may participate in preparing and serving meals), safety and sanitation, and food storage and receiving. It further states that centers will recognize nutritional needs of detainees based on age, activity, physical condition, gender, religious preference, and medical considerations, and that those planning menu cycles "shall accommodate the ethnic and religious diversity of the facility's detainee population" (2011:203). Detention centers are also to arrange for quarterly monitoring of menus by qualified nutritionists or dieticians. Importantly, item number 13 under "expected outcomes" states that "food should never be used for reward or punishment" (2011:204). These guidelines stand in stark contrast to the accounts shared with me by participants in my research, to news accounts of spontaneous hunger strikes breaking out in detention centers all over the U.S. described below, and to earlier research cited elsewhere in this chapter.

This long list of grievances citing malnutrition while in detention does not foreclose moments of protest and resistance by detainees. Recent hunger strikes, for instance, by immigrant detainees underscore the multiple forms of embodied resistance that have become increasingly widespread (Carney, 2014). In March 2014, I attended a rally in support of the 1,200 or so detainees at the Northwest Detention Center who had initiated a hunger strike four days before. Hunger strikers had issued a handwritten list of demands—

including better food, better treatment and medical care—to the private prison company overseeing site operations. Within the first few days of the strike, however, the number of *huelgistas de hambre* (hunger strikers) had dramatically declined; guards were rumored to have intimidated strikers and threatened them with force-feeding. From 2014 to 2015 there were an additional five recorded hunger strikes at detention centers in Texas, Arizona, and Georgia. It is no wonder, then, that detainees and their family members experience bidirectional syndemic suffering related to malnutrition and anxiety, and malnutrition and depression. As shown in Figure 5.2, below, worrying about not having food, and being too hungry to effectively manage anxiety and sadness, affects the stigmatized, detained, and/or socially isolated body at multiple interacting physical, biochemical, and psychological levels.

Instances of food-related abuse inside detention centers are compounded by the already stressful experience of food insecurity plaguing many immigrant communities in the United States. Food insecurity affects immigrant populations disproportionately as a condition of economic poverty and political marginalization (Carney, 2012; 2013; 2014; 2015), and food insecurity is

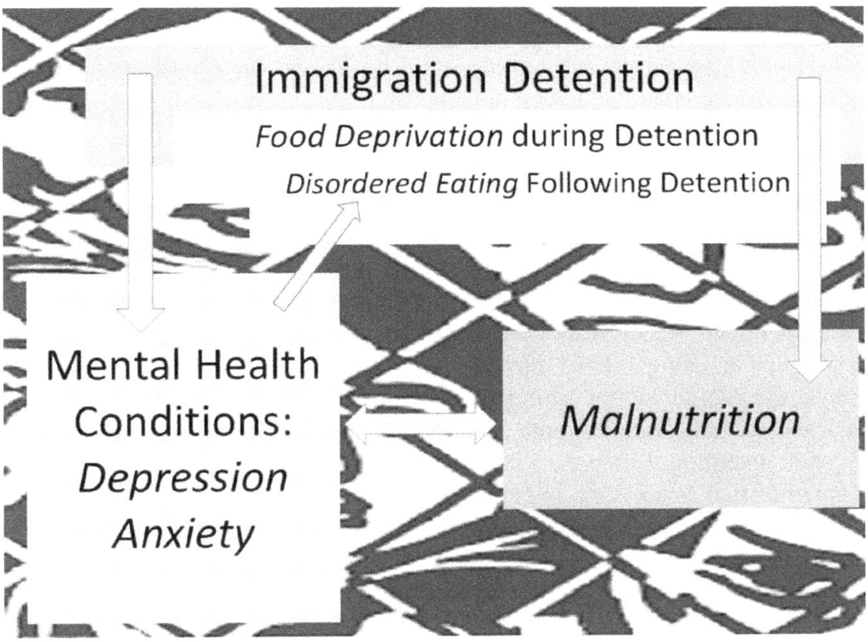

Figure 5.2. Multidirectional interactions between immigration detention, mental health conditions, and food deprivation, resulting in malnutrition and disordered eating.

strongly correlated with depression. Immigrant populations are also susceptible to unhealthy dietary habits when facing heightened levels of fear, anxiety, and depression (Carney, 2014; 2015). Yet immigration stigma, fears about immigration enforcement, and stigmas around welfare prevent many immigrants from seeking government forms of food assistance for which they are eligible. Together these conditions result in avoidance of programs that could help to mitigate the experience of food insecurity and different forms of malnutrition, which may interact syndemically with corresponding stigma-induced risks for mental health conditions including depression and anxiety. The same structural risk factors that increase risks for stigma syndemics inside detention centers may also increase physical and mental suffering for former detainees, and family members of detainees, outside of detention, even when programs exist to mitigate the contributing factor of malnutrition.

CONCLUSION

In this chapter I explored how the stigmas around immigration drive forms of mental distress that produce syndemic interactions malnutrition and contribute to marginalized health status of detained immigrants and immigrant communities in general, to render this population even more vulnerable to physical and psychosocial suffering. The stigma of "illegality" surrounds the treatment of immigrants as an illegitimate population who are rendered undeserving of various rights and entitlements, including health care and adequate nutrition, and perversely deserving of inhumane treatment in the context of detention. The dual stigmas of detention and mental distress silence discussion of much of the psychosocial suffering in immigrant communities that follows experiences of exclusion through immigration policies predicated on stigmatization of immigrants. Malnutrition results from food-related abuses committed against detainees while in detention centers, and interacts syndemically with mental health conditions including depression and anxiety to compound existing mental distress or create risks for mental illness and future disordered eating. In mapping stigma and the spectrum of suffering that afflicts Latino immigrants in the United States, particularly around immigrant detention, I propose a new stigma-driven malnutrition-mental health syndemic that is no way natural but rather produced and perpetuated by policy-driven social stigma and structural profit-making incentives. This syndemic is likely not unique to immigration detention, but is worthy of further research also in other settings of incarceration and exclusion.

Immigrants have long provided a source of cheap labor to the United States, but it is only recently that detaining and stigmatizing immigrants has also translated to direct profits for private interests. As zones of confinement, detention centers represent one of the most egregious contemporary examples of primitive accumulation, or more precisely the accumulation of capital through the rampant exploitation and subjugation of migrant bodies. Recent media coverage even highlights instances of indentured servitude within detention centers, and notes, ironically, how the private prison system is now one of the largest employers of undocumented immigrants in the United States (NPR, 2015).

Privatization of the immigrant detention system presents some major concerns especially for the preservation of basic human rights, and in light of the widespread public health implications of this newly identified syndemic which poses grave health threats to the large and growing immigrant population in our country. The myriad instances of neglect characterizing immigrant detention in the United States, often life-threatening and occasionally resulting in death, certainly represent human rights violations. Ending this wrongdoing should be at the forefront of the United States' attempts at immigration reform, yet so few are actually aware that this system exists or that they are even implicated in its perpetuation vis-à-vis financing through tax dollars. My university students, for instance, are always extremely disturbed and surprised when they learn about the details of the ICE detention system for the first time. This sentiment even holds true among students who perhaps have been persuaded by a conservative political agenda that touts unauthorized immigrants as a morally inferior group that 'deserves' harsh penalties for 'illegally' entering the country. I have yet to meet anyone who, when provided with all the information, feels this system is at all just. A syndemic perspective on the health implications of stigma-driven syndemics of the immigration detention system offers yet another lens through which to examine and critique this unfair and unjust system that threatens the physical and mental health of those caught up in it.

NOTES

1. My use of "formal" in this context refers to the official recognition of immigrants granted by the U.S. government. Examples include temporary visas, residency, and citizenship.
2. Removals averaged 20,000 annually from 1900 to 1990, but began escalating in the 1990s. In 1996, there were 22 times as many returns as removals, but in 2011 the United States removed more people than it returned (Golash-Boza and Hondagneu-Sotelo, 2013). By 2012, the number of removals had increased to 409,849 (Golash-Boza and Hondagneu-Sotelo, 2013).
3. I have replaced study participants' actual names throughout this chapter with pseudonyms to protect their identities.
4. The multiple vulnerabilities characterizing the experiences of detainees and their families pose challenges for documenting human rights abuses in detention centers. These circumstances also pose methodological challenges for those conducting fieldwork. For reasons related to concerns about re-traumatization, it is not always possible to inquire into experiences of detention in an interview context. Thus, accounts of this experience are often filtered through secondary sources such as attorneys or social workers who have helped hundreds of current and former detainees through the legal system in obtaining formal status. Social scientists must continue to privilege this sort of data since obtaining it directly may result in re-traumatization.

5. For the full list of Performance-Based National Detention Standards, visit http://www.ice.gov/detention-standards/2011/.

REFERENCES

Adams, M., et al. Culture of Cruelty: Abuse and Impunity in Short-Term U.S. Border Patrol Custody. No More Deaths, 2011.

Alaimo, K., C. M. Olson, and E. A. Frongillo. "Family food insufficiency, but not low family income, is positively associated with dysthymia and suicide symptoms in adolescents." *Journal of Nutrition* 132(4) (2002):719–725.

Androff, D. K., and K. Y. Tavassoli. "Deaths in the Desert: The Human Rights Crisis on the U.S.-Mexico Border." *Social Work* 57(2)(2012):165–173.

Biehl, J. *Vita: Life in a Zone of Social Abandonment*. Berkeley: University of California Press, 2005.

Bourdieu, P. "Gender and Symbolic Violence." In *Violence in War and Peace: An Anthology*. N. Scheper-Hughes and P. Bourgois, eds. 339–42. Malden, MA: Blackwell, 2004.

Cabot, H. "The social aesthetics of eligibility: NGO aid and indeterminacy in the Greek asylum process." *American Ethnologist* 40(3)(2013):452–466.

Carney, M.A. *The Unending Hunger: Tracing Women and Food Insecurity Across Borders*. Berkeley and Los Angeles: University of California Press, 2015.

———. "Eating and Feeding at the Margins of the State: Barriers to Healthcare for Undocumented Migrant Women and the 'Clinical' Aspects of Food Assistance." *Medical Anthropology Quarterly* 29(2)(2015):196–215.

———. "The Biopolitics of 'Food Insecurity': Towards a Critical Political Ecology of the Body in Studies of Women's Transnational Migration." *Journal of Political Ecology* 21(2014):1–18.

———. Carney, M.A. "Bodies on the Line: Fighting Inhuman Treatment with Hunger in Immigrant Detention." *Access Denied: A Conversation on Unauthorized Im/migration and Health*, 2014. Accessed October 18, 2016: http://accessdeniedblog.wordpress.com/2014/05/04/bodies-on-the-line-fighting-inhumane-treatment-with-hunger-in-immigrant-detention-megan-carney/.

——— "Border Meals: Detention Center Feeding Practices, Migrant Subjectivities, and Questions on Trauma." *Gastronomica* 13(4)(2013):32–46.

———. "Compounding crises of economic recession and food insecurity: a comparative study of three low-income communities in Santa Barbara County." *Agriculture and Human Values* 29(2)(2012):185–201.

Casey, P., et al. "Maternal depression, changing public assistance, food security, and child health status." *Pediatrics* 113(2)(2004):298–304.

Castaneda, H. "'Over-Foreignization' or 'Unused Potential'? A critical review of migrant health in Germany and responses toward unauthorized migration." *Social Science & Medicine* 74(6)(2012):830–838.

Chavez, L. R. "Undocumented immigrants and their use of medical services in Orange County, California." *Social Science & Medicine* 74(6)(2012):887–893.

———. *The Latino Threat: Constructing Immigrants, Citizens, and the Nation*. Stanford: Stanford University Press, 2008.

Chen, J., and A. Vargas-Bustamante. "Estimating the Effects of Immigration Status on Mental Health Care Utilizations in the United States." *Journal of Immigrant and Minority Health* 13(4)(2011):671–680.

City of Seattle. "Office of Immigrant and Refugee Affairs." Accessed on July 28, 2015: http://www.seattle.gov/office-of-immigrant-and-refugee-affairs/2010-census.

Coleman, M., and A. Kocher. "Detention, deportation, devolution and immigrant incapacitation in the US, post 9/11." *Geographical Journal* 177(2011):228–237.

Counterpunch. "Imprisoning Immigrants For Profit." Accessed December 14, 2012: http://www.counterpunch.org/2009/03/13/imprisoning-immigrants-for-profit/.

Coutin, S. B. "Confined within: National territories as zones of confinement." *Political Geography* 29(4)(2010):200–208.
———. *Nations of emigrants: Shifting boundaries of citizenship in El Salvador and the United States*. Ithaca: Cornell University Press, 2007
Das Gupta, M. "'Don't Deport Our Daddies': Gendering State Deportation Practices and Immigrant Organizing." *Gender & Society* 28(1)(2013):83–109.
De Genova, N. "Migrant 'Illegality' and Deportability in Everyday Life." *Annual Review of Anthropology* 31(2013):419–47.
De Genova, N., and N. Peutz. *The Deportation Regime: Sovereignty, Space, and the Freedom of Movement*. Durham: Duke University Press, 2010.
De León, J. "'Better to Be Hot than Caught': Excavating the Conflicting Roles of Migrant Material Culture." *American Anthropologist* 114(3)(2012):477–495.
Detention Watch Network. "About the U.S. Detention and Deportation System." Accessed July 31, 2015: http://www.detentionwatchnetwork.org/resources.
———. "End the Immigrant Detention Bed Quota." Accessed July 31, 2015: http://www.detentionwatchnetwork.org/EndTheQuotaNarrative.
DHS Yearbook of Immigration Statistics. "2012 Yearbook of Immigration Statistics." Accessed July 31, 2015: http://www.dhs.gov/yearbook-immigration-statistics.
Fassin, D. "Policing Borders, Producing Boundaries. The Governmentality of Immigration in Dark Times." *Annual Review of Anthropology*, 40 (2011):213–226.
Fassin, D., and R. Rechtman. *The Empire of Trauma: An Inquiry into the Condition of Victimhood*. Princeton: Princeton University Press, 2009.
Giordano, C. *Migrants in Translation: Caring and the Logics of Difference in Contemporary Italy*. Berkeley and Los Angeles: University of California Press, 2014.
Gleeson, S. "Labor Rights for All? The Role of Undocumented Immigrant Status for Worker Claims-Making." *Law & Social Inquiry* 35(3)(2010):561–602.
Golash-Boza, T., and P. Hondagneu-Sotelo. "Latino immigrant men and the deportation crisis: A gendered racial removal program." *Latino Studies* 11(3)(2013):271–292.
Gonzales, R.G., C. Suarez-Orozco, and M.C. Dedios-Sanguineti. "No Place to Belong: Contextualizing Concepts of Mental Health Among Undocumented Immigrant Youth in the United States." *American Behavioral Scientist* 57(8)(2013):1174–1199.
Gonzales, R.G., and L.R. Chavez. "'Awakening to a Nightmare': Abjectivity and Illegality in the Lives of Undocumented 1.5-Generation Latino Immigrants in the United States." *Current Anthropology* 53(3)(2012):255–281.
Green, L. "The Nobodies: Neoliberalism, Violence, and Migration." *Medical Anthropology* 30(4)(2011):366–385.
Hacker, K., et al. "The impact of Immigration and Customs Enforcement on immigrant health: Perceptions of immigrants in Everett, Massachusetts, USA." *Social Science & Medicine* 73(4)(2011):586–594.
Holmes, S.M. "'Is it worth risking your life?': Ethnography, risk and death on the U.S.-Mexico border." *Social Science & Medicine* 99(2013):153–161.
———. "The clinical gaze in the practice of migrant health: Mexican migrants in the United States." *Social Science & Medicine* 74(6)(2012):873–881.
Horton, S., and J. C. Barker. "Stigmatized Biologies: Examining the Cumulative Effects of Oral Health Disparities for Mexican American Farmworker Children." *Medical Anthropology Quarterly* 24(2)(2010):199–219.
Huddleston-Casas, C., R. Charnigo, and L. A. Simmons. "Food insecurity and maternal depression in rural, low-income families: a longitudinal investigation." *Public Health Nutrition* 12(8)(2009):1133–1140.
Immigration and Customs Enforcement. *Operations Manual Ice Performance-Based National Detention Standards*. Washington, DC: Department of Homeland Security, 2011.
Jenkins, J., and E.A. Carpenter-Song. "Stigma Despite Recovery: Strategies for Living in the Aftermath of Psychosis." *Medical Anthropology Quarterly* 22(4)(2008):381–409.
Kenworthy, N.J. "Asylum's Asylum: Undocumented Immigrants, Belonging, and the Space of Exception at a State Psychiatric Center." *Human Organization* 71(2)(2012):123–134.

Laraia, B.A., et al. "Psychosocial factors and socioeconomic indicators are associated with household food insecurity among pregnant women." *Journal of Nutrition* 136(1)(2012):177–182.

Larchanche, S. "Intangible obstacles: Health implications of stigmatization, structural violence, and fear among undocumented immigrants in France." *Social Science & Medicine* 74(6)(2012):858–863.

Lerman, S. "Disordered Minds and Disordered Bodies: Stigma, Depression, and Obesity Syndemic in Puerto Rico." In *Foundations of Biosocial Health: Stigma and Illness Interactions*. S. Lerman, B. Ostrach, and M. Singer, eds., 47–82. Lanham, MD: Lexington, 2017.

———. *"Un Pueblo Tan Dulce": Diabetes, Depression, and Obesity Syndemics in Puerto Rico*. Storrs: University of Connecticut, 2015. Accessed October 18, 2016: http://digitalcommons.uconn.edu/cgi/viewcontent.cgi?article=1812&context=gs_theses.

Marchevsky, A. and B. Baker. "Why Has President Obama Deported More Immigrants Than Any Other President in US History?" *The Nation*, 2014. Accessed November 11, 2015: http://www.thenation.com/article/why-has-president-obama-deported-more-immigrants-any-president-us-history/.

Mendenhall, E. *Syndemic suffering: Social distress, depression, and diabetes among Mexican immigrant women* (Vol. 4). Left Coast Press, 2012.

Menjívar, C. "Central American immigrant workers and legal violence in Phoenix, Arizona." *Latino Studies* 11(2)(2013):228–252.

Migration Policy Institute. "Post-9/11 Policies Dramatically Alter the U.S. Immigration Landscape." Accessed October 21, 2015: http://www.migrationpolicy.org/article/post-911-policies-dramatically-alter-us-immigration-landscape.

Migration Policy Institute. "State Immigration Data Profiles." Accessed July 31, 2015: http://www.migrationpolicy.org/programs/data-hub/state-immigration-data-profiles.

NPR. "At Low Pay, Government Hires Immigrants Held at Detention Centers." Accessed July 31, 2015: http://www.npr.org/2015/07/23/425511981/at-low-pay-government-hires-immigrants-held-at-detention-centers.

Ostrach, B., and Singer, M. "Syndemics Of War: Malnutrition-Infectious Disease Interactions And The Unintended Health Consequences Of Intentional War Policies." *Annals of Anthropological Practice*, 36(2)(2012), 257–273.

Patel, S., and T. Jawetz. Conditions of Confinement in Immigration Detention Facilities. American Civil Liberties Union, 2008.

Pew Hispanic Center. "Unauthorized Immigrant Population, By State, 2012." Accessed July 28, 2015: http://www.pewhispanic.org/interactives/unauthorized-immigrants-2012/.

Plascencia, L. *Disenchanting Citizenship: Mexican Migrants and the Boundaries of Belonging*. New Brunswick: Rutgers University Press, 2012.

Polivy, J., et al. "Food Restriction and Binge Eating: A Study of Former Prisoners of War." *Journal of Abnormal Psychology* 103(2)(1994):409–411.

Quesada, J., L.K. Hart, and P. Bourgois. "Structural Vulnerability and Health: Latino Migrant Laborers in the United States." *Medical Anthropology* 30(4)(2011):339–362.

Rivera, C. "The Brown Threat: Post-9/11 conflations of Latina/os and Middle Eastern Muslims in the US American imagination." *Latino Studies* 12(1)(2014):44–64.

Silove, D., Z. Steel, and C. Watters. "Policies of deterrence and the mental health of asylum seekers." *Jama-Journal of the American Medical Association* 284(5)(2000):604–611.

Salas, L.M., C. Ayon, and M. Gurrola. "Estamos Traumados: The Effect of Anti-Immigrant Sentiment and Policies on the Mental Health of Mexican Immigrant Families." *Journal of Community Psychology* 41(8)(2013):1005–1020.

Sargent, C., and S. Larchanche. "Transnational Migration and Global Health: The Production and Management of Risk, Illness, and Access to Care." *Annual Review of Anthropology*, 40(2011):345–361.

Sindler, A.J., N.S. Wellman, and O.R. Stier. "Holocaust Survivors Report Long-Term Effects on Attitudes toward Food." *Journal of Nutrition, Education and Behavior* 36(2004):189–196.

Talavera, T., G.G. Núñez-Mchiri, and J. Heyman. "Deportation in the U.S.-Mexico Borderlands: Anticipation, Experience, and Memory." In *The Deportation Regime: Sovereignty,*

Space, and the Freedom of Movement. N. De Genova and N. Peutz, eds., 166–195. Durham and London: Duke University Press, 2010.
Toomey, R.B., et al. "The Impact of Arizona's S.B. 1070 Immigration Law on Utilization of Health Care and Public Assistance among Mexican-Origin Teen Mothers and Their Mother Figures." *American Journal of Public Health* (2013).
US Census Bureau. "American Community Survey, Seattle, Washington." Accessed July, 31, 2015: http://quickfacts.census.gov/qfd/states/53/5363000.html.
Vélez-Ibáñez, C.G. *Border Visions: Mexican Cultures of the Southwest United States*. Tucson: University of Arizona Press, 1996.
Viruell-Fuentes, E. A., P. Y. Miranda, and S. Abdulrahim. "More than culture: Structural racism, intersectionality theory, and immigrant health." *Social Science & Medicine* 75(12)(2012):2099–2106.
Willen, S. S. Migration, "illegality," and health: Mapping embodied vulnerability and debating health-related deservingness Special Issue Introduction." *Social Science & Medicine* 74(6)(2012):805–811.
———. "Toward a Critical Phenomenology of 'Illegality': State Power, Criminalization, and Abjectivity Among Undocumented Migrant Workers in Tel Aviv, Israel." *International Migration* 45(3)(2007):8–38.
Willen, S. S., J. Mulligan, and H. Castaneda. "Take a Stand Commentary: How Can Medical Anthropologists Contribute to Contemporary Conversations on 'Illegal' Im/migration and Health?" *Medical Anthropology Quarterly* 25(3)(2011):331–356.
Zambrana, R.E., C. Dorrington, and D. Hayes-Bautista. "Family and Child Health: A Neglected Vision." In *Understanding Latino Families: Scholarship, Policy and Practice*. R. Zambrana, ed. Thousand Oaks: Sage Publications, 1995.
Zlolniski, C. *Janitors, Street Vendors, and Activists: The Lives of Mexican Immigrants in Silicon Valley*. Berkeley: University of California Press, 2006.

Chapter Six

Stigma Syndemic among People with Intellectual Disability Who Have Been Incarcerated

Fernanda Claudio, Kate van Dooren, Jesse T. Young, and Nick Lennox

"JOHN" (PSEUDONYM) IN HIS WORDS: FRAGMENTS OF A LIFE RETOLD

Prison

Now I got been in prison since I was a ju-bee [juvenile detention] . . . then they decided yeah we'll get John out. John look like he's a capable person to take on his self. To step out. So that one big goal. You know? . . . In a prisons mate, you got nowhere to go. Nowhere to hide. Nowhere to run. You stuck. You stuck in a cell like this *(referring to small interview room). You bed. Toilet. Sink. That's it. That's you. That's all you got.

And when they lock the door on you. Now if you in there with them, right. You in there inside with them . . . a couple of the boys . . . right . . . and you in there with them. They will search you. They come lock you. They come turn the key. Only so much. (He gestures to demonstrate with the interview room door). I can't get out. It's locked.

I was planning to leave here last year [area where he lives]. But, naaahhh. I couldn't do it. I thought, I do it now I'll upset everyone here. Cause I been around they know I gonna sooner or later be for myself. I gotta be myself. My dad say, "you wanna be yourself. You wanna be you." Right. I gotta be me. You gotta be you. Right. Follow? Same conversation. It comes out alright.

Cause they come out and sooner or later that fuck up. I am saying these are my workers. They help me get out of jail. From ju-bee to adult, from adult to ju-bee, from ju-bee to adult. What's that boy gonna do? That boy's gonna turn

> around and go back to jail. Unless someone gonna be there, with him, and talk to him to not. Right. You understand where I'm coming from?

Family

> Oh my family. Don't really see them. But sometime I should be seeing them. Only my old man anyways.
>
> Yeah. Well my old man is alcoholic. Doesn't drink much but I don't know if he drinks much. I don't know if he drinks today. If it, he does drinking. But I gotta go down and see him sometime. But he's in a wheelchair too see. Bit tricky. Hard for the old boy to go shopping cause his electric chair broken. Twit broke down.

Health

> My health was fuckin poo going down. They get me go down and see doctors. I see doctors over at . . . [indigenous health service].

The Future

> And now yeah, now I step up a bit. And I stopped myself. Stepped back a bit. But not too far. Always go forward. And if I push myself too forward I have a good year. This is where I am. So is good. (John, Perth, Western Australia, 2015)

Vulnerabilities exist in many forms, but some individuals experience assemblages of problems that produce, exacerbate, and maintain chronic and seemingly insurmountable disadvantages. One such group is incarcerated people (aka prisoners) with intellectual disability (ID) like John whose life, prison, and transition experiences illustrate a pervasive incongruence with societal expectations and norms. Definitions of ID vary (Cockram 2005; World Health Organization 2012), but a useful approach states that ID:

> Encompasses any set of conditions, resulting from genetic, neurological, nutritional, social, traumatic or other factors occurring prior to birth, at birth, or during childhood up to the age of brain maturity, that affect intellectual development. (WHO, 2000)

ID is a condition characterized by deficits in intellectual functioning and adaptive behavior related to common social and practical skills (American Association on Intellectual and Developmental Disabilities, 2016). However, the influence of ID is not determined in isolation, it synergistically interacts with biological, social, cultural, and political gradients to intensify the burden experienced by individuals who are affected by this characteristic. Specifically, ID coupled with chronic physical and mental health conditions, poor family and community supports, inappropriate or absent services, and Indigeneity contribute to a specific stigma syndemic in Australia. Like John, our informants experience challenges in understanding and navigating social environments. John started life on the biological backfoot, was born into a poor family, had little schooling and is Indigenous. He broke the law, went to prison, received a semblance of care and routine, and was released into a world where he cannot cope by himself. His father cannot practically help his son beyond offering moral support, because of alcohol dependence and physical disability. John was incarcerated because of a combination of factors that preclude his ability to cope and function in a society devoid of sufficiently supportive families, communities, and social and health systems.

Time spent in prison can become a life-course event in lives fraught with difficulties, including for individuals with ID. Gauging the prevalence of ID within prison populations is problematic because of methodological variation across research (Simpson 2014). In a random sample of 140 British prisoners, Hayes et al. (2007) found 30.7 percent were intellectually disabled. In a systematic review comprising 11,969 prisoners, Fazel et al. (2008) found methodological variation across studies precluded calculation of ID prevalence. In Australia, individuals with ID are estimated to range from 3 percent to approximately 9–10 percent of the prison population (Australian Institute of Health and Welfare, 2008) but it is probable that this is an underestimate. In Australian law, cognitive impairment and mental health impairment are merged leading to under-recording of ID (Baldry 2014). However, the New South Wales Law Reform Commission distinguishes between mental and cognitive impairment, classifying the former as temporary and the latter as permanent (Baldry 2014). In Queensland this distinction is non-existent, however cognitive impairment is gauged through IQ testing (Howard and O'Brien 2009). In Western Australia, a distinction exists between mental illness as a mood disorder and ID as a learning deficit (Government of Western Australia ND). Varying measurement practices result in under-ascertainment of ID in prison populations; data on prisoners with ID in Queensland was last gathered in 2002 when 10 percent were found to have intellectual impairment and 29 percent to have borderline impairment (Office of the Public Advocate 2014). Measurement is imprecise; however, a considerable proportion of individuals involved in the criminal justice system experience a level of ID that predicts poor health, social, and justice outcomes upon reintegration to the community. Given that the global prison population is estimated above 10.2 million individuals (Walmsley 2013), gauging and understanding ID is crucial to planning appropriate screening and care, and for equity within judicial systems.

Policing and sentencing impact this group differently. Baldry et al. (2012) found the average age of contact with police to be 16.5 years, but those with complex health and social needs and drug use had earlier contact as victims and/or perpetrators. Police were found to be disrespectful in a study of perpetrators with ID in which 25 percent were Indigenous (Simpson, 2014). With regard to sentencing, as ID-specific supports vary by state, sentencing practices take into account available services. People with ID arrested for the first time were more likely to receive a prison sentence compared to a fine or penalties other than incarceration (Cockram, 2005). The original decision by police to lay charges was the primary predictor of receiving a sentence for people with ID, not their non-ID counterparts (Cockram 2005). Consequently, people with ID are over-represented in the court system (Hayes 1997; Vanny 2009)

In Australia, individuals with ID are disproportionately represented within prison populations and their life trajectories are replete with disadvantage. Social determinants approaches do not fully account for relationships between the various aspects of their disadvantage. Syndemic theory provides a framework to understand this dynamic through its acknowledgment of the interactions between biology, social predicament, and political economy (Singer 2014). We argue that ID syndemics among incarcerated Australians comprise a "quadripartite interaction" of factors that augment burdens of affliction: 1) *biological*: unfavorable inter-relationships among ID, obesity, dental health, hepatitis C, mental illness, substance abuse, and unsafe sex (Bhandari et al. 2014) result in chronic poor health; 2) *social/individual*: difficult childhoods, poor schooling and family supports, homelessness, and a double burden of stigma resulting from ID and incarceration; 3) *socio-political*: inadequately designed social/health services and perceptions of inability of prisoners with ID to fend for themselves, resulting in low expectations of existing interventions and low political will to design improvements; and 4) *racial/ethnic factors*: Indigenous Australians with ID are over-represented in prison experiencing additional stigmatization, often exacerbating extant barriers to healthcare access, systemically eroding the capacity for self-care and further marginalizing their social/political visibility.

The Diagnostic and Statistical Manual, version 5 (DSM-V) of the American Psychiatric Association (APA) and International Classification of Diseases (ICD) of the World Health Organization (WHO) do not account for the biological, socio-cultural and political positioning of this population because their conditions are not discrete entities but, instead, complex predicaments that elude medical understanding, resulting in disconnected, disparate systems of redress. Prisoners with ID encounter significant challenges to successful transition out of incarceration and are at higher risk of recidivism and poorer health/social outcomes following release compared with other prisoners. Specific challenges include the inability to actively seek out social and practical supports, disrupted families and communities, lack of government and other supports in remote areas, and poor overall social functionality and mental health issues. Further, psychological challenges related to poor functionality and stigmas include low self-esteem (Johnson 2012), which conspires to further isolate and marginalize this group.

It is clear that this population is complex and difficult to study. Baldry et al. (2011) used a life-course approach to investigate pathways into prison to overcome limitations of descriptive and single-system studies. While the study uncovered social issues associated with committing crimes, it did not provide a holistic approach. This chapter focuses on ex-prisoners with ID and highlights critical contradictions across the research-policy-practice continuum. We argue that ex-prisoners with ID reveal a syndemic constellation in the Australian population because of negative relationships between their cognitive impairment, disability and health status, and marginal socio-structural position in which stigma predominates. They are multiply stigmatized by: misunderstandings of ID in society, mis-/undiagnosed and marginalization in health systems; and the impact of incarceration and the nature of their offences. If poor or physically disabled they will be further stigmatized (Ali et al. 2015). If Indigenous, they will be incarcerated at higher rates, constituting 27 percent of the prison population, while representing only 3 percent of the Australian population (Australian Bureau of Statistics 2015). Also, they may experience further stigmatization from a lack of culturally safe and appropriate healthcare access. Therefore, socio-economic status, race, and ethnicity are important factors within this population coupling with ID and incarceration, all stigmatized states that exist in a nefarious relationship with poor health. (Baldry et al. 2015). In this syndemic, multiple bodily and social conditions associated with combinations of ID, incarceration, Indigeneity, and stigma, confound diagnosis, treatment, and care within a predominantly biomedically centered policy and practice milieu that is not philosophically and practically structured to respond to this group. We focus on prisoners with ID to examine whether Australian disability/healthcare policy, outlined in the National Disability Plan (2010–2020) (NDIS), can redress shortcomings in current policy and practice. We argue that among prisoners with ID in Australia, personal biologies, histories, and social-political containments need not be destiny. Because of its comprehensive approach, syndemic theory provides an alternate way to understand these needs within their complex subaltern biopolitical and social conditions.

SYNDEMICS

The syndemic approach was introduced to understand complex bodily states, such as the diabetes-poverty nexus, identified in the late twentieth century when it became clear that scientific reductionism and mind-body dualism could not explain the biosocial interconnections characteristic of these conditions (Singer 2009). Researchers using a syndemics perspective sought to overcome the fallacy of the single cause, an approach that precluded seeking multi-causal understanding of physical conditions that interact in conditions of social inequality. As Singer explained:

> Syndemics are defined as the aggregation of two or more diseases in a population in which there is some level of deleterious biological interaction that exacerbates the negative health effects of any or all of the diseases. (2014:1)

Further, Singer (2014) argued that syndemics emerge when there is poverty, stigma, structural violence, and pressures that intensify disease conditions within marginalized populations. Thus, syndemic theory proposes a holistic framework to apprehend and analyze complex disease conditions such as epidemics "that may be the consequence not of single disease but of several diseases acting in tandem in social context" (Singer 2014: 1). Syndemics encompasses the interactive effect of multiple diseases and biological factors, adverse interactions between diseases, multiple exposures, pre-existing immunological damage, poverty, discrimination, and disruptions caused by inadequate livelihoods.

Health policy would benefit from syndemically informed approaches that account for multiple physical and social factors involved in deleterious bodily states. A proper disentanglement of the constitutive syndemic factors is necessary to develop effective intervention strategies, as Ostrach and Singer (2012) have proposed for addressing increased HIV/STI risk among women. These authors established that biological risk, social and structural factors (poverty, malnutrition, coercive contraceptive health promotion) and transactional sex contributed to women's increased susceptibility to HIV/STI interactions. They identified factors associated with "synergistic pathways of interaction that increases women's biopolitical risks for HIV" (Ostrach and Singer 2012:266) to contribute to targeted and effective strategies for treatment, including multi-disease intervention tailored to the contexts that produce and harbor disease states (Ostrach and Singer 2012: 267).

Stigma is one feature of the contexts in which pervasive illness exists among marginalized groups. Stigma serves to create social and psychological boundaries around individuals with ID, contributing to poorer supports and limited medical imaginaries in terms of diagnosis and treatment. Stigma can serve as a limitation on the imagination of policy-makers and practitioners, contributing to complacency with regard to possibility of improved futures.

STIGMA

Stigma is related to discrimination, often directed at weak, vulnerable and marginalized individuals. Goffman (1963/1991) identified three types of stigma: abominations of the body; "blemishes of individual character perceived as weak will, domineering or unnatural passions, treacherous and rigid beliefs, and dishonesty, these being inferred from a known record of, for example, mental disorder, imprisonment, addiction, alcoholism, homosexuality, unemployment, suicidal attempts, and radical political behavior"; and the group stigma of race, national identity, and religion which are inherited and transmissible (Goffman 1991: 5). Prisoners with ID experience significant stigma in terms of the second and third categories: presentations associated with their condition in terms of behavior, demeanor, personal appearance, and individual history of marginalization and incarceration. Recent research from England found that older individuals with moderate ID were potentially at increased risk of becoming targets of stigma (Ali et al. 2016) and stigma was associated with increased psychological distress and reduced quality of life (Ali et al. 2015b).

While Goffman discusses possible responses to stigma by affected individuals, those with ID, including ex-prisoners, are limited by the double constraints resulting from the nature of disability and inequitable social and health system supports. So what "category of person" (Goffman 1991:4) can the individual with ID be or become? Is he or she permanently tainted, discounted and marginalized by having been incarcerated and/or by having ID, or can a future of inclusion be constructed? In Australia, the National Disability Insurance Scheme suggested the possibility of such a future, however, does it actively address the needs of this very vulnerable population?

PRISONERS WITH ID IN AUSTRALIA

In Australia, more people transition in and out of prison each year than are incarcerated at any given time (Kinner and Avery 2015; Steering Committee for the Review of Government Service Provision 2015; Baldry 2014). In a given year between 30,000 and 60,000 individuals move through prisons, the majority on remand in high-security prisons devoid of social supports. Transition out of prison is challenging for most prisoners, as evidenced by high re-incarceration, high morbidity across multiple health-related domains, and elevated mortality compared with age- and sex-matched populations (Merrall, Kariminia et al. 2010). After release, individuals often return to similar or identical situations prior to incarceration, including risky behaviors (Hammett, Roberts et al. 2001; Baldry and Borzycki 2003; Kinner 2006). Although little is known about the post-release conditions of individuals with ID, Australian evidence suggests homelessness, unemployment, and social isolation are prevalent prior to incarceration (Dias et al. 2013; Dias et al. 2014). Substance misuse both prior to and during incarceration are common (Hassiotis, Gazizova et al. 2011; Bhandari, van Dooren et al. 2014) with increased use of cannabis and alcohol (Hassiotis, Gazizova et al. 2011), injecting drug use, and sharing needles in prison (Bhandari et al. 2014) compared to their counterparts without ID. In personal communication, one Queensland doctor who attends to ex-prisoners reported that methamphetamine use, commonly referred to as "ice" occurs amongst her patients, exacerbates chronic health conditions, and can complicate use of health services.

The transitional period provides critical opportunities to improve circumstances responsive to change: procuring accommodation and accessing government payments, employment, support services, and continuity of healthcare (Seal, Eldrige et al. 2007; Kouyoumdjian, Wiwcharuk, Green 2015). Despite evidence suggesting that quality of transition determines success of post-incarceration integration into society, in Australia, transitional planning can be inadequate, particularly for individuals who have served shorter sentences (most of Australia's prison intake is on remand) (Baldry and Borzycki 2003). Failed transition is most evidenced in post-release mortality—especially with regard to preventable causes such as drug-related deaths and suicides (Merrall, Kariminia et al. 2010). Individuals who served sentences of less than one year are at greatest risk of post-release mortality, possibly because of minimal transitional planning and a lack of support services (Graham 2003). Transition is difficult for all prisoners, however, poor understanding of the complexities of ID, and the synergistic role of stigma, exacerbates these common problems.

As of June 2014, Australian adult prison numbers were at a 10-year high with 33,791 individuals incarcerated and the national imprisonment rate 185.6 per 100,000 in the adult population (Australian Bureau of Statistics 2014). Within 10 years of release, approximately three in five people will be re-incarcerated. Rates of re-incarceration are at peak in the years immediately following release (Department of Corrective Services 2014). Racial inequality predominates; younger Indigenous men are more likely to be re-incarcerated, with particularly high recidivism rates observed in northern Queensland and the Northern Territory (Australian Bureau of Statistics 2010). Ex-prisoners with ID have a significantly higher rate of re-arrest and shorter time to re-arrest compared with other ex-prisoners due to their younger age, greater unemployment and/or increased surveillance by the criminal justice system (Cockram 2005; Cockram 2005b). Kilmecki et al. (1994) estimated a 34.6 percent recidivism rate among 75 ex-prisoners with ID in Melbourne suggesting that this figure is likely an underestimate. Nationally in 2014, recidivism for the general prison population was 40.3 percent within two years of release (Steering Committee for the Review of Government Service Provision 2014).

Unemployment, substance misuse, and psychiatric history were listed as important antecedents of recidivism (Klimecki, Jenkinson et al. 1994). In 2009, the UK Prison Reform Trust estimated 61 percent of adults with ID were reconvicted within one year of their release from prison, with poor housing and unemployment important predictors (Louks 2006). In the United States, 84.1 percent of ex-prisoners age <24 at release are re-arrested within 5 years (Durose et al. 2014). Prisoners may lose their homes and family contacts, and be introduced to substance use during incarceration (Kinner 2006; Iorizzo 2012).

Despite the multiple and complex needs of ex-prisoners with ID, the 1996 NSW Law Reform Commission noted paucity of appropriate services and supports (see NSW Ombudsman 2008). Article 9 of the *Convention on the Rights of People with a Disability (United Nations 2006)*, ratified by the Australian Government in March 2008, requires the identification and elimination of barriers to accessibility to information, and promotion of access to new systems for persons with disabilities (World Health Organization 2011).

THE NATIONAL DISABILITY INSURANCE SCHEME

Formerly incarcerated people with ID have histories of disadvantage, are hindered by biology, poor functionality, and stigma. Because of these considerable difficulties, substantial resources are required to address individual needs. The creation of the NDIS, a billion dollar investment from Australian state and federal governments aims to offer flexible and holistic approaches to support individuals to participate in everyday life (National Disability Insurance Agency n.d.). The scheme offers individualized care packages in which control over expenditure is transferred from agencies to individuals (or nominated decision-makers) (National Disability Insurance Agency n.d.). It remains unclear how individuals with ID will be recognized, their representatives appointed, and resources apportioned. Further, funding will be allocated individually, rather than collectively to organizations, which raises questions about provision of social and health response in the context of shortfalls in funding for organizations. However, individualization of approach may, ironically, draw greater attention to very disadvantaged groups such as this one, who are also disproportionately Indigenous.

Eligibility for funding through the NDIS is not clearly defined for individuals in the justice system. Section 34(1) of the *National Disability Insurance Scheme Act 2013* sets out reasonable and necessary resources within the Australian justice system. For individuals transitioning out of prison, NDIS funding includes assistance in life skills and behavioral support specifically related to individual impairment (National Disability Insurance Agency 2014). Eligibility is dependent on assessments by NDIS officers and subject to approval by the Chief Executive Officer. Access requires understanding eligibility requirements, navigation of complex bureaucracies, and advocacy for each ex-prisoner with ID. Challenges that without facilitation by appropriately targeted support, likely remain unattainable.

Once the NDIS is implemented, the Queensland Government will shut its disability department; for those who become ineligible under the NDIS, this closure could have severe consequences. Community and non-government organizations will no longer receive "block" government funding and will rely on individualized NDIS funding for delivery of services (National Disability Insurance Agency n.d.). Consequently, outreach services for those who fall out of the NDIS may disappear. In these cases, reliance on individual funding to support organizations that address the collective needs of vulnerable populations is problematic and probably unsustainable. The NDIS does not present alternative models for the predicted shortfalls in funding to organizations. Additionally, the NDIS is based on federal legislation where states can choose to opt in, which means that there is no nationally coordinated implementation schedule. Queensland implementation will commence in the mid-State in 2016, the west in 2017–2018, and the Far North, southern and metropolitan areas in 2018 (National Disability Insurance Scheme 2016). Implementation in other States follows similar patterns. The rational for this style of scheduling is currently not clear.

Ex-prisoners who avoid alcohol and other drugs, secure stable and safe housing, meaningful employment, steady income, and positive social supports are less likely to reoffend and be re-incarcerated (Baldry and Borzycki 2003; Kinner 2006; Seal, Eldrige et al. 2007; Howerton, Burnett et al. 2009; Ogloff 2015). The withdrawal of support from agencies that work successfully with ex-prisoners with ID, and those who remain undiagnosed but require support, may lead to increased problems post-release, and ultimately higher rates of recidivism.

OUR SYNDEMIC STUDY

In Australia, persons with ID are underserved by health and social services, with the NDIS aiming to address these shortfalls. Proposed assistance is unclear, suggesting a critical need to produce evidence depicting the histories, challenges, and experiences of this group to best advocate for their needs within a seemingly reduced care space. While there is a substantial body of literature on prisoners in Australia, there is very little research on service use. We conducted a literature review of Australian studies on substance use interventions for prisoners with ID transitioning out of prison and found substantial knowledge gaps in this field (van Dooren et al. 2015). Correspondingly, our current study explored post-release needs of adults with ID transitioning out of prisons in Queensland and Western Australia. Specifically, we aimed to (1) understand transition experiences from the perspectives of professionals in the criminal justice, health, and disability sectors; (2) understand transition experiences from the perspectives of ex-prisoners with ID; and (3) compare experiences of professionals and individuals to identify system gaps and suggest appropriate responses to address unmet need.

STUDY PARTICIPANTS

Research in the field of ID is often difficult. Lennox et al. (2005) identified seventeen levels of "gate-keeping" by family members, carers, health workers, and support organization workers that exist around individuals with ID. Gatekeeping of individuals with ID is common in research (Ellem, Wilson et al. 2008; Ellem 2010), providing obstacles to access. Recruitment of service providers was difficult; we approached over fifty organizations to find service providers willing to participate. Recruiting participants with ID was more difficult and we designed our study to first interview service providers to build trust to recruit ex-prisoners with ID for further interviews. We conducted interviews with service providers in Western Australia (WA) and Queensland (QLD). Our questionnaire focused on the transition out of prison for people with ID to determine professionals' perceptions and experiences within the criminal justice, health, and disability systems. We recruited seventeen service providers through purposive sampling of existing networks that serve ex-prisoners with ID. We recruited six participants with ID through service providers and asked them about their life and prison experiences. We did not collect health data on specific individuals because of ethical complexities, relying on their proffered statements of their bodily states and care-seeking. Participants were recruited through non-governmental organizations that provide supports to ex-prisoners with ID. We did not collect data on specific informants with ID from support staff, as doing so would breach Australian privacy laws.

THE CONSTITUENT PARTS OF THE PROPOSED SYNDEMIC

It is clear that prisoners with ID face complicated structural, familial, personal, and social circumstances that can lead to prison. Significant gaps in the Australian literature also suggest they are an under-researched and poorly understood group for whom policy, planning, and delivery of services have been fragmented and inadequate. The issues of indigeneity, race, and ethnicity among this group, and the implications for diagnosis and care, have not been well explored within this literature. Also, the fact that these individuals suffer from disadvantages in various realms means that research within the classical academic domains (law, health, justice, social work) results in disparate sets of data that are difficult to integrate. The "quadripartite interaction" of biological, social, socio-political, and racial/ethnic factors that affect ex-prisoners such as John, require a holistic approach such as syndemic theory to integrate the various levels of disadvantage and lived experiences with health consequences reported by, and observed in this population. We propose that prisoners with ID in Australia, such as John, suffer a stigma syndemic that augments their burden of affliction and argue that holistic approaches to research are necessary to address knowledge gaps about this vulnerable group.

Health: Biologies and Minds

Individuals such as John experience combinations of disease and illness that both result from their ID and are compounded by it. Often their first hurdle is receiving a biomedical diagnosis to explain poor functionality and low cognitive ability in order to gain eligibility for a care pathway within the system. For those with prominent "challenging behavior" in the community, diagnosis often occurs prior to contact with the criminal justice system, usually in their teens, however, mild to borderline ID is difficult to diagnose and a substantial minority remain "hidden" in the criminal justice system (Soldatic et al. 2014). Prisoners with ID also typically suffer from visual impairment, hearing loss, dental disease, musco-skeletal problems, epilepsy, endocrine disorders, obesity (Beange and Lennox 1998), head injury, risky alcohol consumption, psychological disorders, and illicit drug use (Indig et al. 2011). Diabetes is predominant, particularly among the high representation of Indigenous Australians in prisons across Western Australia (Australian Institute of Health and Welfare 2013), Hepatitis C (relating to injecting drug use), problems with medication routines, and dual diagnosis (comorbid mental illness and substance use disorder). Thus, ID is related to risky behaviors, including drug use that can lead to injury and health service inequities that leave many chronic conditions untreated. Beyond risky behaviors associated with substance use, biological conditions such as diabetes co-exist in deleterious relationships with obesity in which one condition exacerbates the other. In this context, poor nutrition and poor ability to seek and follow medication regimes provide multiple exposures to causes of these conditions and serve to sustain ill health.

Mental illness is prevalent in this group and significantly interact with ID (Dias et al. 2013) leading to multiple layers of stigma within the community and in the service sector with practical consequences. One specific problem, "diagnostic overshadowing" (Jones, Howard et al. 2008), occurs when clinicians confuse ID with mental illness, precluding individuals from receiving appropriate care in the community and in prison. Diagnostic overshadowing also occurs when physical symptoms are attributed to underlying mental illness (Giddings 2013), resulting in misdiagnosis and improper care, and is a particular problem when mental illness impedes recording of thorough patient histories because of stigma affecting how patients present (as agitated or uncooperative) both within society and among doctors. Indig et al. (2011) found that overlap between ID and mental illness is problematic because misdiagnosis can result in inappropriately targeted care. Furthermore, we found that psychiatric medication regimes that affect behavior (in terms of both intended effects and side-effects) could further confound the identification of ID. Our study group, who experience multiple mental and physical health disorders and engage in risky substance misuse, began their lives in the context of social disruption, and may lack advocates and/or social supports to navigate complex health and social services in order to meet their multiple and complex needs.

Published literature on the health of "mainstream" prisoners reports that individuals with ID look physically healthier post-release from prison (Hammett, Roberts et al. 2001). Key informants observed that health improved in prison due to decreased alcohol and drug use, but often deteriorated post-release to pre-incarceration levels. In Australia, prisoners with ID often receive the "best health care of their lives" in prison because of frequent access to doctors, dentists, substance abuse programs, and other health supports. However, once they leave prison, health supports are less available due to lack of funding and barriers to access related to impaired functionality. Key informants reported that poor health was related to social exclusion and low socioeconomic status. One key informant referred to ex-prisoners with ID as "people that have sorta lived on the periphery of society" (QLD, disability organization, 2015).

ID is associated with significant limitations in two domains of adaptive functioning affecting independence in vocational, social, and personal activities. In clinical terms, ID may be further defined as severe, moderate, or mild, according to discrete IQ ranges (Schalock, Borthwick-Duffy et al. 2010). Mild ID refers to individuals who have greater functional capacity, independence, and fewer support needs. However, evidence indicates that this group still experiences significant marginalization in the community (Beange, Lennox et al. 1999; Ouellette-Kuntz 2005; Emerson 2007); substantial health inequalities in mortality and morbidity (Beange, Lennox et al. 1999; New South Wales Community Services Commission 2001; Lennox, Bain et al. 2007); and social exclusion, discrimination, and isolation (Ouellette-Kuntz 2005). Many individuals with ID have unrecognized and poorly managed disease and few receive adequate screening and health information (Lennox, Bain et al. 2007). Combinations of social disadvantage, difficulties accessing services, and communication difficulties have been well-documented (Beange, Lennox et al. 1999; Lennox, Taylor et al. 2005; Ouellette-Kuntz 2005; Emerson 2007; Lennox, Bain et al. 2007; Australian Institute of Health and Welfare, 2008). Thus, ID compounds poor physical health conditions, which are, in turn, exacerbated by individuals' inability to seek and self-administer care.

An individual with ID who has not been diagnosed is in a doubly disadvantaged position: distinct and incongruent within society and misunderstood, but lacking the supports to improve his functioning. A formal diagnosis provides the possibility of assistance within the social, healthcare, and prison systems. Absence of diagnosis was one key obstacle to care cited by service providers in the justice sector:

> If someone has a diagnosed disability and they come out of prison and get on the disability support pension rather than Newstart [allowance], I don't have access to them. So I see people with "informal" if you like, ID, but not diagnosed and certainly expected to go out and look for work. (QLD, justice organisation, 2015)

ID has biological origins from birth, and diagnosis depends on the capacity of the family to identify learning deficits, reduced functional capacity, and impaired adaptive behavior in the child, and to access an appropriately trained and qualified clinicians. Residence in remote areas of Australia, alcohol abuse, disruptions within families and communities, a lack of care and appropriate services contribute to high proportions of unidentified ID in ex-prisoners. Individuals without a formal diagnosis might be identified during incarceration, particularly by other inmates, but following release are ineligible and/or do not receive targeted support or funding, whereby by default it rests with organizations and workers to identify ID-related deficits or needs. These service providers may *have suspicions* that an individual has ID, but remain reluctant to make identifications.

> I could tell you about quite a number of clients that do have ID . . . but that's only my diagnosis. I find you don't generally get people volunteering that information. I think it might get identified by others in the system. Often you'll find that they get placed in protection. (QLD, justice organization, 2015)

The need for a formal, clinical identification is problematic within a sector that does not receive training or education specific to ID. A lack of clinical diagnosis means informal and *ad hoc* care is dependent on the service provider's experience, training, and open-mindedness toward a stigmatized group of individuals:

> I don't consider illiteracy to be an ID. But y'know some are illiterate of course, because of their school struggles and maybe never been diagnosed as having difficulties. Or any of those disabilities that we see more often now. (QLD justice organization, 2015)

Individuals who have learned to disguise their disability compound difficulties for carers and service providers, who may not have specific training in this field, and further impede access to services.

> The ID with this fellow . . . he is well practiced at disguising it. If he were sitting in the room here while you and I were chatting he could mimic appropriate responses. (WA, disability organization, 2015)

One informant described the double-edged sword of diagnosis in which care may be provided at the price of an identifiable vulnerability within a prison:

> So that stuff gets pushed into the background. You don't discuss that because, y'know, you push that away 'cause any sign of weakness or any sign of sharing that stuff is . . . not good for your physical health in prison. (QLD, justice organization, 2015)

However, another informant noted that not all prisoners with ID are vulnerable, with some having developed social survival skills prior to incarceration.

> You have some who are quite vulnerable and you have some who have come through the system, understand what it's like in prison, and this is going to sound really terrible, but may have the requisite amount of aggression that can actually mean that they survive within the system. (QLD, justice organization, 2015)

> If you have an intellectual or learning disability you don't know the laws. You don't know your rights. People with ID probably wouldn't be game enough to argue with a police officer about their rights. (QLD, disability organization, 2015)

Regardless of perception of relative advantage of diagnosis, ID entails poor social functionality and poor ability to self-manage their own needs. This manifests in low self-care and lack of access to healthcare resulting in increased chronic disease, injury, and mental illness. Stigma within society, manifested through marginalization, and systemically in support systems, and expressed through weak and *ad hoc* structures that do not address long-term health and social needs of ex-prisoners with ID, maintains a syndemic condition where interacting disease conditions compound and accelerate the aggregate health burden.

Social and Individual Factors

Like John, many prisoners with ID have histories of under-privilege, poor schooling and lack of care, social isolation, and sadness. Their lack of life skills is linked to circumstances experienced prior to incarceration. Key informants raised issues of neglect, poverty, and marginalization stemming from disrupted and unsupportive family backgrounds typified by lack of education and fundamental skills to function as adults. In the words of disability workers:

> One fella that we had . . . he did not know how to use deodorant. Did not know where to apply it. Never had had a hot shower. So he obviously had never had one inside. So that says something. . . . The basic stuff that you assume an adult would be able to do was not there. Stuff that we all take for granted that our guys had never had taught to them. (WA, disability organization, 2015)

> All the ones we work with, bar one fella, have all been brought up in horrific environments from home. So they have not had good role models and learnt skills and things like that. So going into prison and having everything given to them has not enhanced anything. (WA, disability organization, 2015)

Similar to the "mainstream" prison population, ex-prisoners with ID often come from families with entrenched histories of both disadvantage and incarceration.

> I know a lot of their history and I've met a lot of their families. So I know they have not had particularly good upbringings. And, generally the whole family is in and out of prison. So it is like a familial thing that happens. (WA, disability organization, 2015)

Service providers highlighted the need for a sophisticated understanding of the needs, abilities, and complexities of living with ID. One interviewee described teaching an individual with ID to answer the door and to safeguard his home from strangers. He described designing a picture chart to be placed beside the individual's front door, which contained photographs of individuals allowed to visit the house. Another service provider described compiling a recipe book with pictures of healthy meals for a client. One individual described building a gardening box, teaching care for chickens, and applying for permission to obtain a pet greyhound for a client who had engaged in these activities in prison because he thought continuity would ease transition into the community. Yet another interviewee described the need to recognize and address poor cognitive ability:

> When you're often breaking something down that is not necessarily very simple or basic, but it needs to be in that form for him to be able to grasp it

> because he would not grasp it in a way if he was having a conversation like you and I are having now. (WA, disability organization, 2015)

Similarly some service providers perceived that prisoners with ID did not understand social dynamics and were often identified as "different," rendering them vulnerable:

> Other prisoners will sense people's vulnerabilities and weaknesses and yeah, take advantage of that. You know, it's kind of survival of the fittest in there. If you've got an ID, you're at the top of the vulnerability ladder. (QLD, justice organization, 2015)

> I've had other men come out with ID just saying they spent their whole time in protection because they are absolutely scared. (QLD, justice organization, 2015).

Prisoners with ID were sometimes mistakenly identified with sexual offending and stigmatized:

> If they are in the protected side, it is automatically thought that by the mainstreamers that they are sex offenders so they get met up outside and given a hard time. (QLD, justice organization, 2015)

Experiences of disadvantage and poor family support, including being "brought up in government care" (WA, male 3), were themes elicited in discussions with interviewees with ID.

> I suffer from depression. And, I get down sometimes. And, I just got to ring [support person] or parole officer and talk to them. But, apart from that I am quite healthy. I smoke. (WA, male, 2015)

> But I been in and out too. Ah yeah, I couldn't stay away. In and back. In and back. In back, in back. Gave up. Every couple years. Didn't worry about doing 13 years, 14 . . . say 15 years. (WA, male, 2015)

Loneliness and social isolation were also key problems for ex-prisoners with ID in the community prompting some to state that, although they would not want to return to prison, there they had found comfort in companionship. However, incarceration interrupts and severs social networks for prisoners, and if these relationships are not restored or mended, this further drives social isolation, stigma, and marginalization for ex-prisoners.

> Because if I have people to talk to I am fine. Because, I get very lonely sometime. And, I just need to go out and talk to someone. Because you get lonely at home and you get bored. Especially when you are living by yourself. (WA, male, 2015)

Security was raised as important, with individuals and organizations aiming to provide "security of housing, security of home, security of nutrition, and a 'go to' person who had had the chance to get to know them pre-release" (QLD, justice organization, 2015).

Socio-Political Factors and Complex Systems

Stigma is at the heart of socio-political factors contributing to the syndemic of ID amongst ex-prisoners. It is the unspoken negation of the individual with ID; the invisibility that occurs as a result of lack of acknowledgement through medical diagnosis. It is group stigma, in Goffman's framework, in which a group of individuals that are different to others are marginalized and ignored by communities and health systems. The NDIS is unclear on regimes of services for this group. The low priority given to exploring and funding the needs of this population, despite the human rights frameworks to which Australia is signatory, and the fragmented and *ad hoc* nature of care services only sustained through the efforts of workers, are evidence of political marginalization. Ex-prisoners with ID inhabit a peculiarly liminal space at the intersections of health, social, and legal systems. The service delivery sector is an arena of governmental and other agencies, shifting funding regimes within and across states, and poor staffing. These circumstances may render the application of the untested NDIS problematic, especially as it will become the sole form of government support for individuals with disabilities. Individuals without a formal diagnosis of ID may receive no support whatsoever, despite poor functionality and substantial needs. At the same time, if implementation of the NDIS is not evidence-based, it may perpetuate the stigma it was designed to alleviate, especially for ex-prisoners whose entitlements have not been well defined. Service providers interviewed stated that a key aspect of their role was to aid clients to navigate complex systems before they could apply care. Often, they used their own experience, goodwill and ingenuity to help their clients, which indicates a care system that is subjective, lacks integration and formal referral protocols, and provides opportunities for obfuscation.

We found that recent funding cuts in Queensland were associated with combative relationships between service providers, who often lacked funding and clear delivery protocols. Demoralization of staff due to short contracts and poor job security contributed to problems between agencies. Inadequate funding as a result of targeted cuts to this sector demonstrates the low priority attributed to the work done to aid individuals with ID.

In sum, fragmentation within the service provision sector, coupled with clients' high and complex needs leads to absent or inadequate service delivery. Differences between services in and out of prison further complicate care and led one informant to state that, "There is no one model fits all"

(WA, disability organization, 2015) because prison experiences and contexts of release differ. One informant highlighted that Indigenous Australians had specific and different needs across various health and social sectors, often not satisfactorily addressed, a feature common to the care arena extended to all Indigenous populations in Australia.

Racial/Ethnic Factors

> Racism, prejudice. In terms of the government. The government is racist. (WA, disability organization, 2015)

> A bit like racism in Queensland, I suppose. It happens every day but everyone pretends no one is racist. (QLD, disability organization, 2015)

The vulnerabilities of ID (lower functionality, low education, poor personal care, and disease) coupled with criminal justice involvement can lead to stigmatization. However, when ID is combined with Indigenous status, the opportunities for stigma are re-doubled. Firstly, Indigenous Australians are over-represented in prison. Of 33,791 prisoners in Australia in 2014, 9,264 were Indigenous, an over-representation by a factor of 13 compared to the general population (Australian Bureau of Statistics 2014). For this population factors that increase risk of offending include misuse of alcohol, socio-economic disadvantage, exposure to violence and abuse, and psychological distress (Australian Institute of Criminology 2015). Compared to the general prison population, they tend to be younger (80 percent compared to 69 percent), less educated, and have higher rates of recidivism (Australian Institute of Criminology 2008). However, the trajectories that lead to prison start earlier and relate to their marginal position in Australian society. Secondly, Indigenous Australians have much poorer health profiles as compared to the general Australian population. Shorter life expectancy, higher rates of low birth weight, injury and poisoning, respiratory disease, diabetes, kidney disease, and rheumatic fever affect this population (Australian Institute of Health and Welfare, 2015). Further, while data is patchy across Australia, studies using several measures (surveys, referrals to specialist disability services, and data linkage) found 7 percent prevalence of ID amongst Indigenous Australians compared to 1–2 percent in the general population (Roy and Balaratnasingam 2014). These higher proportions are attributed predominantly to social and environmental causes related to poverty, substance abuse, and violence; infections and toxins in utero, nutritional deficiency, perinatal factors, and poor physical environments (Roy and Balaratnasingam 2014).

In this population, the nefarious relationship between poor health in its various physical and mental health dimensions, poor housing and disrupted social environments, cultural marginalization, plus the high rates of offending contribute to stigmatization in Australian society. Definitions of ID in DSM-V and ICD are almost exclusively biological in construct and do not account for the interdependence of biological, socio-cultural, and political positioning because the syndemic of ID is not discrete but, instead, a complex predicament that eludes medical understanding resulting in disconnected, disparate systems of redress. Singular etiological and social determinants approaches have not helped Indigenous Australians because of the complexity of the health-poverty-marginalization-stigma nexus characterizing their experience. The Northern Territory National Emergency Response, a federal government-initiated policy that imposed a number of restrictions on Indigenous areas and inhabitants, demonstrated a clear misunderstanding of the predicament of this population. This policy was meant to re-dress high levels of child abuse through restrictions on alcohol, linking school attendance to welfare payments, and compulsory health checks for children, however, suspension of the Native Title Act effectively removed Indigenous voice on governance, increased policing, prohibited use of customary law, and other restrictions (Edmunds 2010). There is little agreement on the effects of the policy, however, one outcome was that the syndemic causes of social disruption and poor health were overlooked and Indigenous agency reduced (Edmunds 2010), with no improvement in health or criminogenic profiles. Given the over-representation of Indigenous Australians in prisons in Western Australia and Queensland, key informants expressed concerns that systems may not change due to systemic racism within government and the community.

DISCUSSION

John, from the extended ethnographic passage that began this chapter, is a person living in Australia, a country ranked number two in the United Nations Human Development Index (United Nations Development Programme 2017), yet he started his life with biological disadvantage in the form of ID, has little education or family and community care. He committed a crime, and went to prison. There he became another statistic relegated to common descriptions: poor, Indigenous, uneducated, unwell, and unable. Like many of his counterparts, he has a history of deprivation, lack of care, loneliness, and marginality. His health is poor and, despite the efforts of well-meaning workers within justice and health systems, his quality of life has not substantially changed. His ID is forever (static), however many other factors involved are modifiable (dynamic), thus his quality of life could improve. In Australia, the NDIS suggests better futures for persons with disability, however, this policy developed out of a knowledge base built on discipline-centered studies, sometimes taking a social determinants approach that can be instrumental rather than comprehensive. Given the high numbers of prisoners with ID in Australia and worldwide, a syndemic approach to understanding the circumstances of this vulnerable population may improve quality of life and reduce offending. For this group, prison is the "natural" conclusion of lives of stigma and exclusion. It is a containment of a condition that is misunderstood, marginalized, stigmatized, and silenced. However inarticulate, ungrammatical, and confused his narrative may be, John has a voice: he speaks through his body and his history. So what would syndemic theory bring to John's life? The syndemic approach enables understanding of the multiple and interacting aspects of his physicality, environment, and cultural and socio-political space within the Australian state and society. It is a response to compartmentalization of the lives of afflicted individuals and groups, an identification of their marginalized position in society, and an exposure of the antecedents of fragmented and inadequate care. At the biological level, it is insufficient to identify prisoners with ID simply as "complex" cases, but rather necessary to devise consistent diagnostic tools that recognize ID once individuals encounter health, social services, and criminal justice systems across all jurisdictions. Syndemic theory can contribute to avoidance of diagnostic overshadowing so that ID and mental illness are no longer confounded and patients placed on inappropriate medications.

Beyond co-morbidity, studies of the chronic physical disease profile of persons with ID are necessary to understand both the interactions of the diseases they are prone to and the effects of ID on their ability to seek care, participate in the clinical encounter, and subsequently self-manage positive health-related actions to their advantage. At the individual level, the pervasive problem of disrupted contexts that fail at positive social reproduction need to be addressed, especially for the Indigenous sector. Substance abuse, violence, exclusions from economies and communities, inadequate care such that afflictions worsen over time, and poor schooling are matters for the state. However, redress must take into account the biological and cognitive vulnerabilities of individuals with ID and the healthcare inequities propagated by reduced agency to advocate for themselves. The development of life-skills tools to eliminate the *ad hoc* nature of care in order to reduce dependence on the imaginations, time, and goodwill of service providers is necessary. With regard to the socio-political positions of persons with ID, their social and political vulnerability is demonstrated in inadequate care systems characterized by fragmentation, under-resourcing, and *ad hoc* care. Under the NDIS, eligibility and the provisions for prisoners with ID are unclear. Obfuscation of care eligibility is sidestepping the rights of those with ID. In terms of racial and ethnic factors, stigmatized Indigeneity proves to be a specific and prominent vulnerability in Australia, as the disease profile of this population, including ID, is worse compared to the rest of the population. There are specific syndemic reasons for this: poor living conditions that affect every aspect of the life-course from conception, predisposing individuals and communities to disease and scarce resources inadequate to health and prosperity. Marginalization within the Australian state in terms of access to livelihoods, inconsistent recognition in legislation as evidenced by suspension of the Native Title Act during the Intervention, and services augment disease burden. High prevalence of diabetes and other chronic diseases are indicative of relative disadvantage.

Stigma manifests in the actions of individuals structurally and contributes to silencing of the vulnerable. Prisoners with ID are doubly stigmatized by how their specific disability presents: low comprehension; poor self-care; chronic and often untreated sickness; and sometimes homelessness. Poor treatment in prison by other inmates who abuse their vulnerability sometimes requires isolation for their safety. Stigma can also manifest structurally through pervasive unwillingness and/or inability by governments, care and health systems to address specific needs resulting in prolonged suffering. Untreated disease and illness, lack of support resulting in poor self-care and incongruent social presentation, and low cognitive ability all exist in nefarious relationship with stigma to augment marginality.

A syndemic approach, with its holistic orientation, provides a method to disentangle the complexity of combinations of disease states and social disadvantage. An understanding of the stigma syndemic of prisoners with ID could lend insight into the complexities of other vulnerable groups in Australia. A syndemically informed NDIS implementation would fund organizations with an active engagement and holistic needs assessment of individuals, provide funding for screening once symptoms of disability appear, and promote sustainability of care through support for carers and self-care interventions. If John's syndemic condition were recognized for what it is, a history of biological and social disadvantage mediated by a society and government in which he is stigmatized and marginalized, perhaps policy for Australians like him would promise a better and more inclusive future.

REFERENCES

Ali, Afia, and Michael King with Andre Strydom and Angela Hassiotis. 2016. "Self-reported stigma and its association with socio-demographic factors and physical disability in people with intellectual disabilities: results from a cross-sectional study in England." *Social Psychology and Psychiatry Journal*, Apr 30, 2016: 464

Ali, Afia and Mihael King with Andre Strydom and Angela Hassitois. 2015. "Self-reported stigma and symptoms of anxiety and depression in people with intellectual disabilities: Findings from a cross sectional study in England." *Journal of Affective Disorders*. 187: 224–231.

American Association on Intellectual and Developmental Disabilities. 2016. "Definition of Intellectual Disability." Accessed April 17, 2016. http://aaidd.org/intellectual-disability/definition#.VvZNYhJ96WY.

Australian Bureau of Statistics. 2010. "4102.0 - Australian Social Trends, Mar 2010." Canberra, Australia, ABS.

Australian Bureau of Statistics. 2014. "Prisoners in Australia, 2014." Canberra, Australia, ABS. Accessed April 15, 2016. http://www.abs.gov.au/ausstats/abs@.nsf/mf/4517.0/.

Australian Bureau of Statistics. 2014 "Aboriginal and Torres Strait Islander Prisoner Characteristics. 4517.0-Prisoners in Australia, 2015." Canberra, Australia, ABS. Accessed April 14, 2016. http://www.abs.gov.au/ausstats/abs@.nsf/Lookup/by%20Subject/4517.0~2015~Main%20Features~Aboriginal%20and%20Torres%20Strait%20Islander%20prisoner%20characteristics~7.

Australian Federation of Disability Organizations. 2011. "Proposed National Disability Insurance Scheme: Human Rights Analysis." Accessed April 14, 2016. www.pwd.org.au/documents/pubs/RP11-NDIS-HumanRightsAnalysis.doc.

Australian Government. 2011. "Disability Care and Support: Inquiry Report." Canberra: Australia, Productivity Commission. Accessed November 15, 2016. http://www.pc.gov.au/inquiries/completed/disability-support/report.

Australian Institute of Criminology. 2008. "Reintegration of Indigenous prisoners: key findings. Trends and issues in criminal justice. Canberra. Accessed April 17, 2016. http://www.aic.gov.au/media_library/publications/tandi_pdf/tandi364.pdf.

Australian Institute of Criminology. 2015. "Indigenous Justice." Accessed April 12, 2016. http://www.aic.gov.au/crime_types/in_focus/indigenousjustice.html.

Australian Institute of Health and Welfare. 2008. "Disability in Australia: ID" AIHW. Canberra. AIHW bulletin no. 67.

Australian Institute of Health and Welfare. 2013. "The health of Australia's prisoners 2012." Cat. no. PHE 170. Canberra, AIHW.

Australian Institute of Health and Welfare. 2015. "Aboriginal and Torres Strait Islander Health Performance Framework Data." Accessed April 12, 2016. http://www.aihw.gov.au/indigenous-data/health-performance-framework/.

Baldry, Eileen. 2014. "Disability at the margins: Limits of the law." Griffith Law Review 23 (4): 370–388.

Baldry, Eileen and M. Borzycki. 2003. "Promoting Integration: The Provision of Prisoner Post-Release Services. Trends and Issues in Crime and Criminal Justice." Canberra, ACT, Australian Institute of Criminology.

Baldry, Eileen and Leanne Dowse with Melissa Clarence. 2011. "People with mental and cognitive disabilities: pathways into prison." Background Paper for the National Legal Aid Conference Darwin 2011. University of New South Wales, Sydney. Accessed April 15, 2016. http://www.ntlac.nt.gov.au/doco/bpcpapers/People%20With%20Mental%20and%20Cognitive%20Disabilities%20-%20Pathways%20Into%20Prison.pdf.

Baldry Eileen, l. Dowse L and M. Clarence. 2012. "People with intellectual and other cognitive disability in the criminal justice system." Sydney, University of New South Wales. Accessed April 11, 2016. www.adhc.nsw.gov.au/about_us/research/completed_research

Baldry, Eileen and Helen Beange with Nick Lennox. 1998. "Physical Aspects of Health in the Learning Disabled." *Current Opinion in Psychiatry*. 11:531–534.

Baldry, Eileen and Ruth McCausland with Leanne Dowse and Elizabeth McEntyre. 2015. "A predictable and preventable path: Aboriginal people with mental and cognitive disabilities in the criminal justice system." UNSW: Sydney, Australia. Accessed November 15, 2016. https://www.mhdcd.unsw.edu.au/sites/www.mhdcd.unsw.edu.au/files/u18/pdf/a_predictable_and_preventable_path_2nov15.pdf.

Beange, Helen and Nick Lennox with Trevor Parmenter. 1999. "Health targets for people with an ID." *Journal of Intellectual and Developmental Disability* 24(4): 283–297.

Bhandari, A. and Kate van Dooren with N. Eastgate, N, Lennox and S Kinner. 2014. "Comparison of social circumstances, substance use and substance-related harm in soon-to-be-released prisoners with and without ID." *Journal of Intellectual Disability Research*. 59(6): 571–579.

Cockram, J. 2005. "People With an ID in the Prisons." *Psychiatry, Psychology and Law* 12(1): 163–173.

Cockram, J. 2005b. "Careers of offenders with an ID: The probabilities of rearrest." *Journal of Intellectual Disability Research.* 49(7): 525–536.

Department of Corrective Services. 2014. "Recidivism trends in Western Australia with comparisons to national trends." Government of Western Australia, Department of Corrective Services, Perth. Accessed November 15, 2016. https://www.correctiveservices.wa.gov.au/_files/about-us/statistics-publications/statistics/DCS-recidivism-trends-WA-October2014.pdf.

Dias, Shannon and Rob Ware, with Stuart Kinner and Nicholas Lennox. 2013. "Physical health outcomes in prisoners with ID: a cross-sectional study." *Journal of Intellectual Disability Research.* 57(12): 1191–6.

Dias, Shannon, and Rob Ware with Stuart Kinner and Nicholas Lennox. 2013. "Co-occurring mental disorder and intellectual disability in a large sample of Australian prisoners." *Australian and New Zealand Journal of Psychiatry*, 47(10): p. 938–944. doi: 10.1177/0004867413492220

Dias, Shannon and Rob Ware. 2014. "Co-occurring mental disorder and ID in a large sample of Australian prisoners." *Australian and New Zealand Journal of Psychiatry* 47(10): 938–44.

Durose, M. R. and A. D. Cooper with H. N. Snyder. 2014. "Recidivism of Prisoners Released in 30 States in 2005: Patterns from 2005 to 2010." Bureau of Justice Statistics, U.S. Department of Justice, Washington, DC.

Edmunds, Mary. 2010. "The Northern Territory Intervention and Human Rights: An Anthropological Perspective. Canberra:Research School of Humanities and Arts. Australia National University.

Ellem, Karen. 2010. "Life Stories of Ex-Prisoners with Intellectual Disabilty in Queensland. School of Social Work and Human Services. Brisbane, Queensland, The University of Queensland.

Ellem, Karen and Jean Wilson with Wing Hong Chiu and Marie Knox. 2008. "Ethical challenges of life story research with ex-prisoners with ID." *Disability and Society* 23(5): 497–509.

Emerson, E. 2007. "Poverty and people with intellectual disabilities. *Mental Retardation and Developmental Disabilities Research Reviews* 13: 107–113.

Emerson, E. and S. Halpin. 2013. "Anti-Social Behaviour and Police Contact among 13- to 15-Year-old English Adolescents with and Without Mild/Moderate Intellectual Disability." *Journal of Applied Research in Intellectual Disabilities*, 26(5): p. 362–369.

Fazel, Seena and Kiriakos Xenitidis with John Powell. 2008. "The prevalence of intellectual disabilities among 12,000 prisoners - a systematic review." *International Journal of Law Psychiatry* 31(4): 369–73.

Giddings, Gordon. 2013. "Sense and sensitivity." *Canadian Medical Association Journal*, Dec. 10; 185(18):1555

Goffman, Erving. 1963/1991. *Stigma*. New York: Simon and Schuster.

Government of Western Australia N.d. "Operational Instruction 10: Prisoners with Intellectual Disabilities." Department of Corrective Services. Accessed 15 November, 2016. https://www.correctiveservices.wa.gov.au/_files/prisons/adult-custodial-rules/operational-instructions/oi-10.pdf.

Graham, A. 2003. "Post-prison Mortality: Unnatural Death Among People Released from Victorian Prisons Between January 1990 and December 1999." *Australian and New Zealand Journal of Criminology.* 36(1): 94–108.

Hammett, Theodore and Cheryl Roberts with Sofia Kennedy. 2001. "Health-Related Issues in Prisoner Reentry." *Crime and Delinquency* 47(3): 390–409.

Hassiotis, Angela and Dina Gazizova with Leah Akinionu, Paule Bebbington, H. Meltzer, A. Strydom. 2011. "Psychiatric morbidity in prisoners with intellectual disabilities: analysis of prison survey data for England and Wales." *The British Journal of Psychiatry.* 199(2) 156–157. DOI: 10.1192/bjp.bp.110.088039

Hayes, Susan. 1997. "Prevalence of intellectual disability in local courts". *Journal of Intellectual and Developmental Disability*. 22(2): p. 71–85.

Hayes, Susan C. and Phil Shackell with Pat Mottram and Rachel Lancaster. 2007. "The prevalence of Intellectual Disability in a Major UK Prison." *British Journal of Learning Disabilities.* 35(3):p. 162–167.

Howard, Michelle and John O'Brien. 2009. "Criminal Injustice for Vulnerable People. Australian Guardianship and Administration Council." Paper presented at the conference Social Inclusion: The Future of Ageing, Disability and Substituted Decision-Making. The Hilton Hotel, Brisbane, 20 March, 2009.

Howerton, Amanda and Ros Burnett with Richard Byng, John Campbell. 2009. "The Consolations of Going Back to Prison: What 'Revolving Door' Prisoners Think of Their Prospects." *Journal of Offender Rehabilitation* 48(5): 439–461.

Iorizzo, J. 2012. "Helping offenders find a way out of recidivism. *Learning Disability Practice* 15(4): 22–24.

Jacques Baillargeon and Ingrid A. Binswanger with Joseph Penn and Brie William, Owen Murray. 2009. "Psychiatric Disorders and Repeat Incarcerations: The Revolving Prison Door." *American Journal of Psychiatry* 166(1): 103–109.

Johnson, P. 2012. "The prevalence of low self-esteem in an intellectually disabled forensic population." *Journal of Intellectual Disability Research*, 56(3): p. 317–325.

Jones, Simon and Louise Howard with Graham Thornicroft. 2008. "'Diagnostic overshadowing': worse physical health care for people with mental illness."*Acta Psychiatrica Scandinavica* 118(3): 169–171.

Kinner, Stuart. 2006. "Continuity of health impairment and substance misuse among adult prisoners in Queensland, Australia." *International Journal of Prisoner Health* 2(2): 101–113.

Kinner, Stuart and A. Avery. 2015. "A robust estimate of the number and characteristics of persons released from prison in Australia." *Australian and New Zealand Journal of Public Health* 39(4): 315–8.

Klimecki, Megan and Jo Jenkinson with Linda Wilson. 1994. "A Study of Recidivism among Offenders with an Intellectual Disability. *Australia and New Zealand Journal of Developmental Disabilities* 19(3): 209–219.

Kouyoumdjian, F., J. Wiwcharuk, and S. Green. 2015. "Optimizing continuity of care throughout incarceration: Case and opportunities." *Canadian Family Physician*, 61(2): p. 107–109.

Lennox, Nicholas and Christopher Bain with Therese Rey-Conde, D. Purdie, R.Bush and N. Pandeya. 2007. "Effects of a comprehensive health assessment programme for Australian adults with ID: a cluster randomized trial." *International Journal of Epidemiology* 36: 139–146.

Lennox, Nicholas and M. Taylor with Therese Rey-Conde, Christopher Bain, D Purdie and F. Boyle. 2005. "Beating the Barriers: Recruitment of people with ID to participate in research." *Journal of Intellectual Disability Research* 49(4): 296–305.

Louks, N. 2006. "No One Knows: Offenders with learning difficulties and learning disabilities: the prevalence and associated needs of offenders with learning difficulties and learning disabilities." London, Prison Reform Trust. Acessed November 15, 2016. http://www.prisonreformtrust.org.uk/uploads/documents/noknl.pdf.

Merrall, Elizabeth and Azar Kariminia with Ingrid Binswanger, Michael Hobbs, Michael Farrell, John Marsden, Sharon J Hutchinson, Shelia Bird. 2010. "Meta-analysis of drug-related deaths soon after release from prison." *Addiction* (Abingdon, England) 105(9): 1545–1554.

National Disability Insurance Agency. 2014. "Operational Guideline – Planning and Assessment – Supports in the Plan – Interface with Justice." Accessed June 23 2015. http://www.ndis.gov.au/sites/default/files/documents/og_plan_assess_supp_plan_justice.pdf.

National Disability Insurance Agency. N.d. "The National Disability Insurance Scheme." Accessed April 11, 2016, http://www.ndis.gov.au/.

National Disability Insurance Scheme. 2016. "NDIS in Queensland." Accessed April 11, 2016 https://www.ndis.gov.au/document/transition-ndis-queensland.html.

New South Wales Community Services Commission. 2001. "Disability, death and the responsibility of care: A review of the characteristics and circumstances of 211 people with disabilities who died in care between 1991–1998 in NSW." Sydney, New South Wales.

New South Wales Government: Justice. 2014. "2009 NSW Young people in custody health survey: full report." NSW Juvenile Justice and Justice Health. Accessed November 15, 2016. http://www.juvenile.justice.nsw.gov.au/Documents/JH_YPICHSRep2009_D09_01_section1.pdf.

Office of the Public Advocate. 2014. "Inquiry on Strategies to Prevent and Reduce Criminal Activity in Queensland: Report No. 82. Legal Affairs and Community Safety Committee. Accessed April 11, 2016. http://www.parliament.qld.gov.au/documents/committees/lacsc/2014/crimeinquiry2014/rpt-082-28nov2014.pdf.

Ogloff, J. 2015. "Good mental health care in prisons must begin and end in the community. The Conversation. 24 April, 2015. Accessed April 17, 2016. http://theconversation.com/good-mental-health-care-in-prisons-must-begin-and-end-in-the-community-40011.

Ostrach, Bayla and Merrill Singer. 2012. "At Special Risk: Biopolitical Vulnerability and HIV/STI Syndemics Among Women." *Health Sociology Review* 21 (3): 258–271.

Ouellette-Kuntz, H. 2005. "Understanding health disparities and inequities faced by individuals with intellectual disabilities." *Journal of Applied Research in Intellectual Disabilities* (113–121).

Roy, Meera and Sivasankaran Balaratnasingam. 2014. "Intellectual Disability and Indigenous Australian: An Overview." *Asia-Pacific Psychiatry*. 6: 363–372.

Schalock, R., et al. 2010. *Intellectual Disability: Definition, Classification, and Systems of Supports* (11th Edition). American Association on Intellectual and Developmental Disabilities. Washington DC, USA.

Seal, D. W. and G. D. Eldrige with D. Kacanek and D. Binson, R. MacGowan. 2007. "A longitudinal, qualitative analysis of the context of substance use and sexual behavior among 18- to 29-year-old men after their release from prison." *Social Science and Medicine* 65(11): 2394–2406.

Simpson, M. K. and J. Hogg. 2001. "Patterns of offending among people with intellectual disability: a systematic review. Part I: methodology and prevalence data." *Journal of Intellectual Disability Research* 45(5): 384–396.

Simpson, Jim. 2014. *Participants or just policed?: Guide to the role of the NDIS-people with intellectual disability who have contact with the criminal justice system*. Council for Intellectual Disability, Australia. Accessed April 12, 2016. http://www.nswcid.org.au/images/pdf/Participants_or_just_policed_614.pdf.

Singer, Merrill. 2009. "Chapter 1: Learning from Lichen: Reconceptualizing Health and Disease." In *Introduction to Syndemics: A Critical Systems Approach to Public and Community Health*. 1–23. Wiley and Sons, Ltd.

Singer, Merrill. 2014. "Syndemics." In *The Wiley Blackwell Encyclopedia of Health, Illness, Behaviour, and Society*, edited by William C. Cockerham, Robert Dingwall, and Stella R. Quah, 1–4. Wiley and Sons, Ltd.

Soldatic, K., and G.van Toorn, G. with L. Dowse and K. Muir. 2014. "Intellectual Disability and Complex Intersections: Marginalisation under the National Disability Insurance Scheme." *Research and Practice in Intellectual and Developmental Disabilities* 1, 6–16. doi:10.1080/23297018.2014.906050

Steering Committee for the Review of Government Service Provision. 2014. *Report on Government Services 2014, vol. C, Justice*. Canberra, Australian Government Productivity Commission, Canberra.

United Nations. 2005. "Convention on the Rights of Persons with Disabilities." United Nations Development Programme. Accessed 14 April, 2016. http://www.un.org/disabilities/convention/conventionfull.shtml.

United Nations. 2017. "Human Development Reports." *United Nations Development Programme*. Accessed 26 April, 2017. http://hdr.undp.org/en/composite/HDI.

van Dooren, Kate, with Jesse Young and Carmel Blackburn and Fernanda Maria Claudio. 2015. "Substance Use Interventions for People with ID Transitioning Out of Prison." *Australian and New Zealand Journal of Public Health* 39(4): 397.

Vanny, K. A. 2009. "Mental illness and intellectual disability in Magistrates Courts in New South Wales, Australia." *Journal of Intellectual Disability Research*, 53(3): p. 289–297.

Walmsley, Roy. 2013. *World Prison Population List* (10th edition). International Centre for Prison Studies. University of Essex. Accessed 14 April, 2016. http://www.apcca.org/uploads/10th_Edition_2013.pdf.
World Health Organisation. 1992. *The ICD-10 Classification of mental and behavioural disorders: clinical description and diagnostic guidelines*. W. H. Organization. Geneva.
World Health Organisation. 2000. *Ageing and Intellectual Disabilities - Improving Longevity and Promoting Healthy Ageing: Summative Report*. Geneva, Switzerland, World Health Organization.
World Health Organization. 2012. Definition: Intellectual Disability. Geneva, Switzerland, World Health Organization.

Chapter Seven

Exploring the Role of Stigma in Malnutrition-Related Syndemics

Lessons from Guatemala

Elaine M. Bennett

This chapter examines the role of stigma in the perpetuation of a malnutrition/infectious disease syndemic in rural Guatemala. The everyday expression of this syndemic is captured in this episode of healthcare-seeking behavior by Josephina, an indigenous mother in a highland village, as she brought her fourteen-month-old daughter Alicia to the local health post with symptoms of fever and diarrhea. Josephina had risen at 4:00 AM to prepare the morning's tortillas for her family before her husband left for work and to see her other child off to school. Throughout the morning she had changed Alicia's clothing at least five times, vigorously scrubbing away loose stool from diarrhea by hand and setting the cloth out on their corrugated metal roof so it would be dry by the time she ran out of reserves. Each time, she very carefully removed the clothing and cleaned her daughter's body while avoiding exposing her to the chill in the air which could make her fever worse. At the health post's intake desk, the staff asked for Alicia's *carnet,* the government issued card on which they record children's measurements and vaccinations. Josephina murmured that the *carnet* was at home. The intake secretary rolled her eyes and ordered her to go to get it—she should know that you cannot be seen without that *carnet*. Josephina glanced at her sick baby, mustering the energy to hike back up the steep path to their home. As she turned away from the desk, the intake staff noted the brownish liquid that had just begun to seep through Alicia's blanket and added with a tone of disgust, "make sure she is clean the next time you bring her." As Josephina and Alicia left, the woman at the desk commented loudly to another staff member that "these people" wouldn't get sick so often if they would keep themselves clean. When Josephina returned two hours later, with Alicia and the *carnet*, the girl was near dehydration. Measurements would have shown that her length for her age indicated the beginnings of chronic malnutrition, but nobody bothered to check the charts. As the medical staff wrinkled their noses while examining the sick child, they scolded the exhausted Josephina for waiting so long to bring her for medical care. They gave her a prescription for an antibiotic, which she would have to go to another town to purchase, and told her to have the child drink an oral rehydration beverage, which she could purchase from a local *tienda* (a small, convenience store-like shop) for half a day's wages. The medical staff addressed Alicia's problem in the most superficial way, missing the chronic malnutrition that made her vulnerable to the infection, and sending her mother with instructions that they knew she would not be able to follow because of geographic and economic barriers. Nonetheless, they added Josephina to their long list of frustrating cases, in which, in their view, parents just did not bother to care for their children.

I witnessed many such episodes in my twelve years of ethnographic and public health engagement with poor, indigenous communities and argue that social stigmatization of impoverished and indigenous populations in Guatemala both exacerbates and perpetuates malnutrition/infectious disease interactions.

Stigma, as a social process, contributes to malnutrition-related syndemics as it marks and denigrates particular social strata, often based on ethnicity or economic status (Shelton, Alegre, and Son 2010). This social stigma both reflects and contributes to political and ideological superstructures that rationalize low wages, poor public infrastructure, and inadequate educational opportunities (e.g., Parker 2012; Link and Phelan 2001). In a related vein, the long-term outcomes of chronic malnutrition directly affect achievement of human potential and include cognitive deficiencies, susceptibility to infectious and chronic diseases, and reduced adult work capacity. This, in combination with the fact that malnutrition-related syndemics are most prevalent among the poor and marginalized, perpetuates social stigma of these populations as stupid, dirty, and lazy. This stigma, a form of self-fulfilling prophecy, perpetuates various social disadvantages, which perpetuate poverty, which, in turn, perpetuates malnutrition and poor health.

In this chapter, I demonstrate: 1) the nature of a malnutrition/infectious disease syndemic; 2) the role of stigma, in the form of prejudice against the poor and indigenous in Guatemala, in perpetuating poverty and, with it, malnutrition/infectious disease; and 3) the role of stigma processes in undermining potentially effective nutrition/health interventions. I also offer an approach for reframing discourse on efforts to reduce the frequency of malnutrition/infectious disease issues by taking stigma processes into account.

THE SYNDEMIC

A situation can be described as a syndemic when two or more diseases or health conditions interact synergistically and contribute, "as a result of their interaction, to excess burden of disease in a population" (Singer and Clair 2003: 425). Syndemics generally occur when and where people are subjected to poor living conditions or other forms of structural violence. A synergy between chronic malnutrition[1] and infection, particularly diarrheal disease, has long been recognized, and malnutrition is both a cause and a consequence of infectious disease. Children who are malnourished are more likely to succumb to infections, become more severely ill, and take longer to recover than well-nourished children (Schaible and Kaufmann 2007; Black, Morris, and Bryce 2003; Rice et al. 2000). Children who are ill are more likely to become malnourished, especially if they are already close to malnourishment. Scrimshaw (2003:320S), summarizing fifty years of research on the synergistic and cyclical nature of malnutrition and infection, notes that: "Today, the recognition of the synergistic relationship between malnutrition and infection is a strong force in most public health interventions to prevent infection and correct malnutrition."

In combination with infectious disease, malnutrition affects children's development. Impaired cognitive function and school performance are established effects of early childhood malnutrition, especially in situations in which the socio-economic environment in which the child lives creates other risks for cognitive deficits (Wachs 1995; Mendez and Adair 1999; Grantham-McGregor et al. 2007). However, in support of a broadened set of synergistic effects, evidence is also mounting for an association between diarrheal and parasitic infections and impaired cognitive function and school performance (Bulled, Singer, and Dillingham 2008; Lorntz et al. 2006; Niehaus et al. 2002; Guerrant et al. 1999). This impaired cognitive function and school performance, which is now associated with both chronic malnutrition (stunting) and frequent diarrheal infections during childhood, becomes an additional dimension in a malnutrition-infectious disease syndemic (Ostrach and Singer 2012). In sum, malnutrition and infectious disease constitute a bidirectional syndemic, with both conditions impacted by the interaction that is rooted in and perpetuates suboptimal social and economic conditions and from which cognitive impairment and physical vulnerability are potential outcomes.

Immunologists and researchers from various fields studying malnutrition have made significant advances in understanding the connection between nutrition and immune function, emphasizing the molecular mechanisms involved in that synergy (Keusch 2003). There are many ways in which insufficient nutrition affects immune function. One particularly broad effect is seen in the development and function of lymphocytes (immune cells) in the body.

There are many complicated mechanisms by which malnutrition can disrupt the functions of immune cells (Keusch 2003; Solomons and Keusch 2000; Jolly and Fernandes 2000). For example, ß-cells are antigen-specific lymphocytes that produce antibodies against specific pathogens. In order for ß-cells to fully function, they must be complemented by certain types of T-cells, including CD4+ cells. T-cells are another form of lymphocyte (white blood cell) and they are so named because they mature primarily in the thymus. The thymus can involute or shrink in the bodies of malnourished children, an occurrence that is normally seen in aging human adults. This thymic involution leads to a decrease in the number of mature T-cells in malnourished bodies. Because of the critical functions of T-cells in general immunity and in antigen-specific responses, malnutrition directly contributes to a "functional impairment of cell-mediated immunity and diminished antibody response to protein antigens dependent on T-cell mediated help" (Keusch 2003, 338S). In other words, key physiological functions that form the cornerstone of cell-mediated immune function are compromised in a malnourished body, reducing and delaying immune response, and making that body more susceptible to disease.

Diarrheal disease, which occurs frequently among poor, indigenous populations in Guatemala, synergizes with malnutrition in another way, as multiple and repeated enteric (intestinal) infections decrease the body's ability to absorb nutrients (Guerrant et al. 2008). Enteric infections (for which diarrhea is often, but not always, a symptom) damage the lining of the intestines. Repeated infections also affect the ability of the gastro-intestinal tract to protect the body from infection by affecting the barrier functions of the intestinal tract. This negatively affects the ability of the intestinal lining to absorb nutrients, which, in turn, contributes to malnutrition (Guerrant et al. 2008; Solomons and Keusch 2000).

Solomons and Keusch (2000) also point out that infections lead to undernutrition in multiple ways as they reorder the metabolic priorities of the body toward the synthesis of proteins that can defend the body against pathogens. Further, they suggest that infections can induce anorexia (a loss of appetite) by stimulating the production of inflammatory cytokines as indicated by Plata-Salamán (1998). This, in combination with cultural responses which may involve withholding certain types of foods from sick individuals, contributes to worsening nutrition status. All of these processes are more likely to occur in the body of one who has a marginal diet and who lives in marginal conditions because of prevailing structures of social inequality.

The documentation of these biological interactions is certainly important to understanding and solving the problem of the malnutrition infectious disease syndemic, but it is not sufficient for reducing the frequency of this syndemic among poor, indigenous Guatemalans. We need a more detailed examination of the many social processes that contribute to children being in situations in which they can be malnourished and repeatedly exposed to infectious disease agents that their bodies are not equipped to handle. Syndemic theory provides a framework in which we can effectively situate our consideration of the ways in which malnutrition and infectious disease interact synergistically in individual bodies that are living in poor conditions. Integrating that social component makes it easier to demonstrate that malnutrition and infectious disease are simultaneously caused by poverty and by the enactment of stigma on the basis of ethnicity and economic status, that both causes and perpetuates the poverty. This stigma is embedded in long-term discrimination and racism against indigenous people in Guatemala.

THE STIGMA

The malnutrition/infectious disease syndemic is widespread among poor, indigenous children in Guatemala. The stigma under discussion is enacted against the socioeconomic and ethnic identity of those children as poor, indigenous individuals in Guatemala. While this stigma impacts children themselves in many ways, this argument focuses primarily on the effect of stigma as it acts on parents. As Nayar et al. (2014) note, children's health is determined in the context of their environments (e.g., children have limited options to choose "good" health behaviors), and their caretakers are a significant part of those environments. Stigmatization of the caretakers (such as stigma targeting the poor or a certain ethnic group) makes it more difficult for the parents to care for their children, which is a pathway for stigma to impact child health.

Weiss and Ramakrishna (2006, p536) offer a definition of health-related stigma as "a social process or related personal experience characterized by exclusion, rejection, blame, or devaluation that results from experience or reasonable anticipation of an adverse social judgement about a person or group identified with a particular health problem." This helps to expand the discussion of the negative effects of stigma beyond specific diseases such as HIV/AIDS, epilepsy, and mental illnesses to include a call for a better understanding of the contributions of social stigma to the health of marginalized groups, among which certain diseases are more likely to occur (e.g., Keusch, Wilentz, and Kleinman 2006; Weiss and Ramakrishna 2006; Shelton, Alegre, and Son 2010; Nayar et al. 2014).

Link and Phelan (2001, 2006) outline five components of social stigma. The first component involves the identification and labeling of human differences. The second involves stereotyping, which they describe as linking the person who has been labeled to undesirable characteristics. The third component involves the stigmatizing group differentiating themselves from the stigmatized group ("them vs. us," them as "the other"). The fourth component is realized when the stigmatized group experiences discrimination and loss of status based on those identified, labeled, and highlighted differences. Finally, the fifth component involves the stigmatizing group exercising power in ways that harm or put the stigmatized group at a disadvantage.

In Guatemala, the identification of difference, stereotyping, and differentiation of the stigmatized group is the result of a long legacy of oppression, genocide, and exploitation of indigenous peoples and their lands. Through indigenous demands for rights, this history of mistreatment has evolved into a situation in which indigenous cultures are officially recognized by the Guatemalan government under a mantle of multiculturalism; however, this multicultural situation is characterized by economic inequality and racism in which indigenous Guatemalans are at a disadvantage in Guatemalan society (e.g., Hale 2006; Nelson 2001; Menchu, Burgos-Debray, and Wright 2010; Brett 2011; Poder and He 2015). This abbreviated history, discussed in depth in the references cited, among others, establishes the stigma of indigenous people in Guatemala (Link and Phelan's first four components). In the next section, I will focus on the process outlined in that fifth component, in which the stigmatizing group exercises power in ways that harm or put the stigmatized group at a disadvantage, in order to identify the ways in which this stigma becomes a determinant of the malnutrition/infectious disease/stigma syndemic.

Link and Phelan (2001) discuss two major challenges associated with applying the stigma concept. The first challenge, originally raised by Kleinman et al. (1995) and Schneider (1988), is that many social scientists who study stigma do so from theoretical perspectives that are not informed by the lived experiences of the stigmatized people. Given the nature of stigma as a social process that enacts harm on individuals, they identify a need to give priority to the lived experiences of those identified as "stigmatized." This would improve the validity of studies on stigma by minimizing inaccurate or unsupported assumptions. The second is to overcome the individualistic focus of research on stigma, moving from a conceptualization of stigma as connected to the personal attributes of particular people to describing it in terms of "relationships between a set of interrelated concepts" (Link and Phelan, 2001, p366). Following this approach, Kleinman and Clifford-Hall (2009) note that the inclusion of structural discrimination in this model opens the door for us to examine dimensions of power in shaping the distribution of stigma in society and argue for the importance of understanding what stigma means in terms of what matters most to those who live with it. In the following paragraphs, I work both to communicate the lived experiences of stigma among people with whom I have worked and to examine how structural discrimination affects the daily activities of those who live with it.

This structural discrimination as part of the stigmatization of being indigenous and/or poor, contributes to the social, political, and economic determinants of malnutrition in Guatemala, and makes it more difficult for poor, indigenous parents to access valuable resources in preventing and overcoming malnutrition among their children. Pathways by which stigma perpetuates a malnutrition/infectious disease syndemic are both: 1) structural, involving the perpetuation of social and economic conditions in which parents meet many obstacles in attempts to effectively care for their children; and 2) interpersonal, through the ways in which health workers interact with parents of malnourished children. These structural and interpersonal factors serve as pathways for reinforcing inequality that are maintained through the ideological position of moral authority of the non-indigenous and non-poor over the stereotyped poor, indigenous population. Social discourse on malnutrition, as influenced by the government and the media, both reflects and reinforces stigma and contributes to, or rationalizes, the perpetuation of these structural and interpersonal patterns that underlie malnutrition.

STIGMA AS A DETERMINANT OF THE MALNUTRITION/INFECTIOUS DISEASE SYNDEMIC

Among Guatemala's general population the burden of malnutrition is heavy and consistent. Approximately 50 percent of children are chronically malnourished and among the indigenous populations, approximately 66 percent are chronically malnourished (Williams, Stupp, and Pac 2013). Even when controlling for poverty and education level, being indigenous is a significant risk factor for child malnutrition and all of its associated complications (Marini and Gragnolati 2003).

Studying the impact of income inequality in Guatemala, Poder and He (2015) acknowledged that both living in a rural area and being indigenous are associated with discrimination and exploitation. Indigenous status, though, is particularly important as income inequality in Guatemala has stronger negative effects on child growth when the child has at least one indigenous parent or lives in a rural area (Poder and He 2015). The effects are strongest when the child lives in a rural area and has at least one indigenous parent. Poder and He, citing González-izás, note that the longstanding discrimination against rural and indigenous people in Guatemala provides the mechanism by which the elite and some segments of the urban population are, in effect, subsidized by the rural, indigenous populations.

> Given these results, it appears that income inequality and discrimination are mutually reinforcing in Guatemala. Indeed, income inequality reduces access to a large number of fundamental freedoms, which would prevent individuals from fully exercising their abilities. However, rural and indigenous populations are partly judged on their abilities, which are lower precisely because of this inequality, thereby justifying the discrimination that they suffer. If this

> vicious circle is not broken, indigenous and especially rural populations will continue to be exploited, and the fruits of their work will directly subsidize the agro-export oligarchy and indirectly subsidize urban and nonindigenous individuals (González-izás 2010). (Poder and He 2015, 299)

To illustrate how Poder and He's analysis might look in a specific situation, I offer an analysis of my observations in an indigenous village in the western highlands of Guatemala. In this town, most people are employed in construction, hotels, or housekeeping and caretaking for chalets (vacation homes for foreigners and wealthy Guatemalans). A small number maintain subsistence horticulture as part of their livelihood. Some operate their own businesses in the form of *tiendas* (small, convenience store-like shops) or transportation services, in the form of *lanchas* (public boat taxis) or trucks and *tuk-tuks* (small taxis) to take people up and down the long hill from the lake shore to the town. Most people earn no more than the Guatemalan minimum wage, which is generally less than 75 percent of what would be required to purchase the Basic Food Basket for a family (Bennett 2009).

The *chaleteros* (owners of vacation homes) who employ men and women from the village tend to speak condescendingly about their capabilities and work ethic. A stereotype of laziness is expressed when employers rationalize that they pay their *jornaleros*, or day laborers enough, "since they spend half the day just sitting around anyway." Few acknowledge that the *jornaleros'* breaks for rest are usually interspersed among periods of intensive labor, carrying cement blocks, or sacks of gravel long distances on steep paths and steps as the sun beats down on them.[2]

In many cases their skills and manual labor are devalued because they are seen as of low intelligence. This is expressed as employers complain that their employees "can't seem to follow instructions," sometimes even suggesting that this is because they had been malnourished as children and their brains were not as developed. One well-meaning foreigner, who I will refer to as Matilda, had, for years, been operating a cooperative in which women from the village could meet to create beaded jewelry and receive instructions on how to raise their children. One day I encountered Matilda, as I walked along a path in the town, eating a delicious *chicharrone* (fried pork skin) which I had purchased from a woman in the village. Despite this being our first time meeting, she severely admonished me for consuming such garbage and went on to complain to me that she was constantly telling "these women" to stop giving their kids junk food, but that they were so dense that they could not learn. In her opinion, I, as an anthropologist who works on nutrition and public health issues, should have known better than to set such a bad example and potentially confuse them further. I was, apparently, undoing her hard work. Her admonishment reflected an assumption that the women in the village were not capable of nuanced thinking about how an occasional treat is allowable in one's diet.

A friend from the village who had worked with Matilda in the past observed the interaction from a distance and later remarked that I should not worry about what Matilda says—she yells at all of the women and treats them like they are stupid. When I asked why women work with her if she yells at them, my friend explained that the cooperative provided an opportunity to learn a new skill and to sell their handicrafts. Basically, women from the village would put up with the indignity of being scolded and talked down to if it helped them to provide for their families; the stress of the stigma is certainly felt, but the structural factors that shape and limit opportunities for "these women" leave them with few options.

A predisposition to see poor, indigenous Guatemalans as lazy and unintelligent (applying stereotypes to the "other"), in combination with national labor policies that do little to protect or help poor, indigenous Guatemalans (Poder and He 2015) justifies the use of power (on the part of those with the resources to hire employees) in ways that harm or put indigenous Guatemalans at a disadvantage. Further, those national economic policies that concentrate wealth in the hands of a few stifle the economic development of the country, making it easy for employers to further rationalize that their poor, indigenous employees need the low-paid work and would not be able to find it elsewhere.

The stigma and racism targeting poor and indigenous populations also impact the quality, acceptability, and accessibility of health services to these populations. Mistreatment of poor and indigenous populations by health workers in Guatemala has been widely documented. For example, Berry (2006; 2008) reported that health workers at hospitals looked down on and spoke harshly to poor, indigenous patients. Others have documented inferior, inadequate, and dismissive care as well (Chary et al. 2013; van Dijk et al. 2013).

In thinking about the lived experience of stigma, we must remember that even poor people know when they are being spoken down to. They are sensitive to the authoritative tones and exasperated sighs from health workers. They may be exhausted after a long day of heavy labor, or out of breath from carting their children on steep mountain paths to visit a clinic or nutrition center, or hungry themselves, because their morning meal was before dawn. Women expressed to me that they experience fatigue and frustration as they try to keep their children calm and quiet while they are subjected to condescending lectures.[3] In these situations, it would be difficult (even for well-nourished, educated parents) to pay attention to, let alone integrate the pontifications of, health and nutrition workers.

This kind of "experienced stigma" (Nayar et al. 2014) can lead to delayed care or poor adherence to medical prescriptions, a problem that can exacerbate infectious diseases and their interactions with chronically malnourished bodies. This is illustrated in a case from a Ministry of Health medical *jornada* (a day-long medical mission) in a highland village in Guatemala. In this event, a team of health professionals, including a doctor, a nurse, a veterinarian, and a *nutricionista* (nutritionist) set up clinical services on a Saturday in the health post that was primarily used by an NGO clinic. The *nutricionista,* who was a Ladino woman in her early twenties, had learned about my project and invited me to observe their work so I could learn something about malnutrition. During the *jornada*, a mother came in seeking medical care for her 10-month-old baby boy, who had a cough. She was first directed to the *nutricionista*, who measured the baby, checked the growth charts, sighed in frustration and proclaimed to his mother in a harsh, impatient tone, "He isn't growing enough. You need to make him eat more beans." As the mother stared at her blankly (imagine how you would feel if confronted with an accusation that your child is not growing), she repeated, a little more loudly, as if the mother could not hear her "MORE BEANS . . . and don't give him too many tortillas or chips." With these confusing and imprecise instructions, the poor mother was ushered out of the office. The *nutricionista* turned to me and complained that the mother probably wouldn't do what she said and that "these mothers" cannot even follow simple instructions.

In this situation, several barriers to effective nutrition intervention occurred and many of these can be connected to stigma processes. First, we have a Ladino woman, who has provided no context for who she is, lecturing a mother who raises her child in a community in which one's social and kin connections are key to legitimate and authoritative knowledge. The nutritionist made no attempt to introduce herself (by name or any other characteristic), but rather operated on the assumption that, because she sat in the examining room as part of this medical *jornada*, the woman should take her words seriously and implement them. We can analyze this situation using Link and Phelan's (2006) outline of components of stigma. Conditioned by the widespread racism against indigenous Guatemalans, the nutritionist enacted the separation of "the other" ("these mothers"), applying the negative stereotypes associated with indigenous people to this woman. Her confidence in her own authority and the mother's lack of capacity for understanding, and a failure to acknowledge structural factors that would make it difficult for this mother to access high-quality foods for the child, relieved her of any responsibility to make a case to the child's mother. She was able to easily dismiss the mother's stunned expression as a sign of ignorance and stupidity. This likely contributed to the nutritionist's harsh tone when speaking to the indigenous mother. The nutritionist did not take such a tone when conversing with me or with her colleagues—it was reserved for speaking to the indigenous mothers as though they were in need of stern correction, like young children. It reminded me of Rigoberta Menchu's descriptions of how she and her fellow maids were spoken to more harshly than the dogs of the wealthy families for whom they worked (Menchu, Burgos-Debray, and Wright 2010). Finally, stigma had its direct effect on the health of this little boy in the form of a missed opportunity for effective intervention for his developing chronic malnutrition and for his respiratory infection. Stigma, as a social process, deepened the impact of the malnutrition/infectious disease syndemic on this child and his family.

The nutritionist, in large part, because of this deeply embedded stigma, missed an opportunity to effectively counsel the mother. In this case, the nutritionist was not over-worked and trying to serve too many patients—after the woman left, we waited nearly ten minutes for another child to show up. I am not suggesting that this nutritionist specifically be implicated in missing the opportunity. From conversing with her, it seemed more that she lacked the training on how to effectively counsel a mother with a malnourished child. She had been taught how to measure and identify malnutrition, but had little preparation for actually dealing with it in real life situations. This reflects a broader problem, in which there seems to be little real national-level dedication to effective health services for indigenous communities in Guatemala. The effort is focused on being able to complete checklists and say that something has been done, rather than making that "something" effective. This lack of investment is the kind of problem that can constitute an abuse on the part of society that facilitates "neglect" by parents (Nayar et al. 2014).

In another dimension of this case, we have an indigenous mother who brought her little boy to the medical *jornada* because she was concerned about his coughing, but was, instead, confronted with an accusation that her child was not growing well. She had been directed to the nutritionist, rather than a doctor, because the boy was young and the nutritionist needed to see patients. The boy's cough remained unaddressed as his mother carried him out of the health post, stunned by what had transpired. She now possibly had an awareness that her child was "not growing well" but that would have had little meaning for her, since the nutritionist never explained what that meant or why it was a problem and because, from the mother's perspective, her little boy was comparable in size and shape to other local children his age. She likely only half heard what the nutritionist was saying anyway, because she was trying to wipe her son's runny nose and comfort him because he was crying and coughing. He was crying because he did not want to be measured and his crying aggravated his coughing. Over her son's crying and coughing, the indigenous mother may have heard the vague instructions to give him beans, but not too many tortillas or chips. These instructions likely sounded rather silly and irrelevant to her, because they had nothing to do with her son's cough, which was her reason for bringing him to the clinic in the first place and because her son was obviously too young to eat beans. As a member of this community, she had learned that beans can "*empachar*" (give stomach pains and gas[4]) to a child who is not ready to digest them. For this reason, most mothers wait until a child is one year old to introduce them. The risk of *empacho*, which has been discussed in anthropological circles as a folk illness identified with relatively consistent causes and characteristics throughout Latin America (Weller et al. 1993; Weller, Ruebush, and Klein 1991) was not even considered by the nutritionist. She did not engage with local understandings of child feeding because these are seen by many health professionals as "local beliefs" and, by virtue of being simply "beliefs," they are ideas that do not need to be seriously considered, but rather overcome. The mother left with her son, both subjects of a stigma that prevented them from being heard and receiving the help that they were seeking and needed.

In terms of a malnutrition/infectious disease syndemic, the body of this little boy was caught up in a condition in which his malnourished status and immune compromise were interacting and magnifying one another. His mother, recognizing that his body and her ability to care for it needed external support, sought that support and was thwarted by a deeply embedded stigma against poor, indigenous populations. The stigma delayed, and may even have prevented medical intervention for this child.

This part of the stigma process, in which members of the stigmatized group (poor or indigenous Guatemalans) continuously lose status as fully competent members of Guatemalan society, is reflected in the media as well. For example, the *Prensa Libre*, Guatemala's main daily newspaper, occasionally reports on issues related to malnutrition. An article published on February 18, 2015 explained that cases of acute malnutrition[5] are flourishing in Guatemala and that children are being "rescued" from their parents to receive treatment. Below is a quote from this article, followed by a translation:

> Unos 900 niños con desnutrición aguda podrían ser rescatados este año, según estima la Secretaría de Seguridad Alimentaria y Nutricional (Sesán), que en tres años ha registrado 47 mil 574 casos, aunque todavía hay otros sin atender.
>
> La Sesán atiende un promedio de 18 mil niños con malnutrición aguda. Un caso reciente es el de tres hermanos rescatados en El Bejucal, Casillas, Santa Rosa, el martes último.
>
> Germán González, jefe de la Sesán, explicó: "Los rescates de niños con desnutrición aguda en algunos casos son efectuados con orden de juez, porque los padres están desinformados." (Pitán 2015)

> "900 acutely malnourished children could be rescued this year," estimates the Ministry of Food and Nutritional Security (SESAN), which, in three years, has registered 47,574 cases, although there are still others unattended.
>
> SESAN serves an average of 18,000 children with acute malnutrition. A recent case is that of three brothers rescued in El Bejucal, Casillas, Santa Rosa, last Tuesday.

> Germán González, head of the SESAN said: "The rescues of children with acute malnutrition in some cases are made by order of the judge, because parents are uninformed."
> (End translation.)

This public statement by the head of the Ministry of Food and Nutritional Security serves to reinforce to the general public in Guatemala that malnutrition is the result of uninformed, ignorant parenting that persists in spite of attempted interventions by Ministry of Health and SESAN programs.

Consequently, the general attitude toward populations with high rates of malnutrition is that they are inferior and not motivated to do what they need to raise healthy children and that their children will simply be the same. The stigma is so pervasive that, even among indigenous adults, the poorer will be dismissed as hopeless by those who have slightly more education or financial means. For example, a young girl, Cecilia, in an indigenous town had been identified by the indigenous Ministry of Health workers as falling into the category of "*desnutricion aguda*" (acute malnutrition); basically, her weight for her height was quite low. Cecilia was also stunted, indicating a chronic malnutrition that likely interacted with and worsened her infectious disease conditions, although the Ministry of Health workers did not acknowledge the chronic malnutrition at any point; they were entirely focused on her weight-for-height, as that was the condition they were required to act on.[6] Cecilia had been sick, had lost her appetite while she was sick and was slow to regain it. Consequently, she was also slow to regain the weight that would put her into the category of acceptable weight-for-height. I learned of her case when her mother consulted with the free, privately run clinic in the village, because the girl was not gaining weight and the Ministry of Health workers were threatening to take her away to put her in a hospital for nutritional therapy (to rescue her). Since I was pilot testing a digital photography food record method at the time and looking for families to participate in a weighed food record comparison, one of the doctors at the free clinic asked me to work with this family to see how and what the little girl was eating, to help them to better support the mother. The day we did the weighed-food record, I observed that the mother was indeed making an effort to encourage her daughter to eat and that the girl was eating small amounts of food. Cecilia's mother explained the many things she was trying to do to encourage her daughter to eat and showed me the different types of foods they had received from the clinic or purchased themselves to tempt her appetite. Cecilia's mother also expressed her great concern, fear, and sorrow that the Ministry of Health workers were looking to take her daughter.

In addition to conducting an in-depth interview with her mother and weighed-food record for the family, I also measured Cecilia twice a week for two weeks and documented that she was slowly gaining weight. Even with this added information, the Ministry of Health workers were not looking at her weight gain as part of a trend in the right direction; rather, they were looking at her weight-for-height as a binary variable—good or bad. Because it was in the "bad" category for too long, they were threatening to take action.

The stigma and direct threats against the parents contributed to the mother's avoidance of the Ministry of Health services. She feared taking her children to the health post for anything, including growth monitoring and vaccinations, because they "*le regañan*" or scold her and threaten to take her daughter. This scolding approach to communicating with patients has also been reported by others (Chary et al. 2013; Berry 2013). When I attempted to discuss the case with a Ministry of Health worker, who was an indigenous woman from another village, she commented that the mother did not care about her daughter and was not trying hard enough to make her gain weight. As demonstrated by the media reports of malnourished children being "rescued" in various parts of the country, this situation could have feasibly lead to the child being taken. It is also possible that a forcible "rescue" would have been subject to a higher level of review that would have prevented this from happening, as the girl was actually gaining weight; however, the point remains that the threat was made, and the basis of that threat was an ungrounded assumption that this mother (because she was poor and indigenous) did not care enough about her child and did not have the wherewithal to care for her appropriately.

This approach makes for an antagonistic relationship between parents and health workers, in which the health workers, whether Ladino or indigenous, regardless of their training or real expertise, feel a sense of authority and power over the poorer and less formally educated members of the communities that they serve. In terms of stigma processes, the negative stereotypes of impoverished indigenous people contribute to a loss of status in which adults are spoken to and scolded by health workers as if they are children. This puts the stigmatized group at a disadvantage in multiple ways, as the parents are less likely to trust those health workers, and less likely to take advantage of the resources that the workers are gatekeepers for. In this particular case, from a clinical perspective, the fact that Cecilia was gaining weight and "moving up in the charts," would suggest that she was not in immediate danger of death from malnutrition and that her mother should be encouraged and supported, rather than disparaged and threatened. Her status as a poor, indigenous woman with little schooling made her vulnerable to this poor treatment.

In Cecilia's case, I argue that poor training and lack of knowledge on the part of the health workers, in combination with a predisposing stigma against poor mothers, moved the Ministry of Health staff to threaten the family. Training is often insufficient because the programs are not financially well-supported (Martorell 2012), and, with the exceptions of some positions such as the vaccination nurse, there is much turnover in staffing, at least in this particular village. Many positions in the Ministry of Health posts are political appointments which change as municipal or departmental leadership changes. As in the case of the coughing baby boy in the medical *jornada*, stigma against poor, indigenous populations simultaneously operates at interpersonal levels and structural levels, creating a profound barrier to acceptable and effective access to health resources.

Stigma directed at the poor, indigenous communities with high rates of malnutrition is not the exclusive purview of elites and health workers. Stigma is perpetuated within and across communities as well, adding a layer of complication that must be explicated to begin to address the problem. For example, one day I was riding a *lancha* (public boat taxi) across Lake Atitlan, when an indigenous man from a neighboring village asked me about what I was doing in Guatemala. I explained that I was working in one of the villages to understand why so many children in Guatemala are malnourished. With a dismissive laugh, he explained to me that everybody knows the answer to that question. In this particular village, he explained, people are behind the times and not very smart and the men are all lazy and alcoholic and drink away the little money that they do earn. The problem, he said, is the parents. The parents do not care and do not want to do what is right for their children.

This stigmatization of poor and indigenous populations undermines the effectiveness of health programs, even when they are supposed to be "culturally appropriate" by virtue of employing indigenous staff. As noted earlier, in poorer villages, a large portion of the ethnically indigenous staff for NGOs and Ministry of Health programs comes from other less poor towns. The poorer towns do not always have enough qualified individuals. Thus, these indigenous health workers, who have achieved the higher levels of education which qualify them for these positions, move to "separate" themselves from the less educated, poor, indigenous Guatemalans. They, by virtue of having to prove themselves in an environment in which they are being discriminated against, come to see themselves as exceptions to the "*Indio bruto*" stereotype that had been applied to them as they sought higher education (Berry 2013). They differentiate themselves from the population they fear being associated with to deflect the potential stigma their indigenous identity carries. In my repeated visits to a community in Guatemala, I observed an indigenous health worker and friend make this transition. Over a period of four years, during which my friend completed her schooling and achieved a high-level certification in nursing, she transitioned from interacting in an empathetic way with her patients, and discussing their cases and their struggles with respect and deference, to interacting with her patients in an authoritative way and discussing their cases and struggles as though they were individual failings on the part of the patients. Symbolically, during this period, her daily attire also transitioned from the full traditional dress of a *huipil* and *corte* to a white coat and jeans. Her indigenous patients bore the brunt of the stigma she had experienced as an indigenous woman seeking advanced certification.

The size of the thymus or the conditions of the epithelial lining of the intestines are only a small part of the picture of the malnutrition/infectious disease syndemic among poor, indigenous Guatemalans. This syndemic is not an individual problem located in individual bodies; it is a biosocial problem situated in bodies that are subjected to difficult social, physical, and economic conditions that are structured by political factors that operate beyond their control, but for which they are stigmatized. While parental knowledge and attitudes are certainly a factor in the occurrence of chronic malnutrition and infectious diseases, concentrating too much on them as a cause risks denigrating the capacity and motivation of parents to care for their children. The broader social attitudes that perpetuate conditions of poverty and dismissal of impoverished, indigenous populations as incapable or unmotivated are a serious problem here, both in terms of blaming the victim and in making efforts to educate and support parents less effective. The stigma against the indigenous populations deepens with worsened poverty as unhealthy physical bodies come to reflect the inequalities of the social body and the encompassing body politic.

Following Brown's (1987) discussion of microparasitism and macroparasitism, we can think of stigma as part of a macro-level, social, infectious agent that may variably affect individuals and communities. Stigma operating at a social level weakens social (including economic and political) systems in which individual bodies live. In Guatemala, the concentration of wealth in the hands of a few, through the exclusion of many, particularly indigenous individuals, diverts significant natural and economic resources from those populations (Poder and He 2015), in the same way that a parasite diverts nutrients away from the cells of its host to feed itself. This leads to malnutrition and increased vulnerability to pathogens (as in the malnutrition/infectious disease syndemic), but at the level of communities and ethnic groups. Here, the communities, because of the suppressed human capital, are vulnerable to physical, economic, and social pathogens (such as epidemics, recessions, corruption, and violence) as well as to trauma from natural disasters, due to lack of sound infrastructure.

This parasitism is masked, or perhaps more accurately, rationalized, through the process of stigmatization. There is a common attitude that indigenous Guatemalans cause their own problems by not valuing education, by not choosing the correct foods, and by not keeping themselves and their homes clean. An even more insidious attitude is often reflected by those who know something about the effects of chronic malnutrition and infectious diseases, who argue that the indigenous people living in poverty do not have the cognitive or affective capacity to learn better. This includes a belief that they lack the cognitive capacity to understand the problem or implement potential solutions and lack the general wherewithal to care about how malnutrition affects their children. As this impacts the quality of interpersonal interactions with patients and community members, the stigmatization weakens professional health interventions.

REDUCING THE IMPACT OF STIGMA ON A MALNUTRITION/INFECTIOUS DISEASE SYNDEMIC

In the previous sections, I attempted to illustrate how stigma contributes to a malnutrition/infectious disease syndemic by analyzing cases from my ethnographic fieldwork in terms of the process outlined in the stigma and health literature. These personal, lived experiences of mothers and children living in conditions of structural discrimination in highland Guatemala provide a foundation from which to pursue study of the effects of stigma on child health and to identify points of intervention. Since stigma acts at multiple levels of causation, reducing or eliminating stigma could alleviate some of the difficulty in addressing child health issues. This section addresses the implications of considering stigma for discourse and programming for child malnutrition and infectious disease, and recommendations for minimizing effects of stigma on child health in Guatemala.

One important issue to consider in global-level discourse and programing is the degree to which touting the negative impacts of malnutrition, with the intention of motivating policy makers and development organizations to address the issue, might inadvertently reinforce the stigma against these populations. While those setting global health agendas know that not every child who was malnourished will automatically also be cognitively impaired, but are at higher (and unacceptable) risk of this effect, these details get lost in the heuristic statement "malnutrition is associated with long-term cognitive deficiencies." To the untrained ear, "We need to address malnutrition because malnourished children are more susceptible to disease and at risk for reduced cognitive capacity" becomes "malnourished children are sickly and grow up to be unintelligent." This inaccurate interpretation is reflected in the attitudes of many foreigners living in Guatemala, as discussed earlier, and also serves to reinforce existing perceptions of the "*Indio bruto*" among Guatemalans (Berry 2013). This reinforces stigma and rationalizes the poverty and inadequate living conditions that poor, indigenous Guatemalans are subjected to. Preventing this misapplication of nutrition and cognition data requires great care in communication and an emphasis on the fact that cognitive stimulation can significantly mitigate negative effects of the malnutrition/infectious disease syndemic on cognition (e.g., Engle et al. 2007).

Another important step in reducing stigma that impacts child health is to change discourse on malnutrition. In particular the blaming of parents, as in the *Prensa Libre* article cited earlier (Pitán 2015), contributes to an attitude that malnutrition is caused by ignorance or moral failing on the part of the parents. This stigma on the parents is also projected on the children, who can be seen as products of dysfunction and ignorance, and therefore, inferior to children being raised by "better parents." This problem has been recognized in other settings as well; for example, researchers and health workers in Rwanda advocate for actively reducing the stigma associated with malnutrition (Bertrand-Farmer et al. 2014). They found that educating communities about malnutrition can actually increase the experiences of stigma among parents seeking help for their malnourished children. However, they also argue that education that targets reducing stigma of malnutrition can be effective, mitigating the effects of stigma on access to healthcare for malnourished children. They recommend that public service messages specifically attempt to reduce malnutrition-related stigma and that healthcare workers be trained to interact with sensitivity toward families with children who are malnourished.

One way to combat malnutrition/infectious disease related stigma is to emphasize the difference between deliberate withholding of resources and simply not having resources. Golden, Samuels, and Southall (2003) note that "neglect," in popular discourse, has a negative connotation that can feed into stigma. They outline a clinical distinction between "neglect" and "abuse," with "abuse" requiring a deliberate action against or withholding of care from a child. They use "neglect" to refer to situations in which parents do not provide what a child needs (nutrition, emotional security, etc.), but in which this lack of provision is not deliberate and malicious, but rather, the result of circumstances that require the parent to prioritize some needs over others or prevent the parent from meeting the child's needs because of insufficient resources. This is certainly an important distinction to make in an effort to reduce stigma through education, especially in the training of health workers in a setting like Guatemala. However, even when such a theoretical distinction is made, the very act of parents not providing sufficiently for their children is fraught with moral implications across cultures. Overcoming this would require a complete reframing of the efforts to address child malnutrition and infectious disease.

Such a reframing might involve recognizing that, while discussing cycles of poverty with malnutrition and infectious disease is an epidemiologically accurate way to describe the problem, enumerating this cycle also helps to perpetuate a very dangerous and pathogenic social dynamic by situating the cycle in the bodies and homes of those affected by it. Policy discussions and research tend to focus on the individuals involved (parents and children in the context of their communities) because this is where interventions can have the most direct and measurable effect. However, unless we are very careful, by doing this we can contribute to the stigmatization of the poor, and of populations in whom malnutrition frequently occurs. Even the UNICEF Conceptual Framework (United Nations Children's Fund 2006), which frames much of my thinking about malnutrition, falls into this trap. While it recognizes structural, economic, and political forces as basic causes of malnutrition and recognizes the interactions between malnutrition and infectious diseases, the underlying cause categories of Healthy Environment, Care for Women and Children, and Health Services allow for too much blame to be put on the individual families and communities that fail to nourish children. Considering the role of social dynamics, particularly stigma processes, in discussions of child health and in the design of child health programs is critical to avoiding this pitfall. However, since parents are the ones who are closest to the children, especially during critical early years, they make the most sensible point for immediate intervention.

So, if working with parents and communities to solve issues leading to the child malnutrition/infectious disease syndemic is a necessary part of eliminating that syndemic, but nutrition and health programmers inadvertently hold or perpetuate stigmatizing assumptions about the parents and communities of affected children, what can be done? We tend to discuss successful interventions in health education or supplementation as improving "maternal knowledge and care practices," thereby improving child health. This, however, implies that the specific problem was "poor maternal knowledge and care practices" and thereby blames the mother.

At the same time, interventions that focus on maternal knowledge and care practices can increase the likelihood that their children will be healthy. The syndemic approach, which helps us to recognize stigma as a social driver of malnutrition-infectious disease interaction, suggests a need for a different framing. Perhaps, taking a page from Shelton, Alegre, and Son (2010), we should discuss successful interventions in areas such as health education as contributing to maternal resilience in the face of difficult conditions. This framing could change the current dynamic by acknowledging that mothers are working against many difficult conditions to keep their children healthy and that medical or health education interventions are only a small part of the resources they must draw from to accomplish this. With this framing the role and efforts of the mother are something to be supported, a strategy that acknowledges the mother as an asset to her child's health, rather than a detriment that needs to be overcome.

Incorporating this approach into training of local health workers could guide them to reframe their own roles in a more humane and collaborative way. If the leadership in health agencies clearly and deliberately signals a respect for the strength, resilience, and efforts of poor, indigenous mothers, then there could be a shift in the attitude of health workers, many of whom are indigenous, and reacting to stigma against themselves by stigmatizing those who are worse off. This could also be a useful approach to advocating for nutrition to top-level government officials as Martorell (2012) recommends.

In this effort, the anthropologist or ethnographer can contribute by documenting and contextualizing, not only the social and psychological experiences of stigma, but the lived physical experiences of hard labor and fatigue. As noted in discussions on neglect (Nayar et al. 2014), poverty forces parents to prioritize, and often their opportunity to prioritize according to that which they value (such as promoting the health of their children) is thwarted by the physical realities in which they live. Connecting this to the political economic context of a malnutrition/infectious disease syndemic in Guatemala, those physical realities in which they live (e.g., the complications and expenses of transportation, the extra steps needed to secure clean water, the work needed to secure cooking fuel), are shaped by historical, political, and social factors that are beyond their immediate control. It should be made very clear to anyone working on health issues with poor, indigenous Guatemalans that the work of maintaining daily household operations is extensive and that the level of knowledge and organization that most parents have and apply is impressive. It would be better for health workers to see their work not as correcting deficiencies in a stigmatized population, but as supporting the resilience of a strong group of people who are living with the odds stacked against them.

An important motivation for applying the syndemic concept in analyzing health issues is to improve prevention and intervention efforts (Singer, Bulled, and Ostrach 2012). I argue that understanding the interactions between malnutrition and infectious disease and stigma processes can help to identify points for intervention and guide improvements to policies and programs that address child health issues. Addressing and attempting to reduce the role of stigma processes in efforts to improve child health can help to shift attitudes of blame from parents in poor, indigenous populations to broader societal factors and can lead to more constructive, supportive, and effective efforts for child health.

NOTES

1. The term "malnutrition" can include undernutrition of multiple types and over-nutrition (usually obesity). In this paper, I am talking primarily about "chronic malnutrition," a form of undernutrition indicated by stunted growth, measured by a height-for-age z-score (HAZ) of less than –2 on the World Health Organization (WHO 2008) growth charts. Stunting indicates chronic undernutrition caused by an insufficient diet, frequent or chronic illness that interferes with nutrient utilization, or a combination of the two. Over-nutrition in the form of obesity has been unusual in indigenous children in Guatemala, but its prevalence is increasing, even among chronically malnourished children, creating a double burden of malnutrition. Whether under or

over nourished, children may also have deficiencies in one or more micro-nutrients such as iron, iodine, Vitamin A, Vitamin B, or folic acid. Local health services do not test all children for micronutrient deficiencies, but rather operate under the assumption that if a child's diet is deficient in protein and calories, that it is also likely to be deficient in micronutrients.

2. Having carried toddlers in a sling, while carting a measuring board and scale on some of these same paths, I can personally attest to the need for regular rest periods in order to be able to work effectively.

3. This comes from conversations or informal interviews with women who have had regular interactions with health clinics. "*Es difícil*" (it is difficult), they say.

4. Stomach pains and gas only loosely fit into the symptomology of *empacho* as represented in the anthropological literature, but this was the set of symptoms that mothers I interviewed most strongly associated with early consumption of beans.

5. Acute malnutrition is indicated by a weight for age z-score of less than –2, and in severe cases, can lead to death.

6. During this research trip, the Ministry of Health staff kindly agreed to let me copy their growth records for the last several months. As I was doing so, I asked about their thoughts on the current situation of malnutrition in the village. They indicated that it was not bad—they only had three children who were malnourished. My later analysis of the growth data showed that, while there were only three children with acute malnutrition, nearly 50 percent of the children under 36 months were chronically malnourished. The staff did not recognize chronic malnutrition as part of their mission because they were only directed to work with cases of acute malnutrition.

REFERENCES

Bennett, Elaine B. 2009. Understanding Childhood Malnutrition in a Maya Village in Guatemala: A Syndemic Perspective. PhD dissertation, Department of Anthropology, University of Connecticut.

Berry, Nicole S. 2006. Kaqchikel Midwives, Home Births, and Emergency Obstetric Referrals in Guatemala: Contextualizing the Choice to Stay at Home. *Social Science and Medicine* 62(8): 1958–1969.

———. 2008. Who's Judging the Quality of Care? Indigenous Maya and the Problem of "Not Being Attended." *Medical Anthropology* 27(2). Taylor & Francis Group: 164–89.

———. 2013. Unsafe Motherhood: Mayan Maternal Mortality and Subjectivity in Post-War Guatemala. Berghahn Books. https://books.google.com/books?id=IVlFAAAAQBAJ&pgis=1, accessed August 14, 2015.

Bertrand-Farmer, Didi, Grace Ryan, Saleh Niyonzima, et al. 2014. Blaming the Victim: Stigmatization and Food Insecurity in Rwanda Research Aims & Objectives. *Presented at the* 3rd Annual Food and Nutrition Summit. Kigali, Rwanda.

Black, Robert E., Saul S. Morris, and Jennifer Bryce. 2003. Where and Why Are 10 Million Children Dying Every Year? *Lancet* 361(9376): 2226–2234.

Brett, Roddy. 2011. Confronting Racism from within the Guatemalan State: The Challenges Faced by the Defender of Indigenous Rights of Guatemala's Human Rights Ombudsman's Office. *Oxford Development Studies* 39(2): 205–228.

Brown, Peter J. 1987. Microparasites and Macroparasites. *Cultural Anthropology* 2: 155–171.

Bulled, Nicola, Merrill Singer, and Rebecca Dillingham. 2008. The Syndemics of Childhood Diarrhoea: October 141(4): 520–529

Chary, Anita, Sarah Messmer, Eric Sorenson, et al. 2013. The Normalization of Childhood Disease: An Ethnographic Study of Child Malnutrition in Rural Guatemala. *Human Organization* 72(2): 87–97.

Dijk, Marieke van, Marta Julia Ruiz, Diana Letona, and Sandra G. García. 2013. Ensuring Intercultural Maternal Health Care for Mayan Women in Guatemala: A Qualitative Assessment. Culture, Health & Sexuality. Routledge.

Engle, Patrice L., Maureen M. Black, Jere R. Behrman, et al. 2007. Strategies to Avoid the Loss of Developmental Potential in More than 200 Million Children in the Developing World. *Lancet* 369(9557): 229–242.

Golden, M. H., M. P. Samuels, and D. P. Southall. 2003. How to Distinguish between Neglect and Deprivational Abuse. *Archives of Disease in Childhood* 88: 105–107.

González-izás, Matilde. 2010. Guatemala: Modernisation Capitaliste et Racisme Dans Les Circuits Du Café: 119–134.

Grantham-McGregor, Sally, Yin Bun Cheung, Santiago Cueto, et al. 2007. Developmental Potential in the First 5 Years for Children in Developing Countries. *Lancet.*

Guerrant, D. I., S. R. Moore, A. A. Lima, et al. 1999. Association of Early Childhood Diarrhea and Cryptosporidiosis with Impaired Physical Fitness and Cognitive Function Four-Seven Years Later in a Poor Urban Community in Northeast Brazil. *The American Journal of Tropical Medicine and Hygiene* 61(5): 707–13. http://www.ncbi.nlm.nih.gov/pubmed/10586898.

Guerrant, Richard L., Reinaldo B. Oriá, Sean R. Moore, Mônica O. B. Oriá, and Aldo A. M. Lima. 2008. Malnutrition as an Enteric Infectious Disease with Long-Term Effects on Child Development. *Nutrition Reviews* 66(9): 487–505.

Hale, Charles R. 2006. Mas Que Un Indio (More Than An Indian): Racial Ambivalence And The Paradox Of Neoliberal Multiculturalism in Guatemala. Illlustrat. Santa Fe: SAR Press.

Jolly, Christopher A., and Gabriel Fernandes. 2000. Protein-Energy Malnutrition and Infectious Disease: Synergystic Interactions. *In* Nutrition and Immunology: Principles and Practices. M. Eric Gershwin, J. Bruce German, and Carl L. Keen, eds. Pp. 195–201. New Jersey: Humana.

Keusch, Gerald T., Joan Wilentz, and Arthur Kleinman. 2006. Stigma and Global Health: Developing a Research Agenda. *The Lancet* 367(9509): 525–527.

Keusch, Gerald T. 2003. The History of Malnutrition: Malnutrition, Infection and Immunity. *The Journal of Nutrition*: 336S–340S. http://jn.nutrition.org/content/133/1/336S.full.pdf+html.

Kleinman, A., W. Z. Wang, S. C. Li, et al. 1995. The Social Course of Epilepsy: Chronic Illness as Social Experience in Interior China. *Social Science & Medicine* 40(10): 1319–1330.

Kleinman, Arthur, and Rachel Hall-Clifford 2009 Stigma: A Social, Cultural and Moral Process. *Journal of Epidemiology and Community Health* 63(6): 418–9. http://www.ncbi.nlm.nih.gov/pubmed/19439576, accessed June 8, 2015.

Link, Bruce G., and Jo C. Phelan. 2001. Conceptualizing Stigma. *Annual Review of Sociology*. 27:363–385

———. 2006. Stigma and Its Public Health Implications. *The Lancet* 367: 528–529.

Lorntz, Breyette, Alberto M. Soares, Sean R. Moore, et al. 2006. Early Childhood Diarrhea Predicts Impaired School Performance. *The Pediatric Infectious Disease Journal* 25(6): 513–20. http://www.ncbi.nlm.nih.gov/pubmed/16732149, accessed June 7, 2012.

Marini, Alessandra, and Michele Gragnolati. 2003. Malnutrition and Poverty in Guatemala. World Bank (January): 1–54.

Martorell, R. 2012. Interventions and Policy Options for Combating Malnutrition in Guatemala. Washington, D.C. Banco Interamericano Del Desarrollo: 57. http://www.iadb.org/es/publicaciones/detalle,7101.html?id=39166&dcLanguage=es&dcType=All.

Menchu, Rigoberta, Elisabeth Burgos-Debray, and Ann Wright. 2010. I, Rigoberta Menchu: An Indian Woman in Guatemala. 2nd edition. Brooklyn: Verso.

Mendez, M. A., and L. S. Adair. 1999. Severity and Timing of Stunting in the First Two Years of Life Affect Performance on Cognitive Tests in Late Childhood. *The Journal of Nutrition* 129(8): 1555–1562.

Nayar, Usha S., Anne L. Stangl, Barbara De Zalduondo, and Laura M. Brady. 2014. Reducing Stigma and Discrimination to Improve Child Health and Survival in Low- and Middle-Income Countries: Promising Approaches and Implications for Future Research. *Journal of Health Communication* 19(sup1): 142–163.

Nelson, Diane M. 2001. Stumped Identities: Body Image, Bodies Politic, and the Mujer Maya as Prosthetic. *Cultural Anthropology* 16(3): 314–353. http://doi.wiley.com/10.1525/can.2001.16.3.314.

Niehaus, Mark D., Sean R. Moore, Peter D. Patrick, et al. 2002. Early Childhood Diarrhea Is Associated with Diminished Cognitive Function 4 to 7 Years Later in Children in a Northeast Brazilian Shantytown. *American Journal of Tropical Medicine and Hygiene* 66(5): 590–593.

Ostrach, Bayla, and Merrill Singer. 2012. "Syndemics of War: Malnutrition-Infectious Disease Interactions and the Unintended Health Consequences of Intentional War Policies." *Annals of Anthropological Practice* 36(2): 257–273.

Parker, Richard. 2012. Stigma, Prejudice and Discrimination in Global Public Health. *Cadernos de Saúde Pública* 28(1): 164–9. http://www.ncbi.nlm.nih.gov/pubmed/22267076.

Pitán, Edwin. 2015. Casos de desnutrición continúan aflorando. *Prensa Libre*, February 18. http://www.prensalibre.com/guatemala/casos-de-desnutricion-continuan-aflorando.

Plata-Salamán, C. R. 1998. Cytokines and Anorexia: A Brief Overview. *Seminars in Oncology* 25(1 Suppl 1): 64–72. http://europepmc.org/abstract/med/9482542, accessed August 8, 2015.

Poder, Thomas G., and Jie He. 2015. Role of Ethnic and Rural Disctimination in the Relationship Between Income Inequality and Health in Guatemala. *International Journal of Health Services* 45(2): 285–305.

Rice, Amy L., Lisa Sacco, Adnan Hyder, and Robert E. Black. 2000. Malnutrition as an Underlying Cause of Childhood Deaths Associated with Infectious Diseases in Developing Countries. Bulletin of the World Health Organization 78(10): 1207–1221.

Schaible, Ulrich E., and Stefan H. E. Kaufmann. 2007. Malnutrition and Infection: Complex Mechanisms and Global Impacts. *PLoS Medicine* 4(5): 0806–0812.

Schneider, J. W. 1988. Disability as Moral Experience: Epilepsy and Self in Routine Relationships. *Journal of Social Issues* 44: 63–78.

Scrimshaw, Nevin S. 2003. Historical Concepts of Interactions, Synergism and Antagonism between Nutrition and Infection. *The Journal of Nutrition* 133: 316S–321S.

Shelton, J. Nicole, Jan Marie Alegre, and Deborah Son. 2010. Social Stigma and Disadvantage: Current Themes and Future Prospects. *Journal of Social Issues* 66(3): 618–633.

Singer, Merill, and Scott Clair. 2003. Syndemics and Public Health: Reconceptualizing Disease in Bio-Social Context. *Medical Anthropology Quarterly* 17(4): 423–441.http://doi.wiley.com/10.1525/maq.2003.17.4.423, accessed February 25, 2016.

Singer, Merrill, Nicola Bulled, and Bayla Ostrach. 2012. Syndemics and Human Health: Implications for Prevention and Intervention. *Annals of Anthropological Practice* 36(2): 205–211.

Solomons, Noel W., and Gerald T. Keusch. 2000. Childhood Illnesses, Vaccinations, and Nutritional Status. *In* Nutrition and Immunology: Principles and Practices. M Eric Gershwin, J Bruce German, and Carl L Keen, eds. Pp. 181–194. New Jersey: Humana. United Nations Children's Fund 2006 UNICEF Joint Health and Nutrition Strategy for 2006–2015, vol.60563.

Wachs, T. D. 1995. Relation of Mild-to-Moderate Malnutrition to Human Development: Correlational Studies. *The Journal of Nutrition* 125(8 Suppl): 2245S–2254S.

Weiss, Mitchell G., and Jayashree Ramakrishna. 2006. Stigma Interventions and Research for International Health 367(2): 536–538.

Weller, S. C., L. M. Pachter, R. T. Trotter, and R. D. Baer. 1993. Empacho in Four Latino Groups: A Study of Intra- and Inter-Cultural Variation in Beliefs. *Medical Anthropology* 15(2): 109–136.

Weller, S. C., T. K. Ruebush, and R. E. Klein. 1991. An Epidemiological Description of a Folk Illness: A Study of Empacho in Guatemala. *Medical Anthropology* 13(1–2). Taylor & Francis Group: 19–31.

World Health Organization. 2008. Training Course on Child Growth Assessment: Module C Interpreting growth indicators. Geneva: WHO.

Williams, Daniel B., Paul W. Stupp, and Edgar Sajquim Pac. 2013. Revisión Del Estado Nutricional de Niños Y Niñas, ENSMI 2008 / 2009.

Chapter Eight

"Toothless Maw-maw can't eat no more"

Stigma and Synergies of Dental Disease, Diabetes, and Psychosocial Stress among Low-Income Rural Appalachians

Sarah Raskin

In July 2010, in my car with the air conditioner running in a McDonald's parking lot on a thoroughfare transecting the Clinch Mountain valley, Debbie,[1] a 49-year-old white woman, told me about her experiences observing other people's reactions to her teeth, in particular her advanced dental decay. Most folks were initially polite—customers at the Dairy Queen where she relished her second job decorating cakes, or patients at the low-income nursing home where she worked as a health aide, their own ill-fitting dentures tucked into their bedside drawers. Strangers' distanced sympathy frequently yielded to less subtle embarrassment on her behalf, as they turned their eyes downward after glimpsing her mouth. Such mannerly reactions to her dentition contrasted those of a more intimate relation, her husband. "I can feel more comfortable with you and my teeth than with him and my teeth," she said, continuing:

> Everybody else doesn't make me feel that bad about my teeth or my health. It's just him. He says to Autumn (their custodial granddaughter), "Toothless maw-maw. Maw-maw's getting toothless. She can't eat no more." . . . He says it's just joking but, you know, it's like how would he like to be called, if he had a stub? Sooner or later you get tired of hearing it.

Compounding the pain of Debbie's husband's mocking was the impediment he posed to her dental treatment. His addiction to prescription opioids consumed most of their resources, including money that she might have spent on fuel to drive to a far-off dental safety net clinic.

Perhaps unknown to Debbie's patients or customers, or to a social imaginary in which poor dentition indexes personal and moral failings (Heneghan 2007, Horton and Barker 2009, Smarsh 2014), is how cruelty and stigmatization not only are responses to dental problems, but also can contribute to their development. Debbie's synthesis of others' reactions to her dental decay exemplifies the social discomfort, self-consciousness, and internalized disdain that I came to understand as central to the phenomenology of dental suffering while conducting ethnographic fieldwork on dental disparities[2] in far southwest Virginia over fifteen months in 2010 and 2011.[3] So, too, did I learn that the shame often associated with dental decay, breakage, and abscesses was, for many research participants, but one hardship within a lifetime of suffering. Debbie traced her dental problems to her diabetes mellitus, which she developed while pregnant with her second child. These conditions, and others, were aggravated by a stressful prior marriage to a man who "didn't believe in medicine" and isolated her from care. For other research participants such as Tanya, described below, the interminable pain of advanced dental decay and persistent abscesses related not only to diabetes but also to her addiction to prescription opioids and, subsequently, heroin. Her stigmatization, and the internalized loathing it caused, traced not only to her dentition but also to her addiction. In addition to having dental problems, diabetes, and addiction—their own, or someone else's—in common, Debbie and Tanya also grew up in homes characterized by abuse and neglect including medical neglect; they suffered from clinical depression and anxiety and faced the economic, geographic, and social barriers to dental care and other social supports common to low-income rural residents of central Appalachia (Arcury et al. 2005; Behringer and Friedell 2006; Huttlinger et al. 2004).

Dental decay and gum disease, diabetes, addiction, and depression and anxiety interact in complex ways that can worsen each condition, and shape the lived experience of people who have them (D'Amore et al. 2011; Lamster et al. 2008; Peruzzo et al. 2007; USDHHS 2000). Accordingly, interactions among these factors also underlie susceptibility to being stigmatized for having evident decay, missing or broken teeth, and bad breath, because the stress response triggered by stigma can contribute to the development of or can exacerbate health concerns affected by the neural, cardiovascular, autonomic, immune, and metabolic systems (Link and Phelan 2006; McEwen 2008). How can we understand the relationships among dental stigma and interacting health problems, and the intimate and complex microbiological, clinical, social, and structural contexts through which they are shaped? A syndemics approach offers guidance.

Singer defines a syndemic as "the aggregation of two or more diseases in a population in which there is some level of deleterious biological interaction that exacerbates the negative health effects of any or all of the diseases" (2014:2419). He proposed the concept of syndemics in the mid-1990s to examine relationships among substance abuse, violence, and HIV/AIDS, and the social, political, and biological factors underlying these interactions (Singer 1996). Scholars have subsequently used the syndemic framework to examine synergies among other health problems and the contexts through which they occur. For example, Mendenhall situates the synergistic relationships among diabetes, depression, and social distress within contexts of structural, symbolic, and interpersonal violence (see, for example, Mendenhall 2012, Mendenhall 2015). Kline draws on syndemic theory to examine oral health effects of undocumented migration (2012). Hein and Small (2006) and Iacopino (2009) use a syndemics lens to examine two of the conditions addressed in this chapter, dental problems and diabetes.

The mutually worsening effects of dental disease, diabetes, addiction, and anxiety and depression are well documented in the clinical and epidemiologic literatures (see, for example, Chiou et al. 2010). Yet much of this literature overlooks the lived experiences of the people who bear these deleterious biological interactions or fails to situate these synergistic conditions within their social and structural contexts. Using a syndemic framework, in this chapter I examine disease synergies related to dental disease among central Appalachians within the "conditions of health inequality caused by poverty, stigmatization, stress, or structural violence" (Singer 2014:2420). While the region's economic marginalization, maldistribution of health care, environmental contamination, and stigmatized place in the American social imaginary generate chronically stressful living conditions and the persistent health problems that follow (Ludke and Obermiller 2012; Zullig and Hendryx 2011) this chapter focuses on the problem of dental stigma and its relationship with other health problems. Specifically, I trace the stress triggered by dental stigma[4] to the deleterious interactions among four health concerns that inordinately burden the region and its residents: dental disease; diabetes; addiction or, hereafter, substance (mis)use;[5] and depression and/or anxiety (ibid.). In this chapter, I first propose the dental syndemic by synthesizing major findings on interactions among dental disease and diabetes, substance (mis)use, and depression and/or anxiety, as well as existing scholarship on dental disease, dental stigma, and stress, then relate it to the aforementioned health concerns. I then elaborate the dental syndemic through the narratives of two research participants, Debbie and Tanya.

Theorizing the Dental Syndemic: Biological Pathways of Interaction

Dental disease is among the world's most common health problems, in particular dental caries (popularly known as tooth decay or cavities) (USDHHS 2000). The World Health Organization estimates that nearly every adult has had at least one cavity in her lifetime (WHO 2013). Two-thirds of American adults aged 65 years and older have either moderate or severe periodontitis, or inflammation of the gums (Eke et al. 2012). While periodic dental problems are common, chronic, or advanced dental disease is a trenchant marker of social inequality (IOM 2011; USDHHS 2000). For example, 80 percent of cavities diagnosed among U.S. youth are borne by only 25 percent of children, who are almost invariably from low-income households (Kaste et al. 1996).

Dental diseases are complex phenomena for which increasing knowledge about etiology also complicate understandings of pathogenesis, including the interacting roles of other diseases as well as social risk such as stigma and the stress it generates. Tooth decay occurs when naturally occurring oral bacteria, such as *Streptococcus mutans*, *Streptococcus sobrinus*, and lactobacilli, metabolize microscopic bits of food that remain after a person eats or drinks (Selwitz et al. 2007; Tanzer et al. 2001). This process produces acid, which erodes dental enamel and creates tiny holes—cavities—in the teeth. The risk of incipient dental decay becoming entrenched is highly variable and based on other factors such as the frequency and duration of exposure to simple sugars and remineralizing agents such as fluoridated water; "salivary capacity," or neutralization as a function of saliva; genetic predispositions, which are still poorly understood; access to clinical treatment; the heterogeneity of oral bacteria not just by individual person, but by individual tooth *surface*; and co-occurring diseases as well as some medications used to treat them (McLean 2014; Simón-Soro and Mira 2015; Yang et al. 2012). Research on the mutually deleterious interactions among dental disease and the co-occurring conditions presented in this chapter, framed in accordance with syndemic theory's emphasis on social, structural, and political economic determinants of health, offers a useful background for understanding this harmful dynamic.

Dental Disease and Diabetes Mellitus

Evidence increasingly demonstrates the mutually deleterious relationship between poor oral health and diabetes mellitus.[6] For example, diabetes can cause xerostomia, or "dry mouth," which can make dental surfaces more amenable to the "sticking" of simple sugars upon which decay-causing bacteria thrive (Sandberg et al. 2000; Syrjälä et al. 2003). Abscesses and other manifestations of poor oral health can irritate mucosal linings and drive up blood sugar, which can inhibit insulin response (Kidambi and Patel 2008; Lakschevitz et al. 2011). While most scholars use the word "bidirectional" to describe relationships between diabetes mellitus and oral health, cyclical might be a more appropriate adjective. Periodontal disease can worsen insulin resistance, for example, but poor glycemic control also can cause pre-decay lesions to develop and inhibit the periodontum's capacity to self-protect against inflammation and to heal (Lalla and Papanou 2011:738; Lamster et al. 2008). The proliferation of decay-causing oral bacteria can cause long-term changes in the oral microbiome that can depress immune functioning, which can be an effect of diabetes as well (Costalongo and Herzberg 2014; Wellen and Hotamisligil 2005). Given the immune system's role in maintaining overall health, including good oral health and an appropriate level of blood sugar, such suppression can aggravate dental disease and diabetes (Lähteenmäki et al. 2005; Turina et al. 2005).

While the successful management of dental problem and diabetes appears to be mutually beneficial, results vary based on the method of management. Treatment of periodontitis using basic non-surgical means has been demonstrated to have a positive effect on metabolic control not only initially after treatment, but also longitudinally (Darré et al. 2008; Sgolastra et al. 2013; Teeuw et al. 2010). Conversely, insulin therapy can negatively influence the pH balance of saliva and inhibit its capacity as a "buffer" against colonization by harmful oral bacteria (Hintao et al. 2007; Jawed et al. 2011; and Siudikiene et al. 2006). Vulnerability to the dental lesions that precede cavities are most pronounced among people who use insulin therapy exclusively and without accompanying dietary changes (Sandberg et al. 2000). As Debbie and Tanya's narratives demonstrate, below, their awareness of the negative impact of insulin on their oral health, particularly in their home environments of food insecurity, constitutes embodied knowledge that accords with that of experts.

Dental Disease and Substance (Mis)Use

The harmful effects of a variety of substances on dentition are well-documented (D'Amore et al. 2011; Laslett et al. 2008; Rees 2007). For example, the impaired vascular functioning and depression of immune response that can result from heroin use can increase risk of oral abscesses, and inhibit their resolution (Rees 2007; Rosenstein 1975). Oral motor activity associated with stimulants such as methamphetamines can grind down the protective enamel on dentition (Richards and Brofeldt 2000; Shetty et al. 2010). The use of a variety of illicit substances can generate cravings for sugary foods, tobacco, and other substances that increase susceptibility to dental disease (Laslett et al. 2008). Addiction can also inhibit dental home hygiene, as well as the maintenance of material resources that facilitate access to routine care and dental treatment (French et al. 2000; Robinson et al. 2005), as evinced in Debbie's narrative that opened this chapter. As with the cyclical interactions between diabetes and poor oral health, the deleterious effects of substance (mis)use and poor oral health can be mutually constituted. For example, individuals who lack access to dental care, commonly as a result of their low income or contingent employment, may manage dental pain by using cocaine, betel nut, alcohol, or other addictive substances (Agbor and Azodo 2011; Bedos et al. 2003; Cohen et al. 2009). We may understand this technique as both an attempt at self-care and an iatrogenic embodiment of social and structural exclusion.

While illicit substances garner attention for their negative effects on oral health, the adverse effects of legal substances including sugar, now recognized as physiologically addictive (Avena et al. 2008), are also well-documented. For example, tobacco, in both smoked and smokeless forms, contributes to the breakdown of gum tissues, the increased risk of oral cancers, and the development of underlying conditions of dental risk such as xerostemia or "dry mouth" (Winn 2001). Additives commonly used to sweeten chewing tobacco "bathe" the oral mucosa and dentition in the simple carbohydrates upon which acid-producing bacteria thrive (Tomar and Winn 1999); the consumption of smokeless tobacco also predicts diabetes risk, likely due to the metabolic effects of both natural sugars and artificial sweeteners (Brown et al. 2010; Östenson et al. 2012). Excess alcohol can also disrupt oral microbiological balance and overexpose the mouth to excess acids (via vomiting), thus increasing vulnerability to gum recession and dental decay (Dukicá et al. 2010; Smith and Robb 1989).

Dental Disease, and Depression and Anxiety

Associations between oral health and many psychosocial conditions are well-documented. Depression and anxiety[7] can exacerbate periodontal disease (Akcali et al. 2013; Peruzzo et al. 2007; Saletu et al. 2005), while psychosocial fortitude protects against it (Finlayson et al. 2010). Stress is associated with the number of missing teeth, even after controlling for family history of dental disease and frequency of toothbrushing (Rosania et al. 2009; see also Borrell and Crawford 2011). Psychosocial illness and stress do not merely contribute to the development of dental disease. They can also inhibit its treatment. For example, depression and anxiety negatively mediate periodontal therapy (Elter et al. 2002; Vettore et al. 2005).

In terms of the specific mechanisms of the negative influence of psychosocial conditions on oral health, some pathways have been identified. For example, the negative impact of depression on immune function can cause bacterial overgrowths, which can increase risk of dental caries (Kiecolt-

Glaser and Glaser 2002). As with the other health concerns that comprise the dental syndemic, the relationships among dental disease and psychosocial conditions are cyclical and mutually propagating. For example, Berk et al. describe depression as an inflammatory disease and trace dental disease as one possible source of inflammation (2013). Stress has also been found to stimulate inflammation, to negative effect on oral health (Vettore et al. 2005). Psychosocial distress can inhibit self-care regimens, for example tooth-brushing or seeking dental treatment; in the context of care exclusions it can also foment iatrogenic coping methods, for example the self-medicating with addictive substances described above (Chiou et al. 2010; Preeja et al. 2012; Thomson et al. 2000).

Systemic barriers to dental care, such as lack of employer-provided health insurance, dentists' refusals to accept children's comprehensive public dental benefits, or service limitations on adults' public dental benefits, cause considerable stress among low-income patients (Raskin 2015). Financial-related stress and "distress manifest as depression" (Genco 1999:711) track closely with the severity of periodontal disease in adults even after controlling for social, microbiological, and behavioral risk factors (see also Celeste et al. 2011 and Ng and Keung 2006). This finding helps to explicate another: that U.S. adults who earn less than $30,000 per year are twice as likely to lose all of their teeth as those who earn more than that (ADA 2014).

Deleterious Interactions among Diabetes, Substance (Mis)Use, and Depression and Anxiety

The interacting relationships among diabetes, substance (mis)use, and/or depression and anxiety are well-documented elsewhere, including in work that utilizes a syndemic framework; accordingly, my treatment of these relationships here is scant. For example, the mutually worsening relationship between psychosocial conditions and substance (mis)use is long-documented in the epidemiologic, clinical, and social science literatures. Self-medication of mood disorders with addictive substances, like self-medication of dental pain, is a common practice among people who face material, structural, and social barriers to care such as lack of financial resources, lack of health insurance, and internalized feelings of shame (Bolton et al. 2009; Link et al. 1999). Conversely, the use of or dependence upon substances such as alcohol and narcotics (both regulated and illicit) can serve to worsen depression (Boden and Ferguson 2011; Sordo et al. 2012). The physiology of withdrawal can also lead to anxiety and depression (Powell and Taylor 1991).

Interactions between substance (mis)use and diabetes are extremely complex, especially when considered within the social, structural, and political economic contexts through which the maldistribution of these health problems occur as both distinct and interacting concerns. For example, alcohol and tobacco have been associated with the onset of diabetes mellitus, as well as related sequelae including liver cirrhosis and cancer (Johnson et al. 2001; Marrero et al. 2005). Inequality in access to diabetes screening and care, treatment for addiction, liver transplantation, and cancer screening and treatment maldistribute related suffering and premature mortality along racial, ethnic, gender, income-based, and geographic lines (Heisler et al. 2003; Jacobson et al. 2007; Moylan et al. 2008; Ward et al. 2004). Exposure to addiction in one's social environment, and the interpersonal abuse with which it may co-manifest, can also exacerbate the symptoms of diabetes, as well as depression (Mendenhall 2012). Indeed, the mutual and cyclical worsening effects of diabetes, depression and anxiety, and substance (mis)use parallel the mutual and cyclically worsening effects of dental disease and each of these health concerns. With this in mind, we can examine another aspect of the dental syndemic proposed: the stigmatization of poor dentition, the stress that follows, and the resulting health effects.

Stigma, and the Exacerbating Role of Embodied Stress

Singer identifies stigma among the contextual factors that shape syndemics (2014). Link and Phelan argue that stigma takes place "when elements of labeling, stereotyping, separation, status loss, and discrimination co-occur in a power situation" (2001:367, see endnote 4). They identify stigma as a "fundamental cause of population health inequalities" (Hatzenbuehler 2013). Stigma can impede access to care, create discrimination within clinical encounters, and shape pathways through which access to care occurs (Allen et al. 2014; Fay et al. 2011; Hansen et al. 2014; Puhl and Heuer 2010). As Goffman's classic study highlights, and the cases presented in this chapter illustrate, stigma shapes social relations more broadly, for example, influencing others' regard for individuals who have—or are suspected of having—stigmatized illnesses (1963). Stigma can also have physiological effects, as the stress response it can trigger in the body can impede functioning of the neural, cardiovascular, autonomic, immune, and metabolic systems (Link and Phelan 2006; McEwen 2008).

While each of the health concerns addressed in this chapter bears the burden of stigma, I am particularly concerned here with dental-related stigma. Having "good teeth" is considered, in the United States and, increasingly, elsewhere, an aesthetic ideal, a social norm, and a moral imperative (Heneghan 2007; Khalid and Quiñonez 2015; Wickström 2016). Conversely, evident dental disease can powerfully interpellate the bearer into a denigrated social role, in particular for the way that it indexes a lack of self-control, self-interest, and self-care (Horton and Barker 2009; Raskin 2015; Smarsh 2014). For example, public campaigns aimed at reducing methamphetamine use objectify and pathologize low-income rural white people specifically at the site of their dentition (Linneman and Wall 2013; Murakawa 2011); a similar popular discourse, relevant as well to the stigmatization of diabetes as a disease of unrestrained consumption, regards the ingestion of sugary beverages, in particular the Appalachian-originated carbonated beverage Mountain Dew (see Barclay 2013). Such stigmatization fails to account for the structural determinants through which disease, access to treatment, and risk and protective factors—for example, in the case of Mountain Dew, uncontaminated water, nutritious foods, and dental care—are (mal)distributed along economic and other lines. Regardless, it powerfully generates stress (Shetty et al. 2010) that can have profound psychophysiological effect.

Given the propensity of stress to be a precursor to or to worsen dental disease, diabetes, psychosocial conditions, and substance (mis)use, stress derived from dental stigma has particular salience to the syndemic proposed here. These health problems and the related stigma and stress they cause disproportionately burden low-income, rural, and otherwise marginalized populations. So, too, however, do the background conditions against which their daily lives are cast. In the Appalachian context, stigma surrounding health diagnoses and health behaviors collates with the structural violence of living under a regional extraction economy regime that has been described as internal colonization, confronting material and symbolic barriers to health care, and being vilified routinely in the public imaginary for closely-held local traditions, spirituality, and political orientations (Ludke and Obermiller 2012; Zullig and Hendryx 2011). We now turn to two case examples from my research, to explore the lived experiences of the dental syndemic.

Living the Dental Syndemic: Debbie and Tonya's Stories

Clinical and epidemiologic research document numerous harmful interactions among dental disease, diabetes, substance (mis)use, anxiety and depression, and embodied stress, including the stress of dental stigma. In this section, I draw on narrative evidence from my research on dental disparities in far southwest Virginia to examine the lived experiences of these biological interactions and social dynamics. First, I return to the story of Debbie, which opened this chapter. Her narrative portrays how the embodied stress of dental stigma, combined with a lifetime of poverty, health care exclusions and subjugating family relationships coalesce in the manifest interacting illnesses of the dental syndemic. I then share Tanya's story, in which the pharmaceutical management of chronic pain and diabetes iatrogenically underlie mutually exacerbating dental disease, addiction, depression, and a dental stigma that causes her to self-alienate from her beloved social supports. I conclude the chapter by synthesizing observations on the lived experiences of dental syndemics.

Debbie's Narrative: Dental Stigma Amidst a Lifetime of Self-Sacrifice

When I first met Debbie, she attributed breakages in her dentition to the initiation of her use of insulin, five years prior, to manage her diabetes mellitus, a phenomenon described, clinically, above. Soon, however, the contextualization of her dental problems within the longer experience of her life became clear. The third youngest daughter of an alcoholic coal miner who "didn't believe in medicine" and a mother who was powerless against his stance to take her nine children to medical care despite having "a (Medicaid) card," Debbie spent much of her youth parenting her two younger brothers and protecting her twin sisters from their father's sexual abuse. At sixteen Debbie, who did not know how to read, married a man whose skepticism of the medical establishment and control over household decision-making mirrored her father's. When she developed gestational diabetes during her second full-term pregnancy he withheld from her the resources to determine her own care, such as access to her own insurance card or modest amounts of money to make co-payments. He controlled which clinicians she saw, how frequently, and all other aspects of health care. For nearly twenty years, including her first husband's death and her marriage to a second husband who spent their meager resources on the prescription opioids to which he was addicted, Debbie managed her diabetes using the advice of a health educator she knew: by eating no more than 45 grams of carbohydrates per day. It seemed easy at the time, "natural" even to this woman, born and raised in the region, who loved to forage in the hills for blackberries, pecan nuts, and mushrooms.

Five years prior to our interview, however, stressful life events interrupted Debbie's diet-based approach to managing her glucose levels. Following the untimely death of her daughter-in-law, she gained custodianship of her young granddaughter. Accordingly, Debbie found herself with less time to harvest, for free, the healthy foodstuffs she couldn't afford at the grocery store. The unexpected expense of raising her granddaughter caused her to seek out a second job. To save money, Debbie also began eating the $1 meals offered to staff at the low-income nursing home where she worked—soft mushes of overcooked grains, processed meats, and rendered fruits and vegetables. Her blood sugar soon became unmanageable. Debbie turned, reluctantly, to insulin. The symptoms of diabetes that she had kept at bay for two decades began setting in. "It's getting my eyes," she said, "It's done got my leg. It's got my right foot right now. My kidneys is fine, thank God for that." Debbie's mouth, however, was not fine, as evinced in a series of abscesses. As a Medicaid beneficiary in the state of Virginia, Debbie was not entitled to dental coverage beyond emergency extractions, so she asked her primary care provider for antibiotics. Yet one abscess persisted so, she said, "I busted it (she made the motion of jabbing her mouth with a needle) and "spit out" the infection. She continued, "It hurt, but it hurt worse if I didn't do it. (The abscess) tries to come back . . . I'm beginning not to fight off infections really good. It's not just my gums. It's all over my body."

Debbie showed me her forearm, where there also persisted an infected hair follicle that she had also tried, a number of times, to drain herself. She explained that her doctor attributed her uncontrollable glucose and the infections it seemed to be causing, to stress and dental disease, and advised dental extractions. Yet Debbie felt that the proposed "solution" to this set of problems would cause another: profound emotional distress. She said:

> I'm concerned I'll be toothless. I always like to pay attention to peoples' teeth cause mine's so bad. There's a lot of people got real pretty teeth that I always liked to want. I was just infatuated with teeth 'cause I knew mine was so, you know. For people who's got good teeth, I'm glad they got them. It don't make me feel bad as far as mine goes, but . . .

Debbie's narrative turned reflective. Seeing others' good teeth reminded her of her lifetime of deferring self-care to that of others. Her younger twin sisters, who she shielded from their father's sexual abuse and successfully advocated for entry into a foster home, grew up to embody what she saw as the successful middle-class life. They completed college degrees and entered into professional pathways. They received orthodontic treatments to perfect their smiles. Debbie's embodiment of suffering, by contrast, accumulated over time and now stoked discord in her sibling relationships. Her sisters were more polite in their observations of her teeth than was her husband, but they still hounded her to take better care of herself and have "more self-respect." For Debbie, such antagonism countered her understanding of her role as a care-taker, as well as her limited capacity as a result of her health limitations. Diabetes "slowly kills you," she explained, continuing:

> You want to do things but you don't have the energy to do what you need to do for yourself. I guess my kids got me through my life. Now I've got them grown and I don't worry about (self-care) as much as I used to. . . . You know, I had to keep myself really intact so I could work and take care of my kids but now that they're grown and got the life of their own I don't.

Debbie's diminished propensity for self-care notwithstanding, she still felt she was entitled to some dignity, especially in a personal life characterized by self-sacrifice. Instead, she experienced the stress of its denial, and consequential exacerbations of illnesses and suffering.

Debbie's multiple mutually worsening illnesses traced a long life in which she was excluded from health care, obligated to prioritize her siblings and husbands before herself, and ridiculed or pitied for the dental disease that resulted. Contact with people at her workplaces and in her personal life served to remind her of her own marginality, specifically at the site of her mouth, whether the polite, if poorly hidden, pity of strangers, the cruelty of her husband, or the goading of her sisters. Rather than feeling appreciated for her competence, caregiving, or personhood—or, in the case of her family, her self-sacrifice—Debbie endured the public humiliation of her marked dentition.

Concurrently, Debbie tried to manage her multiple interacting illnesses and the stress accrued by both illness and dental stigma, within the context of two additional stressors: economic precarity and traumatic life events. Debbie was excluded from dental care by the structural arrangement of employment and health benefits in the region, as elsewhere in the United States. As a beneficiary of public entitlements in a state that, like many, restricted adult public dental benefits to emergency extractions, Debbie was not entitled to restorative procedures to address the visual and functional problems of her teeth; neither did her benefits cover the preventive or routine procedures that could have encapsulated subsequent dental problems early enough to slow or halt them. Her husband's addiction posed a barrier to care as well, as his consumption of the family's resources left her with no ability to pay for dental care out of pocket. Debbie's increasing dependence upon the low-cost and low-quality foods provided by her employer and insulin to manage her diabetes also contributed to her dental decline and, accordingly, her community's, sisters', and husband's stigmatizing responses to her evident decay and breakage. Moreover, her sense of her decreasing usefulness to others underlay her diminishing self-care.

Tonya's Narrative: Dental Stigma as an Index of Guilt

I met Tonya, a 43-year-old white woman, in the mobile home she shared with her husband, three children, and a toddler granddaughter, on a dead-end gravel path off a tertiary road that led to the federal penitentiary. From the small floral sofa where she spent most of her days, couch-bound by her weight and chronic pain, Tonya told me about her "stomach tooth,"[8] the most recent of her seven remaining teeth to cause her pain in and around her mouth. Unresolved dental problems were not uncommon in Tonya's family since her husband and she had both been retired onto public disability entitlements over five years prior, she from her job as a school bus driver due to chronic knee pain and he from his work as a carpenter and roofer due to chronic obstructive pulmonary disease. Like Debbie, their only covered benefit was emergency extractions. Between this service limitation and their fixed household income, they couldn't find a provider whose charges they could afford.

For six months Tonya treated her stomach tooth herself, as she had done previously with other teeth that eventually broke off at the gum line. She used toothpicks to fish food debris from its hollowed-out structure, rinse it with mouthwash, and pack it with temporary filling material she purchased at the pharmacy. She took antibiotics and prescription painkillers that family members had saved from previous hospitalizations, to treat the abscesses that surrounded her stomach tooth. Eventually, when her self-treatment failed to resolve the infection, and the pain, Tonya found a dentist willing to negotiate cost—and clinical standards. He charged her $35 for the office visit and $95 for a simple extraction without x-rays. The extraction didn't resolve the infection or pain fully, an indicator that the extraction was incomplete due to the lack of the diagnostic guidance. Tonya reluctantly went to the Emergency Room. Aware of her local reputation as a drug seeker, a positionality based on not only her prior behavior but also the evident dental problems caused by drug use, she told the staff, "I'm not here for pain medication." Crying, she begged the staff for a nerve blocker. They acquiesced.

Tonya's request for a nerve blocker did not derive merely from her savvy navigation of a health care system in which her experience of stigmatization, as a recovering addict to opioids, had become commonplace. It was also a pragmatic decision based on her commitment to maintaining her hard-won sobriety. Having been investigated by social services during her active periods of drug abuse, and threatened with removal of her children, Tonya was determined to stay sober so her family could continue to live together. She attributed her sobriety to her faith in God, a faith she fortified by attending church. Yet she increasingly felt inhibited from going out in public, as a result of her evident dental disease and the stigma associated with it. This feeling of alienation from one of the foremost sites of her self-care was especially concerning when Tonya's dental decay got so painful that she felt she had to address it. Reluctantly, she utilized off-label prescription medications, aware of the risk that they might foment the return of her addiction. "I regret the day I started (taking drugs)," she said, "I regret the day I ever even knew what a Tylenol was. I would rather just be off everything, not be on nothing."

Yet, Tonya was not able to be off everything. She took Xanax for anxiety, Tylox for chronic knee pain, and "shots in (her) stomach all the time" for diabetes. Like Debbie, Tonya had observed the negative effects of insulin on her teeth. She experienced this decline as harder to bear than others. "I'm a big woman so I feel insecure about myself," she explained, continuing:

> When I go out in public I like dressing nice. If I go to church I like dressing in suits or if I go to meetings or something like that. But my teeth is so embarrassing to me, where I can't smile and I always have to hold my hand over my mouth, you know, 'cause I don't want people to see my teeth. I like feeling

> good, and dressing up is feeling good to me. It's not being a snob, wanting to feel good. But my teeth is the only thing now that's gotten to me. The not smiling, you know, not smiling like I want to. I'm really discouraged about my teeth, really bad.

Tonya's discouragement indexed the same double bind of managing her diabetes or her oral health that occupied Debbie's thoughts as well. Tonya's discouragement also derived from another source: her guilt over her former addiction to drugs, now marked upon her dentition. "My teeth was really good when I was younger," she explained, continuing:

> Then I got out there, got some experience in the world, I'm not gonna lie, doing some illegal things and that's what I think happened to my teeth. I was hooked on heroin for a long time and that's what made my body go downhill. I put on the weight and started going into depression. . . . I've gained over 200 pounds because dope will make you get depressed. I'd just lay in bed and get my dope going. Now I've noticed I can't get up and move around anymore because of what I've done to my body. And you can't get up and move around when you're on dope because you're depressed and I think 'cause you feel guilty. I feel guilty when I do it.

For Tonya, the complex interactions among various illnesses, framed within her life circumstances, left indelible marks on both her body and her sense of self. Her dental disease was neither a bounded phenomenon nor primarily a co-morbidity through which the management of her diabetes became fraught. Together with her depression, addiction, and diabetes, as well as obesity and chronic pain, her dental disease and the stigmatization that resulted reminded Tonya of an extended marginalization in which she felt complicit.

Tonya's rampant dental decay was a painful testament to her history of addiction, for which she blamed herself, as well as its major sequelae, obesity and depression, to which she attributed the need to manage her diabetes using insulin. Thus, her dental decay was a constant reminder of the inherent trade-off between the self-caring person she felt she used to be, one energized by engagement with her faith community, and the self-isolating and only moderately self-efficacious person she considered herself when I met her. Tonya felt guilty for not being able to work a job that maintained benefits, and vulnerable to a dental market in which she had to "shop" for care whose low cost, she suspected, turned out to be an indicator of low quality. Having formerly developed a reputation for drug-seeking among local providers, Tonya had to frame her care-seeking for advanced dental pain at the emergency room with her specific need, so as to preempt her providers' judgment and, she feared, stigmatized withholding of care. Despite Tonya's efforts to resolve her various problems—the sobriety she tried to maintain despite her enduring chronic pain, the exacting rituals she used to keep her few remaining teeth clean and healthy, or the conditioned frame through which she sought care at the Emergency Room—her teeth powerfully symbolized feelings of shame and inefficacy.

Evincing the Dental Syndemic Ethnographically: Narratives in Dialogue

Reading Debbie and Tonya's narratives together provide insight into the dental syndemic I propose, consisting of multi-layered, overlapping and intersecting biological and biomedical interactions between dental disease, diabetes, substance (mis)use, and psychosocial illness, driven by dental stigma as well as a longer life of social marginalization and economic precarity. For example while both women attribute their most noticeable dental decline to the introduction of insulin to manage their diabetes, the origins of their dental disease, as well as of their diabetes, depression, and encounters with substance (mis)use trace much further back in their lives. Both women's lives are characterized, in addition to the presence of these diseases, by significant social and economic barriers to the routine access to a dentist who could have caught incipient decay or periodontal disease, attempted to control it, and provided restorative solutions so that they could feel "normal" in social settings. Instead, both women found themselves bearing the evidence of rampant decay, dental breakages, and abscesses that subjected them to the humiliation of both strangers' and intimates' responses, as well as the internalized stress of this stigma that exacerbated the harm of their other diseases. On the rare occasion that they could access dental treatment as provided by their public insurance, they found themselves the objects of extractions *as* treatment, in some cases risky extractions performed at a low cost because they did not meet the basic standard of care to confirm, through radiographic evidence, the resolution of infection. Even in situations in which these standards had been met the visual result, toothlessness, was the same, and contributed, for lack of access to restorative procedures, to the dental stigmatization.

For many participants in my research, and even more people I met through everyday interactions in far southwest Virginia, the experience of toothlessness is common. During fieldwork I would occasionally wonder if its ubiquity served to reduce the stigma associated with it, at least locally, while also driving broader stereotypes in the local imaginary. Yet Debbie and Tonya's testimony demonstrates the opposite: not only is a lack of dentition continually stigmatizing in and of itself, toothlessness also indexes social ideas about failures of self-care and self-worth, as well as, in Tonya's case, addiction, a disease widely regarded as a personal and moral failing. Debbie and Tonya's examples demonstrate not only how they are stigmatized on account of their dentition, but also how they come to embody that stigmatization by internalizing it, and the powerful feelings of guilt, shame, and regret that it evokes.

Conclusion

In this chapter, I have proposed a dental syndemic through which dental disease, diabetes, substance (mis)use, and depression interact in mutually deleterious ways, and through which dental stigma transpires as a causal and exacerbating contributor to the suffering in which they result. I have drawn upon epidemiological, clinical, and social science research to describe interactions among these diseases and their disproportionate burdens on marginalized populations who face numerous economic and social barriers to care, such as low-income rural Appalachians, and to examine dentition as a social index through which personal attributes such as, on one hand, prestige, pride, and vitality are assumed among those whose dentition is deemed beautiful or at least unmarked, and, on the other hand, irresponsibility, immorality, and self-loathing among those whose teeth are noticeably cavitated, broken, or missing altogether. Often lost in these social translations are other causes of dental decline, from childhoods and intimate relationships characterized by neglect and abuse, to their exclusion from systems of care that stratify care by type of employment and income level. Yet these stereotypes about dentition persist, and, as I have shown, underlie the worsening of other health conditions.

Applying a syndemic framework allows us to elaborate the deleterious interactions among dental disease, diabetes, substance (mis)use, and depression, and situate them within social and structural contexts such as stigma, income inequality, and an organization of dental care in the United States that ties access, vis-à-vis insurance, to specific forms of employment. For Debbie and Tonya, the dental syndemic is far more than the conceptualization I have presented here. It is a lived experience that inflects their daily live, from the ways in which they interact with their social contacts to the ways in which their internalized shame inhibits their propensity for self-care. The dental syndemic shapes fraught decision-making about how to manage one illness at potential cost to another, as well as their presentations of self to clinicians occasioned by unbearable pain. As I have shown, just as people's lives are shaped by experiences of having dental disease, managing diabetes, encountering substances, and dealing with depression and anxiety, so too do these illnesses reflect their daily lives, in particular the dental stigma they routinely encounter. As a complex phenomenon at the intersection of biology and the stratified distribution of risk and suffering, the dental syndemic offers a lens through which to understand the sociobiology and embodiment of these diseases interactions, and the specific dental stigma that is woven through them.

NOTES

1. All names used in this chapter are pseudonyms.

2. While dental *disease* disparities and dental *treatment* disparities are, technically, distinct concepts, they are mutually implicated (IOM 2011; USDHHS 2000). The advancement of dental disease most commonly occurs among people who lack access to care because they do not receive the preventive benefit of routine cleanings or minor procedures to encapsulate nascent disease. Accordingly, I collapse these concepts into the term dental disparities.

3. This research was conducted under the approval of the University of Arizona Institutional Review Board (Project No. 09-1151-02). It was supported by the National Science Foundation (Award ID 0961762), the Agency for Healthcare Research and Quality (Grant Number R36 HS19117-01A1) and the UA School of Anthropology and Social and Behavioral Science Research Award. Project design also benefited from my participation in the NSF Summer Institute in Research Design in Cultural Anthropology.

4. I follow Link and Phelan's conceptualization of stigma. They advise: "Stigma exists when the following interrelated components converge. In the first component, people distinguish and label human differences. In the second, dominant cultural beliefs link labeled persons to undesirable characteristics—to negative stereotypes. In the third, labeled persons are placed in distinct categories so as to accomplish some degree of separation of "us" from "them." In the fourth, labeled persons experience status loss and discrimination that lead to unequal outcomes. Finally, stigmatization is entirely contingent on access to social, economic, and political power that allows the identification of differentness, the construction of stereotypes, the separation of labeled persons into distinct categories, and the full execution of disapproval, rejection, exclusion, and discrimination. Thus, we apply the term stigma when elements of labeling, stereotyping, separation, status loss, and discrimination co-occur in a power situation that allows the components of stigma to unfold" (2001: 367).

5. As opposed to "addiction," an illness from which some participants in my research also suffer, I use the term substance (mis)use to include in this category the active and engaged determinations through which dentally underserved populations try to manage their dental pain and infection, typically in lieu of access to clinical care. Examining individuals' engagement with addictive substances from the use-framework of self-medication as a management technique may shed light on how the utilization of substances, which may ultimately give way to addiction, are, far from the qualities of personal weakness with which they are often associated, logical approaches to the self-initiated care of diagnosed mental illness, psychosocial trauma, and other embodied manifestations of suffering, particularly among socially marginalized people.

6. Some scholars have also examined the relationship between oral health and obesity and metabolic disorders, both independent of and in relation to diabetes. See, for example, Keller et al. 2015 and Nascimento et al. 2014.

7. There is a prolific literature on the adverse effects of dental-specific fear on oral health. The embodied psychosocial distress I address here is deliberately more general. In fact, while dental-related fear was a theme that emerged in the data, research participants' fear had to do more specifically with the fear of not being able to access care or the fear of being shamed and blamed by dental providers, rather than the fear of dental procedures.

8. "Stomach tooth" is a local term for the lower canine tooth.

WORKS CITED

Agbor, Michael Ashu, and Clement Chinedu Azodo. 2011. "Self Medication for Oral Health Problems in Cameroon." *International Dental Journal* 61:204–9. doi: 10.1111/j.1875–595X.2011.00058.x.

Akcali, Aliye, Olivier Huck, Henri Tenenbaum, Jean-Luc Davideau, and Nurcan Buduneli. 2013. "Periodontal Diseases and Stress: A Brief Review." *Journal of Oral Rehabilitation* 40:60–68. doi: 10.1111/j.1365–2842.2012.02341.x.

Allen, Heidi, Bill J. Wright, Kristin Harding, and Lauren Broffman. 2014. "The Role of Stigma in Access to Health Care for the Poor." *Milbank Quarterly* 92:289–318. doi: 10.1111/1468–0009.12059.

American Dental Association. 2014. "Action for Dental Health." Accessed June 10, 2015 http://www.ada.org/en/public-programs/action-for-dental-health/.

Arcury, Thomas A., Wilbert M. Gesler, John S. Preisser, Jill Sherman, John Spender, and Jamie Perin. 2005. "The Effects of Geography and Spatial Behavior on Health Care Utilization Among the Residents of a Rural Region." *Health Services Research* 40:135–156. doi: 10.1111/j.1475–6773.2005.00346.x

Avena, Nicole M., Pedro Rada, and Bartley G. Hoebel. 2008. "Evidence for Sugar Addiction: Behavioral and Neurochemical Effects of Intermittent, Excessive Sugar Intake." *Neuroscience & Biobehavioral Reviews* 32: 20–39. doi: 10.1016/j.neubiorev.2007.04.019

Barclay, Eliza. 2013. "'Soda Mouth' Can Look A Lot Like 'Meth Mouth.'" *The Salt Blog*, May 29. http://www.npr.org/blogs/thesalt/2013/05/29/187050058/soda-mouth-can-look-a-lot-like-meth-mouth.

Bedos, Christophe, Jean-Marc Brodeur, Laurence Boucheron, Lucie Richard, Mike Benigeri, Marie Olivier, and Slim Haddad. 2003. "The Dental Care Pathway of Welfare Recipients in Quebec." *Social Science & Medicine* 57:2089–99. doi: http://dx.doi.org/10.1016/S0277-9536(03)00066-2.

Behringer, Bruce and Gilbert H. Friedell. 2006. "Appalachia: Where Place Matters in Health." *Preventing Chronic Disease* 3:1–4.

Berk, Michael, Lana J. Williams, Felice N. Jacka, Adrienne O'Neil, Julie A. Pasco, Steven Moylan, Nicholas B. Allen, Amanda L. Stuart, Amie C. Hayley, Michelle L. Byrne, and Michael Maes. 2013. "So Depression is an Inflammatory Disease, but Where Does the Inflammation Come From?" *BMC Medicine* 11:200. doi: 10.1186/1741–7015–11–200.

Boden, Joseph and David Fergusson. 2011. "Alcohol and Depression." *Addiction* 106: 906–914. doi: 10.1111/j.1360-0443.2010.03351.x

Bolton, James M., Jennifer Robinson, and Jitender Sareen. 2009. "Self-medication of Mood Disorders with Alcohol and Drugs in the National Epidemiologic Survey on Alcohol and Related Conditions." *Journal of Affective Disorders* 115: 367–375. doi: 10.1016/j.jad.2008.10.003.

Borrell, Luisa N. and Natalie D. Crawford. 2011. "Social Disparities in Periodontitis Among US Adults: The Effect of Allostatic Load." *Journal of Epidemiology and Community Health* 65:144–49. doi: 10.1136/jech.2009.098269.

Brown, Rebecca J., Mary Ann De Banate, and Kristina I. Rother. 2010. "Artificial Sweeteners: A Systematic Review of Metabolic Effects in Youth." *International Journal of Pediatric Obesity* 5: 305–312. doi: 10.3109/17477160903497027.

Celeste, Roger Keller, Johan Fritzell, and Paulo Nadanovsky. 2011. "The Relationship Between Levels of Income Inequality and Dental Caries and Periodontal Diseases." *Cad. Saúde Pública* 27:1111–20. doi: 10.1590/S0102-311X2011000600008.

Chiou L.J., Y.H. Yang, H.C. Hung, C.C. Tsai, T.Y. Shieh, Y.M. Wu, W.C. Wang, and T.C. Hsu. 2010. "The Association of Psychosocial Factors and Smoking with Periodontal Health in a Community Population." *Journal of Periodontal Research* 45:16–22. doi: 10.1111/j.1600-0765.2008.01194.x

Cohen Leonard A., Arthur J. Bonito, Donald R. Akin, Richard J. Manski, Mark D. Macek, Robert R. Edwards, and Llewellyn J. Cornelius. 2009. "Toothache Pain: Behavioral Impact and Self-care Strategies." *Special Care in Dentistry* 29:85–95. doi: 10.1111/j.1754-4505.2008.00068.x

Costalongo, Massimo and Mark C. Herzberg. 2014. "The Oral Microbiome and the Immunobiology of Periodontal Disease and Caries." *Immunology Letters* 162:22–38. doi: 10.1016/j.imlet.2014.08.017

D'Amore, Meredith M., Debbie M. Cheng, Nancy R. Kressin, Judith Jones, Jeffrey H. Samet, Michael Winter, Theresa W. Kim, and Richard Saitz. 2011. "Oral Health of Substance-Dependent Individuals: Impact of Specific Substances." *Journal of Substance Abuse Treatment* 41:179–185. doi: 10.1016/j.jsat.2011.02.005.

Darré, L., J.-N. Vergnes, P. Gourdy, and M. Sixou. 2008. "Efficacy of Periodontal Treatment on Glycaemic Control in Diabetic Patients: A Meta-analysis of Interventional Studies." *Diabetes & Metabolism* 34:497–506. doi: 10.1016/j.diabet.2008.03.006.

Dukicá, Walter, Tanja Trivanovicá Dobrijevicá, Marina Katunaricá, Sladana Milardovicá, and Sanja Segovicá. 2010. "Erosive Lesions in Patients with Alcoholism." *Journal of the American Dental Association* 141:1452–1458. doi: 10.14219/jada.archive.2010.0107.

Eke, Paul I., Bruce A. Dye, Liang Wei, Gina O. Thornton-Evans, and Robert J. Genco. 2012. "Prevalence of Periodontitis in Adults in the United States: 2009 and 2010." *Journal of Dental Research* 91:914–20. doi: 10.1177/0022034512457373.

Elter, John R., B. Alex White, Bradley N. Gaynes, and James D. Bader. 2002. "Relationship of Clinical Depression to Periodontal Treatment Outcome." *Journal of Periodontology* 73:441–449. doi: 10.1902/jop.2002.73.4.441.

Fay, Heather, Stefan D. Baral, Gift Trapence, Felistus Motimedi, Eric Umar, Scholastika Iipinge, Friedel Dausab, Andrea Wirtz, and Chris Beyrer. 2011. "Stigma, Health Care Access, and HIV knowledge Among Men Who Have Sex With Men in Malawi, Namibia, and Botswana." *AIDS and Behavior* 15: 1088–1097. doi: 10.1007/s10461-010-9861-2.

Finlayson, Tracy L., David R. Williams, Kristine Siefert, James S. Jackson, and Ruth Nowjack-Raymer. 2010. "Oral Health Disparities and Psychosocial Correlates of Self-Rated Oral Health in the National Survey of American Life." *American Journal of Public Health* 100:S246–S255. doi: 10.2105/AJPH.2009.167783.

French, Michael T., Kerry Anne McGeary, Dale D. Chitwood, and Clyde B. McCoy. 2000. "Chronic Illicit Drug Use, Health Services Utilization and the Cost of Medical Care." *Social Science & Medicine* 50: 1703–1713. doi: 10.1016/S0277-9536(99)00411-6.

Genco, R.J., A.W. Ho, S.G. Grossi, R.G. Dunford, and L.A. Tedesco. 1999. "Relationship of Stress, Distress, and Inadequate Coping Behaviors to Periodontal Disease." *Journal of Periodontology* 70:711–723. doi: 10.1902/jop.1999.70.1.100.

Goffman, Erving. 1963. *Stigma: Notes on the Management of Spoiled Identity*. New York: Simon & Schuster, Inc.

Hansen, Helena, Philippe Bourgois, and Ernest Drucker. 2014. "Pathologizing Poverty: New Forms of Diagnosis, Disability, and Structural Stigma Under Welfare Reform." *Social Science & Medicine* 103:76–83. doi: 10.1016/j.socscimed.2013.06.033.

Hatzenbuehler, Mark L., Jo C. Phelan, and Bruce G. Link. 2013. "Stigma as a Fundamental Cause of Population Health Inequalities." *American Journal of Public Health* 103: 813–821. doi: 10.2105/AJPH.2012.301069.

Hein, Casey and Doreen Small. 2006. "Combating Diabetes, Obesity, Periodontal Disease and Interrelated Inflammatory Conditions with a Syndemic Approach." *Grand Rounds Oral-Sys Med.* 1:36–47.

Heisler, Michele, Dylan M. Smith, Rodney A. Hayward, Sarah L. Krein, and Eve A. Kerr. 2003. "Racial Disparities in Diabetes Care Processes, Outcomes, and Treatment Intensity." *Medical Care* 41: 1221–1232. doi: 10.1097/01.MLR.0000093421.64618.9C

Heneghan, Bridget T. 2007. *Whitewashing America: Material Culture and Race in the Antebellum Imagination.* Jackson MS: University Press of Mississippi.

Hintao, J., R. Teanpaisan, V. Chongsuvivatwong, C. Ratarasan, and G. Dahlen. 2007. "The Microbiological Profiles of Saliva, Supragingival and Subgingival Plaque and Dental Caries in Adults With and Without Type 2 Diabetes Mellitus." *Oral Microbiology and Immunology* 22:175–181. doi: 10.1111/j.1399-302X.2007.00341.x

Horton, Sarah and Judith C. Barker. 2009. "'Stains' on Their Self-Discipline: Public Health, Hygiene, and the Disciplining of Undocumented Immigrant Parents in the Nation's Internal Borderlands." *American Ethnologist* 36:784–798. doi: 10.1111/j.1548-1425.2009.01210.x

Huttlinger, Kathleen, Jennifer Schaller-Ayers and Tony Lawson. 2004. "Health Care in Appalachia: A Population-Based Approach." *Public Health Nursing* 21(2):103–110. doi: 10.1111/j.0737-1209.2004.021203.x

Iacopino, Anthony. 2009. "New 'Syndemic' Paradigm for Interprofessional Management of Chronic Inflammatory Disease." *Journal of the Canadian Dental Association* 75:632–633.

Institute of Medicine. 2011. *Advancing Oral Health in America.* Washington, DC: The National Academies Press.

Jacobson, Jerry Owen, Paul Robinson, and Ricky N. Bluthenthal. 2007. "A Multilevel Decomposition Approach to Estimate the Role of Program Location and Neighborhood Disadvantage in Racial Disparities in Alcohol Treatment Completion." *Social Science & Medicine* 64: 462–476. doi: 10.1016/j.socscimed.2006.08.032.

Jawed, Muhammed, Syed M. Shahid, Shah A. Qader, and Abid Azhar. 2011. "Dental Caries in Diabetes Mellitus: Role of Salivary Flow Rate and Minerals." *Journal of Diabetes and its Complications* 25:183–186. doi: 10.1016/j.jdiacomp.2010.07.001

Johnson, Karlon H., Mohsen Bazargan, and Cheryl J. Cherpitel. 2001. "Alcohol, Tobacco, and Drug Use and the Onset of Type 2 Diabetes Among Inner-city Minority Patients." *The Journal of the American Board of Family Practice* 14: 430–436.

Kaste, Linda M., Robert H. Selwitz, Richard J. Oldakowski, J.A. Brunelle, Deborah M. Winn, and Laura J. Brown. 1996. "Coronal Caries in the Primary and Permanent Dentition of Children and Adolescents 1–17 Years of Aage: United States, 1988–1991." *Journal of Dental Research* 1996:631–41.

Khalid, Abeer and Carlos Quiñonez. 2015. "Straight, White Teeth as a Social Prerogative." *Sociology of Health & Illness* 37:782–796. doi: 10.1111/1467-9566.12238.

Kidambi, Srividya and Shailendra B. Patel. 2008. "Diabetes Mellitus: Considerations for Dentistry." *Journal of the American Dental Association* 139:8S–18S. doi: 10.14219/jada.archive.2008.0364

Kiecolt-Glaser, Janice K. and Ronald Glaser. 2002. "Depression and Immune Function: Central Pathways to Morbidity and Mortality." *Journal of Psychosomatic Research* 53:873–876. doi: 10.1016/S0022-3999(02)00309-4

Kline, Nolan. 2012. "'There's Nowhere I Can Go to Get Help, and I Have Tooth Pain Right Now': The Oral Health Syndemic Among Migrant Farmworkers in Florida." *Annals of Anthropological Practice* 36:387–401. doi: 10.1111/napa.12010

Lähteenmäki, Kaarina, Sanna Edelman and Timo K. Korhonen. 2005. "Bacterial Metastasis: The Host Plasminogen System in Bacterial Invasion." *Trends in Microbiology* 13:79–85. doi: 10.1016/j.tim.2004.12.003

Lakschevitz, Flavia, Guy Aboodi, Howard Tenenbaum, and Michael Glogauer. 2011. "Diabetes and Periodontal Diseases: Interplay and Links." *Current Diabetes Review* 7:433–439. doi: 10.2174/157339911797579205

Lalla, Evanthia and Panos N. Papapanou. 2011. "Diabetes Mellitus and Periodontitis: A Tale of Two Common Interrelated Diseases." *Nature Reviews Endocrinology* 7:738–748. doi:10.1038/nrendo.2011.106

Lamster, Ira B., Evanthia Lalla, Wenche S. Borgnakke, and George W. Taylor. 2008. "The Relationship Between Oral Health and Diabetes Mellitus." *Journal of the American Dental Association* 139:19S–24S. doi: 10.14219/jada.archive.2008.0363

Laslett, Anne-Marie, Paul Dietze, and Robyn Dwyer. 2008. "The Oral Health of Street-Recruited Injecting Drug Users: Prevalence and Correlates of Problems." *Addiction* 103:1821–1825. doi: 10.1111/j.1360-0443.2008.02339.x

Link, Bruce G., and Jo C. Phelan. 2001. "Conceptualizing Stigma." *Annual Review of Sociology* 27: 363–385.

——— 2006. "Stigma and its Public Health Implications." *The Lancet* 367.9509 (2006): 528–529. doi: 10.1016/S0140-6736(06)68184-1

Link, Bruce G., Jo C. Phelan, Michaeline Bresnahan, Ann Stueve, and Bernice A. Pescosolido. 1999. "Public Conceptions of Mental Illness: Labels, Causes, Dangerousness, and Social Distance." *American Journal of Public Health* 89: 1328–1333. doi: 10.2105/AJPH.89.9.1328

Linneman, Travis and Tyler Wall. 2013. "'This is Your Face on Meth': The Punitive Spectacle of 'White Trash' in the Rural War on Drugs." *Theoretical Criminology* 17:315–334. doi: 10.1177/1362480612468934

Ludke, Robert L. and Phillip J. Obermiller, eds. 2012. *Appalachian Health and Well-Being.* Lexington KY: University of Kentucky Press.

Marrero, Jorge A., Robert J. Fontana, Sherry Fu, Hari S. Conjeevaram, Grace L. Su, and Anna S. Lok. 2005. "Alcohol, Tobacco and Obesity are Synergistic Risk Factors for Hepatocellular Carcinoma." *Journal of Hepatology* 42: 218–224. doi: 10.1016/j.jhep.2004.10.005

McEwen, Bruce S. 2008. "Central Effects of Stress Hormones in Health and Disease: Understanding the Protective and Damaging Effects of Stress and Stress Mediators." *European Journal of Pharmacology* 583: 174–185. doi: 10.1016/j.ejphar.2007.11.071

McLean, Jeffrey S. 2014. "Advancements Toward a Systems Level Understanding of the Human Oral Microbiome." *Frontiers in Cellular and Infection Microbiology* 4:98.

Mendenhall, Emily. 2012. *Syndemic Suffering: Distress, Depression, and Diabetes among Mexican Women in Chicago*. Walnut Creek, CA: Left Coast Press.

Mendenhall, Emily. 2015. "Beyond Comorbidity: A Critical Perspective of Syndemic Depression and Diabetes in Cross-cultural Contexts." *Medical Anthropology Quarterly*. Epub ahead of print. doi: 10.1111/maq.12215

Moylan, Cynthia A., Carla W. Brady, Jeffrey L. Johnson, Alastair D. Smith, Janet E. Tuttle-Newhall, and Andrew J. Muir. 2008. "Disparities in Liver Transplantation Before and After Introduction of the MELD Score." *JAMA* 300: 2371–2378. doi: 10.1001/jama.2008.720

Murakawa, Naomi. 2011. "Toothless: The Methamphetamine 'Epidemic,' 'Meth Mouth' and the Racial Construction of Drug Scares." *Du Bois Review: Social Science Research on Race* 8:219–228. doi: 10.1017/S1742058X11000208

Ng, Sam K. S. and W. Keung Leung. 2006. "A Community Study on the Relationship Between Stress, Coping, Affective Dispositions and Periodontal Attachment Loss." *Community Dentistry and Oral Epidemiology* 34:252–66. doi: 10.1111/j.1600-0528.2006.00282.x

Östenson, Claes-Göran, Agneta Hilding, Valdemar Grill, and Suad Efendic. 2012. "High Consumption of Smokeless Tobacco ('Snus') Predicts Increased Risk of Type 2 Diabetes in a 10-year Prospective Study of Middle-aged Swedish Men." *Scandinavian Journal of Public Health* 40: 730–737. doi: 10.1177/1403494812459814

Peruzzo, Daiane C., Bruno B. Benatti, Glaucia M.B. Ambrosano, Getúlio R. Nogueira-Filho, Enilson A. Sallum, Márcio Z. Casati, and Francisco H. Nociti Jr. 2007. "A Systematic Review of Stress and Psychological Factors as Possible Risk Factors for Periodontal Disease." *Journal of Periodontology* 78:1491–1504. doi:10.1902/jop.2007.060371

Powell, Janet E. and Daniel Taylor. 1991. "Anger, Depression, and Anxiety following Heroin Withdrawal." *International Journal of the Addictions* 27: 25–35. doi: 10.3109/10826089109063460

Preeja, C., R. Ambili, K. J. Nisha, Abraham Seba, and Vilasan Archana. 2012. "Unveiling the Role of Stress in Periodontal Etiopathogenesis: An Evidence-based Review." *Journal of Investigative and Clinical Dentistry* 4:78–83. doi: 10.1111/jicd.12000

Puhl, Rebecca M., and Chelsea A. Heuer. 2010. "Obesity Stigma: Important Considerations for Public Health." *American Journal of Public Health* 100:1019–1028. doi: 10.2105/AJPH.2009.159491

Raskin, Sarah E. 2015. "Decayed, missing, and filled: Subjectivity and the dental safety net in central Appalachia." PhD. Dissertation. School of Anthropology, University of Arizona.

Rees, Terry D. 2007. "Drugs and Oral Disorders." *Periodontology* 2000 18:21–36. doi: 10.1111/j.1600-0757.1998.tb00136.x

Richards, John R. and B. Tomas Brofeldt. 2000. "Patterns of Tooth Wear Associated with Methamphetamine Use." *Journal of Periodontology* 71:1371–1374. doi:10.1902/jop.2000.71.8.1371

Robinson, P. G., S. Acquah, and B. Gibson. 2005. "Drug Users: Oral Health-related Attitudes and Behaviours." *British Dental Journal*. 2005: 219–224. doi:10.1038/sj.bdj.4812090

Rosania, Amy E., Kathryn G. Low, Cheryl M. McCormick, and David A. Rosania. 2009. "Stress, Depression, Cortisol, and Periodontal Disease." *Journal of Periodontology* 80:260–66. doi:10.1902/jop.2009.080334

Rosenstein, David I. 1975. "Effects of Long-term Addiction to Heroin on Oral Tissues." *Journal of Public Health Dentistry* 35:118–122. doi: 10.1111/j.1752-7325.1975.tb04035.x

Saletu, Alexander, Helene Pirker-Frühauf, Franziska Saletu, Leopold Linzmayer, Peter Anderer,, and Michael Matejka. 2005. "Controlled Clinical and Psychometric Studies on the Relation Between Periodontitis and Depressive Mood." *Journal of Clinical Periodontology* 12:1219–1225. doi: 10.1111/j.1600-051X.2005.00855.x

Sandberg, Gun E., Hans E. Sundberg, Carl A. Fjellstrom, and Karin F. Wikblad. 2000. "Type 2 Diabetes and Oral Health: A Comparison Between Diabetic and Non-diabetic Subjects." *Diabetes Research and Clinical Practice* 50:27–34. doi: 10.1016/S0168-8227(00)00159-5

Selwitz, Robert H., Amid I. Ismail, and Nigel B. Pitts. 2007. "Dental Caries." *Lancet* 369:51–59. doi: 10.1016/S0140-6736(07)60031-2

Sgolastra, Fabrizio, Marco Severino, Davide Pietropaoli, Roberto Gatto, and Annalisa Monaco. 2013. "Effectiveness of Periodontal Treatment to Improve Metabolic Control in Patients With Chronic Periodontitis and Type 2 Diabetes: A Meta-Analysis of Randomized Clinical Trials." *Journal of Periodontology* 84:958–973. doi:10.1902/jop.2012.120377

Shetty, Vivek, Larissa J. Mooney, Corwin M. Zigler, Thomas R. Belin, Debra Murphy, and Richard Rawson. 2010. "The Relationship Between Methamphetamine Use and Increased Dental Disease." *Journal of the American Dental Association* 141:307–318. doi: 10.14219/jada.archive.2010.0165

Simón-Soro, Aurea and Alex Mira. 2015. "Solving the Etiology of Dental Caries." *Trends in Microbiology* 23:76–82. doi: 10.1016/j.tim.2014.10.010

Singer, Merrill. 1996. "A Dose of Drugs, a Touch of Violence, a Case of AIDS: Conceptualizing the SAVA Syndemic." *Free Inquiry in Creative Sociology* 24: 99–110.

——— 2014. "Syndemics." In: *The Wiley Blackwell Encyclopedia of Health, Illness, Behavior, and Society,* First Edition. Eds: William C. Cockerham, Robert Dingwall, and Stella R. Quah.

Siudikiene, Jolanta, Vita Machiulskiene, Bente Nyvad, Jorma Tenovuo, and Irena Nedzelskiene. 2006. "Dental Caries and Salivary Status in Children with Type 1 Diabetes Mellitus, Related to the Metabolic Control of the Disease." *European Journal of Oral Sciences.* 114:8–14. doi: 10.1111/j.1600-0722.2006.00277.x

Smarsh, Sarah. 2014. "Poor teeth." Aeon Magazine. https://aeon.co/essays/there-is-no-shame-worse-than-poor-teeth-in-a-rich-world. Accessed October 25, 2014.

Smith, B.G.N. and N.D. Robb. 1989. "Dental Erosion in Patients with Chronic Alcoholism." *Journal of Dentistry* 17:219–221. doi:10.1016/0300-5712(89)90168-1

Sordo, L., M. Chahua, M. J. Bravo, G. Barrio, M. T. Brugal, A. Domingo-Salvany, G. Molist, L+ De la Fuente, and ITINERE Project Group. 2012. "Depression Among Regular Heroin Users: The Influence of Gender." *Addictive Behaviors* 37: 148–152. doi: 10.1016/j.addbeh.2011.09.009

Syrjälä Anna-Maija H., Mirka C. Niskanen, Pekka Ylöstalo, Matti L. E. Knuuttila. 2003. "Metabolic Control as a Modifier of the Association between Salivary Factors and Dental Caries among Diabetic Patients." *Caries Research* 37:142–147. doi: 10.1159/000069020

Tanzer, Jason M., Jill Livingston, and Angela M. Thompson. 2001. "The Microbiology of Primary Dental Caries in Humans." *Journal of Dental Education* 65:1028–1037.

Teeuw, Wijnand, Victor E.A. Gerdes, and Bruno G. Loos. 2010. "Effect of Periodontal Treatment on Glycemic Control of Diabetic Patients: A Systematic Review and Meta-analysis." *Diabetes Care* 33:421–427. doi: 10.2337/dc09-1378

Thomson, W. Murray, Aubrey Sheiham, and A. John Spencer. 2000. "Sociobehavioral Aspects of Periodontal Disease." *Periodontology* 60:54–63. doi: 10.1111/j.1600-0757.2011.00405.x

Tomar, Scott L., and Deborah M. Winn. 1999. "Chewing Tobacco Use and Dental Caries Among US Men." *The Journal of the American Dental Association* 130: 1601–1610. doi:10.14219/jada.archive.1999.0099

Turina, Matthias, Donald E. Fry, and Hiram C. Polk. 2005. "Acute Hyperglycemia and the Innate Immune System: Clinical, Cellular, and Molecular Aspects." *Critical Care Medicine* 33: 1624–1633. doi: 10.1097/01.CCM.0000170106.61978.D8

US Department of Health and Human Services. 2000. "Oral Health in America: A Report of the Surgeon General." U.S. Department Of Health And Human Services National Institute of Dental and Craniofacial Research National Institutes of Health.

Vettore, M., R. S. Quintanilha, A. M. Monteiro da Silva, G. A. Lamarca, A. T. T. Leão. 2005. "The Influence of Stress and Anxiety on the Response of Non-surgical Periodontal Treatment." *Journal of Clinical Periodontology* 32:1226–35. doi: 10.1111/j.1600-051X.2005.00852.x

Ward, Elizabeth, Ahmedin Jemal, Vilma Cokkinides, Gopal K. Singh, Cheryll Cardinez, Asma Ghafoor, and Michael Thun. 2004. "Cancer Disparities by Race/Ethnicity and Socioeconomic Status." *CA: A Cancer Journal for Clinicians* 54: 78–93. doi: 10.3322/canjclin.54.2.78

Wellen, Kathryn E. and Gökhan S. Hotamisligil. 2005. "Inflammation, Stress, and Diabetes." *The Journal of Clinical Investigation* 115:1111–1119. doi:10.1172/JCI87439

Wickström, Anette. 2016. "'I Hope I Get Movie-Star Teeth': Doing the Exceptional Normal in Orthodontic Practice for Young People." *Medical Anthropology Quarterly* 30:285–302. doi: 10.1111/maq.12247

Winn, Deborah M. 2001. "Tobacco Use and Oral Disease. *Journal of Dental Education* 65: 306–312.

World Health Organization. 2013. Oral Health Fact Sheet N°318.

Xiong, Xu, Karen E. Elkind-Hirsch, Sotirios Vastardis, Robert L. Delarosa, Gabriella Pridjian, and Pierre Buekens. 2009. "Periodontal Disease is Associated with Gestational Diabetes Mellitus: A Case-Control Study." *Journal of Periodontology* 80:1742–1749. doi: 10.1902/jop.2009.090250

Yang, Fang, Xiaowei Zeng, Kang Ning, Kuan-Liang Liu, Chien-Chi Lo, Wei Wang, Jie Chen, Dongmei Wang, Ranran Huang, Xingzhi Chang, Patrick S Chain, Gary Xie, Junqi Ling, and Jian Xu. 2012. "Saliva Microbiomes Distinguish Caries-active From Healthy Human Populations." *The ISME Journal* 6:1–10. doi: 10.1038/ismej.2011.71

Zullig, Keith J. and Michael Hendryx. 2011. "Health-Related Quality of Life Among Central Appalachian Residents in Mountaintop Mining Counties." *American Journal of Public Health* 101:848–853. doi: 10.2105/AJPH.2010.300073

Conclusion

Bayla Ostrach, Merrill Singer, and Shir Lerman

Socially enforced stigma at the individual, interpersonal, societal, and structural levels negatively affects health, not only by enabling the isolation of and discrimination toward those with particular illnesses, but also, entire categories of people deemed by others to be different, unworthy, and commonly the cause of their own social failings. People marked by stigma suffer from biological conditions and in living conditions that put them at increased risk for multiple diseases, disease interactions, and a resulting heightened disease burden. Stigma, a socially constructed and structurally produced phenomenon, becomes a critical cog in the machine of structural violence, producing and contributing to damaging syndemics. As the authors in this volume and its companion volume powerfully show, stigma syndemics affect people living with illnesses or conditions already widely understood as susceptible to stigmatization—sexually transmitted infections, drug abuse, or mental health problems, to cite a few examples. Contributing to an expanded understanding of both the health effects of stigma and syndemics, however, our contributors in this volume particularly illuminated the devastating role of stigma, and the political-economic structures that perpetuate its influence in people's day-to-day lives, in new areas of biosocial health interactions: detention and in carceral settings, pregnancy-related health outcomes, oral health, and malnutrition. Obesity, diabetes, substance use, HIV, mental illness, and other known stigmatized illnesses are all arenas in which how sufferers are viewed and treated by those in power and society at large determines their access to resources and potential for worsened outcomes. Here we extended this analysis to people currently incarcerated/detained, or who have been in the past; people affected by infertility and poorly understood gynecological conditions; those experiencing pregnancies stigmatized by those around them because of the person in whose body it occurs or because of the intentions for the pregnancy itself; people denied adequate, often life-saving care because of their oral health and what it signifies, and families whose nutritional status is assumed to indicate something about what quality and quantity of care they deserve, demonstrating the power of a biosocial framework for health research, advocacy, and policy expands to encompass a much wider range of lived experiences.

All stigma does not look the same and all suffering and discrimination do not affect health through the same pathways of biosocial interaction. The value of a syndemics perspective lies in its dual specificity and universality—each particular circumstance of disease-disease, disease-health condition, or condition-condition interaction in a given structural environment may be analyzed through the lens of a given population's specific experience of suffering: in these cases, suffering increased by stigma. But the ability to pay attention in the grounded, multi-layered syndemic model—attentive to physical, environmental, structural, and uniquely biosocial linkages, offers a vital opportunity to analyze stigmatized experiences and how they affect disease interactions for individuals, populations, and health outcomes.

Offering a glimpse of the future of syndemics research across disciplines, a biannual graduate-level syndemics seminar taught by one of the editors at Boston University recently included students from pre-med, health sciences, public health, medical anthropology, biology, and health services fields. This diverse group of interdisciplinary scholars collaborated to closely examine the history and contributions of syndemics research, and, through a literature review and analysis, identified and proposed their own new syndemic, that of tuberculosis-malnutrition-diabetes interactions in immigration detention settings—where sufferers are highly stigmatized as both undocumented immigrants, and then as detainees. Demonstrating the growing recognition and relevance of the syndemic concept in interdisciplinary research, the majority of students in the seminar (87 percent) indicated on course evaluations they thought syndemics might relate to their planned thesis work or be relevant to future clinical practice. In short, they had come to see health on multiple levels and in terms of consequential interactions, as well as to understand that social inequality and the concentration of power in society were determinant factors in disease clustering, interaction, and outcome.

Chapters in this volume outlined but a few of what we anticipate are many more stigma-linked syndemics which remain to be proposed. We are confident stigma may well be an underlying or additive social factor in many already identified syndemics, which now merit re-examination with this additional lens of analysis. Conversely, existing discussions of stigma and health warrant re-examination in light of the syndemic model.

Index

About the Contributors

Roula AbiSamra, MPH, serves on the board of *Access Reproductive Care-Southeast*, a reproductive justice organization that supports people in navigating the pathways to abortion and other reproductive care in the South. Her interest in abortion stigma developed during her time as a clinic worker at the Atlanta Feminist Women's Health Center and a case manager with the National Abortion Federation Hotline. More recently she worked with a research project of Advancing New Standards In Reproductive Health (ANSIRH) at the University of California, San Francisco, and with the Sea Change Program managing the Untold Stories Project, which engages communities to foster empathy and visibility around reproductive experiences. She earned her BA and MPH at Emory University, and has spent her career working in reproductive health research, education, and service provision.

Elaine M. Bennett, PhD, MPH, is an associate professor of Anthropology and director of the minor in Public Health at Saint Vincent College, Latrobe, Pennsylvania. Her research interests include child health and nutrition in Guatemala, using ethnographic research to develop and evaluate community health programming, and the role of service-learning in higher education. She regularly leads interdisciplinary teams of students in conducting applied research for community partners in Southwestern Pennsylvania and in Guatemala. She is a member of the Society for Applied Anthropology, American Anthropological Association, Society for Medical Anthropology, and the Council for Anthropology and Education.

Megan A. Carney is a medical and sociocultural anthropologist. She has been a faculty member at the University of Washington since 2012. Her research focuses on gendered and transnational migration, migrant health, social movements, and biopolitics, both in the Western United States and Southern Italy. In 2015, she published *The Unending of Hunger: Tracing Women and Food Insecurity Across Borders* (University of California Press) which received the 2015 Outstanding Academic Title by Choice Magazine. Her work has appeared in a wide range of sources, such as *Medical Anthropology Quarterly*, *The Journal of Political Ecology*, and *Gender, Sexuality and Feminism*. Currently, she is working on another book project about the migrant solidarity movement in Sicily. Since 2013, she has been a contributing editor of *Anthropology News* and a board member of the Society for Medical Anthropology. She also serves as an advisory member of the new Public Education Initiative of the American Anthropological Association "World on the Move: 100,000 Years of Human Migration" that is striving to educate a wider public about migration.

Fernanda Claudio is an anthropologist who teaches and researches in the School of Social Science at The University of Queensland in the fields of medical anthropology, global health and development. Her current research focuses on ethnographic approaches to vulnerable groups, including African refugees in Australia and prisoners with intellectual disability. Fernanda also conducts mixed-method research on child-feeding practices in Nigeria and chronic kidney disease amongst agricultural workers. She studied anthropology at McGill University, the University of Montreal, and the London School of Economics.

Pamela I. Erickson, DrPH, PhD, is a medical anthropologist at the University of Connecticut, Storrs in the department of Anthropology. She is also affiliated with the Institute for Collaboration on Health, Intervention, and Policy (Storrs campus) and the Department of Community Health in the School of Medicine (Farmington Campus). Her research interests include human reproduction, sexual decision-making and risk reduction among adolescents and emerging adults, global health, the impact of global climate change on health, health and human rights, qualitative research methods, ethnomedicine, and the causes and implications of Waorani raiding in Amazonian Ecuador. She has conducted research in East Los Angeles, CA, Hartford, CT, Ecuador, India, Mexico, Panama, the Philippines, and Nepal.

Courtney L. Everson, PhD, is a biocultural medical anthropologist and the Dean of Graduate Studies at the Midwives College of Utah (Salt Lake City, UT—global campus). Dr. Everson is also the Director of Research Education for the Midwives Alliance of North America (MANA) Division of Research; a birth and postpartum doula; a perinatal health educator; an anti-oppression trainer; and serves on the Board of Directors for the Australasian Professional Doula Regulatory Association (APDRA), the Association of Midwifery

Educators (AME), the Midwifery Education Accreditation Council (MEAC), and the Academic Collaborative for Integrative Health (ACIH). Dr. Everson's research, teaching and activism address the stigma and systemic oppression encountered by pregnant/parenting adolescents and other marginalized communities in accessing supportive, non-violent reproductive health care. Dr. Everson explores doula, midwifery, and community-based care as models for reducing health inequities and advancing reproductive justice. She actively publishes in academic forums, and is an invited, avid speaker at local, national, and international venues. Dr. Everson has won multiple awards for her teaching, research, and service, including being named "Teacher of the Year" at the Midwives College of Utah, and receiving the "Our Future, Award of Excellence" from the Oregon Women in Higher Education Consortium.

Dr. **Véronique A. S. Griffith**, MD, MSc, completed her undergraduate degree at Harvard University in 2002 and her medical degree at Yale School of Medicine in 2009. She is currently studying for her PhD in medical anthropology at Durham University. Her research focuses on endometriosis, illness narratives, and doctor-patient interactions. She is particularly interested in biosociality, biopower, and how gendered understandings of stigma impact on experiences of endometriosis.

Nick Lennox is the director of the Queensland Centre for Intellectual and Developmental Disability at the Mater Misericordiae Hospital, Brisbane. Nicholas is a researcher, educator, advocate, and clinician. He has specialised in the health of adults with intellectual disability since 1992. He trained in general practice and also for a time in psychiatry. In 2007, he completed his PhD based on a randomised controlled trial of the Comprehensive Health Assessment Program (CHAP). Nicholas has been instrumental in the IASSIDD (International Association for the Scientific Study of Intellectual and Developmental Disabilities) ratification of health guidelines and has successfully advocated for systemic change at a local, state, national, and international level. He is foundation vice-president and immediate past president of the Australian Association of Developmental Disability Medicine (AADDM) and remains on the committee.

Shir Lerman, PhD, MPH, is a PRACCTIS postdoctoral fellow in implementation science at the University of Massachusetts Medical School. Trained as a medical anthropologist, her research centers on chronic illness syndemics in Puerto Rico, particularly framed within Puerto Rico's political and economic crises. More broadly, her research focuses on mental health, syndemics, and structural inequalities in ethnic minorities. She also conducts research on mindfulness in underserved communities and on the Zika Virus in Puerto Rico.

Bayla Ostrach, MA, PhD, is appointed as an assistant professor in the Family Medicine Department at Boston University School of Medicine, and Affiliated Faculty with the Medical Anthropology and Cross-Cultural Practice Program. Dr. Ostrach works as a Research Scientist in the Division of Research at the Mountain Area Health Education Center in Asheville, North Carolina. Her research explores health inequality, access to care, syndemics, sexual and reproductive health, rural health, publicly funded health systems, and the role of social and mutual support in people's ability to overcome obstacles. She began working directly in the field of reproductive health and abortion care in 1999, and has since worked with and volunteered at multiple clinics in Oregon, Connecticut, and Catalunya. She is the author of *Health Policy in a Time of Crisis: Abortion, Austerity, and Access*.

Sarah Raskin, PhD, MPH is an assistant professor in the iCubed Program, L. Douglas Wilder School of Government and Public Affairs at Virginia Commonwealth University, where she collaborates on a multi-disciplinary community partnership to address oral health disparities among children and adolescents in Richmond, VA, and elsewhere. Her research interests include access to health care, race and the body, and the health care workforce. Previously, Sarah was a research scientist, Patient Reported Outcomes, at the Institute for Patient-Centered Initiatives and Health Equity at the George Washington University Cancer Center, where she directed a small portfolio of applied health services research, dissemination, and tool development projects for patient navigation and cancer survivorship. Sarah completed her PhD in medical anthropology at University of Arizona, where one of her dissertation chapters on oral health disparities and dental services in central Appalachia won the Society for Medical Anthropology's Rudolf Virchow graduate student paper award. Previously, she completed her MPH at Emory University, where she won the Eugene J. Gangarosa, M.D. student award for Excellence in International Health.

Merrill Singer, PhD, is a professor in the Department of Anthropology at the University of Connecticut and Senior Research Scientist at the UConn Center for Health, Intervention and Prevention, University of Connecticut, and is an applied medical anthropologist and co-founder of Critical Medical Anthropology. Dr. Singer developed the concept of syndemics and was the first to publish the term in 1996. His research focuses on structural and biosocial factors in health, syndemics, health effects of substance use and HIV/AIDS, anthropogenic climate change and ecosyndemics, and health inequality. He is the author of more than 20 books and more than 200 articles.

Kate van Dooren is a public health specialist who researches health-related experiences of young people transitioning out of prison and children with developmental disorders. Kate has published on autism, prisoner health, intellectual disability and health service use amongst vulnerable populations. Kate holds degrees from the Australian National University and The University of Queensland. She has worked at the Queensland Centre for Intellectual and Developmental Disability, Mater Misericordiae Hospital, Brisbane.

Jesse T. Young is a public health researcher specializing in psychiatric epidemiology. His research areas include justice health, emerging drug trends and dependency, and intellectual and developmental disabilities. Jesse is currently undertaking a PhD at the Melbourne School of Population and Global Health, The University of Melbourne. He has eight years' experience in the substance use and mental health research field and held positions at the Centre for Health Services research (UWA), NDRI, a World Health Organization Collaborating Centre, and the Centre for Addictions research of British Columbia.

www.ingramcontent.com/pod-product-compliance
Ingram Content Group UK Ltd.
Pitfield, Milton Keynes, MK11 3LW, UK
UKHW020213290926
15470UKWH00001B/157

9 781498 552141